EDITING TURGENEV, DOSTOEVSKY, AND TOLSTOY

Editing Turgenev, Dostoevsky, and Tolstoy

Mikhail Katkov and the Great Russian Novel

Susanne Fusso

NIU Press, Dekalb IL

Northern Illinois University Press, DeKalb 60115
© 2017 by Northern Illinois University Press
All rights reserved
Printed in the United States of America
26 25 24 23 22 21 20 19 18 17   1 2 3 4 5
978-0-87580-766-9 (cloth)
978-1-60909-225-2 (e-book)
Book and cover design by Yuni Dorr

Library of Congress Cataloging-in-Publication Data
Names: Fusso, Susanne, author.
Title: Editing Turgenev, Dostoevsky, and Tolstoy : Mikhail Katkov and the great Russian novel / Susanne Fusso.
Description: DeKalb, IL : Northern Illinois University Press, 2017. | Includes bibliographical references and index.
Identifiers: LCCN 2017011529 (print) | LCCN 2017027553 (ebook) | ISBN 9781609092252 (ebook) | ISBN 9780875807669 (cloth : alk. paper)
Subjects: LCSH: Katkov, M. N. (Mikhail Nikiforovich), 1818–1887. | Editors—Russia. | Turgenev, Ivan Sergeevich, 1818–1883—Relations with editors. | Dostoyevsky, Fyodor, 1821–1881—Relations with editors. | Tolstoy, Leo, graf, 1828-1910—Relations with editors. | Russian literature—Publishing—History—19th century. | Nationalism and literature—Russia—History—19th century. | Authors and publishers—Russia—History—19th century. | Russki?i vestnik (Moscow, Russia : 1856–)
Classification: LCC PN5276.K38 (ebook) | LCC PN5276.K38 F87 2017 (print) | DDC 891.73/309—dc23
LC record available at https://lccn.loc.gov/2017011529

FOR JOE

Contents

Acknowledgments ix
Note on Transliteration and Dates xii

INTRODUCTION
FROM PARIAH TO PARAGON 3

CHAPTER 1
KATKOV AND BELINSKY | LOVE, FRIENDSHIP, AND THE WORLD-HISTORICAL NATION 21

CHAPTER 2
KATKOV AND EVGENIIA TUR | A PERSONA SHAPED IN POLEMICS 46

CHAPTER 3
KATKOV AND TURGENEV | THE CONCEPTION OF *ON THE EVE* AND *FATHERS AND SONS* 70

CHAPTER 4
KATKOV AND DOSTOEVSKY | THEIR POLEMICS OF 1861–63 98

CHAPTER 5
KATKOV AND DOSTOEVSKY | PATRONAGE AND INTERFERENCE (*CRIME AND PUNISHMENT* AND *THE DEVILS*) 137

CHAPTER 6
KATKOV AND TOLSTOY | *ANNA KARENINA* AGAINST THE RUSSIAN HERALD 163

CHAPTER 7
KATKOV AND PUSHKIN | THE END OF KATKOV'S LITERARY CAREER 204

CONCLUSION
THE EDITOR AS PATRON 242

Notes 247
Bibliography 289
Index 303

Acknowledgments

This project was first conceived and developed during my fellowship at the Center for the Humanities, Wesleyan University, in 2008. I would like to thank the Director, Jill Morawski, and all the faculty and student fellows for their incisive and stimulating responses and suggestions. Jill created an atmosphere of warmth and free intellectual inquiry that I will always remember and be most grateful for. Throughout my work I have been supported, challenged, and inspired by my colleagues in the Russian, East European, and Eurasian Studies Program: Irina Aleshkovsky, Sergei Bunaev, Priscilla Meyer, Philip Pomper, Justine Quijada, Peter Rutland, Victoria Smolkin-Rothrock, and Duffield White. Debra Pozzetti has provided invaluable administrative help. Irina, Priscilla, and Duffy, and their spouses Yuz Aleshkovsky, Bill Trousdale, and Isabel Guy, have offered mentorship, hospitality, and moral support from the day I arrived at Wesleyan in 1985.

The staff of Wesleyan's Olin Library have been of indispensable help. I would like to thank Kate Wolfe and Lisa Pinette in the Interlibrary Loan Office, as well as Pat Tully, Rebecca McCallum, and Dianne Kelly. At the Yale University Library, Stephen Ross, Manager, Public Services, Manuscripts and Archives, kindly helped me with access to the *Russian Herald* and other nineteenth-century Russian journals, which about halfway through the eight years of my work on this book miraculously became available online via HathiTrust.

Eric Naiman invited me to give a lecture on Katkov at the Department of Slavic Languages and Literatures, University of California, Berkeley, in October 2014. The interaction with faculty and students there gave me an inspiring push toward completing the manuscript of this book. Thanks especially to Eric, David Frick, Luba Golburt, Olga Matich, and Irina Paperno for their insightful comments and intellectual hospitality. Thanks also to Ian Duncan and Ayşe Agiş for their comments and warm encouragement on the same occasion.

Catherine Ciepiela and Lazar Fleishman published my essay on Katkov's literary relationship with Dostoevsky in their Festschrift for Stanley J. Rabinowitz. I thank them for this opportunity to share my ongoing work on Katkov.

Svetlana Evdokimova and Vladimir Golstein invited me to their conference at Brown University in March 2014, "Dostoevsky Beyond Dostoevsky," where I was able to connect with distinguished Dostoevsky scholars. Thanks to the participants at this gathering, especially Carol Apollonio, Marina Kostalevsky, Deborah Martinsen, Robin Feuer Miller, and Donna Orwin, for their encouragement.

I am grateful to Donna T. Orwin for putting me in touch with Liudmila Viktorovna Gladkova and Tatiana Georgievna Nikiforova at the State Tolstoy Museum in Moscow. They promptly and generously answered my queries about the spelling of a particular word in Tolstoy's drafts of *Anna Karenina*.

Thanks are also due to the following colleagues, who helped me in various ways in the writing of this book: Nadja Akšamija, Robert Conn, Bruce Masters, James McGuire, and Michael J. Roberts. My brother Jim Fusso and his husband Richard Barry, as well as my dear friends Susan Amert, Olga Peters Hasty, Nancy Pollak, Olga Monina, and Alexandra Semenova, provide constant sympathetic conversation and counsel, and I thank them from the bottom of my heart. I have been learning from Robert Louis Jackson for many years, and his approach to Russian literature has been my guiding spirit.

The administration of Wesleyan University has supported me every step of the way, beginning with the fellowship at the Center for the Humanities in 2008. President Michael S. Roth invited me to share my work at a President's Lunch Series talk in 2013. Deans Andrew Curran, Marc Eisner, and Gary Shaw, and Provosts Ruth Weissman and Joyce Jacobsen, have provided funds for research on numerous occasions. This book could not have been written without Wesleyan's generous sabbatical policy, which helps us all embody the teacher-scholar ideal.

This book develops ideas that grow out of more than thirty years of teaching Wesleyan's incomparable students. I have had the priceless opportunity of introducing these brilliant young people to the great works of Turgenev, Dostoevsky, and Tolstoy, and of watching them respond and rise to the challenge of these novels. The students who have contributed to the ideas and interpretations presented here are too numerous to name. I thank them all, but in particular those who have gone on to make contributions to the field: Lindsay Ceballos, Elizabeth Papazian, Emily Wang, and Matvei Yankelevich.

Thanks are also due to the two readers of my manuscript for their valuable comments. Amy Farranto, Russian Studies Editor; Nathan Holmes, Managing Editor; and Linda Manning, Director, NIU Press, have been helpful and responsive during the shepherding of this book to publication. Yuni Dorr provided an elegant book design.

It is not a cliché but the simple truth to say that this book would not have been written without the participation of my husband, Joseph M. Siry. Joe is a peerless scholar of architectural history, and he has set an example for me of what historical scholarship can and should be. He took a shine to Mikhail Katkov from the day I started studying him. At times when I was ready to give up, Joe would intone, "No Katkov, no canon!" He has read these chapters in all their versions, and has offered astute editorial advice and criticism. This book is dedicated to him with the deepest love and gratitude.

A version of chapter 4 appeared as "Prelude to a Collaboration: Dostoevsky's Aesthetic Polemic with Mikhail Katkov," in *Dostoevsky Beyond Dostoevsky: Science, Religion, Philosophy*, ed. Vladimir Golstein and Svetlana Evdokimova (Boston: Academic Studies Press, 2016), 193–212. Permission granted by Academic Studies Press. A version of chapter 5 appeared as "Dostoevsky and Mikhail Katkov: Their Literary Partnership (*Crime and Punishment* and *The Devils*)," in *New Studies in Russian Literature and Culture: Essays in Honor of Stanley J. Rabinowitz*, ed. Catherine Ciepiela and Lazar Fleishman, vol. 45 of *Stanford Slavic Studies* (Oakland: Berkeley Slavic Specialties, 2014), 35–69. A version of chapter 6 will appear as "Mikhail Katkov and Lev Tolstoy: *Anna Karenina* Against the *Russian Herald*," forthcoming from Uppsala: Acta Universitatis Upsaliensis.

Note on Transliteration and Dates

A modified Library of Congress standard has been used for bibliographical items in the footnotes and for all words and untranslated titles. The same system has been used for names and toponyms except for the following:

ский = sky: Dostoevsky
ъ (omitted): Gorkii
ё = io: Gumiliov
ье/ьё/ьи = ie/io/i: Leontiev/Soloviov/Ilich
Марья: Maria
Мария: Mariia
Софья: Sofia
Certain names with time-honored transliterations: Herzen, Tolstoy, etc.
Russian orthography has been modernized throughout.

In the nineteenth century, Russia used a calendar that was twelve days behind the calendar used in Western Europe (conventionally represented as "Old Style" and "New Style," or "O.S." and "N.S.," respectively). In this book, dates are O.S., with the exception of letters written from Western Europe to Russia, which give two dates, of which the earlier is the O.S. date.

EDITING TURGENEV, DOSTOEVSKY, AND TOLSTOY

INTRODUCTION

FROM PARIAH TO PARAGON

Fathers and Sons by Turgenev. *Crime and Punishment, The Idiot, The Devils,* and *The Brothers Karamazov* by Dostoevsky. *War and Peace* and *Anna Karenina* by Tolstoy. This list sounds like an excellent syllabus for a course on the nineteenth-century Russian novel after 1850. Here are virtually all the major, canonical works that have made the international reputation of Russian literature, all the works that are translated into many languages and that earn Russian literature a place in world literature. This list is also the list of Russian novels that first appeared in the journal founded and edited by Mikhail Nikiforovich Katkov (1818–87), the *Russian Herald*. Yet most people in the West who are not specialists in Russian literary history have never heard of Katkov, and those who are specialists know him mainly through the fixed epithet "reactionary Russian publisher," a publisher who caused distress to Russia's great writers through his insistence on interfering with the artistic integrity of their literary texts. Most famously, he refused to print a central chapter in Dostoevsky's *Devils* as well as the final part of *Anna Karenina*. Our understanding of Katkov's literary activity and contribution has been greatly complicated by his vigorous political activity. In parallel with his literary efforts, as the editor of the daily newspaper the *Moscow News*, he was a towering political figure who advocated Russian nationalism and autocracy and agitated vigorously against radical and revolutionary movements. Because of this, seventy years of Soviet-era Russian literary history had to treat him as *persona non grata*. His literary role was consistently minimized or presented in its most unfavorable light. The situation in the West has been somewhat similar. Throughout the twentieth century, Western literary scholars tried to take a critical, objective approach to the ideologically constrained productions of Soviet scholars while still relying on their formidable archival, historical, and philological resources. No matter how objective one's approach, it was very hard not to be influenced by the incessant negativity surrounding the image of a figure like Katkov (a negativity that he in many ways deserved). But that list of canonical novels with which we began remains. Somehow, Katkov was the man who provided the venue, the financing, the possibility for the emergence of Russian literature on the world scene. This book had its origins in my curiosity about the positive side of Katkov's activity. What was it about this man that made it possible for him to play a role in the production of the great Russian novel?

Western and, until recently, Russian literary scholarship has overlooked a major figure in the development of the canonical Russian novel in the second half of the nineteenth century. Because of Katkov's conservative nationalist politics, Soviet scholarship was forced to minimize and demonize his role in the careers of Turgenev, Dostoevsky, and Tolstoy, and Western scholarship has followed that lead. This book strives to correct this blind spot by elucidating in depth and in specific textual detail the ways in which Katkov's own political-philological program, which strove to exalt Russian nationality via the creation of a world-class literature in the Russian language, played an active role in the conception and creation of the major Russian novels. I have thoroughly studied Katkov's writings related to literature, and to political issues relevant to the novels he published. This book uses Katkov's writings, largely unknown today but prominent and influential in their time, to help us understand the context in which the Russian novel flowered. The following chapters explore the literary side of Katkov's career and his interactions with some of Russia's major literary figures: Vissarion Belinsky, Evgeniia Tur, Ivan Turgenev, Fyodor Dostoevsky, and Lev Tolstoy. Each chapter has a different structure because of the differing nature of Katkov's relationship with each figure. The final chapter describes the end of Katkov's relationships with Turgenev and Dostoevsky, as all three men came together at the 1880 Pushkin celebrations in Moscow.

Katkov's Early Career

Katkov was born in 1818 in Moscow, the son of a humble civil servant who had earned personal (nonhereditary) nobility; his mother, Varvara Akimovna Katkova (née Tulaeva), belonged to an impoverished Georgian noble family.[1] Katkov's father died when he and his younger brother Mefodii were under the age of five. Between 1823 and 1828, six notices were published in the *Ladies' Journal* (*Damskii zhurnal*), edited by a friend of Katkova's, asking for charity for the "homeless widow with little orphans" and listing a number of addresses over that brief period. Finally Katkova found a position as linen-keeper in the Butyrka Prison Fortress in Moscow, where the boys spent their early years.[2] A family friend, Tatiana Petrovna Passek, recalls Katkov as a preternaturally quiet and reserved little boy, "seemingly wrapped up in himself."[3] The Russian scholar E. V. Perevalova interestingly suggests that the character of the mature Katkov, often described as haughty, proud, and self-willed, had its roots in this pensive, impoverished child: "It is possible that the cause of Katkov's [proud] behavior was the feeling of dependence on others that he constantly felt in his youth, his poverty, the necessity for self-limitation; he often came up against the indifference of people, felt his own powerlessness to help his loved ones in any way, and all of this called forth in his proud, ambitious nature a certain irritable and embittered attitude toward life."[4]

Although Katkov's family background was not distinguished by either wealth or social position, his intellectual talents were manifested at an early age; by twenty-seven he was adjunct professor of philosophy at Moscow University, after having studied philosophy in Germany. His university career was broken off in 1850, after the revolutionary events of 1848 in Western Europe, when a crackdown on the educational system deprived him of his position as the teaching of philosophy became the province of professors of theology. He moved into journalism, first as editor of the *Moscow News*, a daily that suffered all the strict censorship of the reign of Nicholas I. In 1856 he founded the *Russian Herald (Russkii vestnik)*, a biweekly (later monthly) journal that soon became a major organ of literary, political, and social discourse, a notable player in the discussions surrounding the 1861 emancipation of the serfs, for which Katkov advocated as part of the needed modernization of Russia.

In 1863, while maintaining his control of the *Russian Herald*, Katkov returned as editor of the *Moscow News* in the more open press climate of the reign of Alexander II. Soon after he assumed the editorship, the Polish uprising of 1863 catalyzed what had been Katkov's fairly liberal social position into something more radically conservative, or at least made his essential conservative nationalism widely known to the public. Katkov's editorials galvanized Russian public opinion against the Poles and successfully urged the government to take strict measures against them. From 1863 until the end of his life in 1887, Katkov poured enormous energy into his editorials for the *Moscow News*. Although he never held a government position, he was extremely influential in promoting his pet causes, most of which were directed toward preserving the Russian autocracy and Russian supremacy within the multiethnic empire of the tsars. He called himself "the watchdog of the state, guarding the master's property and sensing if something is wrong in the house."[5] It is hard to glean from the existing documents a clear picture of Katkov's personality. His supporters depict a kind, noble, hard-working person who was dedicated to the highest ideals; other accounts paint him as cold, haughty, overbearing, and politically ruthless. What is consistent not only in contemporaneous descriptions of him but also in his own writings is the force of his intellect and the vigor of his polemical arguments.

It is not surprising that Katkov is remembered both in Russia and the West primarily as a political figure; his editorials for the *Moscow News*, published by his widow, fill twenty-five large-format volumes, and they are mostly devoted to political, economic, and social issues.[6] But his earlier career and writings provide clues to how the apparently divided halves of Katkov's life activity, the literary and the political, are in fact deeply connected. Katkov's early interests were not just philosophical but philological. One of his first publications was a translation of Act I of *Romeo and Juliet*; he also translated Heine and other German poets. His master's thesis, *On the Elements and Forms of the Slavo-Russian Language* (1845), is a serious exercise in historical-comparative linguistics.[7] Philosophy was not divorced from philology in Katkov's time or in his personal ambitions; his profound interest in the coming-into-being of the Russian language was part of his hope, framed in Hegelian terms, that the Russian nation could achieve world-historical status.[8] These hopes are reflected in his articles of the 1830s and early 1840s.

The Project of the *Russian Herald*

In 1855, Katkov petitioned the minister of education for permission to begin what became the *Russian Herald*. As William Mills Todd III has pointed out, journalism was growing rapidly at precisely this time, due to "relaxed censorship practices and a new tolerance of political reporting in the press" in the wake of the death of the repressive Nicholas I and the accession to the throne of Alexander II.[9] Katkov was choosing the most direct and effective field for his activity, far more vital and influential than the university (although his connections to university professors proved to be of essential importance in maintaining the quality of the journal's contents).

In the early years of the *Russian Herald*, Katkov's articles continued to develop the theme of nation-formation through language and literature. His first contribution to the journal was a lengthy article on Pushkin, who had died in 1837 and whose collected works were published by P. V. Annenkov in 1855. The high point of Katkov's article is his discussion of Pushkin's work as the culminating stage in the formation of the Russian literary language. Katkov stresses that (as his 1845 thesis had investigated at length) the modern Russian language had been formed from two different branches of the Slavic family: the indigenous Russian dialect of the northeast and the imported Church Slavic element originating in the southwest. To these basic elements, according to Katkov, were later added the influence of classical grammar and of modern European literatures. This chaotic mix had already been somewhat ordered before Pushkin, but in him, Katkov writes, "the inner labor of forming the language finally came to rest." He continues: "An established literary language is a great deed in the life of a people. The formation of a literary language strengthens national [*narodnoe*] unity like nothing else. While this work of formation was going on, we seemed backward in the family of historical peoples, we were timid pupils and imitators. When this work was accomplished, Russian thought found in itself inner power for original living movement, and the national physiognomy emerged clearly out of the fog."[10]

Although many studies of Katkov see his stress on Russian supremacy as developing after the Polish rebellion of 1863, this 1856 article contains a passage that suggests otherwise. Katkov quotes Pushkin's "monument" poem, itself a free translation of Horace's *Exegi monumentum*, in which Pushkin claims that his "monument not made by hands," his poetic legacy, will survive him and will cause "every tongue" throughout great Russia, the Slav, the Finn, the savage Tungus, and the Kalmyk, to "call my name." Katkov writes, "The multitude of multifarious tribes that populate our fatherland must completely, intellectually and morally, subject themselves to the Russian nationality, as they are now subjected to the Russian state. For these tribes the Russian nationality is the sole path to human formation, and they 'will call the name of Pushkin.'"[11] Perevalova notes, "In this article Katkov announced himself as the representative of the ideology of state nationalism [*gosudarstvennyi natsionalizm*]. Nationality [*natsional'nost'*] in Katkov's conception is a state concept, and tribal origin, language, the historically formed peculiarities of character, mores and customs, and religion play no role in the given case. One tribe that has historically taken the lead lays the foundation of the state, unites around itself and subjects to itself the other tribes in the name of state unity. This tribe achieves the significance of a state nation [*gosudarstvennaia natsiia*]."[12]

By the 1860s, the discourse of the radicals associated with the rival journal the *Contemporary* was arousing Katkov to ever greater polemical heights. In the course of his polemics he returned to the theme of language as the legitimator of

Russian national aspirations. In articles published in the *Russian Herald* in 1861, Katkov compared the potential significance of Russian among Slavic languages to that of High German, the importance and dominance of which was guaranteed by the literature written in it. Although German has many dialects, Katkov writes, "in the High German language, the common language of Germany, were expressed so many treasures of knowledge and thought, it was the field of such a rich development, it took in so many impressions of creative power, that all the different languages fell silent before it, and it became the palladium of a great nationality [*narodnost'*]."[13] Katkov is flaunting his classical erudition here. The word "palladium," derived from the statue of Pallas Athena that was believed to protect Troy, means a safeguard that guarantees the integrity of social institutions, as in "The Bill of Rights, palladium of American civil liberties." Katkov aspires to the same role for the Russian language. According to Katkov, the Slavic world has been "forgotten or suppressed by history" because "not one of its tribal elements has achieved indisputable power." Because of its emergence as a "great state power," Russia might play this role, becoming "the indisputable center of unification" for the Slavic world: "But when will this Russian language, which was formed over so long and with such difficulty, as if predestined for something great and universal, when will it prove in its literature to be worthy of this predestination? When will this thousand-year-old child be acknowledged as a person come of age, capable of independent life and thought? ... Will it truly become the instrument of mature thought and knowledge, a living expression of the great interests of civil society [*grazhdanstvennost'*], will there turn out to be a truly universal, binding, and creating force in it?"[14] Katkov outlines here a problem, a task, and a call to action.

The program that Katkov outlines in these writings of 1839–61, and that, as this study will demonstrate, he proceeded to put into practice through his editorial and publishing activity in the golden age of the Russian novel, never disappeared from his mind even as he turned to more obviously political activity. Near the end of his life, in 1880, he wrote an essay on Pushkin on the occasion of the plan to erect a monument to the poet. In this essay the clearly defined program of the young Katkov is still being affirmed, even as Katkov discusses not Turgenev, Dostoevsky, or Tolstoy, but Pushkin, the writer who initially gave him the idea that it was possible for Russian literature to achieve world status. Katkov describes the life of a nation as consisting of a body (state power and armed force) and a soul or spirit ("the development of the gifts of human nature"). The nation proves its right to existence not by state power alone but also by its artistic heritage: "No one brought so much true benefit to the Russian nationality [*narodnost'*] as Pushkin during the time God granted him to live, and his works are worth many battles won."[15]

In a study of Katkov's version of Russian nationalism, Andreas Renner describes Katkov's contribution, influential and widely accepted in its time, as his "redefining [of] traditional imperial unity as national unity," overcoming the heterogeneity of the Russian Empire with an overarching conception of Russian nationality. As Renner writes, "For Katkov the 'unity of Russia' . . . was fundamental to a programme for building a nation-empire with several co-existing nationalities (*narodnosti*) of which, however, only one could be politically decisive: Russia. For centuries Russia had been gathering the territories of the tsarist empire. The time had come to unite its disparate parts into one nation as other European states had done."[16] Renner only briefly mentions the role of language and literature in this process of redefinition, but Katkov's own writings clearly show that in his mind it was a decisive and central one. Years before the Polish rebellion, Katkov had laid out his program for ensuring the supremacy of the Russian language, and consequently the Russian nation, through the medium of a great literature.

So how did Katkov go about implementing this program? An important factor in the development of his relationship with the major Russian writers was his ability to offer financial support. Already in his 1855 petition to the minister of education, Katkov explained that his efforts to improve the *Moscow News* had been hampered by the fact that, since he did not own the newspaper (it was a state organ belonging to Moscow University), he could not improve the publication by paying writers more.[17] As the *Russian Herald* developed and grew stronger over the course of the 1860s, its reputation spread as the journal that paid more, and more reliably, than any of its competitors. Turgenev, Tolstoy, and Dostoevsky all attested to this, usually while defending themselves for the crime of publishing in the journal of such a retrograde figure. Dostoevsky's letters from 1865 on make it clear that he relied on Katkov for virtually continuous financial support through payment of advances on his work in progress.[18]

But Turgenev, Dostoevsky, and Tolstoy, who all admitted that they carefully read the *Russian Herald*, were responding to something more than just the money it could offer. From its beginnings the journal was engaging not only with literature but also with the vital social issues facing Russia: modernization, industrialization, economic development, reform of the courts and of the government. Of course all the so-called "thick" journals were doing something similar, but as both Turgenev's and Tolstoy's letters testify, it was the *Russian Herald* that was dominating the attention of the serious readers of Russia.[19] Dostoevsky wrote in 1869,

"It is definitely the best journal in Russia and the one that firmly knows its own tendency.... All the most important things appeared in their journal: *War and Peace, Fathers and Sons*, etc.... The main thing is that reliably every year, every subscriber knows, three or four articles will appear, the most apt, the most characteristic and necessary at the present time, and the newest, and, the main thing, they will be only in their journal and not in any other—the public knows this."[20]

In the years 1856–62, the years immediately preceding the great flowering of the Russian novel, Katkov's journal was permeated with his powerful personality and aspirations for the Russian nation. Many of these aspirations were expressed in political terms, but we can also find his literary program in these pages. Already in 1856, in the article on Pushkin, in criticizing Pushkin's experiments in prose Katkov seems to be calling for the lengthy novel of psychological, political, and philosophical complexity, that novel that was to become the dominant mode of Russian literature. He writes of Pushkin's laconic and terse prose works, "In [*The Captain's Daughter*] you cannot help but notice that same dryness from which all Pushkin's prose experiments suffer. The depictions are too petty, or too summary, or too general. Here as well we do not notice those powerful outlines that give us the living person, or depict the complex connection of the phenomena of life and everyday existence. It was not only the natural character of Pushkin's talent that was to blame for the above indicated deficiency in his works; of course, also to blame was the insufficient development of intellectual and moral interests in the social consciousness whose organ Pushkin was."[21] An improved, "formed" society, of the kind being nurtured by the *Russian Herald*, would in Katkov's view give rise to more developed works of prose fiction—and it is emphatically prose fiction, not poetry, on which Katkov fixed his attention in the coming years (although the *Russian Herald* also published a wide array of very fine poetry by the likes of A. A. Fet, Karolina Pavlova, and A. K. Tolstoy).

The Reception of Katkov: The Late Imperial Period

In order to understand the present-day perception of Katkov, it will help to review how his legacy was understood in the years immediately after his death. Katkov made many friends and enemies during his long career, and the attitudes of both camps are vividly displayed in works about him from the last decades of the Russian Empire. Less easy to find are dispassionate, objective studies of a man who aroused great passion. Many of these books and memoirs include a wealth of useful detail (even if some of it must be taken with caution, and many contradict each other), but they devote vastly more attention to Katkov's political activity than to his role in helping to create the great Russian novel. On the hagiographic side, the most important publication is by Katkov's close associate N. A. Liubimov, who ran the day-to-day editorial affairs of the *Russian Herald* after Katkov became the editor of the *Moscow News* in 1863. As Catharine Theimer Nepomnyashchy writes in her pioneering 1977 article on Katkov's literary activity, "Lyubimov includes a number of useful documents, quoted in full in the text, and is especially helpful in tracing the events leading up to the founding of the *Russian [Herald]*."[22] Liubimov largely ends his account in 1866, and says virtually nothing about Katkov's literary work, perhaps not wishing to draw attention to the fact (evident in letters) that when it came to the most important writers such as Dostoevsky and Tolstoy, Katkov did not at all allow Liubimov a free hand in important decisions at the *Russian Herald*. Liubimov's work, as Martin Katz writes, "is a classic apologia," as are the biographical essays by Prince N. P. Meshchersky and others, published in the *Russian Herald* in August 1897.[23] A typical passage from Meshchersky's contribution, presented in the form of letters to Katkov's widow, is the following patch of sanctimoniously purple prose: "The Lord God gave bountiful gifts to the great fighter for truth, and as a humble servant, he greatly multiplied the talents that had been granted him. Without doubt, he was the ideal of what is demanded for the gigantic work to which he selflessly dedicated himself."[24]

More influential in the Soviet period were memoirs by disenchanted former collaborators like B. N. Chicherin, who wrote (with a dig at Meshchersky's eulogy), "He lowered the holy feeling of love for fatherland to the level of purely animal instinct, in which any idea of truth and goodness disappeared and there remained only national egoism [*narodnyi egoizm*], which has contempt for everything but itself.... I think that history will pronounce a severe verdict on Katkov. He was given talent by God, and what did he use it for?"[25] The 1888 study by "S. Nevedensky" (pseudonym of S. G. Shcheglovitov) is full of valuable information, mostly devoted to Katkov's political activity, but as Katz writes, "[It] was primarily responsible for the judgment that Katkov was an 'opportunist,' whose so-called 'national direction' could not be taken seriously, but attested to the publicist's political immaturity and shallow convictions. Such a judgment, which [Nevedensky] at times himself contradicts, only tends to obscure the importance of ideas as determinants in Katkov's life."[26] Katz is similarly skeptical of the highly influential 1892 work by R. I. Sementkovsky: "[It] expresses in essay form the liberal view of a Katkov who was not only an opportunist, but one of the worst kind.

Sementkovskii's primary hypothesis is that Katkov never had an idea of his own, not to speak of a direction, but rather made skillful use of those attitudes, trends, and programs which he felt had the best chance of success; according to this extreme view, 'he almost always sang another's tune.'"[27] Like Katz, recent Russian scholars have convincingly countered the "opportunist" accusation by tracing the continuities in Katkov's thought and the principles on which he relied.[28]

It should be noted, given the tendency of Russian conservatives to be anti-Semitic, that Sementkovsky singles out Katkov's relatively liberal position on the "Jewish question" as the only area in which he "remained true to himself from the beginning of his journalistic career to his very death." In the early 1860s, Katkov "quite decisively spoke out in favor of expanding the rights of the Jews, in particular for the abolition of the notorious Pale of Settlement, demonstrating all the harm it causes in the economic respect and its groundlessness from the point of view of Russian state interests, which require the merging of non-Russians in the Russian Empire [*inorodtsy*] with the native population, and not their artificial separation.... He attacked the Poles, the Baltic Germans, the Finns, the Georgians, the Armenians, but left the Jews alone, and neither at the time of the Polish rebellion, nor later, did he accuse the Jews of inciting disorders." Katkov condemned the pogroms of 1881, attributing them to revolutionary agitation and denying any economic, religious, or ethnic causes.[29]

The ambivalent feelings that Katkov inspired even in some people who might be his natural allies are perhaps best expressed in a brief, thoughtful memoir by the philosopher Vladimir Soloviov, whose works Katkov published in the *Russian Herald* very early in his career. Their connection was broken after Soloviov publicly expressed his opposition to the death penalty soon after the assassination of Tsar Alexander II in March 1881. Soloviov heard that Katkov had tearfully told Liubimov that Soloviov's speech was an insult to national feeling [*narodnoe chuvstvo*]. Soloviov caustically remarks, "For Katkov the supposed opinion of the nation [*mnenie naroda*], that is, Katkov's personal opinion about the opinion of the nation, was the highest criterion of truth and goodness."[30] But Soloviov also writes, "At the same time that I was indignant at Katkov, suddenly there rose up in my memory the spiritual image of this person, as I knew him in his best moments, with his deep piety, his sincere kindness in personal relations, and his lofty understanding of Christian ideas. I felt that he was under the delusion of an evil power. I wrote him a long letter with the main thought—You are carried away by a political idea, it seems to you to be the most important thing, but imagine yourself on your deathbed, passing to the other world, would then the idea of *extreme* nationalism [*natsionalizm*] toward non-Russians in the Russian Empire [*inorodtsy*] really preserve its importance for you? And if not, then that means it is a temporary, passing idea, not worthy of carrying away a thinking person and a Christian."[31] Soloviov received no answer, and Katkov died a year later, on July 20 (O.S.), 1887.

The Reception of Katkov: The Soviet Period

Katkov's conservative politics made him a virtually untouchable subject for Soviet scholars until the 1970s, when two monographs appeared, by V. A. Kitaev in 1972 and V. A. Tvardovskaia in 1978, both of which were devoted mainly to his political thought and activity.[32] These works are full of useful information but are also laced with the obligatory quotations from Lenin and characterizations such as "Katkov's conservative liberalism, which closed ranks with the government reaction in order to persecute the revolutionary democrats," and "Katkov's life path is an instructive example of how serving a historically unjust and doomed cause places an ineradicable and irreversible stamp of impoverishment on a personality."[33] The most important freestanding work devoted to Katkov's literary activity is an article by Vladimir Kantor, which somewhat misleadingly labels Katkov an adherent of "art for art's sake" who "exploded this movement from within, intensifying its reactionary aspects and, decisively bringing them to their logical conclusion, moved as a result not only to political but also to aesthetic reaction." Since Katkov was never an adherent of "art for art's sake" and from the beginning of his career always insisted on the embeddedness of art in historical and social consciousness, the premise of Kantor's argument (that Katkov betrayed his early aestheticism by interpreting works like *Fathers and Sons* in a political context) is questionable. But he takes Katkov's literary career more seriously than perhaps any other Soviet-era scholar. His conclusion is scathing. Speaking of Katkov's grand funeral, which surpassed any given for the great Russian writers, Kantor writes, "Katkov's very funeral turned out to be insulting for the memory of the best representatives of Russian art. And Russian culture repaid Katkov with oblivion."[34]

More pervasive and influential than any single work of scholarship, though, is the way Katkov appears as a supporting player in the scholarly apparatus to Soviet editions of Turgenev, Dostoevsky, Tolstoy, and other writers. When you are a scholar interested in one of these writers and you spend time consulting the notes to their complete works published in the Soviet era, you form a mental image of a man whose name cannot be mentioned without the epithets "reactionary" and "obscurantist" or "enemy of progress" (*mrakobes*, an expressive Russian word that combines "*mrak*," "darkness," and "*bes*," "demon"). According to V. V. Vinogradov, the noun *mrakobesie* (obscurantism) derives from the title of an 1818 play by Hyacinthe-François-Isaac Decomberousse, *L'Ultra, ou la Manie des Ténèbres* (the mania of darkness).[35] But to someone ignorant of this etymology, it conjures the phrase "demon of darkness." Katkov, this demon of darkness, is constantly doing battle with the "revolutionary democrats"—that is, radical journalists, particularly N. G. Chernyshevsky, N. A. Dobroliubov, and D. I. Pisarev. He does nothing positive for Turgenev, Dostoevsky, or Tolstoy; he just keeps trying to infringe on their artistic freedom in pursuit of his own reactionary aims.

The Reception of Katkov: The Post-Soviet Period

Soviet-era scholars were under an ideological constraint dictating that they minimize Katkov's positive role. And since by the end of his career Katkov had emerged as an enemy of the liberal intelligentsia, he had no natural constituency in Russian émigré cultural circles either. So when I began this project in 2008, I had to read Katkov's works in their original nineteenth-century publications. There was no Collected Works, no modern biography, and no scholarly commentary on his works. In the intervening years, there has been a significant rediscovery of Katkov in Russia, with new books, biographical works, and articles coming out every year, mostly devoted to his political activity, but with some contributions about his literary career as well. Most centrally, in 2010–12 a six-volume collection of his works appeared, which contains an annotated selection of his articles, editorials, and letters.[36] According to the editors, the complete works of Katkov are now being prepared for publication. But my reading of these recent publications suggests that, with some notable exceptions, Katkov is still being seen through a veil of ideology. The man who was labeled by Soviet-era scholars as an evil reactionary who tried to crush the "revolutionary democrats" is now in the post-Soviet era a hero who struggled against "sedition" and the "destroyers of Russia"—the same people, that is, whom the Soviets praised as revolutionary democrats.[37] In the Soviet period, Katkov was a *mrakobes*; the new mood can be summed up by the title of a 2013 article on him titled "Savior of the Fatherland" ("*Spasitel' otechestva*").[38]

The main editor of the six-volume collection, A. N. Nikoliukin, gave an interview in 2013 that described how in the Soviet period he chose to specialize in

American rather than Russian literature, because "[For a Soviet scholar] It wasn't Tolstoy that was important so much as Lenin's articles on Tolstoy.... No one interfered in what I wrote about American literature."[39] With the coming of *perestroika*, he was able to edit and publish writers like Vasilii Rozanov, Iurii Samarin, and Katkov, who belong to what he calls the line of "preservers of Russia," stemming from Karamzin and Pushkin (in opposition to the line of "destroyers of Russia," stemming from the Decembrists and Alexander Herzen). He says, "To preserve is not only to remember, but also to return to Russia the extremely rich heritage that was rejected in the twentieth century."[40]

A striking example of the way Katkov is being presented in the Putin era is the introduction to a collection of articles published in 2008, in honor of the 190th anniversary of Katkov's birth. The volume collects papers read at a conference on Katkov held at the Moscow Cathedral of All Saints in the Alekseevsky Monastery, where Katkov was buried. It contains an introduction and afterword by Archpriest Artemii Vladimirov. Father Artemii writes, "I would call him the true mentor of the Russian nation [*natsiia*], because sitting for several decades at the helm of the *Moscow News*, dictating his articles, he truly formed the national [*natsional'noe*] worldview. And, thanks be to God, without any computers or Internets [sic], he truly was the ideologue of our state, who was not afraid to utter the truth, for which he always experienced a great deal of unpleasantness."[41] In his conclusion Father Artemii makes the connection to Putin and the new atmosphere of Orthodox religiosity explicit. He asks what would happen if Katkov were to rise from the grave today: "We, fathers, would probably send him straight to the president and to the government commission where the strategies, tactics, and ideology of our society are being formulated. I think that Mikhail Nikiforovich, a brave and uncompromising person, would immediately drive away with his fiery word all the hacks, scribblers, and mercenary newspapermen. As an incorporeal spirit, he would not be afraid of attempts on his life, and in five to ten years would be able to accomplish a great deal, if he were supported by patriotically inclined politicians, the military, and representatives of the clergy." Katkov would foster "a conscious and profound religiosity" and a correct interpretation of Russian history.[42]

This connection of Katkov's role in the nineteenth century to the situation in post-Soviet Russia is vividly on display in a television program in the series "*Istoricheskii protsess*" (which can be translated as either "The Historical Process" or "Historical Trial"), broadcast on March 28, 2012, on the Rossiia 1 channel. On this program, titled "Political Journalism: From 'The Barbarian Intelligentsia' of

Katkov to 'Anatomy of a Protest' on NTV," a debate is conducted between two television personalities, the liberal Nikolai Svanidze and the pro-Putin Dmitrii Kiseliov, each backed up by a panel of three experts.[43] In the first half of the program, Svanidze and Kiseliov debate (using the term loosely) the significance of Katkov, particularly his critique of the Russian intelligentsia in the 1870s. In the second half, they debate the value of the documentary *Anatomy of a Protest* (dir. Iurii Shalimov), broadcast on NTV on March 15 and October 5, 2012, which attempted to prove that the Russian protest movement of 2011–12 was financed by Western interests.

In Svanidze's opening statement, he commends Katkov (inaccurately) for being the first person to publish Turgenev, Tolstoy, and Dostoevsky. But although Katkov was important and talented, "his views were obscurantist [*mrakobesnye*] and ruinous for the country." Svanidze and the other liberal panelists take the line of Sementkovsky, that Katkov was a disingenuous opportunist, whose anti-Polish feelings "grew into savage hatred for the Russian intelligentsia." Kiseliov and the other pro-Putin panelists keep returning to Katkov's literary contributions. In response to a particularly pointed attack on Katkov by Dmitrii Muratov, chief editor of *Novaia gazeta*, the right-wing journalist Maksim Shevchenko says, "This person, this monster, publishes the novels of Leskov, the novels of Dostoevsky, which completely refute what we've just been told about him. Precisely thanks to this supposed sycophantically loyal lackey, as they're trying to represent him, we understood how the Russian people in the nineteenth century felt and tragically suffered."

Watching the program creates an uneasy feeling in a person who is trying to understand Katkov's contribution objectively. Gratifying as it is to see that people can still be passionately shouting at each other over Katkov's legacy, my personal sympathies are entirely with the anti-Katkov participants, who are trying to defend the right of the Russian people to work openly to change their society for the better. As the liberal panelist A. A. Nechaev (Russian minister of the economy, 1992–93) says, "People aren't protesting because the [US] State Department paid them.... They're going out onto the street because their elemental rights are being violated, because lawlessness reigns in the country, because the Ministry of Internal Affairs has turned into an organization that doesn't defend society, but is dangerous for society.... They are going out into the street because they want to have a normal life in this country." Perhaps the wisest comment in the entire program is made by Andrei Vasiliev, producer of the satirical "Citizen Poet" project, who says, "[Katkov's ideas] might have had some rationale in their day, 150 years ago. But when people in power or close to power try to apply these terrifying, outmoded, ancient ideas to the present day, that is truly quite dangerous." The anachronism of the right-wing panelists enlisting themselves in Katkov's "Russian party," with the tsarist autocracy as its central article of faith, in a supposedly modern, democratic Russia that Katkov would not be able to recognize, is poignant and dismaying. Even more poignant is the thought that in the present climate, only a few years later, it would be unthinkable for the liberal position to be represented so fully and vigorously on such a program (the liberals "win" the debate, based on audience voting, by 77.9 percent to 22.1 percent).

Despite the sometimes horrifying use to which Katkov's legacy is being put in present-day Russia, his place in Russian literary history needs to be reevaluated soberly and thoroughly. My plan in this study is to offer a view of Katkov's literary activity that avoids the extremes of "*mrakobes*" and "savior of the fatherland," giving him his due as the important figure he was, without vilification or canonization.

In the first chapter I trace the intellectual and personal intimacy between Katkov and the pioneering critic Vissarion Belinsky at the very beginning of Katkov's career, when he was part of the circle of young Russian thinkers who were trying to assimilate German idealist philosophy in both their lives and their understanding of art. Most works dealing with the interlacing of the philosophical and the personal in 1830s Russia mention Katkov sparingly or not at all. In fact he was at the heart of these entanglements. Belinsky has been enshrined by Soviet scholarship as a major figure of the 1830s while Katkov has been ignored; this chapter shows the similar role the two played in the 1830s. Even readers who are aware of Katkov's relationship with Turgenev, Dostoevsky, and Tolstoy will likely be surprised to learn in detail of his close working and personal relationship with Belinsky, who is seen as the progenitor of Russian literary criticism.

The second chapter focuses on a very public controversy between Katkov and the novelist and critic Evgeniia Tur in the summer and fall of 1860, upon her departure from working as an editor and contributor at the *Russian Herald*. This polemic, which involved several writers including Chernyshevsky, was an open and quite pointed discussion of Katkov's editing practice, a discussion that created his public persona and revealed the fundamental habits and traits that would plague his relationship with Turgenev, Dostoevsky, and Tolstoy.

Chapter 3 investigates the ways in which Turgenev responded in the conception of his novels to the discourse of the *Russian Herald*. In particular, the question asked by many critics about *On the Eve* (1860), "Why a Bulgarian?" can be answered at least in part by the sustained attention that was being paid in the *Russian Herald* in the late 1850s to the plight of Slavic Christians and especially Bulgarians in the Ottoman Empire. Similarly, the conception of *Fathers and Sons* was in harmony with Katkov's battles with the young radicals who would be forever given Turgenev's label "nihilists," a term reaffirmed and popularized by Katkov in his own writings.

Chapter 4 traces a kind of dialogue between Katkov and Dostoevsky in their journalistic polemics of 1861–63, a dialogue that preceded a long and productive working relationship. In this chapter I consider the issues that Katkov and Dostoevsky clashed over, as well as the points of inner, fundamental agreement that can help us understand what made possible their fruitful, if sometimes contentious, partnership. Chapter 5 deals with the famous episodes of Katkov's interference in the artistic realization of two of Dostoevsky's most important novels, *Crime and Punishment* (1866) and *The Devils* (1871–72). In this chapter I revisit Soviet literary historiography of these moments of conflict and attempt to restore a more balanced view of Katkov's interventions.

Chapter 6 analyzes Katkov's relationship with Tolstoy. Tolstoy published several works in the *Russian Herald* starting in 1859, including the first parts of *War and Peace*, published in 1865 and 1866, partly overlapping with Dostoevsky's *Crime and Punishment*. It is easy to see how *War and Peace* suits the Russian national program of Katkov: vast and imposing in size and scope, it is beautifully designed to promote the national "self-consciousness" that Katkov called for in his earliest articles on Pushkin. *Anna Karenina* (1875–77), the work that led to Tolstoy's violent break with Katkov, is something different. Dostoevsky clashed with Katkov over a single chapter in *The Devils* that departed from Katkov's program, but a close look at *Anna Karenina* reveals that the entire novel is ideologically opposed to many of Katkov's most cherished plans and ideals. It is well known that Katkov refused to publish the eighth and final part of *Anna Karenina*, and that Tolstoy had to resort to publishing it as a separate brochure. In Part 8, Liovin's drama plays out against the backdrop of Russian volunteers traveling to Serbia to fight with the Serbs against their Turkish overlords; this movement eventually led to Russia's being drawn into war with Turkey. Tolstoy expresses through Liovin and other "positive" characters his disapproval and condemnation of this movement, which he depicts as an empty fad of idle circles in the capitals and completely out of touch with the needs and desires of the Russian people. The movement, however, was dear to Katkov's heart and one of his most important propaganda themes at the time. Unsurprisingly, Katkov refused to publish this direct attack on his own ideological program.

What is less obvious about *Anna Karenina* in relation to Katkov is that Part 8 is only the most blatant and explicit attack on Katkov's favorite programs to be found in it. Chapter 6 delves into articles in the *Russian Herald* and the *Moscow News* about railroads, industrialization, credit operations, classical education, education of women, spiritualism, and the Russian volunteer movement in Serbia, showing in detail how Tolstoy's treatment of these issues in *Anna Karenina* is directed against Katkov's policies and programs. The attack on the Russian volunteer movement in the epilogue was not a sudden, unanticipated burst of negativity towards one of Katkov's pet causes; it was only the last in a series of such attacks in the novel, and no doubt had the effect of a last straw.

In chapter 7 I describe the Pushkin Celebration of 1880, in which Turgenev, Dostoevsky, and Katkov all played prominent roles, from the viewpoint of its status as a kind of summing-up of Katkov's literary career. *The Brothers Karamazov*, the last important literary work to be published in the *Russian Herald*, was appearing in installments at the time of the Pushkin Celebration, and it was a major factor in the way that Dostoevsky's Pushkin speech was received. In particular, I read Turgenev's and Dostoevsky's Pushkin speeches, as well as Katkov's own 1880 essay on Pushkin, against the background of the appreciation of Pushkin by the German critic Varnhagen von Ense that was translated and published by Katkov in 1839.

The conclusion considers the nature of Katkov's role as both editor and patron. As a writer of articles and editorials, Katkov presented a clear program for Russian literature, which was to affirm the political and historical importance of the Russian nationality as expressed through its language. As a powerful and entrepreneurial publisher, he also sought, encouraged, and paid for the writing of the works that were to embody that program, the works we now recognize as among the greatest achievements of Russian literature.

This book is an introduction to Katkov and his writings, in particular the role he played in the creation of some of the most significant works of Russian literature. Although this is not a biography of Katkov, it will be necessary to provide a certain amount of biographical information in order to illuminate the career of a man who is not as well known as his importance warrants. The primary texts that form the basis of this book are the journalistic articles of the time, which are of essential significance to the context in which the Russian novel was conceived and executed. My goal is to provide as dispassionate an account as possible of a man who inspired vehement passions, both positive and negative, and to provide a basis for further investigation that will relate Katkov more organically to the study of readership, serialization, print culture, and canonicity in the nineteenth-century Russian context. The goal of this book is to elucidate the molding of Katkov as a literary figure, and how he became the person who enabled the creation of the great Russian novel in the second half of the nineteenth century.[44]

CHAPTER 1

KATKOV AND BELINSKY

LOVE, FRIENDSHIP, AND THE WORLD-HISTORICAL NATION

In the obituary for Mikhail Nikiforovich Katkov that appeared in the *Times* of London on August 2, 1887, one day after he had died of stomach cancer, he is characterized as "a statesman who started from the assumption that Russia is to maintain her present greatness and to become greater in the eyes of the world by nationalizing the different elements of the Empire."[1] Most of the obituary describes Katkov's political journalism, a paragraph is devoted to his educational reform program, but no mention is made of his literary activity, of the fact that he was the editor who published the greatest works of Turgenev, Dostoevsky, and Tolstoy. This omission is not accidental, but reflects the way in which Katkov has been represented in history, in Russia and, as a result, in the West. Katkov is indeed remembered for his political activity, not his literary activity. Yet anyone looking at the career of the twenty-year-old Katkov would hardly predict such an outcome. In the years 1838–40, the person Katkov most resembles in his intellectual preoccupations and writings is Vissarion Grigorievich Belinsky (1811–48), who became the first major Russian literary critic and theorist. Thanks to his eventual identification with the politically radical camp in Russian letters, over the course of the twentieth century Belinsky was canonized by Soviet literary scholarship, while the early writings of Katkov, who eventually became a fierce and influential conservative and defender of autocracy, were left in obscurity. How did Katkov become the person who enabled the creation of the great Russian novel in the second half of the nineteenth century? In this chapter I will consider first Katkov's deeply personal involvement with Belinsky and other young Russian thinkers who were trying to assimilate German idealist philosophy in both their lives and their understanding of art. Then I will examine the theoretical principles, largely inspired by Hegel, that emerge from Katkov's early journalistic writings and translations.

Love and Philosophy

In his recent study *The House in the Garden: The Bakunin Family and the Romance of Russian Idealism*, John Randolph explores the domestic dramas that accompanied the reception of German idealist philosophy in Russia in the 1830s and 1840s, with particular emphasis on the Bakunin family and Belinsky's relations with them.[2] Randolph writes of the loose circle of students and ex-students of Moscow University, sometimes labeled the Stankevich Circle after one of their important figures, Nikolai Vladimirovich Stankevich (1813–40),

> Not only did these charismatic students show a dangerously independent streak, they also seemed oblivious to the conventional limits of philosophical activity. In its native Germany, post-Kantian Idealism was practiced in public institutions, such as university lecture halls and scientific publications. Russian analogues to this institutionalized Idealism existed, inside of the Imperial Academy; yet the most famous and charismatic traditions surrounding Russian Idealism were produced more intimately, on the stage of private life.

Randolph continues,

> On the one hand, this private cult of philosophy seemed to violate what many regarded to be the proper limits of abstract thought by pulling it so deeply into the sphere of intimate relations. On the other hand, ... there was something progressive—if comical—about this idealistic habit of "living through" philosophy. It had allowed its practitioners to break their subservience to the Empire's religious and political dogmas. In the process it made them independent, "complete," and fully "modern" men (to borrow Herzen's phrases), and prepared their subsequent, autonomous role in Russian life.[3]

One of Katkov's biographers writes that in this period, "Philosophical systems were not only being thought through [*peredumyvalis'*] but being lived through [*perezhivalis'*], so to speak."[4] Randolph's book does not mention Katkov, but Katkov was involved with both Belinsky and Bakunin in personal dramas that reveal his embeddedness in the "private cult of philosophy" in which Russian literary theory, among other major currents in Russian thought, was being born.[5]

Belinsky's letters in the late 1830s are documents of his inner life and his struggles to explain that life in terms of his own understanding of Hegel's philosophy. It has often been pointed out that Belinsky, who was from a poor background and whose education was spotty, did not know German well enough to master Hegel in the original. He was dependent on friends like Mikhail Bakunin and, as he mentions several times, Katkov, to form his conception of Hegel. As Herbert Bowman writes,

> The power of the circle to arouse intense interest in works of philosophical speculation to which it did not always provide an authoritative guide worked to place a member like Belinski in an unfortunate position of intellectual dependence. Such intellectual dependence carried with it a psychological dependence upon more learned friends; and to this dependence Belinski's imperfect education made him particularly susceptible. The fact that such a large measure of Belinski's philosophical knowledge thus came to him at second hand was to constitute one of the principal sources of the extravagance and frequent distortion of his philosophical creed.[6]

Katkov's contributions to Belinsky's understanding of Hegel tended to be in the realm of aesthetics, but by 1837 Bakunin had developed a way of applying Hegel to the art of living. As Randolph writes, "Mikhail [Bakunin] had hit upon the ideal for which he would become famous in the literary circles of the 1830s and early 1840s: the call to reconcile oneself with reality and thereby become a 'real man.' It was an ambition he translated with celebrated ease from technical German into Romantic Russian, projecting both himself and Hegel into the foreground of Russian thought for the first time."[7]

Aileen Kelly has lucidly described Bakunin's "new understanding of reality, based on Hegel's famous dictum in the *Introduction to the Philosophy of Right*: 'The real is the rational and the rational is real.'"[8] As Kelly explains, Hegel's dictum meant only "that there is a logical order in the development of all things, in which all historical forms and institutions have their necessary place as successive expressions of the dialectical development of Absolute Reason."[9] But Bakunin and other early Russian students of Hegel understood it to mean that one must accept the status quo; the catch phrase for this in Russia was "reconciliation with reality," which allowed Russian thinkers to overcome their alienation from "the repugnant world around them."[10] In the period of his discipleship to Bakunin, Belinsky wholeheartedly accepted the need for "reconciliation with reality," the conservative interpretation of Hegel to which he clung until 1840.

Even after Belinsky emerged from under Bakunin's spell, the influence of his teacher can still be detected in his correspondence. Belinsky wrote voluminous letters both to Bakunin and to other friends in which he painstakingly analyzed his own life experiences, testing them against his understanding of "*deistvitel'nost*", Bakunin's rendering of Hegel's *Wirklichkeit*, "reality" or more precisely "actuality"; the Russian word "*deistvitel'nost*'" is usually translated as "reality." In relation to Katkov, the most important of Belinsky's letters concern their rivalry in the fall of 1838 and winter of 1839 over the actress Aleksandra Mikhailovna Shchepkina (1816–41), daughter of the great actor Mikhail Semionovich Shchepkin (1788–1863). Twenty-three-year-old Shchepkina was first in love with twenty-one-year-old Moscow University student Katkov. As Belinsky tells it, "*The young lady* [his constant epithet for Shchepkina] loved another, and that other loved her, but he conducted himself so *realistically* [*deistvitel'no*] that she thought he didn't love her."[11] At this juncture twenty-eight-year-old Belinsky, an old friend of her family, expressed romantic interest in her. Again in Belinsky's account, "Concluding from my wild behavior that I *adored* her, she decided to love me, with the thought that if I were to marry her, she could be happy with me, a noble person who loved her, as happy as one can be in a loveless marriage."[12] In Belinsky's complex world of emotion, "when she almost clearly expressed to me that she loved me ... I came to know what hell is and what true suffering is, suffering without sadness, without any moisture, but with only dry, burning despair."[13]

Learning of Belinsky's interest, Katkov renewed his attentions to Shchepkina, and Belinsky (with apparent relief) stepped aside. In the September–October 1839 letter in which Belinsky recounted the affair to Stankevich, he describes the dénouement as follows: "[Katkov's] love was a religious ecstasy; our *young lady* turned out to be a creature who was in the objective sense beautiful [*prekrasnoe*], passionate, and, in the area of passion, profound, but not at all of our world, and we both saw that we had been fools and bottom feeders [*griazoedy*, lit. "mud-eaters"]. He was the first to realize it—first he got angry at himself, cursed his feelings for all he was worth, and now he laughs." Belinsky goes on to offer the Bakuninesque moral of the story: "Oh, brother, what a person he is! You knew him as a kind of embryo. He is angry at his feelings and this whole affair, but it turned him upside down, pierced his coarse mass with rays of light, and now he is a marvelous young man.... He is still a child, but his childhood promises an impending and powerful manhood."[14] In Belinsky's version, Katkov's love for Shchepkina had been a necessary stage in the spiritual development of Katkov the man. Belinsky's final words on her are written three years later, on the occasion of her death, to Katkov himself: "In Moscow I found myself at a funeral—of Aleksandra Mikhailovna Shchepkina. The poor girl—she so much wanted to live, she so much wanted not to die; but she died!"[15]

The Fifty-Year-Old Uncle

Belinsky's letters are not the only venue he chose for describing the Shchepkina episode. In November 1838, while the affair was still in progress, Belinsky used it as material for one of his few artistic works, the play *The Fifty-Year-Old Uncle; or a Strange Illness* (*Piatidesiatiletnii diadiushka, ili Strannaia bolezn'*), written to be performed at M. S. Shchepkin's benefit on January 27, 1839, in Moscow. In his September–October 1839 letter to Stankevich describing his involvement with Shchepkina, Belinsky calls the real-life drama a "tragicomedy with vaudeville couplets." His play, which attempts with moderate success to be both tragic and comic, presents the Belinsky-Shchepkina-Katkov triangle through the characters of Nikolai Matveevich Gorsky, Lizanka Dumskaia, and Vladimir Dmitrievich Malsky. Gorsky is the "uncle" of the play's title, the guardian of the orphaned Lizanka and her sister Katenka. It is telling that the twenty-eight-year-old Belinsky depicts himself as fifty years old, moreover as not just a suitor but a father figure. Lizanka is presented as the pensive, quiet sister who resembles Pushkin's Tatiana (from *Eugene Onegin*) while Katenka takes the role of the frivolous, humorous counterpart of Pushkin's Olga. And Malsky, a student at Moscow University who is also Gorsky's "nephew and ward," is Katkov, "sketched in almost portrait-like fashion."[16] The play was first performed at Shchepkin's benefit, with Aleksandra Shchepkina playing her fictional double, Lizanka Dumskaia.

The plot of Belinsky's play is simple: Lizanka, Katenka, and Malsky have grown up under Gorsky's roof, and family tradition has destined Katenka to marry Malsky. But in the course of the play it becomes clear that frivolous Katenka does not really know her own mind, while Malsky is beginning to realize that his true love is Lizanka. Meanwhile Gorsky, Malsky's uncle and the guardian of Katenka and Lizanka, is overcome by passion for Lizanka. He confesses his love to her, and she initially recoils in horror. But as she comes to believe that Katenka loves Malsky, whom she herself loves, she decides that a loveless marriage to her kind guardian is the best fate for her. There are feeble complications in the form of a meddling woman and her son, but in the end Katenka and Malsky make it clear to each other that they are not in love (another suitor for Katenka conveniently turns up at the right moment), and Gorsky, having overheard Malsky talking to himself about his love for Lizanka, magnanimously steps aside so that Malsky and Lizanka can be united.

The play is an intriguing document of Belinsky's feelings about himself and about Katkov at a moment when the outcome of their own real-life drama had not yet been determined. The age difference between them is exaggerated, and the Katkov figure is depicted as a handsome, vigorous, and (unlike Katkov) rich young man. Gorsky says at one point, "That young rogue with his pretty little mug wants to torment me ... torture me ..."[17] His own appearance, in contrast, is far from attractive in his own eyes. Looking into a mirror, he says, "What is that over there—let me see ... Bah! It's me—what a good-looking fellow, devil take it! ... (*He hits himself on the head.*) What's that? A bald spot ... (*He hits himself on the stomach.*) And that? A fat, fifty-year-old belly! Well, what a fine lover, what a fine suitor!"[18]

Like an eighteenth-century Russian playwright, Belinsky gives his characters speaking names. Gorsky could be derived from "*gora*," "mountain," but it also evokes "*gore*," "sorrow," and "*gor'kii*," "bitter." Dumskaia evokes "*duma*," "thought, meditation." Most tellingly, the name of the Katkov figure, Malsky, is derived from the root meaning "small," and includes the first syllable of "*mal'chik*," "little boy." This is consonant with Belinsky's attitude in his letters, where he harps on Katkov's youth and greenness and most often refers to him as "the youth." A year later, in fall 1839, Belinsky would describe his feelings on seeing Katkov and Shchepkina commune lovingly: "I could not stand to see the agitation and alarm with which she would wait for her youth [Katkov], how, *sensing* his arrival, she would run out of the room in order to hide her agitation, how later they would talk to each other, their faces shining with bliss."[19] Something similar is experienced by Gorsky: "Who could have foreseen it? No, rather—who could have helped but see it! She has loved him for a long time, but she hid it. ... He has also loved her for a long time—before he even realized it. ... You can't deceive the heart—it has a thousand eyes ... a thousand ears—it sees everything, hears everything."[20]

In the description of Malsky, the play also reproduces the ambivalent attitude toward Katkov that Belinsky evinces in his letters. Despite his attractiveness, Malsky is accused repeatedly of being proud and pompous, and Katenka adds the accusation of "lack of candor and secretiveness."[21] Gorsky's hostility to his "nephew and ward," even before the rivalry over Lizanka develops fully, bursts out in a remarkable speech to Malsky: "All you know how to do is to have fun, pick flowers ... for uncle, read Pushkin with [the girls], fantasize, daydream, be carried away beyond the clouds, discourse beautifully about love ... according to professors' lectures. ... You're a learned man, you know how to talk, one listens to you spellbound.... You're a master at paying compliments and fawning ... but when misfortune comes, you don't give a damn ... the devil take you, you damned dreamer ... half-baked philosopher ... homespun poet!"[22] The hostility breaks out even more openly later in the play, without provocation by Malsky. Overcome by jealousy, Gorsky cries, "You are disgusting to me, repulsive.... I hate you! Yes! Even if you're right ... noble ... pure ..."[23] Even when he acknowledges Malsky's virtues, Gorsky cannot avoid a tinge of irony and sarcasm: "He's a splendid young man—intelligent, educated, sensitive—in a word, a real hero of a novel."[24]

Belinsky's play is a trifle; in the words of Belinsky's friend V. P. Botkin, "it has some decent scenes for the theater, but it is not an artistic work."[25] The most powerful moments convey Gorsky's tormenting passion for Lizanka, his hatred of both himself and his rival, and his gloomy resignation to a sad old age. Malsky and Lizanka are given the happy ending that was denied to Katkov and Shchepkina in life, while Belinsky faithfully reproduces his own sense of futility and despair. But there is no denying that as an artist Belinsky could not express himself with the passion and strangeness that he displays in his letters. His expression of his feelings toward Katkov in February 1839, as the rivalry was ending, far surpasses anything in *The Fifty-Year-Old Uncle* for power and self-torturing complexity:

> Truly, I am not guilty toward him in the slightest, and if I am guilty, then it's toward myself; but even toward myself my reason completely justifies me, and it justifies me freely, without any strain. But I have deeply understood the words of Werder—the reason justifies, but all the same, love produces the consciousness of guilt. And in this sense I deeply feel my guilt toward Katkov, and I have more than once in my thoughts lain sobbing at his feet, and like a slave begged for his forgiveness, not considering myself worthy of looking at him.... I was vulgar, low, base, nasty before him; obscurely sensing his superiority over me, I found my defense against his power, which irresistibly pursued me, in rotten, onanistic constructions. I didn't understand why myself, but he disturbed me, I was afraid of him, and I was ready to escape from his noble directness wherever I could, even into a latrine or under the skirt of the first wench I could find, in order to stick out my tongue at him from there, knowing that he is too holy and noble to follow me into such a disgusting refuge.[26]

Belinsky's attitude toward Katkov is a mix of attraction, exaggerated admiration, envy, and fear.

The Youth and the Eunuch

This same complex mixture is manifested in another personal drama in which the two took part, not long after the Shchepkina affair. In the winter of 1839–40, a rumor was spread in Moscow, apparently by Bakunin, that Katkov was having an affair with Mariia Lvovna Ogariova, wife of Nikolai Platonovich Ogariov (1813–77), a friend and close associate of Alexander Herzen. Perhaps the most detailed account of the gossip was given to the conservative memoirist Evgenii Mikhailovich Feoktistov (1829–98) by Elizaveta Vasilievna Salias-de-Turnemir [Sailhas de Tournemire] (1815–92, pen name Evgeniia Tur), who had a romantic relationship with Ogariov in the late 1840s. Feoktistov writes: "Countess Salias told me the following in this connection: soon after Ogariov's marriage, a discord arose between his wife, a young society lady who loved amusement, and her husband's friends, which grew stronger every day." Feoktistov continues,

> Of all the people who visited her husband, she valued highly only Katkov, who fell passionately in love with her. Once the well-known M. Bakunin came into Mme Ogariova's study and saw Katkov sitting on a bench at her feet, with his head on her knees; he [Bakunin] quickly retreated, but did not delay in telling people about the scene he had had occasion to witness. [Ogariov]'s friends were filled with indignation, although from the point of view of their theories they shouldn't have displayed any severity in this regard; they were enraptured by the sermons of George Sand.[27]

By most accounts the indignation of Ogariov and his friends was directed mainly at Bakunin for his gossip, not at Katkov for his indiscretion. In particular, Belinsky, who was estranged from Bakunin at this point, entered into the drama as an active supporter of Katkov and provided the venue for a physical clash between Bakunin and Katkov, described in one of Belinsky's letters, a letter that has had an inordinate influence on the historical interpretation of Bakunin's sexuality.

Belinsky's initial reaction to the rumors about Katkov and Ogariova, in a letter of December 1839–February 1840, was not in Katkov's favor. Belinsky writes that he feels the incident casts an "unpleasant light" on Katkov, who should be spiritually developed enough to avoid being tempted by "one moment of sensual ecstasy." Katkov's actions injure a husband who is "a noble person, trusting not out of weakness but out of the nobility of his soul." Nevertheless, Belinsky envies Katkov his ability to be carried away: "But with all this ... I envy him—and I envy, agonizingly envy this idiotic ability to give oneself up completely, without reflection, if only to a vulgar feeling. Why was I never able to give myself up entirely and completely to any feeling at all, although the worst of my foolish actions was more reasonable and more humane than the *youth* in question [Katkov]."[28] By June 1840, however, Belinsky had entered the conflict on the side of Katkov, as described in a letter written, again to his friend V. P. Botkin, two months after the fact, in August.

Katkov was apparently quite friendly with Bakunin before this, and even took his side in his conflict with Belinsky in the winter of 1838–39, the same time, of course, as Katkov's rivalry with Belinsky over Shchepkina. In one of Katkov's letters of the time, written to Bakunin in January 1839, he seems to be speaking the common Bakuninesque-Hegelian discourse of "reality" or "actuality":

> There can be nothing higher or sweeter than the feeling when you begin to recognize yourself as a legitimate citizen in the realm of the spirit, when you begin to deeply respect your *I*, not the former, immediate, natural one, which has been conquered (at least at those moments), but the enlightened, spiritual one, the concrete form of the general life.... The main mistake we have all made is that we worried too much about circumstances: they should freely emerge out of a person's personality and be considered actual [or real] in direct proportion to the actuality [reality] of that personality.[29]

But in June 1840, incensed by the rumors spread by Bakunin about his relations with Mariia Ogariova, and learning of Bakunin's arrival in St. Petersburg in anticipation of his departure for Germany, Katkov arranged to lie in wait for Bakunin in Belinsky's apartment.

As the editor of Bakunin's letters notes, Belinsky "played the role if not of an instigator, then of an active accomplice of the side hostile to Bakunin. The second day after his arrival in Petersburg, that is probably June 27, Bakunin went to say goodbye to Belinsky, where something like a trap had been set for him."[30] In Belinsky's study, Bakunin was unexpectedly confronted by Katkov. In Belinsky's account, Katkov challenged Bakunin about his interference in Katkov's affairs:

> Bakunin, like someone suddenly burned by heavenly fire, backed up and entered the bedroom rear end first, and sat on the divan, saying with a changed face and voice and with feigned indifference: "Facts, facts, I would like some little facts, my dear sir!" [Katkov said,] "What facts! You sold me out for small change—you are a scoundrel, sir!" B. jumped up[, saying,] "You're a scoundrel yourself!" [Katkov said:]

"Eunuch! [*skopets*]"—this acted on [Bakunin] more powerfully than "scoundrel": he shuddered as if from an electric shock.[31]

A physical clash ensued, in which, according to Belinsky, Katkov obtained the upper hand, slapping Bakunin twice in the face. The scene ended with Katkov's strong hint that Bakunin was obligated to fight a duel with him.

In the letter to Botkin describing this incident, Belinsky expresses some ambivalence about the role he has played. He felt a pity for Bakunin that was "more insulting than any offense" and regret that as a guest in Belinsky's home Bakunin "had been subjected to a shameful beating." As for Katkov, "I was irritated with him for choosing my apartment as the theater for such an explanation, and meanwhile at the same time I felt that there are certain situations in life when only philistines think about the proprieties and relationships."[32] The conclusion to Belinsky's account recalls the mix of sexual jealousy of and sexual admiration for Katkov that he displayed in the Shchepkina affair:

> Well ... I will not forget that day. I played the role of a wet chicken. I should either have watched the entertaining spectacle silently, with the learned air of an expert, or thrown myself between the knights in order to separate them, but I stood firmly on the threshold of the room, as if riveted to it; only my arms freely stretched out to the fighters, but didn't reach them. Yes, Botkin, for the first time I looked life in the face, for the first time I learned the significance of a man who is worthy of the love of a woman.[33]

Belinsky's strong reaction to Katkov's young and virile persona was surely one frame of reference that he brought to his concurrent assessment of Katkov's early writings, which we will discuss shortly.

In a later letter to Botkin, Belinsky again exalts Katkov's virility, this time in comparison not with the "eunuch" Bakunin but with the supposedly wronged husband Ogariov. Belinsky calls Ogariov "a brood-hen incapable of satisfying the needs either of the most profound and spiritual woman or of a passionate woman," who got married based on abstract ideas. He asks why Mariia Ogariova should have to die without knowing "the caresses of a man whom her soul and heart so thirst for"—that is, Katkov. Belinsky asks,

> If our youth [Katkov], in your opinion, acted ignobly with O[gariov], then did O[gariov] act nobly with *her*? ... I understand now how George Sand could dedicate

the activity of her whole life to a war with marriage. In general all the social bases of our time demand the strictest reconsideration and radical rebuilding [*perestroika*], which will happen sooner or later. It's time to liberate the human personality, which is unhappy even without this, from the vile fetters of irrational actuality—the opinion of the mob and the traditions of the barbaric ages.

Belinsky here anticipates the radical attempts to explode traditional family arrangements that would later be the subject of Nikolai Chernyshevsky's highly influential novel *What Is To Be Done?* (*Chto delat'*, 1863). Ironically, given what Belinsky sees as Katkov's potentially "liberating" role in the Ogariov marriage, Katkov was to be Chernyshevsky's chief antagonist in the 1860s.[34]

Ogariov himself displays an attitude toward Katkov that recalls Belinsky's in its ambivalence. Something about Katkov continued to attract Ogariov long after their friendship had been damaged by whatever may have happened in the winter of 1839–40. Ogariov, now separated from Mariia Lvovna but still faithfully corresponding with her, writes her from Berlin in December 1841:

> It seems I already wrote to you that at a lecture by Schelling I bowed to Katkov. I am a foolish child. I loved him and forgave him. Yesterday we met on the street and talked; he was polite and embarrassed, but joy was also visible on his face; I was touched, but adopted a calm appearance; we said a few words and parted. The insult inflicted [*nanesennoe*] by Katkov is completely personal; his childish self-esteem could not arouse any anger in me, but only extract a smile. That is why one can forgive Katkov. The insult being inflicted [*nanosimoe*] by Bakunin is much worse. It cannot be forgiven; [it is] an insult to everything that is deeply human in us.[35]

Two months later, in February 1842, Ogariov seems to echo Belinsky's criticism of his own inability to satisfy a woman (although here the context is spiritual rather than sexual). At the same time, he compares Katkov to Franz Liszt, the great composer and pianist and an acquaintance of the Ogariovs, who was famous for his powerful magnetism and sexual attractiveness. Ogariov tells Mariia that he is not offended by the fact that he does not "satisfy all the needs of [her] soul." He is offended only by "your attraction to Lizst and to Katkov." Ogariov acknowledges the similarities between the two men, and continues,

> But can you really be attracted to these purely external natures, not penetrated by any love? These are will o' the wisps, Masha. You have to run after them over barren

soil, and then only in order to convince yourself that they don't exist. Earlier it seemed to me that Katkov was capable of loving; I was forced to lose faith in that. I bowed to him because you can't deny that he has at least external nobility; but what can you do with the fact that there is a lot in him that is nasty, and in me too. But I never had a moment of doubt about Liszt—he is a brilliant man from the outside, but without any human interior.[36]

Like Belinsky, Ogariov deeply feels Katkov's charisma but is also disturbed by it and suspicious that it masks either "nastiness" or, worse, emptiness.

In Belinsky's mythologizing of Katkov's clash with Bakunin, Katkov emerges as the youthful, virile figure who flings the accusation "eunuch" (or "castrate") at Bakunin at the height of their quarrel. As Marshall S. Shatz has demonstrated, this passage in Belinsky's letter, along with other bits of flimsy evidence, has been used to build a theory of Bakunin's supposed sexual impotence, and his consequent channeling of his sexual energies into revolutionary political activity. Shatz rightly argues that "we cannot be certain that Belinskii was reporting Katkov's exact words and not his own embellishment of them."[37] Shatz points out that in the same letter to Botkin in which Belinsky describes the clash between Katkov and Bakunin, he himself a bit later refers to Bakunin as writing a note to Katkov "in the style of a masturbator and eunuch" [*onanisticheskim i skopecheskim slogom*]. Shatz concludes that for Belinsky, "eunuch" could not possibly refer literally to sexual impotence: "One does not have to be a physiologist to suggest that it is really rather difficult to be both a 'masturbator' and a 'eunuch' at the same time."[38] In fact, however, in nineteenth-century discourse about masturbation, the connection between masturbation and impotence was clearly established; sexual impotence was one of the many disorders masturbation was believed to cause.[39]

In 1992 (four years after Shatz's article was published), a previously suppressed portion of a letter from Belinsky to Bakunin was published that illuminates Belinsky's preoccupation with the idea of masturbation and shows that it is not purely metaphorical. In the summer and fall of 1837, Belinsky and Bakunin were competing with each other in letters as to who had the most vices to overcome in order to achieve a truly spiritual existence. In a letter that has been lost but whose content is clear from Belinsky's reply, Bakunin attempted to top Belinsky's sordid confessions with his trump card: that he had been an "onanist" until the age of nineteen. In the newly published portion of his letter of November 15–20, 1837, to Bakunin, Belinsky tops him by confessing that he *began* masturbating at the age of nineteen and only stopped recently: "No, Michel, say what you wish, but I am more outstanding than you: I wasn't a cadet, I wasn't an officer in Moscow, without books, without people, without money and boots, I began not as a young boy but as a youth—no, I am higher than you."[40] Belinsky is using the words "outstanding" and "higher" ironically here; in fact, it would be considered much more shameful to indulge in masturbation as a mature man than as a young boy, hence he has topped Bakunin in abjectness. To say that Belinsky meant it literally when he called Bakunin a masturbator is not to deny that he sometimes lends masturbation a metaphorical meaning as well. In Belinsky's letters, the idea of masturbation is often linked with fruitless, abstract reasoning; the connection between onanism and impotence is not for him an oxymoron but a causality: "I am definitely going to write a big article about onanism, or *raisonneur* idealism, which makes a heavy dream of life, makes phantoms out of joys."[41]

The Great Hope of Russian Literature

Just as Katkov emerges in Belinsky's version of the romantic dramas of 1838–40 as young and virile, not impotent like his "onanistic" elders, at the same time his literary and journalistic productivity arouses Belinsky's admiration and envy. In the same fall 1839 letter to Stankevich in which Belinsky describes the Shchepkina affair, he writes, "He [Katkov] is still a child, but his childhood promises an impending and powerful manhood. What talent, what profundity, how much spiritual fire, what an inexhaustible, fruitful, and manly activity! In everything he writes, there is such presence of thought, his first attempts are much more manly [*muzhestvennee*] than the ones I'm making now."[42] In 1838–40, Katkov was trying his hand at literary translation and literary criticism, and his efforts evoked Belinsky's sometimes wholehearted, sometimes grudging admiration. Belinsky praised several of Katkov's works: his review of I. Sakharov's edition of *Songs of the Russian People* (1839); his introduction to and translation of Karl August Varnhagen von Ense's article on Pushkin (1839); his review of Mikhail Maksimovich, *History of Old Russian Literature* (1840); and his translation of Shakespeare's *Romeo and Juliet* (1838–41).[43] Perhaps the most enthusiastic endorsement of Katkov by Belinsky comes in a letter of spring 1840:

> I see in him the great hope of scholarship and of Russian literature. He will go far, far, farther than the likes of us have even dreamed of going or ever will. His article about Maksimovich's little book is marvelous—an excellent article: thought just shines in

every word. In general, the predominance of thought in a definite and vivid word is the distinguishing character of his articles and their lofty virtue; and the absence of concentrated spontaneous heartfelt warmth is their fault, but it is a fault not of his nature but of his years. The general [*obshchee*] devours his spirit and, so to say, deprives his individuality of personality. This miraculous beginning—it will always remain with him, being strengthened by his scholarship, and when he stops raising dust and turns from a nasty piglet into a respected hog like you and me—then even the fault I spoke of and which I don't know how to name precisely will disappear. I read his articles with particular respect—I delight in them and learn how to think. Yes, brother, this nasty piglet, the Devil take him, is looking to become a mentor for some hogs, of which the first is yours truly.[44]

Belinsky's statement that Katkov was "the great hope ... of Russian literature" would surely have been repudiated by him a few years later, when he decisively broke with Katkov. But the statement has lasting validity if we take seriously Katkov's accomplishment in fostering the emergence of the great Russian novel in the second half of the nineteenth century.

It is useful to look closely at some of Katkov's early literary exercises, to understand his formation as an aspiring critic. His work was not destined to continue along the same lines, and Katkov, unlike Belinsky, was not to find his calling as a literary critic or theorist. But there is no doubt that his eventual goals and mission as an editor and publisher had their birth in these early writings.

Katkov's Translation of Rötscher, *Philosophy of Art*

The first of Katkov's publications we will consider is his translation of part of Heinrich Theodor Rötscher, *Abhandlungen zur Philosophie der Kunst* (Berlin, 1837), which appeared with his introduction and commentary in the *Moscow Observer*, a journal edited by Belinsky, in 1838.[45] As Katkov explains in his introduction, Rötscher was one of a number of German thinkers who were trying to popularize philosophical ideas by "adapting philosophical results to general comprehension." For Katkov, the most powerful of these attempts are those, like Rötscher's, that deal with the study of art, "because their main goal consists not simply in adapting the idea for general comprehension, but in a scientific development of its content, a development that must make the concrete even more concrete."[46]

In the course of translating Rötscher, a disciple of Hegel, Katkov has to do his own work of popularization, finding Russian equivalents for specific Hegelian terms such as *Verstand* (understanding), *Vernunft* (reason), *Moralität* (morality), *Sittlichkeit* (ethics), and *Totalität* (totality; Katkov chooses "*rassudok*," "*razum*," "*moral'nost'*," "*nravstvennost'*," and "*totalitet*," the latter a neologism).[47] In a footnote, Katkov explains,

> We would not wish to weary our readers with foreign words that are not yet in use here, but these words are necessary terms of philosophy, the roots of which are deeply buried in its soil.... We are not undertaking to invent words: that right belongs either to a whole people, or to the representatives of the people's consciousness. Of course the word *Totalität* could be conveyed faithfully by the Russian word *tselost'* [wholeness]; but that word has not yet attained the necessary flexibility, and therefore in certain meanings it would be too strange for the unaccustomed ear.[48]

The central idea of Rötscher's essay is that the student of art, specifically literary art, must respect the wholeness of the artistic work, and not be content with what, in a paraphrase of Goethe, Rötscher calls "fragmentary praise and fragmentary censure."[49] In Katkov's introduction, he summarizes Rötscher's ideas in a way that would not be alien to many modern students of literary art: The task of aesthetics is to delve deeply into the particularity and detail of art, to understand the great works in "their rational architectonics," and "through the enrichment of the general with the living content of the particular, grasped in all its necessity, the cognition of the general principles of this science will also be broadened."[50]

As Rötscher explains, in order to understand "the idea of the whole," the philosophical student of art must first "extract this concrete idea out of the beautiful world of its living images and be able to keep hold of it." He admits that this process of analysis can seem painful. The form must first be broken down, "the beautiful construction is deconstructed": "At first a person is embraced by the elegant work in all its wholeness and is sated by its fullness; but being a spirit, he feels a deep need to recognize the content of his enjoyment and as it were *justify* it to himself. And this same spirit necessarily inspires a person to break the precious vessel, so that, without being blinded by its magnificence and beauty, he may contemplate its content in all its nakedness."[51] Then the form that has been destroyed for an instant is restored: "The spirit, having voluntarily banished itself from the country of beauty and from the circle of living images, returns to live independently in that world and to understand the language and the sounds that resound in that world."[52] Rötscher later compares this process to the dismemberment and revivification of Dionysus: "In the scientific study of the artistic work it is not enough to preserve the *general* life of the concrete idea—this is the work of *wisdom*; but also besides wisdom is needed a *creative* activity, which would restore the magnificent construction of the body and through this would return the images, preserved in the fire of thought, in a new, enlightened form."[53]

In a footnote to this passage, Katkov uses the analogy of the "living water" of Russian folklore, which has the power to bring dead members back to life. The action of the reason [*razum*], like the supernatural power of living water, has the superintellectual [*sverkhrassudochnyi*] power to overcome the deadening action of the intellect; *Vernunft* is the living water that counteracts the ruinous decomposing effects of the *Verstand*. Katkov's deep understanding of literary analysis, as displayed by his translation of and commentary on Rötscher, was an important grounding for his later career of editorial discernment and cultivation of the best Russian writers.

Yet another of Rötscher's main ideas also has important implications for Katkov's later work as an editor. After offering interpretations of *Romeo and Juliet* and Goethe's *Elective Affinities* using his "philosophical" method, Rötscher answers the anticipated objection that the artist himself probably did not think of all the details and interpretations offered by the philosophical critic. Of course, Rötscher replies, the artist did not know about these connections, because he is an artist and not a philosopher. The moment the artist recognizes "with the power of thought in all its wholeness" the interconnection of all the "inner phenomena of his work, the laws of these phenomena, the necessity by which they can only be these and not others," he ceases to be a creative artist and becomes a philosopher. The artist contemplates the world in concrete images and is not conscious of "the general content of the whole." As an artist, he "cannot determine in advance for his work some thought and then search out for it separate images and distribute them according to their mission.... The artist does not recognize pure thought and cannot philosophically define the inner relations of the parts of his work."[54]

Here Rötscher provides the basis for arguing that the artist does not have complete control over interpretations of his work once it has been made public. The critic-philosopher is free to find connections and interpretations that the artist himself might not recognize as being part of his plan, because "*as* an artist he does not have and cannot have a *consciousness* of his creative activity in general, and even less at the moment of inspired creation, to be aware of the rational unity of the particular images with the general idea of the whole. If an artist strives to recognize the nature of his activity or its products, then he is located outside of his realm and enters into the realm of philosophy. Moving onto the ground of philosophy, now as a philosopher, he goes to meet his artistic activity and makes it an object for *thinking consciousness*."[55] In other words, the artist has no privileged position in the interpretation of his art. He is free to interpret it himself, but his interpretation has no priority over those of other "philosophers." In his later activity as an editor, Katkov was famous for what was perceived as high-handed interference in artistic creation, for seeming to regard himself as knowing better than the artist what the work should contain or not contain. Although such interference goes beyond what Rötscher prescribes here, since it goes beyond interpretation into cocreation, Katkov's apparent sense that he had superior knowledge of what belonged and did not belong in an artistic work may well have its origins here.

A problem arises for the Russian critic who wishes to put Rötscher's ideas to the test, since he tends to take his examples from the realm of "eternal" works of art, works by Goethe and Shakespeare that have attained universal significance in the Western world. The constant refrain of Russian writers, particularly Belinsky, in the first decades of the nineteenth century was, "We have no literature!" Despite individual geniuses like Lomonosov, Derzhavin, and of course Pushkin, Russian literature had not yet assembled a corpus that could compare with the works of classical Greece, Elizabethan England, and the contemporary German-speaking lands. But toward the very end of the articles translated by Katkov, Rötscher offers a hint that Katkov was to take up in his further literary writings. Rötscher defines three types of criticism: the type that must mercilessly destroy works "that try to cover their emptiness with a phrase-making membrane, to cover the poverty of their content with the tinsel glitter of form"; the type that has the aim of "uncovering the positive within the negative, of removing the kernel from its shell"; and the type that considers works that are "eternal revelations of the absolute idea."[56]

The second type of criticism finds its highest expression as "a criticism that understands an individual work or an artist in their historical significance," that defines a work's negative aspects as part of historical development, so that criticism "becomes in a sense a dialectic of the world-historical process." This kind of criticism "leaves the indication of the negative aspects to the most objective power—history itself; renouncing any subjectivity, it only repeats and brings into an inner connection what is expressed by the facts of history."[57] In his following works on Russian literature, which deal with the pre-modern tradition of folk songs and knightly tales, Katkov clearly models himself as the critic who understands art "in its historical significance."

Literature and the World-Historical Nation

In his reviews of Sakharov's *Songs of the Russian People* and Maksimovich's *History of Old Russian Literature*, Katkov uses the Hegelian terminology of the "world-historical nation," as expounded in *Elements of the Philosophy of Right* (1820). In Hegel's formulation,

> Since history is the process whereby the spirit assumes the shape of events and of immediate natural actuality, the stages of its development are present as *immediate natural principles*; and since these are natural, they constitute a plurality of separate entities such that *one of them is allotted to each nation* in its geographical and anthropological existence. The nation to which such a moment is allotted as a natural principle is given the task of implementing this principle in the course of the self-development of the world spirit's self-consciousness. This nation is the dominant one in world history for this epoch, and only once in history can it have this epoch-making role.[58]

Katkov uses the term "world-historical nation" sometimes in a strictly Hegelian sense, and sometimes more loosely, to mean "a nation with universal cultural significance."

In both reviews Katkov identifies the reign of Peter the Great as the moment at which Russia moved out of its primordial state and began to enter into world-historical status: "Only from Peter's time did Russia arise, a powerful, giantlike state; only from Peter's time did the Russian people become a nation [*natsiia*], become one of the representatives of humanity, which developed one of the aspects of the spirit through its life; only from Peter's time did higher spiritual interests enter its organism; only from his time did it accept into itself the content of the development of humanity." According to Katkov, neither art nor science truly existed in Russia before Peter's reign: "We have no Gothic churches, we have no works of the artistic brush or sculptor's chisel, we had no music. The people had not yet matured for such manifestations of its essence; it was all submerged into its natural life, which can be revealed also in a natural, in a naïve form. This naïve form of expression of the people's life is the people's [folk] poetry."[59]

In the review of Maksimovich, Katkov asserts that achieving world-historical status is the only way for a people to preserve its language. According to Katkov, if a people "is animated by the world-historical spirit," it may die physically but it will "remain eternally alive in the spirit": "Ancient Greece no longer exists on the earth, but its essence, the immortal idea that animated it, shines with blessed glory in the self-consciousness of the spirit." A people that lives only an external existence disappears without a trace. He sees language in the same terms: "Language is exactly the same: either it disappears completely and forever, having resounded in space, or, ceasing to resound and fly from mouth to mouth, *remains for all eternity imprinted in indestructible monuments*. In the latter case, although a language is called dead, it is dead only because it does not resound in empirical life and lives, together with the spirit of the people, in spirit, which has been manifested in verbal works."[60] In other words, the way to preserve a language as the sign of a world-historical nation is to produce a great literature written in that language. This conviction will remain with Katkov as he changes careers from literary critic to professor and finally to journal editor and publisher.

In the course of his analysis, Katkov indicates an adoption of the conservative interpretation of Hegel, the idea of "reconciliation with reality" that Bakunin and Belinsky had promoted. He writes, "Whatever is must be, and—if you look closely, you will be convinced of the rationality and necessity of what is and what must be."[61] In his review of Russian history, Katkov argues that the Mongol invasion of Kievan *Rus'* (the ancient name for the Russian lands) in the thirteenth–fifteenth centuries was a necessary component of Russia's development, because after the fragmentation of the body of Russia through the *udel* system of princely holdings that arose in the twelfth century, an external force was needed that would stop the centrifugal movement. This external force needed to act on Rus' without affecting its internal nature, "so that Rus' would not cease being Rus'." Thus it was providential not only that there was an invasion, but that it was the Mongols who invaded: "Only a nomadic people could create the consequences that conditioned the character of the further development of Rus'." The Mongols fenced Rus' off "by the terrible wall of their might," defining its borders and concentrating it, while not disturbing the essence of its character; "they left everything just as it was."[62] In consonance with "reconciliation with reality," at the end of this article Katkov enthusiastically affirms the slogan "Orthodoxy, autocracy, and nationality," shorthand for the doctrine of "official nationality" proposed by Minister of Education Sergei Semionovich Uvarov in 1833, which had become the dominant ideology of the reign of Nicholas I (r. 1825–55). This slogan, Katkov asserts, "must be imprinted in the heart of every true Russian."[63]

In the review of Maksimovich, Katkov singles out literature as "the expression of the self-consciousness of the spirit," "the living aggregate of works that explore the various tendencies of the developing spirit." In studying literature, we study not works in their separateness, but "literature as a living organism."[64] Katkov acknowledges that the Slavic tribes do not yet have world-historical status: "Not a single people has had such an enigmatic and unfortunate fate as the Slavic tribes. Gifted by nature with the richest talents, they have remained somehow an unsolved mystery [*nerazgadanny*], at least until Russia began to justify their existence on the earth." The Slavic tribes have not a history but a collection of random events. But the future is promising: "It would be sinful of us, living in the bosom of this tribe, not to sense the power contained in it, and not to have a premonition of its blessed future. It will be great in spirit and in humanity, the Slavic tribe—this premonition of ours tells us powerfully. With this inner voice, how understandable is the desire to learn about and preserve the fates of the former life of the people, even if nothing world-historical has yet been opened up in it!"[65] In this prediction of the coming to world-historical status of the Slavic tribes, with Russia as their head, we can see the later political preoccupations of Katkov in embryo. It is important to note, however, that at this stage of his career he is focused on literature, not politics, as the proper field in which Russia was to attain its world-historical status. According to Shlomo Avineri, this focus is consonant with an accurate reading of Hegel: "Hegel never ascribed *political domination* to what he termed world-historical nations.... The *absolute right* is not in the realm of international politics, but in the sphere of cultural leadership."[66]

The Greatness of Pushkin

Another important publication by Katkov in these years addresses the question of Russia's own literary contribution head-on. In 1838 Karl August Varnhagen von Ense (1785–1858) had published a review of a posthumous edition of Pushkin's works soon after Pushkin died in a duel in 1837. The review appeared in *Jahrbücher für wissenschaftliche Kritik*, the Berlin journal that served as the major venue for Hegelian criticism. A Russian translation had appeared in 1839 in the journal *Son of the Fatherland* (*Syn otechestva*). Dissatisfied with this translation, Belinsky asked Katkov to do a new translation of the essay for his own journal the *Moscow Observer*, but it was not passed by the censor. Katkov's translation, with his own introduction, appeared in *Notes of the Fatherland*, also in 1839.[67] Belinsky wrote of the original translation, "[Varnhagen's article] has already been translated in *Son of the Fatherland*, but translated *in such a way* that if Varnhagen himself knew Russian as well as he knows German, he would not at all recognize his article."[68] No doubt Belinsky's opinion of the quality of the translation was influenced by Katkov himself, who wrote in his introduction, "Some kind of pitiful, unfaithful translation has without authorization called itself Varnhagen's article on Pushkin and has set off, together with the journal that accepted it into its embraces, to wander about the world and mislead honest people."[69]

In his introduction to his translation of Varnhagen's article, Katkov expresses great pride that "the famous German biographer and critic" has shown an appreciation of "our Pushkin, our great Pushkin." This affirmation by a foreigner provides justification for claiming Pushkin's universal significance:

> It would seem ludicrous to many if we said that Pushkin is a universal poet who ranks with those few on whom all of humanity looks with reverence.... What if we say to them what we have just said, in the voice of a foreigner who is alien to all bias, a foreigner who judges Russia and its phenomena not as a member of the nation but as a member of all humanity—what will they say then?... Just as the people of Russia are not lower than any nation in the world, so Pushkin is not lower than any poet in the world.[70]

After pointing out the Hegelian provenance of the journal in which Varnhagen's article appeared, Katkov rejoices in Russia's incipient universal significance (implying that if Russia has been acknowledged by Germany, it has become truly universal):

> In the person of Hegel, Germany extends its hand to us, in the person of Germany— all of Europe and all humanity extends its hand to us.... Do you hear? Our teachers call out to us as equals to equals.... For shame! We were forestalled in the evaluation of our Pushkin! But may God grant that this is the last time, may God grant that we finally feel in ourselves the strength for original and self-conscious intellectual activity. With this sweet hope we conclude our short introduction to the article by Varnhagen von Ense, an article in which we hear as if from another world, resounding in greeting to Russia and its great poet—the voice of Hegel himself.[71]

In his introduction, Katkov notes that during Pushkin's lifetime many Russian critics did not fully appreciate his greatness: "With pitiful pomposity they analyzed his creations, or with a cloying smile of insulting condescension they would praise them, adding that Pushkin is a poet, a good poet."[72] Belinsky himself had fallen into this category during Pushkin's lifetime, but by 1839 he seemed to share Katkov's enthusiasm for the significance of Varnhagen's acclamation of Pushkin.[73] After quoting in his 1839 overview of Russian journals Katkov's exaltation of Pushkin as the "poet of all humanity," Belinsky writes, "These lines are a fiery expression of a deep heartfelt conviction—we are completely, *literally* in agreement with them; they constitute one of the most basic supports of our inner life, one of the most ardent beliefs by which our spirit lives."[74] Although Katkov (and Belinsky) seem confident that Varnhagen's seal of approval makes Pushkin a poet of universal significance, one writer does not make a world-historical nation. Katkov had to feel that there was a need for the canon to be augmented, so that Russia could attain the bright future he foretold in the review of Maksimovich.

The Parting of the Ways

Belinsky acknowledged Katkov's influence on him in several letters of 1837–40: "Katkov has forced me to move forward a lot, without knowing it"; "He awoke a lot in me, and out of this lot the greater part was resurrected and independently reworked in me after his departure."[75] Katkov's notes on Hegel's aesthetics and his translation of Rötscher's essay on the philosophy of art helped shape Belinsky's conception of literary criticism in these years.[76] But Katkov had left for Germany in October 1840, and it seems that without his charismatic, magnetic presence, Belinsky began to feel disillusioned. By the end of 1840, a note of criticism appears in Belinsky's letters: "I wish I could borrow Katkov's style: I'd make better use of it. By the way, tell me frankly: what did you think of his article about Sarra Tolstaia? No one likes it—I myself can see that there are a lot of ideas, but they pass through the reader's head as if through a sieve, and don't stay there. I begin reading—it's marvelous; I close the book—I don't remember anything I read. What do you think?"[77] Although he had praised Katkov's translation of *Romeo and Juliet* to Stankevich in fall 1839, now he eagerly asks Botkin to convey negative gossip about it: "What are you saying there about Katkov's *Romeo and Juliet*—is it really awfully inaccurate?"[78]

Belinsky's most expansive critique of Katkov appears in a letter of December 1840–January 1841 to Botkin. Here he reinterprets his earlier admiration of Katkov as a symptom of his own psychic need to exalt those he sees as competitors: "I have a strange habit of taking self-advertisement in others for proof of merit—and I believed that he was a statue more masterly than the Apollo Belvedere itself, so why not spit on myself and humble myself before him.... Don't forget that Katkov and I are rivals in our craft, and because of my nature, I am always capable of seeing in a rival God knows what, and in myself less than nothing."[79] This is the same letter in which Belinsky compares Katkov favorably with the "brood-hen" Ogariov, and in which he speaks of how "Katkov awoke a lot in me." His analysis of Katkov still contains much that is positive and admiring, even as he predicts that Katkov's downfall will be caused by his exaggerated self-esteem:

> Yes, there are many, many blemishes on this otherwise excellent character. Time is forming it. There are characters that develop with difficulty and slowly [*tugo*]—to such belongs the character of our youth [Katkov]. And meanwhile it is a character full of strength, energy, power, a broad nature, if not yet profound; he will never become either a pietist or a *raisonneur* or a sentimental buffoon. Only he carries in himself a terrible enemy—self-esteem [*samoliubie*], which with his raw, animal organism can lead him to the Devil knows what.[80]

The word Belinsky uses to characterize Katkov, *samoliubie*, lit. "self-love" (a calque of the French *amour propre*), can be translated as self-esteem, ambition, vanity, pride, or self-respect. It is probably the word most often used to describe Katkov in the coming years, when his public persona as the editor of the *Russian Herald* and the *Moscow News* becomes defined. It will appear in these pages often, and although it may be translated in different ways, I will note its recurrence by giving the Russian whenever it appears.

By the time of Katkov's return to Russia in early 1843, Belinsky can find nothing good to say about him. His reaction now contains an element of physical revulsion that contrasts starkly with the quasi-sexual attraction Belinsky felt for Katkov in 1839: "You saw Katkov. I saw him too. A splendid subject for psychological observation. He is Khlestakov in the German style. I now understand why at the height of my supposed friendship with him I was wildly struck by his green glassy eyes.... This person has not changed, but only become himself. Now he is a pile of philosophical shit: watch out and don't step in it—it will dirty you and begin to stink."[81] In comparing Katkov to Khlestakov, the wildly imaginative and boastful liar in Gogol's 1836 play *The Government Inspector*, Belinsky seemingly repudiated the weighty significance he had lent the man he called "the great hope of scholarship and of Russian literature." He also gave Soviet critics the label, "Khlestakov in the German style," that would invariably accompany their characterizations of the Belinsky-Katkov relationship.

It is no coincidence that Belinsky's rejection of Katkov happened in the period 1840-43, at the same time as his rejection of the conservative-Hegelian idea of "reconciliation with reality." Although Belinsky was really only rejecting a myth of Hegel, in 1841 he saw it as a repudiation of Hegel himself:

> I have particularly important reasons to be furious at Hegel, because I feel that I was faithful to him (in sensation), by reconciling with Russian reality. . . . The fate of the subject, of the individual, of the personality is more important than the fates of the whole world and the health of the Chinese emperor (that is Hegel's *Allgemeinheit*).[82]

It is hardly surprising that along with Hegel, Belinsky would discard Katkov, the man who had helped to introduce him to Hegel's thought. Katkov was also a man who, although he favored moderate reform in the 1850s, never stopped believing that the Russian autocracy was a "rational reality" that should be preserved. Belinsky, meanwhile, aligned himself with the more radical critique of the Russian status quo that centered around the journal the *Contemporary* (*Sovremennik*). In 1847 in his famous letter to Gogol, Belinsky offered his view of the Russian writer as a bulwark against "official nationality": "[The public] sees in Russian writers its only leaders, defenders, and saviors from Russian autocracy, Orthodoxy, and nationalism."[83]

In the 1840–41 letter to Botkin in which Belinsky criticizes Katkov at length, his final words on Katkov are significant: "The more I think about it, the more clearly I see that Katkov's stay in Piter [St. Petersburg] gave a powerful shove [or stimulus] to the movement of my consciousness. His personality slid over me without leaving a trace; but his views on many things—truly, it seems to me that they gave me more than they did to him."[84] Katkov played a key role in the formative years of the man who was to be recognized as Russia's greatest literary critic of the nineteenth century. The question of what Katkov's ideas gave to Belinsky deserves more serious study, freed of the need felt by Soviet scholars to dismiss Katkov's contributions and demonize his personality. In the late 1830s, after the death of Pushkin in 1837, both Belinsky and Katkov were moved by the feeling that, as Belinsky wrote, "Russia has no literature!"[85] Belinsky's response, until his untimely death in 1848, was to foster Russian literature through philosophically informed discussion, criticism, and theory formation. Katkov's next phase of activity sees him departing from the path of critical writing onto the path of education, a path he would never fully abandon even after he became Russia's most powerful publisher.

CHAPTER 2

KATKOV AND EVGENIIA TUR

A PERSONA SHAPED IN POLEMICS

Katkov, who made his major contribution to Russian literary, intellectual, and political life as a journalist, took a while to find his way to that profession, first studying philosophy in Berlin for a year and a half and then teaching philosophy at Moscow University until losing his position for political reasons. In this chapter we will briefly review the period of his life between his early literary activity and his founding of the *Russian Herald* in 1856. Then we will consider the role played in the early years of the journal by the writer Evgeniia Tur (pseudonym of Elizaveta Vasilievna Salias-de-Turnemir [Sailhas de Tournemire], 1815–92). Tur's collaboration with Katkov on the *Russian Herald* ended in an extensive journal polemic that helped to create Katkov's public image, and in particular Dostoevsky's image of him and his editing practice. Tur's polemic with Katkov revealed the fundamental conflicts that would plague his relationships with Turgenev, Dostoevsky, and Tolstoy.

Katkov in Berlin

Katkov went to Berlin in October 1841 with almost no money in his pockets, relying on an honorarium that he expected would be sent to him for the publication of his translation of *Romeo and Juliet* and also on his planned work for *Notes of the Fatherland*.[1] The payment for the translation never came, and it was impossible for him to write the kind of extensive book reviews for *Notes of the Fatherland* that he had produced in Russia, since he could not afford to buy books to review. His entire stay in Germany was marked by severe financial need. His one lifeline was A. A. Kraevsky, the editor of *Notes of the Fatherland*, who provided him with some scanty financial support. As Katkov wrote later to Kraevsky, "With an empty pocket and, what's still worse, with a head full of extravagant fantasizing and drunken hopes, I left for a foreign land. All I could dream of was leaving, and then I would fly throughout God's world lightly and freely."[2] In a letter of March 1842, Katkov looks back soberly on the reality of his experience: "My patience is being exhausted, the struggle with destitution has worn me out. My God, how much have I endured, how many deprivations, humiliations, insults! I don't even know how to go back. Oh, money—that devil's invention—how very much depends on it. Sometimes I have moments of such despair that I need all my strength of will, all the aid of my education, in order not to crown the comedy with a bad ending."[3] In his later practice as editor and publisher, one can see the lasting impression that these years of deprivation had on Katkov, particularly in his willingness to advance money to Dostoevsky when he wrote Katkov the kind of desperate letters from Western Europe that Katkov himself had once sent Kraevsky.

Despite the material difficulties of his stay in Berlin, Katkov highly valued the opportunity to study idealist philosophy at its source: "The living and serious occupation with philosophy, not as before—in a vulgar form, based on brochures—has acted on my whole being beneficially and profoundly."[4] The farewell lecture of Karl Friedrich Werder (1806–93) had a particularly strong impact on Katkov: "Whoever participated in that moment [the ovation for Werder] will never allow it to be lost from his memories."[5] In the quotation from Werder's lecture provided by Katkov's biographer Nevedensky [S. G. Shcheglovitov], we can see some of the elements of character and personality that Katkov was to carry into his mature journalistic practice:

> [The goal of philosophy] is to make us devoted to God, joyful for life and for death, ready for sacrifice and renunciation, strong and great in creative activity. ... The greatest enemy of man is timidity, timidity is the devil, the progeny of lies, and its punishment is moral enslavement; the friend of man, his savior and deliverer, is boldness; boldness is love; it is born out of truth, and its bliss is called freedom.... Whoever thinks nobly, whoever thinks authentically, whoever has transformed the free power of thought into the life force of the soul, that person will not act basely, and whoever does not act basely himself will not allow others to treat him basely.[6]

In his later career Katkov could never be accused of timidity; boldness based on a conviction of rightness was his hallmark and, to some of his critics, his greatest fault.

Katkov also attended lectures by F. W. J. Schelling (1775–1854) in the fall of 1841 and summer of 1842, which apparently supported his "conservative" interpretation of Hegel.[7] Throughout his time in Berlin, Katkov never ceased to think of how he would one day play an important role in the fate of his country. He wrote to his mother and brother, "I think and dream of Russia very often and every time I feel even more the strength of the bonds uniting me with my people; ... I am convinced—the best reward for all my labors, of course in the future, would be at least some kind of useful service that I could contribute. The thought of that acts beneficially on me and gives me an objective support and goal. I am ready to collect the slightest trifle, everything that could in some degree relate to the benefit of Russia, just as now beneath my window the Germans are collecting little tufts of hay that remained on the pavement after the unloading of a wagon, with unusual care and thoroughness."[8]

Katkov in the University

Katkov returned to Russia in early 1843 with a vague intention of entering the civil service. But Count S. G. Stroganov, administrator of the Moscow Educational District, who had known Katkov as a student, persuaded him to embark on a scholarly career, hinting at a chair at Moscow University.[9] While working as a tutor in the Golitsyn family, Katkov wrote a master's thesis, *On the Elements and Forms of the Slavo-Russian Language* (published in 1845), that was a serious exercise in historical-comparative linguistics.[10] Philosophy was not divorced from philology in Katkov's time or in his personal ambitions, as is evident in his early translations of English and German literature and of Rötscher's work on literary theory. Katkov's profound interest in the coming-to-being of the Russian language is part of his hope, framed in Hegelian terms in his essays on old Russian literature, that the Russian nation could achieve world-historical status.

The chair in Russian literature was not available to Katkov, since it was already occupied by two professors, I. I. Davydov and S. P. Shevyriov. He was talked about as a candidate for the chair in literature at the University of Kiev, but instead he became an adjunct professor of philosophy at Moscow University.[11] Katkov did not find his new role immediately comfortable. In 1846 he wrote of his difficulties in adapting his abstruse subject matter to an unaccustomed audience "for whom I had to masticate a lot, cut short a lot, taking into account their level of understanding.... My lectures, especially the first ones, were so scandalously garbled in the students' notes that I fell into despair."[12] Evaluations of Katkov's teaching differ greatly. According to Nevedensky, "Katkov was not distinguished by the gift of oral exposition."[13] He had a soft voice, and his students recalled trying to get a place close to the lectern so as not to miss a single word of his lectures; in his later writings they recognized what one critic has called his "mercilessly logical mind."[14] Most accounts seem to agree that, whatever his faults as an orator, Katkov impressed students with the power of his intellect and with his attention to students in more personal interactions.

Katkov's Return to Journalism

In 1850, as part of a governmental reaction to the revolutions of 1848 in Western Europe, a new regulation was imposed that deprived Katkov of his position teaching philosophy. The teaching of philosophy, a potentially subversive topic in the eyes of the government, was now reserved for professors of theology—that is, members of the clergy. As the censor and St. Petersburg professor of literature A. V. Nikitenko (1804?-77) wrote in his diary for March 16, 1850, "Again persecution of philosophy. It is proposed that its teaching in universities be limited to logic and psychology, entrusting both to ecclesiastics."[15] Professors of philosophy were offered the opportunity to transfer into departments of pedagogy, but Shevyriov maneuvered to get that chair for himself, in addition to his chair in literature, and Katkov ended up without a position. Nikitenko's reaction to this was probably typical: "It's interesting that [Shevyriov] justifies all his unattractive acts by the idea that he is supposedly acting in the name of some higher principle, for the sake of which he even sacrifices his good name."[16] Katkov managed to land on his feet, and in 1851 he was offered the position of editor of the official Moscow University newspaper *Moscow News* (*Moskovskie vedomosti*). As Nevedensky writes, "By such a twisting path did fate lead him finally to his true calling—social and political journalism."[17] Now established in a fairly secure position, Katkov married the Princess Sofia Petrovna Shalikova in 1852.

Katkov had little room for creativity or enterprise while editing the *Moscow News* during the last days of the repressive reign of Nicholas I. During the national crisis that was the Crimean War (1853–56), the censorship did not permit public discussion of the most vital issues facing Russia. A contemporary memoirist recounts an anecdote that is apocryphal but nevertheless telling; as he introduces it, "*Se non è vero, è ben trovato*": "The story is that the emperor once asked Count

A. F. Orlov what the public was interested in, and when [Orlov] answered that people everywhere were thinking and talking only about the war, [the emperor] remarked, 'But what business is that of theirs?'"[18] Russia's terrible defeat in the war, whose probability was evident by 1855, and the beginning of the reign of the new Tsar Alexander II in March of that year, changed everything. Now it was recognized that Russia desperately needed for its people to make the country's policies and administrative structures "their business," in the interest of reforming a backward society. In 1855, Katkov saw his opportunity to start a journal that would play a vital role in that process. Here again, as at the beginning of his career, he saw literature as one of the most important components in the building of a nation of world-historical significance.

In 1839, in his introduction to his own translation of Varnhagen's article on Pushkin, Katkov heralded a new role for Russia on the world stage: "They [foreigners] are no longer calling us pupils and imitators.... May God grant that we finally feel in ourselves the strength for original and self-conscious intellectual activity."[19] Sixteen years later in 1855, when Katkov petitioned the minister of education for permission to begin what became the *Russian Herald*, he spoke of the mission of the journal in similar terms. The task of the journal was to help Russia come into its own through the medium of language, which attains its highest expression in literature. In the petition Katkov repeatedly uses the word *obrazovanie*, which is usually translated as "education," but which literally means "formation." It is a key word in his discourse of nationhood, as Russia is always contrasted to the already "formed [*obrazovannye*]" nations of Western Europe. He writes, "In our formation in the last thirty years there has taken place a very significant revolution. Enlightenment, dispersed superficially and directly from foreign sources, has now been felt in the depths of our own nationality [*narodnost'*]. The beautiful gleams of poetry and art have announced to the world the presence of a new spiritual actor in the family of humanity. The Russian word has unfolded its wealth and variety; it has become a living and flexible tool of creation." Katkov calls for "a peculiarly Russian view of things" to be clarified, for "the Russian intellect [to] throw off the yoke of foreign thought just as it has already thrown off the yoke of the foreign word," and for "our literature, maturing and becoming richer, [to] provide satisfaction to all the intellectual needs of the Russian person."[20]

Katkov eloquently describes the vital role that "the living organs of literature, periodical publications," can play in this process. These publications "call forth capable people to labor and open them a field for it. Very often significant works drowse at their beginning or are broken off because of a lack of moral and material support, which they could find in a broad and conscientious literary enterprise.... A journal cannot create talents, but it can call them forth and give them a direction.... The work of the editor is not visible to everyone, and only the person who looks more deeply can understand how great is his obligation and how much both the tendency and form of a work can depend on him."[21]

When he speaks of the way that journals can "call forth capable people to labor and open them a field for it," offering "moral and material support," we can hear an echo of what the young Katkov felt in 1839 when the editor Kraevsky gave him an opportunity to write for *Notes of the Fatherland*. As Nevedensky describes it, "Katkov, who had to support not only himself but his aged mother and his brother by his own labor while preparing for the university, was very needy. He accepted [Kraevsky's offer] like manna from heaven."[22] After an 1839 visit to Kraevsky in St. Petersburg, Katkov expressed his gratitude with an allusion to his own long memory: "There are few such beautiful meetings in life as my meeting with you. The cordial reception you gave to an unknown person, completely alien to you, the friendly courtesy with which you adorned my stay in an unknown city—I feel all this very deeply. I ask you only to be assured that the person in whom you produced this feeling has a good memory."[23] No doubt this memory was still alive as Katkov wrote his petition to start his new journal.

As William Mills Todd III has pointed out, journalism was growing rapidly at precisely this time, due to "relaxed censorship practices and a new tolerance of political reporting in the press."[24] Katkov was choosing the most direct and effective field for his activity, far more vital and influential than the university. On October 31, 1855, he received permission to publish the *Russian Herald*, with the proviso that he would give up the editorship of the university's daily *Moscow News* and that the new independent journal would appear no more than twice a month.[25] The first issue appeared in January 1856.

The *Russian Herald*

In his first contribution to the journal, his 1856 article on Pushkin, Katkov speaks of the true poet as "a great expert in language, even if he has never studied grammar."[26] He defends art from demands that it serve didactic ends, arguing that the "nobility of social relations" in the "formed" nations was first developed in art. "The lines of Raphael did not solve any practical question from the everyday life contemporary to him; but they brought great good and great usefulness for life with the course of time; they powerfully contributed to the humanization of life. The action of great works of art remains not only in the sphere closest to them but spreads far and turns out to be there where there is not so much as a mention of the ideals of the artist."[27] Although Katkov's views in this period are sometimes characterized as "art for art's sake," he explicitly rejects this rubric, saying that an art that is focused *only* on elegance of form is just as far from the true inner goal of art as didactic art is. He defines the goal of "true art" as "bring[ing] life into human consciousness and consciousness into the most secret convolutions of life."[28]

As previously noted, the high point of Katkov's article is his discussion of Pushkin's work as the culminating stage in the formation of the Russian literary language. For Katkov, the magnitude of this accomplishment cannot be overestimated. The creation of a literary language strengthens national unity and defines a "national [*narodnaia*] physiognomy."[29] This process of national definition is the precondition for the predominance of the Russian ethnos within the multiethnic empire. As Pushkin's "monument" poem predicts, "The multitude of multifarious tribes that populate our fatherland must completely, intellectually and morally, subject themselves to the Russian nationality [*narodnost'*], as they are now subjected to the Russian state. For these tribes the Russian nationality is the sole path to human formation, and they 'will call the name of Pushkin.'"[30]

This emphasis on the theme of language as the legitimator of Russian national aspirations appears again in articles published in the *Russian Herald* in 1861, as discussed in the introduction to the present work. Katkov compares the potential significance of literary Russian among Slavic languages to that of High German, the importance and dominance of which was guaranteed by the literature written in it. He writes, "Thanks to what was done in this language [High German], it truly acquired immortal significance, it is now not simply the language of some nationality or other, it has become one of the universal languages." He goes on to say that Russian has not become that strong yet, but that there is hope for its future.[31]

From its beginnings the *Russian Herald* engaged not only with literature but with the vital social issues facing Russia: modernization, industrialization, the emancipation of the serfs, economic development, reform of the courts and of the government. In the years 1856–62, the years immediately preceding the great flowering of the Russian novel, the journal was permeated with Katkov's powerful personality and aspirations for the Russian nation. Many of these aspirations were expressed in political terms, but Katkov's literary program can also be found in these pages. Perevalova gives a good description of the blossoming of Katkov as a journalist in these years:

It was probably a great surprise for those who knew Katkov intimately, when in the boring and incomprehensible lecturer, the interlocutor who was taciturn and even somewhat tongue-tied in ordinary conversation, a person who seemed to be cold and indifferent, there was suddenly revealed the talent of a brilliant publicist, who combined journalistic mastery with perceptiveness and a political mind, capable of making the reader trust him, of convincingly and cogently defending his point of view, subordinating other people's opinions and convictions in the process.[32]

In pursuing his aims, Katkov strove to maintain a uniform ideological stance throughout all the articles he published. This understandably led to conflict as the editor tried to get every contributor to fall into line, while some resisted his intense involvement with the content of their writings. In the first years of the *Russian Herald*, several prominent contributors left the journal. The public discussion surrounding these departures, when there was any, centered on the substance of the issues—for example, in the case of Boris Isaakovich Utin, the institution of justices of the peace in England.[33] In 1860, however, Katkov's polemic with his contributor Evgeniia Tur began with substance but very soon involved public discussion by several writers of Katkov's journalistic principles and practices. In this complex and multivoiced discussion, we get a foretaste of the conflicts that would attend Katkov's involvement with three of Russia's greatest novelists, Ivan Turgenev, Fyodor Dostoevsky, and Lev Tolstoy.

Tur at the *Russian Herald*

Evgeniia Tur had become acquainted with Katkov through the lively salon she had hosted in Moscow in the 1840s and 1850s.[34] Although sources focused on Katkov refer to her merely as a contributor to the *Russian Herald*, according to D. Iazykov she was a member of the editorial board entrusted with the review, evaluation, and sometimes even the editing of the literary texts submitted to the journal.[35] Certainly the prominence given to women writers in the years of Tur's association with the journal supports this claim. As Jehanne Gheith points out, these writers included Marko Vovchok, Iuliia Zhadovskaia, Tur herself, and the non-Russian authors Elizabeth Gaskell, George Sand, and Harriet Beecher Stowe.[36] Many of Karolina Pavlova's most important poems were published in the *Russian Herald* during Tur's association with the journal in 1856–60.[37] Katkov had earlier shown an interest in literature by women in his 1840 article on the poetry of Sarra

Tolstaia, and the fact that he would invite Tur to oversee the literary section of the *Russian Herald* indicates that this interest was still alive in him.

Gheith makes the important point that "the search for a native woman author" was part of the attempt to define a national literature: "England had Jane Austen, the Brontës, and George Eliot, France had George Sand, and Russian critics saw female authorship as part and parcel of establishing a legitimate literature: Russia, too, needed a female author."[38] Unfortunately, in Katkov's article on Tolstaia, while he takes a somewhat liberal line for 1840 on the question of women's writing, arguing that women should not be arbitrarily confined to the traditional sphere of home and family, he also betrays a condescending attitude toward the limits of feminine literary talent. He claims that it is impossible for women to display genius in science, art, and other spheres of "external activity," because "genius presumes a full correspondence with one's gender, with the idea of one's purpose." Woman's calling is in a different sphere, and "her genius is expressed in a different form." Nevertheless, there is a place for women in "external activity," as long as they do not aspire to "world-historical grandeur": "There are very few geniuses, and one should not confuse them with talents, gifts, capabilities, and let us add, with a passing need to express oneself that may be forced by some necessity."[39] We can hear the echoes of this condescension in his polemic with Tur, as he refers to her repeatedly as "the gifted authoress" or "the energetic authoress."

In addition to her novellas "Starushka" ("The Old Woman," 1856) and "Na rubezhe" ("On the Boundary," 1857), Tur published a number of substantial articles in the *Russian Herald*, many of which were devoted to women writers like George Sand and Charlotte Brontë.[40] Gheith has thoroughly discussed these articles from the point of view of the "woman question" and Tur's working out of a feminine aesthetic.[41] From the point of view of the "tendency" [*napravlenie*], or ideological line, that Katkov prescribed for the *Russian Herald*, Tur seems to be upholding his endeavors to discredit France as a viable social model for Russia.

As Feoktistov describes Katkov's views, after the "judgment day" of Russia's loss at Sevastopol in 1855, faith in the Russian order of things had been undermined.

> Katkov set his mind to the idea that for Russia a system of self-government [*samoupravlenie*] on a broad scale was necessary.... Self-government had blossomed luxuriantly in English soil—that is the source of Mikhail Nikiforovich's admiration of England, a rather strange admiration almost the day after England had been our most fierce and implacable enemy in bloody battle.... [In private conversations] one could abuse France, the country of administrative centralization,

as much as you liked, but Katkov assiduously deleted from the articles of his contributors any unfavorable opinions about England out of the fear that these opinions might undermine faith and respect for the country whose internal organization was to serve as a model for Russia.[42]

Tur does not write much about England as a society, but she does "abuse France" repeatedly, possibly in an attempt to keep in harmony with the tendency of the *Russian Herald*.

In her essay on Flaubert's 1856–57 novel *Madame Bovary*, Tur begins with the general principle that the novel of *moeurs* reveals much about the "level of moral grandeur or decline" of the country depicted: "These thoughts came to us by chance as we were reading the French novel *Madame Bovary*, which recently appeared and which aroused much talk and occasioned a trial from which the author emerged as the victor."[43] Given Tur's verdict on *Madame Bovary*, her conclusions about France's "level of moral grandeur or decline" are hardly flattering: "How can we forgive a writer who has taken up the pen indifferently, and indifferently drawn hideous scenes in which there is nothing but shameless, obvious debauchery? How can we forgive him his careless ignorance that a moral feeling has been invested into human nature, and that in a writer it should be developed more strongly than in anyone else? How can we forgive him his truly criminal contempt for everything that is holy in life?" She accuses Flaubert of "unconditional and amazing disrespect for the feeling of human dignity, and for everything that all educated, highly moral and mature people have become accustomed to honor and respect." Flaubert's novel leaves the reader with "a kind of mixture of repulsion and contempt, something oppressive as a nightmare, and wearying as a hot day without a drop of water for quenching one's thirst—something that insults the soul and frightens the imagination.... Is such moral decline, such corruption really eating away at French society?"[44]

Even in a review of a work she approves of, Émile Augier's 1858 play *La Jeunesse*, Tur finds an opportunity to take a swipe at the moral condition of France. She claims that Augier's play "sharply contrasts with the present strivings of Parisian society, infected with a greedy thirst for gold, a thirst for power and truly horrifying egoism."[45] The conclusion to her review of an 1858 play by Alexandre Dumas *fils*, *Le fils naturel*, contains perhaps her most wholesale condemnation of the moral bankruptcy and hypocrisy of French society: "A strange thing! France, the land of all emancipations, extreme emancipations that lead nowhere, as for example the emancipation of women, the land of all possible encroachments and liberties (but not at all of freedom), is at the same time the land of the most implacable prejudices, the most inexorable and constraining conventions and an unusual narrowness in the understanding of life."[46]

The Polemic over Svechina

The article by Tur that gave rise to her polemic with Katkov and her eventual break with the *Russian Herald* would seem at first glance to be another example of her adherence to the journal's tendency, as it continues to pursue the attack on France. Yet in this piece, which Tur likely offered in the spirit of what she understood to be Katkov's editorial tendency, she ventured, possibly inadvertently, into issues that ran afoul of Katkov's inclinations. This set up a pattern of disagreement between them, which was partly played out in print, and came to involve some of their mutual literary colleagues. What happened between Tur and Katkov vividly illustrated the kind of difficulties that Katkov would have with later collaborators and contributors to the *Russian Herald*. In tracing their exchanges, we see Katkov being defined publicly by writers hostile to him. We also see Katkov defining a professional editorial persona that, in its mature state, he would bring to his dealings with Turgenev and others.

Tur's review of the biography and writings of Sofia Petrovna Svechina (1782–1857), known as Madame Swetchine, was the point of departure for a polemic that extended over the summer of 1860 and into the fall and involved not just Tur and Katkov but at least five other people.[47] Svechina was a Russian noblewoman who converted to Catholicism in 1815 under the influence of Count Joseph de Maistre and other Jesuits who had found refuge in St. Petersburg in the late eighteenth and early nineteenth centuries after being suppressed by the pope in 1773. Although Tsar Alexander I had been somewhat tolerant of Russian nobility, especially women, converting to Catholicism, in the same year as Svechina's conversion he expelled the Jesuits from St. Petersburg and Moscow, and in 1820 he expelled them from the Russian Empire.[48] Svechina and her husband (who never left the Orthodox faith) emigrated to France in 1816, and she spent the rest of her life in Paris. Although Tur represents Svechina's emigration as a free choice to leave her homeland for the country whose language, culture, and religion she had already adopted, it is likely that the unpropitious climate in Russia for Catholic converts, especially members of the nobility, left Svechina and others no choice but to leave.[49] In Paris, Svechina devoted herself to charitable works and also maintained a lively salon. Here she associated with many important cultural figures such as Chateaubriand and Tocqueville, but Tur emphasizes her connections to the Ultramontane Party, which favored the subordination of temporal authority to the authority of the pope.

Tur's essay on Svechina continues the negative presentation of France that is a theme in her other *Russian Herald* articles. To give just one of many examples, Tur recounts one of Svechina's witticisms as relayed by Svechina's biographer Comte de Falloux, and comments, "The French like all such affectations, unbearable for us. For a Frenchman there is nothing higher than a *bon mot*, even if this *bon mot* has been thought up, specially composed, forcibly fitted to the occasion.... That is the kind of apothegm that creates the reputation of intellect in Paris. A simple, serious person, deeply intelligent but not brilliant, can seldom be appreciated on his merits in this so-called capital of the world."[50]

Even more savage than such attacks on France in general are Tur's attacks on Catholicism, as well as her personal disparagement of Svechina's intellect and talents. An incident from Svechina's childhood in which she renounces the gift of a watch is interpreted as showing "the stamp of the Catholic spirit": "Here one can clearly see pride, exactingness if not toward others, then toward oneself, an unreasonable exactingness, a love for fruitless renunciations, a passion for fruitless sacrifices, which only nourish self-esteem and vanity. It has always seemed to us that despite the external appearance of humility that the Catholic clergy flaunts so much, it is especially distinguished by pride, self-esteem, and vanity."[51] She attributes Svechina's conversion to "the fruitless philosophizing of a sick mind that had been sent in a crooked direction and devoted itself to some kind of casuistic hair-splitting."[52] Her summing-up of the process of Svechina's conversion is devastating: "Everything led her inexorably to the bosom of the Roman church—the wavering of her mind, the disorder of her fragmentary knowledge, the absence of any understanding formed with the aid of education, the insufficiency of a normal, healthy development, and the desire to come to rest on something indisputable, narrow, and close, the desire to freeze [*zameret'*], having put oneself into a framework prepared in advance. Catholicism is a superb framework, excellently devised; whoever has fallen into it will die in it, constantly revolving within its closed-in space."[53]

Tur dismisses not only the depth and sincerity of Svechina's religious convictions but also the quality of her mind and writings (which were not intended for publication): "This is a conventional mind, conventional truths, and phrases, and affectations, and an unbearable pretension to depth of thought."[54] She suggests that de Falloux made a grave mistake in publishing Svechina's works, since they reveal to us that the unusual intelligence he speaks of is "a phantom, a mirage." For Tur, "This unusual intellect evaporates upon reading her works, and it becomes clear to everyone that it was neither mature, nor profound, nor broad, nor clear, in a word, did not have a single one of those properties that are the conditions for a full conception of intellect. It was petty, intricate, affected, inconsistent. Mrs. Svechina didn't even know how to express herself simply and clearly."[55]

At the end of Tur's article, Katkov appended a note. Since this note evoked Tur's furious response and gave rise to a polemic that spread to several other publications, it is worth quoting in full.

> In printing this interesting article, we consider it our duty to declare that we do not share all the opinions of its gifted author. They seem to us to be somewhat one-sided and not completely fair. Perhaps they have been evoked as a reaction against the excessive raptures of Mrs. Svechina's admirers; but if one extreme is not fair, then the other extreme is just as unfair. Mrs. Tur's article is very interesting, but it hardly gives a completely faithful conception of the subject that gave rise to it. It is a pity that instead of the petty aphorisms taken from [the collection] *Airelles*, which Svechina wrote in 1811, in the first period of her life, the critic did not choose many passages, for example from her discourse *Le progrès, la civilisation et le christianisme*. In general it is a pity that the critic chose from the author's works only that which seemed weak to her and could cast a shadow on the author, without dealing with other aspects that could present the author in a better light or at least could give grounds for serious discussion. Religious interest, if it is sincere and not united with fanaticism, deserves respect not only in the opinion of religious people, even if of different creeds, but even in the opinion of those who are indifferent to that interest. *Ed*.[56]

Katkov had not warned Tur that he was appending this note, even though she lived in Moscow, where the *Russian Herald* was published, and it should not have been difficult to do so. His note is framed in polite terms, but certainly any author would be shocked and dismayed to see such a note at the end of an article. Throughout the polemic, Katkov never directly addresses the issue of why he did not warn Tur. As the polemic develops, it becomes clear that Katkov considered himself to have the right to frame and comment on any writing presented under the aegis of the *Russian Herald*, and that he saw himself as a kind of super-author of all the articles and *belles-lettres* that appeared in the journal.[57]

When Katkov neglects to answer the charge of not warning Tur, it could be simply that he has no good explanation to offer. But it is also consistent with his general polemical style, as described much later by his colleague and biographer Liubimov. According to Liubimov, Katkov's method was not to remain in a defensive position, but to "quickly move to the attack," making the opponent think not of attacking but of defending himself. He also tried not to "dissipate his energies in details," but to attack the general thrust of his opponent's argument. Liubimov describes Katkov's distinctive way of preparing for a polemic: "Later he established a rather original practice. Mikhail Nikiforovich avoided reading the articles to which he retorted with such force. One of his close colleagues would relate the content of the article to him. Mikhail Nikiforovich would pause on the salient points, ask that they be marked, and would familiarize himself only with those passages when he himself read the article. Otherwise he would want to answer everything, and that would keep him from concentrating."[58] Liubimov is speaking here of Katkov's later practice when he again became the editor of the *Moscow News*, but one can see similar methods at work in his polemic with Tur. He avoids responding to each individual accusation of his opponents, so as "not to dissipate his energies in details."

Tur insisted on answering Katkov, in a letter published in the "Contemporary Chronicle" supplement to the *Russian Herald*, also in April 1860; her letter was followed in the same publication by Katkov's answer to it.[59] Aside from her objection to the very publication of Katkov's note without consulting her, Tur's two main points are, first, that she was shocked to discover that Katkov did not share her convictions [*ubezhdeniia*], her opposition to what she calls the "dark doctrine" ["*mrachnoe uchenie*"] of Catholicism; and, second, that he could not possibly have read Svechina's *Le progrès, la civilisation, et le christianisme*, or he would have known that it is not a weighty treatise but a short pamphlet. She quotes some passages from the work with derisive commentary, and dismisses it as "the exercises of a French boarding-school girl on a topic assigned to her by a Catholic priest."[60]

Katkov responds first by rather insultingly professing ignorance about Tur's convictions that he is supposed to have shared: "The editor of the *Russian Herald* is very pleased to learn that his convictions coincided with the views and convictions of Mrs. Evgeniia Tur, although for his part he does not presume to define exactly to what degree they coincided."[61] The condescending tone of this statement can also be heard in his reference to "the agitated tone" of Tur's letter, his description of her as "our staunch [*ubezhdennaia*] and energetic authoress," and his statement that Tur's remarks on Svechina's writings reflect a *jalousie de métier* [professional jealousy] that is out of place, since Svechina never intended her works for publication.[62] The major portion of Katkov's response is devoted to a defense of Svechina's treatise on Christianity and civilization. Katkov provides a more accurate context for the passages that Tur had quoted, and offers many more extensive quotations in a fairly successful effort to show that Svechina's short work is worthy of respect.[63] These quotations demonstrate to some extent what Katkov might have found attractive in Svechina's writings. Her idea that Christianity fosters the development of civilization not through direct political action but through "transforming the conscience" recollects Katkov's conception of the indirect and spiritual action of art on society, as expounded in his article on Pushkin, where he spoke of how Raphael's art did not solve any practical questions but "powerfully contributed to the humanization of life."[64]

The next phase of the polemic moved beyond the dialogue of Tur and Katkov to encompass other voices, and at the same time the focus shifted from the substance of their disagreement over Svechina and Catholicism to the very nature of Katkov's editing practice. Before discussing these developments, though, we should pause for a moment to consider what lay behind the disagreement. As discussed above, Tur's earlier articles demonstrate that she was trying to fall in with Katkov's "tendency" for his journal, in contributing evidence for the decadence of French society and implying the unsuitability of France as a model for Russia. She must have seen herself as pursuing the same line in her article on Svechina, but Katkov resists the part of her attack that has Catholicism, not just French civilization, as its target.

Much is made later in the polemic of Katkov's having unforgivably referred to a private letter in his published response to Tur. The passage in question reads as follows in Katkov's article: "Mrs. Evgeniia Tur has set herself the goal of tirelessly waging war against darkness and evil—a splendid goal!"[65] It is not entirely fair to say, as one of Tur's defenders does, that this had to come from a private letter, given that Tur's battle with the "dark doctrine" of Catholicism emerges quite clearly in her published article on Svechina as well as in her letter to the editor. But a private letter she wrote to Katkov, apparently right after the publication of her article on Svechina, does seem to be the direct source for Katkov's sarcastic remark. Tur writes to Katkov that she attacked Svechina because "her works, which everyone is vying with each other to read, especially women, I consider to be harmful and *corrupting* of the mind." Tur declares war on Svechina and Catholicism as a whole: "I don't care about Russian ladies and whether they change their religion or not, I have always hated Catholic priests, the darkness of that doctrine, and I will prosecute it everywhere, and ridicule it (to the best of my powers).... I have been and will be the enemy of narrow and obscure theories, the enemy of narrow and conventional morals, and I hope to die with my convictions, no matter what they shout about me."[66] This letter clearly demonstrates, and must have demonstrated to Katkov, that in writing her article on Svechina, Tur was pursuing not only Katkov's ideological line but her own project, which she apparently assumed he would agree with. The question remains why Katkov rejected Tur's project of attacking Catholicism. For one thing, Catholicism had traditionally been associated in Russia with Katkov's favored path of modernization and Westernization, as the actions of several tsars attest.[67] Katkov may also have been concerned to defend Christianity in any of its forms from an attack that would give comfort to those "indifferent to [religion]," as his note to Tur's article implies.

The Polemic Expands

The response to Katkov's answer to Tur came not from Tur herself but from Genrikh Vikentievich Vyzinsky (1834–79), writing in the *Moscow News* under the pseudonym I. Mai.[68] Vyzinsky was a young professor of history at Moscow University, a protégé of Katkov's friend and coeditor, P. M. Leontiev, who had until recently been a contributor to the *Russian Herald*. According to Feoktistov's memoirs, Vyzinsky, who was of Polish origin and who later became active in the Polish movement for independence from Russia, could sense that Katkov and Leontiev would not be sympathetic to his cause, and thus not only broke with them but also set Tur against Katkov and inspired her to become involved with the radical movement. Feoktistov writes, "Perhaps she would have preserved her equilibrium in part, if not for the fatal influence on her of the Moscow University professor Vyzinsky, who was then the closest of her friends."[69] Certainly Tur had enough reason to be upset with Katkov without any outside influence, but Vyzinsky's article demonstrates his eagerness to join the fight against Katkov and his entire editorial practice. It is with Vyzinsky's article that the dispute becomes intensely personal.

Vyzinsky broadens the discussion by invoking two other writers, the classical philologist N. M. Blagoveshchensky (1821–92) and the legal scholar Boris Isaakovich Utin (1832–72), who like Tur had been distressed by the way their writings were handled in the *Russian Herald*.[70] Vyzinsky draws a picture not of a dispute between one contributor and her editor, but of a journal that has made a general practice of riding roughshod over its contributing writers. He makes the discussion quite personal, indicating that the reason for the situation prevailing in the journal is "of a psychological nature." The success of the *Russian Herald*, he writes, has had a bad influence on the journal's editors: "To speak in the language of the simple people, they've gotten a big head [*oni zaznalis'*]."[71]

Although Vyzinsky and others involved in the polemic always refer either to "editors" in the plural or "the editorial board" ["*redaktsiia*"], it is clear throughout that they have Katkov specifically in mind. Vyzinsky's explication of the "psychology" of the *Russian Herald* points directly at Katkov and his personality. Vyzinsky speaks of some of the same traits of arrogance and intellectual superiority that had once disturbed Belinsky in Katkov: "Having attained a high position in literature, [the editors] have become a bit deluded, have submitted to an innocent temptation—they have attributed the success of the journal exclusively to themselves, solely to their own grandeur, and not at all, not even in part, to the contributors who have nourished the journal with their works. Their spirit has become proud. Little by little the conviction has lodged in them that they are more intelligent, more learned, more profound not only than their contributors, but than everyone ... in general."[72]

According to Vyzinsky, the idea that the editors are omniscient has been fostered in them not by their extensive reading but by their training in philosophy. One senses that Vyzinsky had heard a lot from Katkov about the superiority of a philosophical education during the time he worked for him: "For the acquisition of this universal knowledge, books are not at all necessary. [The editors] have what no one in our land has—a philosophical education. They have bathed for a long time in the sea of philosophy, enlightened their intellect with philosophy, and been penetrated through and through with philosophy. And philosophy is the kind of knowledge that replaces and makes superfluous all other kinds. Philosophy easily and quickly elucidates for the editors of the *Russian Herald* that which others are forced to acquire for themselves by difficult labor and many years' study of the facts of scholarship."[73]

Vyzinsky also maintains that the editors of the *Russian Herald* have an inflated sense of the importance of the role of the editor, evidenced by Katkov's supercilious reaction to Tur's claim that her convictions might coincide with his. Here Vyzinsky hits upon Katkov's greatest strength as an editor as well as his greatest failing, the total control that he sought to exert over everything that appeared in his journal: "The contributors are unskilled laborers [*chernorabochii narod*], who lighten the work of the editor and take upon themselves tasks of a lower sort. They exist for this: after all, the editor himself can't write all the articles! They only prepare the background for him, upon which he paints his 'elucubrations.' To borrow a comparison from English life, so dear to the *Russian Herald*, one might say that the editor is a rich landlord and his contributors are farmers who work for him but also enjoy his powerful patronage."[74] In pursuing the theme of "psychology" (a relatively new and modish discipline at the time), Vyzinsky pathologizes Katkov's need to correct the work of his contributors: "The passion [*strast'*] to correct everything has turned into a chronic ailment [*stradanie*], which one might call *mania emendatoria*, or better *lues emendatoria*."[75] This is probably Vyzinsky's cheapest shot, when one considers that "*lues*" means "syphilis."

Vyzinsky's article clearly stung Katkov in a way that Tur's letter to the editor had not. In his response he descends to Vyzinsky's level in making personal allusions, no doubt based on his having correctly guessed who was behind the pseudonym "Mai." Katkov reinterprets Vyzinsky's attack on him as a slander against the contributors to the *Russian Herald*, because free people would never tolerate the kind of tyranny that Vyzinsky describes as holding sway there: "The worse the despot, the more contemptible are the subjects who bear his yoke."[76] In rejecting Vyzinsky's charge that the contributors to the *Russian Herald* are a class of oppressed laborers, Katkov accuses Vyzinsky himself of being enslaved: "Despite the tone of bullying and familiarity, many people unfortunately saw in this article a certain unpleasant servility, some echoes of grumbling that are unseemly for a free man."[77] Katkov also alludes in several passages to the "youthful inexperience" that is evident in Vyzinsky's article, and even hints at an improper relationship between him and Tur. After dismissing the stories of Blagoveshchensky and Utin as a smokescreen, Katkov writes, "An apologia for Mrs. Evgeniia Tur is the sole subject and sole pretext for the ardent attack against the *Russian Herald*," and hints that Vyzinsky may have helped Tur write her letter to the editor.[78] He also accuses Vyzinsky of having listened at doors and peeked at other people's letters, because of Vyzinsky's allusion to Tur's private letter to Katkov.[79]

Most surprising for a man of Katkov's stature is the ending of his response to Vyzinsky. Since Vyzinsky had announced that his article was being published in the interests of public knowledge [*glasnost'*], Katkov invites the editor of the *Moscow News*, also in the interests of public knowledge, to visit him in his office to inspect his books and research the state of his scholarly attainments. He goes on: "He won't find the second volume of Gneist in our study at this time.... By the way, on the topic of books. Could the editors of the *Moscow News*, through this gentleman [Vyzinsky], the lover of information and inquiries, track down the location of a book by the Hungarian Eötvös that someone borrowed from us, the book we spoke about in our article on the Austrian state council? We are in extreme need of it at the present moment for certain references, and there is no possibility of obtaining another copy in Moscow."[80]

Perhaps Katkov intended to end his article on a humorous note, but this petulant reference to books that Vyzinsky apparently borrowed from him and didn't return creates a very strange and jarring impression. A measure of the extent to which Katkov had lowered his dignity with these remarks is a humorous letter that appeared in the *Moscow News* in June 1860, in which the writer, a certain Piotr Ivanov from Kostroma province, complains that he can never build up his library because people are always borrowing books and not returning them. He rejoices that Katkov's article has given him an idea for solving his problem. When he read it, he realized that he could simply ask, "by means of the press," all those who had borrowed books from him to return them: "Encouraged by the example of the *Russian Herald*, I made up my mind, my dear sir, to appeal to you and ask you to publish that So-and-so asks his acquaintances, whoever has his books, to return them, for he has a great need of them. I hope you won't refuse me this favor, and will not cause me to envy the editors of the *Russian Herald*, who will certainly get their books back only because they have their own journal to meet their needs; I don't belong to any editorial boards, and all my hope is in you."[81]

Through the summer of 1860, the polemic continued to spread beyond the dispute between Katkov and Tur. Both Utin and Blagoveshchensky published articles in the *Moscow News* supporting Vyzinsky's contention that they had been unhappy about their treatment in the *Russian Herald*. Utin's article, titled "A Witness's Testimony" ["*Svidetel'skoe pokazanie*"], ends with his announcement that he will no longer submit articles to the *Russian Herald*. Katkov answered both Utin and Blagoveshchensky in his own journal. In the case of Utin, he returned to the substance of their disagreement and tried to demonstrate to Utin the error of his opinions on the English institution of justices of the peace. As far as we know, Utin did not engage any further with Katkov. Katkov had greater success with Blagoveshchensky, obtaining what amounted to a retraction in the pages of the *Moscow News* after confronting Blagoveshchensky with his own letters, which apparently could be read as giving the editors of the *Russian Herald* the authority to alter his text.[82]

Vyzinsky answered Katkov's response to him with an article that clearly demonstrated that Katkov's personal references had hit home. Vyzinsky writes that the editors of the *Russian Herald* had called him "a gossip, a slanderer, a detective and nearly a spy," accusing him of eavesdropping on other people's conversations from behind doors and peeking at other people's letters.[83] But Vyzinsky mainly uses this article to rehash the same accusations he made in his first article, and to express disingenuous concern for the *Russian Herald*, whose contributors, according to him, are abandoning it: "It is not hard for anyone to notice that various contributors in turn are leaving the *Russian Herald*. Almost all Russian men of letters have passed through this journal, but many have passed through and are not returning again.... Not everyone wants to part with the editors *avec éclat*, like Mrs. Evgeniia Tur; not everyone wants the irascible editors to dress them down in their journal.... Some prefer to leave quietly, without any demonstrations."[84] Vyzinsky ends with expressions of concern for the future of the *Russian Herald*, "a serious journal, with an excellent tendency, always interesting content, and of great benefit to very many people."[85] Such concern sounds somewhat insincere after the harsh attacks Vyzinsky has made in his two articles. But the intervention, also in June 1860, by one of Katkov's greatest rivals, Nikolai Gavrilovich Chernyshevsky (1828–89), took the activity of imparting disingenuous "friendly advice" to a new level.

Chernyshevsky Gives Katkov Friendly Advice

Since 1853 Chernyshevsky had been the editor of the *Contemporary* (*Sovremennik*), a journal founded by Pushkin in 1836 that often jousted with the *Russian Herald* on political and social issues from the position of the incipient radical movement. Chernyshevsky jumped on the Katkov–Tur polemic as an opportunity to amplify the accusations of Tur and Vyzinsky. Chernyshevsky begins by expressing his desire that the *Russian Herald* succeed, since it serves as a useful intermediate stage that prepares readers for the more advanced ideas of the *Contemporary*. According to Chernyshevsky, it is hard for people who are just awakening from a long intellectual sleep to leap at once to "the full truth." The *Russian Herald* serves as a crossroads at which the reader can rest on his way from ignorance to "the clear consciousness of his deeds and the means of satisfying his needs": "May the *Russian Herald* forgive us, but we consider it a very useful preparation of serious people for the acceptance of our ideas: we consider it a pedagogical institution in which a preparatory course is offered."[86]

Chernyshevsky adds very little to the substance of the polemic. It seems that the main object of his article is to provide yet another venue for the arguments of Tur in her letter to the editor of the *Russian Herald* and Vyzinsky in his article in the *Moscow News* for any readers who missed them the first time, as he rehearses the details of both publications at great length.[87] Chernyshevsky, like Vyzinsky in his second article, is eager to create the impression of the *Russian Herald* as a journal in trouble, whose contributors and readers are abandoning it. He reproaches the editors of the *Russian Herald* for "harming the journal itself" by not treating its contributors fairly, since it is those contributors who constitute "the main strength" of the journal: "Unfortunately, the editors did not know how to appreciate their position and conducted their business in such a way that soon quite a few of the people on whose assistance the power of the *Russian Herald* was based left the journal."[88]

Chernyshevsky describes a journal that has "not preserved even half of the previous interest it held for the public," and like Vyzinsky, he advises the editors to change their ways: "If the editors of the *Russian Herald* understand their own interests, they will give the contributors who have left them the possibility to join them again. We are forced to wish this by the interests of literature in general and our own interests: we already said that we consider the *Russian Herald* a very useful preparation of the public for the acceptance of the ideas that we defend."[89] Katkov did not answer Chernyshevsky directly, but one can see a reference to Chernyshevsky's disingenuous solicitude in a remark Katkov makes in his answer to Utin: "The editors are obliged to carefully preserve the purity of tendency of their journal; they not only have the right, but are obligated to declare on all such questions definite opinions and not under any circumstances, not out of any considerations to depart from this obligation or to ease it for themselves. That is how we understand our business, that is how we have conducted it, that is how we will continue to conduct it, without heeding various dear, friendly pieces of advice that are given us from various sides."[90]

Tur's Rival Journal

Chernyshevsky speaks in his article of Tur's plans to start a new journal.[91] Indeed, in the fall of 1860 Tur published announcements of her new newspaper, to be called *Russkaia rech'* (*Russian Speech*).[92] In describing the program of her new publication, Tur echoes the words of Vyzinsky and Chernyshevsky in characterizing the type of editorial program she is reacting against. Without mentioning the *Russian Herald* by name, she is obviously referring to it when she speaks of an ideological line that has avoided the extremes of the earlier standoff between Westernizers and Slavophiles, but that has unfortunately fallen into its own excesses: "The desire to follow through on [this line] with inflexible strictness not only in the main bases but in the smallest details and trivia, the desire to subsume all heterogeneity of thought under one scale and an intolerance toward any opinion that departs in the slightest from that scale—that is the onesidedness against which voices have often resounded recently in our literature."[93] Her own paper is to provide a very different alternative:

> Our publication will serve, to the best of our powers, as an organ of reconciliation for all people who desire gradual and correct progress in Russia. Without allowing any harsh extremes, any doctrinaire attitudes, penetrated by the conviction of the necessity of all-round, independent development of social interests, of the excesses of inordinate centralization, our publication will never betray one great principle: it will not forget that respect for another's opinion, respect for the right to independent thought of each of the people who are striving together with us to a single goal, is the main basis for freedom of opinion.[94]

This is a direct challenge to the *Russian Herald*, which had so recently been accused by Tur and her allies of the desire to control all the "details and trivia" of the articles published in the journal, of doctrinaire attitudes, and of denial of contributors' right to think independently. Tur ended her announcement with a list of thirty-eight people who had promised "active and constant participation."[95] These thirty-eight people included twelve who had been associated with the *Russian Herald*, including one member of its editorial board as well as the important writer Ivan Turgenev, who in January 1860 had published his novel *On the Eve* in Katkov's journal. (Vyzinsky is also listed.)

Katkov predictably reacted negatively to this announcement; it was clearly an attack on his journal that continued the attacks of the previous summer by Tur, Vyzinsky, and Chernyshevsky. Vyzinsky and Chernyshevsky had reveled in the departure of Katkov's most important contributors and predicted the demise of the *Russian Herald*; Tur's announcement, with its list of contributors, obviously exacerbated this sore spot. Katkov claimed that the contributors Tur listed who were associated with him were amazed to find themselves presented as protestors against the intolerance of the *Russian Herald*.[96]

In her response, Tur disingenuously claims that she had not been aiming her remarks at the *Russian Herald*, and that she had no intention of enlisting her contributors in any kind of protest.[97] As a sign of her desire to avoid any appearance of leading a protest, she mentions that she left the names of Utin and

Blagoveshchensky out of her list, despite their willingness to participate. Gheith has found evidence in Tur's private correspondence, however, that she did indeed try to organize a protest that would involve those two writers.[98] In his response to Tur's response, Katkov openly linked her announcement of her new publication with the attacks by Vyzinsky and Chernyshevsky, reminding the reader of their accusations that Katkov maintained an oppressed class of tormented contributors, and their descriptions of the *Russian Herald* as a journal in decline. In accepting Tur's affirmation that she had no intention of leading a protest, Katkov at the same time accuses her of being a mouthpiece for others: "We do not have the slightest basis for doubting the sincerity of the publisher's own words, and we can't help but think that the program was written not by her herself; we are convinced of this also by the circumstance that this program is not distinguished by those virtues of exposition that our readers have come to expect from the skillful and experienced pen of Mrs. Evgeniia Tur."[99] Just as the polemic had grown beyond the dialogue between Tur and Katkov, Katkov saw her establishment of a new publication as representing more than just her own personal ambitions. It represented a larger power struggle that involved Chernyshevsky and the *Contemporary* as well.

Around the same time as Tur's program announcement, Katkov felt compelled to issue a disclaimer similar to Mark Twain's famous statement, "The report of my death was an exaggeration." Referring to yet another newspaper that had jumped into the fray against the *Russian Herald*, Katkov writes, "We recently read in the *Russian Invalid* a rather definite notification of our imminent demise." He then quoted in full the item from the *Russian Invalid*, which refers to the *Russian Herald* as "a declining journal" that is "very successfully digging its own grave" because of its treatment of Tur and other contributors.[100] Contrary to the predictions (and desires) of Tur's allies, however, the *Russian Herald* was about to enter into its most glorious phase. In the next two decades the journal was to publish the most important works by the three writers who produced the canon of the great Russian novel, Turgenev, Dostoevsky, and Tolstoy.

In their exchange about Tur's announcement of her new publication, she and Katkov spar most acrimoniously over the participation of Ivan Turgenev. Katkov writes, "As for I. S. Turgenev, whose popular name has become the indispensable appurtenance of all sorts of programs, he recently wrote to us from Paris, where he is now, about an extensive work he has started which he hopes to finish and send to the *Russian Herald* for February or March of the coming year."[101] Tur replies that she too had been promised future works by various writers, but had refrained from exhibiting names purely "for cunning advertisement." She continues, mocking Katkov by using his own phrases in italics, "We did not announce what articles were lying *in our portfolios*, did not expatiate about what *someone wrote us from Paris* that they were *promising us for February or March*, but only followed the customary practice of clearly indicating that our journal has the purpose of being an organ of reconciliation for people who are uniformly respected by the Russian public."[102]

The letter from Turgenev that Katkov refers to has apparently not survived, but the work in question is *Fathers and Sons* (*Ottsy i deti*), which was to appear in the *Russian Herald* in February 1862, initiating the series of landmark publications that was to include parts of *War and Peace*, *Anna Karenina*, and all Dostoevsky's major novels except *A Raw Youth*. Throughout the period during which these novels appeared in the *Russian Herald*, Katkov continued to display the single-minded will to control that had led to the public dispute with Evgeniia Tur. As in his relationship with Tur, his skill at identifying and encouraging literary talent was combined with an overbearing need to be a coauthor, to use other people's gifts in the service of his own ideological line. Both the creative energies that Katkov released and nurtured through his editorial patronage, and the way that that patronage caused conflict with the writers whose works he published, are the subject of the following chapters.

CHAPTER 3

KATKOV AND TURGENEV

THE CONCEPTION OF *ON THE EVE* AND *FATHERS AND SONS*

In his 1856 article on Pushkin, the major thrust of which was to exalt Pushkin as the creator of the Russian literary language, Katkov criticized Pushkin's experiments in prose as being too dry, sketchy, and simple, failing to depict "the complex connection of the phenomena of life and everyday existence." In doing so he seemed to be calling for the lengthy novel of psychological, political, and philosophical complexity, the kind of novel that in the second half of the century was to become the dominant mode of Russian literature, represented most significantly by works published in the *Russian Herald*. Pushkin was not entirely to blame for this, according to Katkov; it was also due to "the insufficient development of intellectual and moral interests in the social consciousness whose organ Pushkin was."[1] An improved, "formed" society, of the kind being nurtured by the *Russian Herald*, would in Katkov's view give rise to more developed works of prose fiction, which would in turn strengthen the position of Russia among the "formed" nations.

A number of notable works of prose fiction were published in the *Russian Herald* starting in 1856, but none of them rose to the level of national cultural significance until Ivan Sergeevich Turgenev's *Fathers and Sons* (*Ottsy i deti*) was published in its entirety in the February 1862 issue. A few months after the novel appeared, Katkov took the unusual step of writing and publishing two serious and sophisticated essays on it. (Normally a journal would not publish a review of a novel that had appeared in its own pages.) His evaluation of its significance was unusually insightful not only about the novel's intrinsic merits, but also about how it would be perceived by later generations: "[In Mr. Turgenev's novel] is captured the current moment, the fleeting moment is caught, a transient phase of our life has been depicted typically and engraved forever. That is the task of the artist who wishes to act on his time directly; that is the true meaning of the demand that the artist remain a son of his time, a citizen of his country."[2] Turgenev's novel seems to Katkov to be continuing through the response and commentary on it, which constitute a kind of epilogue: "Taken out of current life, it enters into it again and produces a powerful practical effect in all directions, an effect the likes of which hardly any literary work has ever produced here.... In later times, the historian of our literature will speak of this novel in no other way than in connection with the phenomena it has called forth in that milieu from which it takes its content."[3] Turgenev had produced the novel that Pushkin had failed to produce, the one that "depicted the complex connection of the phenomena of life and everyday existence," the one that Katkov correctly predicted would live in Russian history as a true mirror of its times. In this chapter we will examine Turgenev's relationship with Katkov and the *Russian Herald* leading up to his publication of *Fathers and Sons*, particularly the genesis of *On the Eve* (*Nakanune*, 1860), the first novel that Turgenev published with Katkov. We will demonstrate that in conceiving *On the Eve*, Turgenev took into account the political preoccupations of the *Russian Herald*. Understanding that process is helpful for understanding how Turgenev's next novel, *Fathers and Sons*, was conceived. We will also revisit the topic of Katkov's role in the creation and subsequent evaluation of *Fathers and Sons*.

On the Eve: Why a Bulgarian?

The literary relationship between Turgenev and Katkov had begun inauspiciously with a public squabble in the pages of the *Russian Herald* and the *Moscow News* in 1856–57. Katkov announced to his readers that Turgenev had promised a new work called "Phantoms" ("Prizraki"), to be published in the *Russian Herald* in 1856, but had failed to deliver. Moreover, he implied that Turgenev had reneged on his promise by publishing the story under a different title ("Faust") in the *Contemporary*. Turgenev publicly declared that he had been unable to finish "Phantoms," and that "Faust" was a completely different story. He added that Katkov's insulting accusation had absolved him of his obligation to the *Russian Herald*. In Turgenev's letters there is evidence that this clash was deeply painful to him.[4] The coldness in the relations between Turgenev and Katkov continued until the fall of 1858, when Katkov sent Turgenev an elaborately polite invitation to contribute to the *Russian Herald*.[5] Turgenev's growing dissatisfaction with the editors of the *Contemporary* inclined him to accept Katkov's offer, and by

December 1858 Turgenev had promised his next work, which turned out to be *On the Eve*, to the *Russian Herald*.[6]

On the Eve, set in 1853 near the beginning of the Crimean War, is the story of an unusual young woman, Elena Nikolaevna Stakhova, who feels a deep need to do good in the world that she attempts to satisfy by adopting stray animals. She is courted by three young men who, as a contemporary review noted, rather schematically represent scholarship (Bersenev), art (Shubin), and the practical world of affairs (Kurnatovsky).[7] She chooses none of these worthy Russians, but instead falls passionately in love with a young student from Bulgaria, Dmitrii Nikanorovich Insarov, who is consumed with a burning desire to return to his homeland and liberate his Orthodox Christian people from the domination of the Ottoman Empire. In a turn of the plot that scandalized conservative readers, Elena gives herself sexually to Insarov in his lodgings, marries him secretly, and sets off with him for Bulgaria, leaving her family and her homeland behind with scarcely a backward glance.[8] The couple never makes it to Bulgaria. In scenes inspired by Turgenev's journey to Venice in March 1858, they visit the Lido, ride in a gondola along the Grand Canal, and attend a performance of *La Traviata* before Insarov dies of tuberculosis (like Violetta in the opera). Elena's further fate is left unclear, but it is implied that she either dies in a shipwreck or is later sighted, dressed all in black, in the midst of the uprising in Herzegovina.

The contemporary reaction to *On the Eve* reflects a great deal of confusion and bewilderment among Turgenev's readers. If the response were to be condensed into a single question, it might be, "Why a Bulgarian?" The title *On the Eve* would seem to be pointing to the "eve" of reform in Russia, as the emancipation of the serfs and other transformations of society were being planned and hotly discussed in journals like the *Contemporary* and the *Russian Herald*. Yet, as D. I. Pisarev wrote in 1861, for some reason Turgenev decided to "send away to Bulgaria for the impossible and completely unnecessary Insarov [*vypisyvaet iz Bolgarii nevozmozhnogo i ni na chto ne nuzhnogo Insarova*]."[9]

One of the earliest and certainly most influential readings of the novel, by N. A. Dobroliubov in 1860, provided an answer to the question "Why a Bulgarian?" that would become entrenched in the Soviet critical literature. Dobroliubov uses Insarov and his mission of liberation to speak in allegorical terms about Russia. The problem for Russian readers in feeling close to Insarov, according to Dobroliubov, is that they cannot share the seeming simplicity and single-mindedness of his struggle with Ottoman domination: "All the charm of Insarov is contained in the grandeur and holiness of that idea with which his whole being is penetrated."[10]

Dobroliubov contrasts Insarov's task with the situation of a typical Russian, using heavy irony to describe the current state of Russian society:

> Bulgaria is enslaved, it suffers under the Turkish yoke. We, thank God, are not enslaved by anyone, we are free, we are a great people who have more than once decided with our arms the fates of kingdoms and peoples; we rule over others, and no one rules over us.... In Bulgaria there are no social rights and guarantees.... Russia, on the contrary, is a well-ordered state, in it exist wise laws that protect the rights of the citizens and determine their obligations, justice reigns in it, and beneficial *glasnost'* [open public discourse] flourishes. No one takes away our churches, and our faith is not constrained by anything ... not only are rights and lands not taken away, but they are given to those who did not have them before.[11]

As the editors of a 1935 edition of Dobroliubov's works point out, this passage is an example of the advice he gave another writer about how to get around the censorship, telling him, "You have to speak in facts and figures, not only without calling things by their names, but even sometimes calling them by names that are opposite to their essential character."[12] The description of Russia as a "well-ordered state" in which "justice reigns" clearly does not correspond to Dobroliubov's own opinion of it.

Dobroliubov's allegorical reading calls for Russian Insarovs to take up a more difficult task than that of Insarov, a struggle against one's own people. Insarov is striving against the oppressors of his homeland, the Turks, with whom he has nothing in common. "But a Russian hero, usually coming from educated society, is himself intimately connected to that against which he must rebel. He is in the same situation as would be, for example, one of the sons of a Turkish agha who took it into his head to liberate Bulgaria from the Turks.... He would have to renounce everything that connected him to the Turks: his faith, and his nationality, and the circle of his relatives, and his friends, and the worldly advantages of his situation."[13] It is significant that near the beginning of his essay Dobroliubov mentions "new people [*novye liudi*] for whom love for truth and honorable strivings are no longer an oddity."[14] His description of the "Russian Insarov" who renounces nation and family to struggle against an internal enemy foreshadows the ascetic, single-minded "new people" who will be depicted in Chernyshevsky's answer to *Fathers and Sons*, *What Is To Be Done? (Chto delat'*, 1863).

Dobroliubov's most pointed reference to the applicability of Insarov's struggle to Russian society comes in passages that were censored from the journal publication but appeared in the 1862 edition of Dobroliubov's works. After acknowledging that Russia is well armed and not threatened by a foreign enemy, Dobroliubov continues: "But don't we have plenty of internal enemies? Don't we need a struggle with them, and isn't heroism needed for that struggle? But where are people capable of the deed? Where are people of integrity, gripped from childhood by a single idea, so accustomed to it that they have to either attain the victory of that idea or die? There are no such people, because our social milieu up to this time has not favored their development. And it is from it, from that milieu, from its vulgarity and pettiness, that we must be liberated by the *new people* whose appearance is so impatiently and passionately awaited by everything that is best and most fresh in our society."[15] This is a veiled or not-so-veiled call for revolution.

Dobroliubov's allegorical reading, or variants of it, became entrenched in Soviet (and to some extent Western and post-Soviet) interpretations of *On the Eve*. The commentary to Turgenev's complete works provides numerous examples. Elena Stakhova is presented as a prototype of the "*nigilistka*," the "nihilist girl" in Turgenev's later poem in prose, "The Threshold" ("*Porog*," 1878). Dobroliubov's article is seen as helping Turgenev to develop the conception of *Fathers and Sons*, defining the views of the "new people" and offering harsh criticism of the liberal nobility: "This was conducive to a deeper penetration by Turgenev of the essence of the social conflict that predetermined the plot basis of his next novel, *Fathers and Sons*.... Turgenev the artist could not help but take into account the general aims of Dobroliubov's article, which amounted to a demand that he depict the Russian Insarov in the struggle with internal Turks."[16]

The inclination to read *On the Eve* as being much more about Russia than about Bulgaria is not unwarranted. Turgenev himself said in a letter that the basis of the novel was the idea of the need for "*consciously*-heroic natures" in order to move Russia forward.[17] Moreover, except for the final scenes in Venice, the novel takes place entirely in Russia, and most of the discussions of social issues concern Russia, not Bulgaria. Turgenev himself, however, was horrified by Dobroliubov's allegorical reading. After seeing an earlier, more severe version of the review that has not survived, Turgenev wrote to the editor of the *Contemporary*, N. A. Nekrasov, begging him not to publish it: "[This article] can cause nothing but trouble, it is unjust and harsh—I won't know what to do with myself if it is published."[18] According to the memoirs of A. Ia. Panaeva, the wife of I. I. Panaev, one of the editors of the *Contemporary*, after Nekrasov wrote to Turgenev trying to work things out, Turgenev sent him a note that said, "Choose: either me or Dobroliubov."[19] Nekrasov apparently "chose" Dobroliubov: his review did appear, and is usually considered one of the reasons for Turgenev's final break with the *Contemporary*.

If one thinks carefully about the implications of Dobroliubov's analogy, it is not hard to understand Turgenev's horror, which goes far beyond what an experienced writer would feel about a mere negative review. On Dobroliubov's reading, Insarov is to the oppressive Ottoman Empire as the desired "Russian Insarov" is to the oppressive Russian Empire. Just as Insarov's singleminded goal is to liberate Bulgarians from the yoke of the infidel Turks, a Russian Insarov would have the goal of liberating Russians from—from what, if not the tsarist state? Turgenev could not possibly have intended such a message, certainly not in a novel that was destined from its inception for the pages of the *Russian Herald*, with its moderate-liberal editor Katkov. Obviously writers lose control of the possible meanings of their work once it is published. But in order to understand the dynamics of the relationship between Turgenev and Katkov, it might be helpful to ask the question "Why a Bulgarian?" once again, within the context of the *Russian Herald* of 1858, the year in which Turgenev decided to begin contributing to it.

"Turkish Affairs" in the *Russian Herald*

From January to May 1858, a number of articles were published in the *Russian Herald*, mostly in the current-events section called the *Contemporary Chronicle* (*Sovremennaia letopis'*), that dealt in various ways with the Ottoman Empire, especially vis-à-vis Russia. In January, I. Beriozin's travelogue "Scenes in the Desert: Between Basra and Baghdad" discussed the "laziness" of Ottoman governance, Muslim hatred of "infidels," and English imperial interests in the region (represented by English plans to build a railroad from Baghdad to Damascus, thus strengthening the connections between colonial India and the metropolis).[20] In three separate articles in February and March, K. Ugrinovich reported on Russian military operations in the Caucasus, with a constant eye to the importance of the region for Russian, Turkish, and British imperial interests.[21]

In March 1858, M. Kapustin published a review of a book titled *Le passé et l'avenir de l'Empire Byzantin*, which argues that the only salvation for the Ottoman Empire lies in the acceptance of Christianity by the Sultan. Kapustin summarizes the author's conclusion: "The Sultan must either accept Christianity or yield to a Christian government. Islamism is the enemy of social order, it contradicts the natural, state, and international law; there is too much republicanism in it, even more, it leads to communism!"[22] In April, a "Letter from Bolgrad" related the plight of the majority Bulgarian population in this city in Moldavia, which after the Crimean War was removed by the Treaty of Paris from Russian domination and was now under Ottoman suzerainty. The author laments Russian inaction with respect to Bulgarian affairs and the growing threats to the Orthodox religion from Islam and the West. He depicts Slavic Orthodoxy as oppressed by the domination of the Greek Phanariote hierarchy. (The Phanariotes were Greek subjects loyal to Ottoman authorities, who controlled the Orthodox *millet*, or confessional community.) The author writes: "By the way, excuse me if I say that you Russian gentlemen opine about Bulgarians without doing anything; and meanwhile the propaganda of the Western powers never sleeps: they want to take advantage of the present relationship of the Byzantine church to the Bulgarians, to tear them away from it and join them to the Latin church in a kind of uniate."[23] The letter ends with a plea for Bulgarian–Russian cooperation: "May our prayers be heard and may our wishes be fulfilled; may Russians and Bulgarians serve each other mutually and may the inner union between us grow and become stronger. Bulgaria is poor and weak in comparison with the colossus Russia, but it has often happened that even the weak one saved the strong one."[24]

Also in April, the *Russian Herald* published "The History of a Serbian Village" by P. Sretkovich, which offered a vivid and gruesome account of the Turkish conquest of Serbia through the experiences of the village of Karchmar: "In the sixteenth and seventeenth centuries ... the Turks devastated Serbia with impunity, they beat, murdered, took people away to slavery. In the sixteenth century it happened that at one time 200,000 Serbs were taken captive and made into slaves. No one in all of Serbia could take off their boots at night, so as to be ready at any minute to flee. The churches were turned into Turkish stables.... But all these oppressions for the whole people were nothing in comparison with the violence that the Turks permitted themselves with individuals." Sretkovich then describes a punitive raid after Greek monks raped "the wife of some bey": "The Turks came, burned down the monastery, attacked the Karchmarians. Some tried to rush into the forest, but this did not help: the Turks always brought with them a multitude of dogs, who soon searched out the escapees. They burned the village, defiled the women and led them away to slavery, slaughtered all the adults, trampled the old men and women with horses, and the children they either carried around on their knives or made into slaves. Thus did the Turks take vengeance for the wife of their bey."[25]

The most sustained treatment of the situation of Orthodox Christian Slavic peoples in the Ottoman Empire came in three articles published in February,

March, and May 1858 under the title "Turkish Affairs [*Turetskie dela*]."[26] The themes of poor Ottoman administration, unjust Phanariote domination of the Orthodox church hierarchy, and oppressive taxation of Christian subjects, which appear scattered throughout the articles cited above, are the intense focus of these three articles. The author describes unrest and uprisings among Christian Slavs in Bulgaria, Bosnia, and Herzegovina, and likens the situation to that of 1853 (the year in which *On the Eve* is set, a time of uprisings in the Balkans): "On the one hand, the government of the Sultan, as the supreme temporal power, and on the other, the Phanariote clergy, which exercises dominion over the southern Slavs, watch the events taking place within the country with bewilderment, and are trying by all means to conceal the bloody drama that is now being played out on the Balkan peninsula ... in all spheres one notes exactly the same kind of activity as at the end of 1853."[27] He compares the Bulgarians and their educational strivings to the Greeks, who had won their independence in the 1820s: "The Bulgarian people, like new Greeks, for some time now have occupied themselves with education as the sole means that can lead them out of the depths of that insignificance into which they have been plunged not so much by the Turks as by the Phanariotes. In this respect the Bulgarians, despite all the persecutions to which the Slavic language is subjected in Turkey on the part of the local Phanariote bishops, have made progress that is worthy of amazement."[28] He speaks of the need for Bulgarians to be provided with books in Church Slavic, since that language has been supplanted in the church by Greek.[29]

The theme of the development of Bulgarian literary culture as a means of national liberation is continued in the May installment: "With the appearance of a new Bulgarian literary culture [*pis'mennost'*], which is making an effort to resurrect the forgotten and downtrodden Slavic dialect, which once was classic, the Bulgarian has seized upon his education as the anchor of salvation, and has become convinced that he will have to perform a great feat in the milieu of rotting Mohammedanism and the scrivener's life of the bearded Phanariote."[30] The author describes the founding of journals and literary societies that engage in publishing books, collecting ancient documents, disseminating literacy among the people, and establishing libraries and museums. In particular, he describes a new literary journal, *Bl"garski knizhitsy* (*Bulgarian Library*), which comes out on the fifth and twentieth of each month and consists of two sections: sciences and literature, and "contemporary chronicle." He adds, "At first glance one cannot help but notice a certain similarity to the *Russian Herald*."[31] The words the author quotes from the journal's editor make him sound like a Bulgarian Katkov, calling for the awakening of his people so that they can take their place among the enlightened nations of the world. Another important point made by the author of the article is that the solidarity of Bulgarians, based on ethnicity, religion, and language, transcends class divisions. Although the Muslim yoke and the Phanariote oppression have "laid the stamp of abasement and sycophancy on the Bulgarians for a whole century," the lower classes have preserved their dignity: "Only the simple people, in the purity and chastity of their feelings, which were not touched by the luxurious intoxication of Phanariote life, remain true to the traditions of their homeland, preserve the language of their ancestors, and find consolation in religion. [The struggle with the Phanariote clergy] revealed the precious remnants of nationality [*national'nost'*] that still glimmered in the breast of the undebauched villager." This in turn, in the author's view, led to the flowering of Bulgarian literary culture that he outlines in his article.[32]

We know that Turgenev was a writer who cared about the opinions of others. As M. Klevensky concluded in a 1923 article about Turgenev's literary advisers, "Not a single important Russian writer attributed so much significance to the preliminary judgment of close friends about his work, or so insistently sought advice and instructions, or so willingly followed those instructions, as Turgenev."[33] Klevensky is speaking about friends like P. V. Annenkov and Countess E. E. Lambert, who read and commented on many of Turgenev's works in manuscript. But it is just as likely that Turgenev cared about what his prospective editor and publisher Katkov would think about his work, and would try to tailor the plot of his first novel for the *Russian Herald* to Katkov's interests, as reflected in the journal.

Katkov's invitation to contribute to the *Russian Herald* came in October 1858; based on his letters, Turgenev seems to have begun writing *On the Eve* in December 1858, and finished the rough draft in October 1859. The plot was based on a manuscript conveyed to him by a neighbor of his country estate, V. Karateev, in 1853 or 1854, before Karateev's departure to fight in the Crimean War.[34] After an unsuccessful attempt to publish Karateev's story, which Annenkov describes as "an incompetent, clumsy, bad tale," Turgenev appears to have put it on the shelf until 1858. Among his Paris manuscripts is a list of characters for the novel that André Mazon has dated to January 1858. But Turgenev only begins to speak in his letters about working on the novel at the end of 1858, after Katkov's invitation.[35] Karateev's autobiographical story told of his love for a young woman who jilted him for a Bulgarian named Katranov and went with him to Bulgaria, where he soon died.[36]

When Katkov's invitation came to him in fall 1858, Turgenev would have had at hand the kernel of a plot that dealt with the question of Bulgaria and the oppression of Slavic Christians in the Ottoman Empire, a question that had been raised again and again in the *Russian Herald* over the course of 1858.[37] *On the Eve* reflects many of the issues discussed in the *Russian Herald* that year: Turkish oppression of the Christian Slav Bulgarians, the drive for Bulgarian literary culture (Insarov is studying Bulgarian folk songs and chronicles), the need for Russians and Bulgarians to strengthen their ties (Insarov is writing a Russian grammar for Bulgarians and a Bulgarian grammar for Russians), and the solidarity among Bulgarians that transcends class differences. As Insarov says in one of the novel's most famous passages, "The lowest peasant, the lowest beggar in Bulgaria and I—we desire one and the same thing. All of us have a single goal. Understand how much confidence and strength that gives!"[38] Katkov's drive to bring the Slavic "dialects" together under Great Russian finds its reflection when Insarov tells Elena, "It's shameful for a Russian not to know Bulgarian. A Russian should know all the Slavic dialects."[39] At one point Insarov describes the depredations of the Turks to Elena: "If you knew what a land of plenty is ours. But meanwhile it is trampled on, it is tormented, they have taken everything from us, everything: our churches, our rights, our lands; the unclean Turks drive us like a herd, they slaughter us." This passage did not appear in the manuscript and was added for the journal publication, possibly at the suggestion of Katkov.[40]

For anyone attuned to Katkov's preoccupations in 1858, the question "Why a Bulgarian?" should not have required Dobroliubov's resort to allegory. To paraphrase a witticism attributed to Freud, sometimes a Bulgarian is just a Bulgarian. Questions of Slavic solidarity, of Russian imperial interests, and of the development of Slavic literacy, although they may have lacked interest for most of Turgenev's reviewers, were at the center of the interests of his publisher Katkov. The muddle in the reception of *On the Eve*, though, has to be laid at Turgenev's feet, because as many contemporary reviewers noted, he really wasn't that interested in the Bulgarian situation, and it does not achieve a full, powerful realization in the novel's pages. N. F. Pavlov made this point most forcefully, and seems here to detect Turgenev's journalistic inspiration:

> Where is the idea, where is the enchanting charm, where is the living aspect of the matter? Is Bulgaria really suffering, how is it suffering, from what is it suffering, is it really necessary to save it, in what does the importance of that salvation consist— this is not visible in the tale.... The author of an artistic work has no right to rely on

information drawn from books and newspapers. The work must stand completely independently and have its own fullness. Therefore it would not be a bad thing to acquaint not only us but the heroine of the tale with the calamities of Bulgaria.[41]

We do not have any evidence of Katkov's own reaction to *On the Eve*, although Turgenev heard a rumor that the editors of the *Russian Herald* considered it "a specimen of absurd talentlessness."[42] Turgenev was never personally fond of Katkov, and by the time *On the Eve* was in press he was complaining bitterly about the editor's arrogance. Angry that proofs were not ready for him although he had notified Katkov of his coming to Moscow, Turgenev wrote to Annenkov: "Nekrasov and Kraevsky never attained such Olympian heights of rudeness, never forced an ill man to gallop more than 600 versts, etc."[43] But despite Katkov's supposedly cool response to *On the Eve* and Turgenev's growing irritation at Katkov's famously high-handed manners, the two men needed each other. As Evgeniia Tur caustically noted to Turgenev when he asked Katkov's permission to publish a chapter of *Fathers and Sons* in her periodical *Russian Speech*, "Katkov doesn't have many contributors—he values the ones that are left and you all the more. After all there are no novelists, and no one writes novels better than you—of course you know this."[44] As for Turgenev, with his relations with the *Contemporary* severely damaged after Dobroliubov's review, the *Russian Herald* was the only journal left with the kind of stability and wide readership that a writer of his stature could consider having as his regular publisher.

Fathers and Sons and the Birth of "Nihilism"

The Soviet editors of Turgenev's complete works saw the origins of *Fathers and Sons* (*Ottsy i deti*, 1862) in Turgenev's response to Dobroliubov's call to depict the struggle with "internal Turks."[45] But from the viewpoint of Katkov, the internal threat to Russia was not an oppressive government but young radicals like Dobroliubov himself and Nikolai Chernyshevsky, who were propagating their ideas by means of the *Contemporary*. Throughout 1861, Katkov did battle with the editors of the *Contemporary*, particularly Chernyshevsky, in the pages of the *Russian Herald*.[46] (Dobroliubov died in November of that year.) He also published lengthy excerpts from a treatise by P. D. Iurkevich, a philosopher who was teaching at the Kiev Religious Academy, that attacked materialism in general and Chernyshevsky's articles on the "anthropological principle in philosophy" in particular.[47] Virtually simultaneously, Turgenev was writing *Fathers and Sons*, from August 1860 to July 1861 (he continued revising it up until publication at the beginning of 1862). In his initial materials for the novel, Turgenev describes the character of Bazarov as "Nihilist. Self-confident, speaks in fragments and not much—a hard worker.—(A mixture of Dobroliubov, Pavlov, and Preobrazhenskii) ... has no artistic element and does not recognize [the artistic element]."[48] Pavlov may be the provincial doctor "D." who Turgenev claimed was his prototype in his 1869 literary memoirs, in a clear attempt to ward off accusations that in depicting Bazarov he was attacking Dobroliubov.[49] But at least in its initial conception, *Fathers and Sons* was indeed intended as a response to the circle of the *Contemporary*.

Fathers and Sons centers around the character of Evgenii Vasilievich Bazarov, a young *raznochinets* student of natural sciences who typifies the characteristics of the "new people," whom Turgenev indelibly labeled as "nihilists." While visiting his university friend and devoted intellectual disciple Arkadii Nikolaevich Kirsanov, Bazarov engages in fierce debate with Arkadii's father Nikolai Petrovich and his uncle Pavel Petrovich. In a plot development that seems to discredit Bazarov's loudly stated antiromantic principles, he falls passionately in love with the bored society lady Anna Sergeevna Odintsova and is spiritually broken by her rejection. He returns to the humble home of his parents and dies after accidentally cutting himself during the autopsy of a typhus victim. The novel ends with the joyful celebration of two weddings, that of Nikolai Petrovich and his peasant mistress, and that of Arkadii and Odintsova's younger sister Katia.

Both Katkov in his journal polemics and Turgenev in his novel use the term "nihilist" to describe the young generation of radicals. The word had never before been used in this sense in Russian, and most scholars attribute the coinage to Turgenev, as did he himself. In 1951 the Soviet scholar B. P. Kozmin argued that Turgenev had borrowed the term from Katkov, who used it in his October 1861 article "A Little Something about Progress."[50] In responding to Kozmin in the same journal, A. I. Batiuto pointed out that Katkov's use of the term in October 1861 proved nothing, since Turgenev had given Katkov the completed manuscript in August 1861, and that consequently Katkov probably borrowed the term "nihilism" from Turgenev, not the other way around. Batiuto also pointed out that in fact Katkov had used the term earlier, in his February 1861 article "Old Gods and New Gods," but that his use of it there did not refer to the young radicals but to materialism and idealism in general.[51] Kozmin responded that the reference in "Old Gods and New Gods" was indeed directed against Chernyshevsky and M. A. Antonovich of the *Contemporary*.[52] Kozmin's argument hinges on Turgenev's having added the word "nihilism" to the manuscript of *Fathers and Sons* after Katkov's article appeared in February 1861, but this does not appear to have been the case.

More important than who borrowed "nihilism" from whom, however, is the fact that both men were using the term in the same sense at the same time, a fact that indicates that in 1861 they were thinking along similar lines with respect to the young radicals. Both Turgenev and Katkov studied German philosophy in Berlin in the 1840s, and it is no coincidence that the term was used in German thought in the early nineteenth century. According to M. P. Alekseev, who traced the earliest uses of the term in Russian literature, the German philosopher Wilhelm Krug (1770–1841) "opposes nihilism to materialism, and sees in it only the extreme manifestation of idealistic thought, which assumes the idea as something first, absolute, and attempts from it to explain the origins of reality."[53] This association of nihilism with idealism in early nineteenth-century German philosophy helps to explain Katkov's reference in "Old Gods and New Gods" to "idealistic systems that lead thought to the kind of nihilism that the most desperate of the materialists could not imagine."[54] Turgenev stresses the materialism and empiricism of the radicals as embodied in Bazarov, but in the scene where the term "nihilism" first appears, he brings out the "nothingness" of their philosophy by having Nikolai Petrovich Kirsanov say, "Nihilist—that's from the Latin *nihil, nothing*, as far as I can judge."[55] Katkov's view, while in line with Turgenev's, is more philosophically complex. This emerges most clearly in the October article "A Little Something about Progress," in which Katkov explains more fully the extreme idealism that lies at the heart of the philosophy of those who "take pride in and admire their own nihilism." He writes that negation is a "weapon of success" and a "force for life" only when it is connected to something positive: "But negation for the sake of negation—destruction and decomposition—is the business of death, not life."[56] The seemingly counterintuitive link between idealism and the nihilism of the young radicals, who vaunt their materialism, becomes clearer at the end of the article: "Our social development will be both more fruitful and more conservative to the same degree that we recognize that progress takes place in life and for life, not in the clouds, but on the earth, not in airy constructions, but in the data of real experience. The more we recognize this, the less we will strain our vision looking into the empty distance without seeing anything, or seeing only phantasmagorias; the more we will investigate the surrounding milieu, bring our thought close to reality, and make it an organ of life and of true movement forward."[57]

The intellectual solidarity of Katkov and Turgenev in the months during which *Fathers and Sons* was being written was described in 1958 by the Soviet scholar V.

Arkhipov, who noted both men's use of the term "nihilism," Turgenev's willingness to make changes to the manuscript in response to Katkov's suggestions, and Turgenev's fairly substantial working relationship with the *Russian Herald*. Arkhipov writes: "Although Turgenev did not like Katkov personally, the writer was not much bothered by this, and he firmly became a contributor to the *Russian Herald*, where he published his three main novels, which are landmarks both on the path of the writer's evolution and on the path of the evolution of the *Russian Herald*."[58] Arkhipov's article had a clear ideological purpose: the political discrediting of Turgenev and his relegation to the ranks of those who stood against the revolutionary movement. The article appeared in the first issue of the important new journal *Russian Literature* [*Russkaia literatura*], and it evoked a furious response from other scholars of Turgenev, who had to quickly suppress the suggestion that the great Russian writer could have been in a kind of conspiracy with Katkov, whose name was anathema for the Soviet establishment in 1958.[59]

Arkhipov's article appeared during the so-called "Thaw," when, in line with Khrushchev's attempt to overcome the Stalin era, literary culture was being mildly liberalized. V. M. Markovich, who in 2008 published a fascinating account of the uproar over Arkhipov's article, clearly describes the danger that faced Turgenev's reputation (and the careers of Turgenev scholars) after Arkhipov's article was published: "We do not know Arkhipov's subjective intentions, but the objective meaning of his article [*vystuplenie*] was clear: it was one of the rather frequent attempts at the time to master the liberalization of the regime that had been outlined in 1956, and thereby to recover the 'Stalinist' 1940s."[60] He continues, "Arkhipov ... was trying to restore the atmosphere of ideological 'campaigns' of the 1940s. And everyone could still remember the example of Dostoevsky, who was then crossed out of the Russian classics."[61] Turgenev's defenders won the day, and Turgenev remained in the pantheon of Russian classics as codified by Soviet literary scholarship. But in defending against Arkhipov's malicious attack, Soviet scholarship had to close its eyes to the essence of his insight about the relations between Turgenev and Katkov. It is one of the aims of this study to restore a more objective approach, now that the danger from Soviet "campaigns" has passed. It is worth reexamining the question of Katkov's influence on the creation of *Fathers and Sons*, without Arkhipov's malign political purpose in doing so.

The conservative and not entirely reliable memoirist E. M. Feoktistov recalled that Turgenev's initial conception of the novel was that it would expose the new type of the nihilist, and that Turgenev said, "only Russian life was capable of producing such an abomination [*merzost'*]."[62] Feoktistov was astounded by Turgenev's assertion in his 1869 memoir "Apropos of *Fathers and Sons*" that his sympathies were entirely with the nihilist Bazarov.[63] Feoktistov claims that he confronted Turgenev in 1870, saying, "'Do you remember with what revulsion you reacted then to the nihilism that was just then arising in Russia, and what a great contribution you considered it to be to expose it ... and now suddenly you want to assure us that you sympathize with everything in Bazarov, decidedly everything, therefore even his views on art, in which he sees nothing other than an idle amusement: well, tell me please, why did you need to do this?' Turgenev laughed and waved his hand. 'Well,' he said, 'I really did go too far.'"[64]

Feoktistov's bewilderment was shared by Nikolai Strakhov, who had written one of the finest responses to *Fathers and Sons* in Dostoevsky's journal *Time* in 1862. After Turgenev's 1869 essay appeared, Strakhov wrote that he refused to allow Turgenev to enroll in the nihilist movement. Strakhov goes on to provide a pithy description of what Turgenev's avowed "sympathies" with Bazarov entail. It would be deplorable if a man "who for so long has occupied the first place" among Russian writers and "achieved considerable fame even in enlightened Europe" really wanted to enter posterity as "a secret nihilist" who believed neither in philosophy nor history, "who of all the sciences respected only natural sciences," and who had no reverence for "love, friendship, family, the beauties of nature and the inspirations of art."[65] Most tellingly for the purposes of this discussion, Strakhov refuses to believe that Katkov could have been deceived by Turgenev to such a degree that he would allow a "secret nihilist" to publish a novel in the pages of the *Russian Herald*. Strakhov writes, "This nihilist at first hid his desperate opinions, pretended to be a completely different person, so that he succeeded in deceiving even the shrewd and incorruptible Mr. Katkov, who thought that the author of *Fathers and Sons* sincerely desired a different impression, desired in his tale to expose and castigate nihilism."[66]

Bazarov as Apotheosis

Despite Feoktistov's and Strakhov's confidence that Turgenev's initial conception of *Fathers and Sons* was as an exposure and castigation of nihilism, both "Apropos of *Fathers and Sons*" and Annenkov's memoirs provide evidence that Katkov was not pleased with the manuscript he received in the fall of 1861. Turgenev quotes a letter from Katkov that has not survived, in which Katkov says that, even if Bazarov has not been elevated "to an apotheosis," he has nevertheless "accidentally ended up on a very high pedestal": "He truly crushes everything around him. Everything compared to him is either old trash or weak and green. Is that the impression that should be desired? In the tale one senses that the author wanted to characterize a principle with which he hardly sympathizes, but he seems to waver in the choice of tone and has unconsciously submitted to that principle. One senses something unfree in the author's relationship with the hero of the tale, a kind of awkwardness and constraint. The author seems to become flustered in his presence, and he doesn't love him but even more he fears him!"[67]

A similar reaction by Katkov is vividly described by Annenkov, who recalls meeting with Katkov in the fall of 1861, soon after he received the manuscript. Annenkov recalls that Katkov received him in a friendly but restrained manner, and did not express any delight in the new novel. According to Annenkov, Katkov said, "'Isn't Turgenev ashamed of lowering the flag before a radical and saluting him as a meritorious warrior?'" Annenkov replied that in fact the figure of Bazarov evoked horror and revulsion. "'That's true,' he replied, 'but secret goodwill can disguise itself as horror and revulsion, and an experienced eye recognizes the bird in that form.'" Annenkov objected that Turgenev could not have lowered himself to creating an apotheosis of radicalism or to the patronage of intellectual and moral dissoluteness. "'I didn't say that,' Katkov answered passionately, and becoming obviously animated, 'but it comes out resembling that. Just think, this young hero, Bazarov, rules unconditionally over everyone and never encounters any sensible resistance. Even his death is a triumph, a crown to this glorious life, and it is a self-sacrifice, although an accidental one. One cannot go any further!'" Annenkov replied that in an artistic work one has to show one's enemies from their best side. "'Very well,' Mr. Katkov responded half-ironically and half-seriously, 'but besides art, please remember, there is also a political question here. Who knows what this type may turn into? After all, this is only its beginning. To hastily extol him and adorn him with the flowers of creativity means to make the struggle with him twice as hard later. But,' Mr. Katkov added, rising from the sofa, 'I will write to Turgenev about this and will await his reply.'"[68]

Katkov did of course write to Turgenev, and although his letters have not survived, we can see in Turgenev's own letters something of the process that ensued. Soviet literary scholarship has devoted enormous effort to parsing the changes that Turgenev made to the manuscript of *Fathers and Sons* in response to suggestions by Katkov and Annenkov, but it does not appear that any fundamental alteration was made to the novel's outline or even to the general character of Bazarov. One might characterize the effect of the changes as leading to a more fuzzy outline of Bazarov's character, but he remains basically the same somewhat contradictory figure.[69] And whatever his initial negative reaction, after the novel was published Katkov embraced it wholeheartedly and explicated it in his two lengthy articles, articles that used the novel as part of his continued polemic against the radicals of the *Contemporary*.

As we have seen, in "Apropos of *Fathers and Sons*" in 1869, Turgenev used Katkov's initial negative reaction to the novel as a defense against the criticism by young radical youth that he had caricatured their movement. Already in April 1862 he wrote to the venerable émigré leader Alexander Herzen, "While composing Bazarov I not only was not angry at him, but I felt toward him 'an attraction, a sort of sickness'—so that Katkov at first was horrified and saw in him the *apotheosis* of the *Contemporary* and later persuaded me to discard not a few extenuating features, of which I repent."[70]

Whenever Turgenev makes a similar remark to someone in the radical camp, he seems to be saying that he *wanted* Bazarov to be an apotheosis and was only thwarted by Katkov. But his letters to Katkov at the time say something different. While working on revising the manuscript in October 1861, he writes to Katkov, "I hope that as a result of my corrections the figure of Bazarov will be clarified for you and will not produce on you the impression of an apotheosis, *which was not my intention*."[71] In asking for publication of the novel to be put off for various reasons, including his own dissatisfaction with the work, Turgenev speaks in terms that imply that he knew that with this work he was going into battle, and on Katkov's side: "With this plot in particular one must go out before the reader fully armed (as fully as possible)." He goes on to speak in unmistakably negative terms about the figure of Bazarov. We may gather from what Turgenev says that Katkov had suggested that Odintsova make fun of Bazarov and that he be described as inferior to the Russian peasant. In his reply, even as he defends against Katkov's suggestions, Turgenev provides a fairly damning summation of Bazarov's character: "Odintsova must not ironize Bazarov, nor the peasant stand higher than him, although he is himself empty and barren. . . . Perhaps my view of Russia is more misanthropic than you suppose: he—in my view—is truly the hero of our time. A fine hero and a fine time, you will say. But that is how it is."[72]

Katkov and Pavel Petrovich

In his letters to Katkov, Turgenev does not discuss the character of Pavel Petrovich Kirsanov, Bazarov's main antagonist, but it would appear that Katkov was not entirely satisfied with his depiction either. Annenkov recalled Katkov as saying that Bazarov meets no "sensible resistance [*del'nyi otpor*]" in the novel. This implies that Katkov considered Pavel Petrovich to be an unworthy spokesman for the antiradical position. Hidden here may be another reason for Katkov's initial, viscerally negative response to the novel, for Pavel Petrovich bears many of the traits of Katkov himself, starting with his pronounced Anglomania (not mentioned among the traits of this character in Turgenev's initial notes toward the novel).[73] He wears English clothing (Turgenev even uses the English word "suit" in his Russian text), reads an English-language newspaper, and ends up socializing with English people in Dresden.[74] Most importantly, in his most extended argument with Bazarov, he exalts English aristocratic principles, thus echoing the "line" of Katkov's *Russian Herald*, which Herzen mockingly called the "Westminster Herald."[75] Pavel Petrovich is arrogant, high-handed, and cold, all qualities attested of Katkov by his contemporaries: "[Pavel Petrovich] was self-assured, a bit mocking, and somehow amusingly irritable."[76] In his amazement that an ill-bred, uncultured "*lekarishka* [pejorative word for doctor]" dares to challenge him intellectually and makes light of something as serious as a duel, Pavel Petrovich evokes the image of the proud, self-assured Katkov in his polemics with the "whistlers" of the *Contemporary*.[77] It was not only Dobroliubov who provided inspiration for the characters in *Fathers and Sons*, but also Katkov and his indignant, furious defense of traditional values.

In his lengthy letter to the young poet and student K. K. Sluchevsky defending *Fathers and Sons* against its critics, Turgenev compared Pavel Petrovich not to Katkov but to "Stolypin, Esakov, and Rosset" (the aristocratic military men Aleksei Arkadievich Stolypin [1816–58], Piotr Semionovich Esakov [1806–42], and one of the three Rosset brothers, probably Aleksandr Osipovich Rosset [1811–81]).[78] One could, of course, hardly expect Turgenev to admit, even in a private letter, to using his own publisher as a model for the dignified but somewhat ridiculous figure of Pavel Petrovich. Yet the similarity between Pavel Petrovich and Katkov was discerned by no less a reader than Dostoevsky, who according to Turgenev himself was one of only two people who fully understood his conception of Bazarov.[79]

In 1862 Dostoevsky published an article, "A Ticklish Question: An Article with Whistling, with Transformations and Disguises [*Shchekotlivyi vopros: Stat'ia so svistom, s prevrashcheniiami i pereodevan'iami*]," that was the culmination of his own polemic with Katkov.[80] Katkov's 1861 polemic with the *Contemporary* had overlapped and intersected with his polemic with Dostoevsky and his own journal

Time, a polemic that will be discussed in chapter 4. In "A Ticklish Question," Dostoevsky creates an artistic image of Katkov that develops and extends the portraiture provided in Belinsky's play *The Fifty-Year-Old Uncle* and in Vyzinsky's contributions to the Tur controversy. He also blends his caricatured figure of Katkov with Turgenev's Pavel Petrovich, thus laying bare a genealogy that both Turgenev and Katkov would probably have preferred not to emphasize.[81]

Dostoevsky's article was inspired by an article titled "Who Is To Blame?" ("*Kto vinovat?*") that had appeared in the newspaper *Contemporary Word* (*Sovremennoe slovo*). The anonymous author absurdly tried to blame Katkov for the rise of nihilism, because he had nurtured liberal ideas in the *Russian Herald*, and in conclusion called for the *Russian Herald* to provide an accounting for its past actions. Dostoevsky uses a fantastic imagining of this "accounting" as the basis for his biting caricature of Katkov.[82] Katkov's Anglomania is foregrounded, as the fantasy is cast in the form of an English-style parliamentary session, with speakers asking for the floor and indications in parentheses of the responses of the listeners, such as "Hear, hear!" (The *Russian Herald* often published summaries of English parliamentary sessions that were presented in a similar form.) The Katkov figure, called "the Orator," constantly speaks of his admiration for "English principles" and the merit he has earned by introducing them into Russian life. In the announcement of *Time* for 1862, Dostoevsky had spoken of people in public life who "want to send for Russian nationality [*narodnost'*] from England, since it's agreed that English goods are the very best."[83]

The Orator possesses all the traits of pride, arrogance, and self-assurance that are so prevalent in contemporary portraits of Katkov. Dostoevsky wickedly parodies Katkov's polemical voice: "I won't hide that I am proud [*samoliubiv*, lit. self-loving] and very much like to daydream sometimes about my significance and my fame. But speak—oh, I speak only on rare occasions, when I have to, so to speak, shoot from the cannon, when I have to crush, mow down, destroy."[84] The Orator brags of his literary activities, his translation of *Romeo and Juliet* and his article on Pushkin. He says, "What good is false delicacy: I frankly considered and consider myself higher than all my contemporaries.... All my literary activity can be explained by that same selfish pride [*samoliubie*]. I founded a journal out of selfish pride. I wanted to take first place, to shine and to subjugate."[85] Dostoevsky parodies Katkov's style, with its use of neologistic borrowings like "abstruozno."[86] Dostoevsky even refers to the ludicrous moment in the Tur polemic when Katkov demanded that Vyzinsky return his books. The Orator, speaking of his acquaintance with an anglomaniacal character in Griboedov's *Woe from Wit*, says, "I knew this superb and unforgettable nobleman, Prince Grigorii. He even borrowed a book from me, which he forgot to return; but I have long ago forgiven him for that."[87]

Part of "A Ticklish Question" is cast in the form of a dialogue with a "Nihilist" among the listeners, thus evoking the argument between Pavel Petrovich and Bazarov in chapter 10 of *Fathers and Sons*. In defending "English principles," the Orator comes close to quoting Pavel Petrovich word for word. Pavel Petrovich says in defending English aristocratic principles: "'Remember, my dear sir' (at these words Bazarov lifted his eyes to Pavel Petrovich), 'remember, my dear sir'— he repeated with bitterness—'the English aristocrats. They do not yield one iota of their rights [*ne ustupaiut ioty ot prav svoikh*], and therefore they respect the rights of others; they demand the fulfillment of obligations in relation to themselves, and therefore they themselves fulfill their own obligations. The aristocracy gave freedom to England and supports it.'"[88] Dostoevsky's Orator, using the same unusual borrowed word "iota," says in response to the Nihilist, "In Anglomania there is yet another precious quality (oh, God, how many precious qualities it has!), namely: it is a finished business, arranged, finalized. I speak, I preach, and of course I do not yield one iota of my convictions [*ni odnoi ioty ne ustupaesh' iz svoikh ubezhdenii*]."[89]

Katkov's Commentary on *Fathers and Sons*

We have no evidence that Katkov recognized himself in Pavel Petrovich, but it is likely that his incisive mind would have noticed the same similarities that Dostoevsky perceived. Nevertheless, whatever disagreements Katkov had with Turgenev's depiction of Bazarov and Pavel Petrovich, once the novel was published he devoted himself to directing its reception into channels that were appropriate for the program of the *Russian Herald*. The first step was the highlighting of the discord that the novel had evoked in the camp of the radicals.

The reviewer for the *Contemporary*, M. A. Antonovich, wrote a highly negative review that accused Turgenev of making Bazarov as unattractive as possible. Antonovich absurdly exaggerates every last detail of Turgenev's narrative to support his claim: Bazarov loses at cards, he's a glutton and a drunkard, Odintsova is revolted by his advances, and on his deathbed he can't restrain his lust for her.[90] Writing in the *Russian Word* (*Russkoe slovo*), D. I. Pisarev, to the contrary, embraced Turgenev's portrait of Bazarov as an ideal for the young generation, "a person strong in intellect and character." In his interpretation, Bazarov is a phenomenon that, like it or not, cannot be stopped, "the same as cholera."[91] The *Russian Herald* gleefully seized upon the disagreement among the radicals, and published excerpts from Antonovich's and Pisarev's dueling articles in the form of a dialogue. The commentator (not Katkov, but someone who signed himself "I. V.") concluded, "For any unprejudiced eye, Bazarov is an unpleasant personality.... As Mr. Pisarev says quite correctly, ... he's the same as cholera." The commentator goes on to say that to claim such a representative would compromise and lower any cause. He writes that Pisarev was carried away by youthful enthusiasm and decided to applaud Bazarov and claim him as one of his own. The more cautious and experienced Antonovich decided to cry out that real Bazarovs are not like that, that Turgenev slandered the young generation. But according to the commentator, Antonovich was just pretending: "In his soul he recognizes that Bazarov is a good likeness, and he sympathizes with him even more intimately than Mr. Pisarev does, and complains only as a way of diverting attention."[92]

In his first article, "Turgenev's Novel and Its Critics" (May 1862), Katkov also dwells on Antonovich's and Pisarev's responses. He sees Antonovich as a blind follower who does not want his idol to be depicted in artistic detail. A principle that "has pretensions to dominance" fears being brought to public light:

> To become the object of observation, to be shown in a definite form, means to come down from the heights and to be transformed from a dominant principle into a simple object. It is well known that a person cannot be liberated from blind enthusiasms in any other way than through consciousness.... That is why any blind power fears becoming the object of consciousness and does not like being represented. That is why people who are blindly subjected to such a force fight hand and foot, become angry and indignant, when it is called out onto the stage.[93]

As a result of seeing such an accurate depiction of the "blind force" of nihilism, Antonovich has produced an article that is "not criticism but a convulsion."[94]

Katkov goes on to explain that Pisarev, in contrast to Antonovich, is delighted with Bazarov and merely regrets that Turgenev, "because of his age and soft-heartedness, cannot experience all the sweetness of Bazarov's thought process and live his life."[95] Katkov resolves the paradox of the diametrically opposite reactions of Antonovich and Pisarev in the following way: "They felt the same thing in opposite ways. One recognized the future hero with joyful exultation; the other also recognized him, but with gnashing of teeth. One is calm and happy; the other is agitated, and tormented, and pours forth curses."[96] In fact, however, the "cursing" critic, Antonovich, also deeply sympathizes with Bazarov; he simply cannot bear "this harsh, energetically outlined figure; he cannot bear that now thousands of eyes are turned on this figure, that everyone can inspect it from all sides.... The temple has been thrown open, the idol has been carried outside! How can the priest remain indifferent, not rend his raiment, not pour ashes on his head! How can he not be indignant at the profaner of the sacred thing!"[97]

Katkov goes on to discuss the characters in the novel other than Bazarov, interestingly saying of Pavel Petrovich, "If he had been born an English squire, he perhaps would have been a marvelous justice of the peace and trusty organ of a political party."[98] But Katkov sees Pavel Petrovich as a person who has little real strength, "a phantom among the living," not up to the contest with Bazarov, whom he describes as "a robust and capable person who cannot be accused of any vulgarity [*poshlost'*]." Katkov promises in the next installment to discuss the question, "Is this a real force, or only an optical illusion, the result of comparing him with the surrounding softness and powerlessness?"[99]

In his second article, "On Our Nihilism Apropos of Turgenev's Novel" (July 1862), Katkov scoffs at Bazarov's scientific research, which he equates to the dabbling in German philosophy of an earlier generation. Bazarov's dissecting of frogs reminds him of how in the past "young and even rather mature people assiduously occupied themselves with philosophy, travelled from one German university to another, listened, took notes, and religiously reread in their little notebooks the teachings about *Sein* and *Nichts*."[100] According to Katkov, this lack of seriousness is characteristic of Russian intellectual life as a whole, and explains why the pitiful doctrine of nihilism is gaining a foothold.

Katkov draws a strong distinction between negation for negation's sake and true doubt, the kind of doubt of which Descartes and Kant were capable: "Doubt neither assumes nor negates; doubt, real, true doubt admits the possibility of opposite resolutions." If doubt has been resolved, either negatively or positively, that means "that we have already made a decision and that a dogmatic element is already present in our criticism.... If we negate, then that means that the matter has already been decided by us in advance, decided without doubt; we are only deceiving ourselves in imagining that we are doubting; we have decided the matter simply and directly.... The negating tendency is a kind of religion—religion turned upside down, full of internal contradiction and senselessness, but a religion all the same, which may have its teachers and fanatics."[101]

As in "A Little Something about Progress," here Katkov identifies nihilism with unrealistic, utopian schemes, which form part of its dogmatic "religion turned upside down." In describing the attraction of utopias for people's minds, Katkov anticipates Dostoevsky's Grand Inquisitor, who speaks of the "intelligent people" who guard the secret of the emptiness of their teachings from the childlike masses. Katkov argues that utopias "serve as the best weapon of negation and destruction." When the impossible and unrealizable is presented as possible and natural, people's minds are intoxicated and decomposed: "Everything close, practical, possible, everything actual, is more easily rejected because of the distant and the dreamy that intoxicates people—and that is where the interest of nihilism lies.... The intelligent people [*liudi umnye*], the priests and teachers, cannot help but recognize in the depths of their souls all the vanity of these fantasies, but they do not consider it necessary to undermine this faith in them; on the contrary, they consider it necessary and obligatory to support this faith and even to encourage others in all possible absurdities."[102]

Katkov sees the only resistance to nihilism in the positive interests of society: "Education, science, political and industrial life, the development and competition of all sorts of interests, freedom of conscience, the educational influence of the milieu, the living force of tradition—these are the obstacles that come to meet this phenomenon [nihilism] in the formed societies of our time."[103] Given that the *Russian Herald* from its inception devoted itself precisely to these subjects, it is not surprising that Katkov returns to a similar idea to conclude his article. He explains that one cannot use negative means against negative phenomena, and that any kind of persecution would only intensify the illness and make it chronic. The negative must be resisted with the positive: "There is only one sure and drastic remedy against these phenomena—the strengthening of all positive interests of public life. The more richly life develops in all its normal interests, in all its positive strivings—religious, intellectual, political, economic—the less room will remain for negative forces in public life. In such circumstances, the Bazarovs would be extremely uncomfortable: they would have to feel themselves to be in a contemptible and powerless position, and for them that is the cruelest death."[104]

Turgenev's Commentary on *Fathers and Sons*

After the first of Katkov's two articles appeared, Turgenev wrote him that he liked it very much and was awaiting the second with impatience.[105] But as we have seen, in his 1869 memoir "Apropos of *Fathers and Sons*," Turgenev tried to direct the reception of the novel in a very different way than Katkov had in 1862. In 1869, Turgenev attempts to "enroll in the nihilist movement," as Strakhov put it, or at least to claim a more unambiguously positive attitude toward the character of Bazarov than most readers of the novel have perceived, saying that aside from Bazarov's views on art, he personally shares almost all his convictions.[106] He cites at length Katkov's initial negative reaction to the novel as a means of distancing himself from an association that he no longer found useful (he had published his novel *Smoke* in the *Russian Herald* in 1867, and his final work published there, the story "An Unfortunate Girl [*Neschastnaia*]," was published in January 1869).

By 1869, Katkov was a much more polarizing figure than he had been in 1858, when Turgenev began working with him. Soon after Katkov assumed the editorship of the *Moscow News* in 1863, the Polish uprising led him to move more decisively into politics. The role Katkov played in 1863, in galvanizing public opinion against the Poles and successfully urging the government to take strict measures against them, had given him the reputation not of a moderate-liberal Anglomane but of a reactionary. Already in 1867, at the time of the publication of *Smoke* and two years before "Apropos of *Fathers and Sons*," Turgenev felt it necessary to explain and almost apologize to Herzen for his association with Katkov. After pointing out that he was publishing not in the *Moscow News* but in the *Russian Herald*, which he disingenuously claimed had "no political coloration," he continued, "At the present time the *Russian Herald* is the sole journal that is read by the public—and that pays."[107]

"Apropos of *Fathers and Sons*" could certainly be read as Turgenev's repudiation of Katkov. Katkov himself in later years said that Turgenev had "betrayed [*vydal*]" his publisher by highlighting his disagreements with him at the time of publication.[108] But although Turgenev had complained in private letters to correspondents such as Herzen and Dostoevsky that Katkov and other critical readers (like Annenkov, no doubt) had caused him to make changes that rendered the character of Bazarov more negative, he did not make such an accusation publicly until several years later, in 1874.[109] Any reader who compared the *Russian Herald* edition of *Fathers and Sons* with the separate edition published later in 1862 would see that Turgenev had introduced some minor changes, some of which probably represented restoration of passages that had been omitted in the course of publication in the *Russian Herald*. (The question of which changes had been made to the *Russian Herald* edition at the insistence of Katkov and which were either Turgenev's own or ones suggested by Annenkov is still a vexed one.)[110]

But the general reader's attention was not drawn to this issue until 1874, when Turgenev sanctioned a very public airing of the question of Katkov's imposition of changes to the novel during its publication.

For the separate publication of the novel in September 1862, Turgenev had made notations in the margins of an offprint of the novel as it appeared in the *Russian Herald*, restoring some of the original passages that had been changed in the process of publication. In 1874, V. V. Stasov, who as director of the Artistic Section of the Imperial Public Library was in charge of collecting and curating manuscripts by important Russian cultural figures, asked Turgenev to write and sign the following notation on the inside cover of the offprint, which was in the library's collection: "All the corrections that have been made in pencil in this book were written by me; and the other corrections, although not written by me, were done according to my instructions. May 20, 1874. Iv. Turgenev."[111] Stasov then published an announcement in the *St. Petersburg News* that the Imperial Public Library had this offprint in its possession, "in the same form as it was published in 1862 in the *Russian Herald*, that is, with the omission of many passages relating to Bazarov that were cut (without the author's permission) by the editors of the Moscow journal. On the margins of this copy all these passages have been restored by the hand of the author."[112]

Katkov responded in the *Moscow News*, which he had begun to edit in 1863 in addition to the *Russian Herald*, in a manner calculated to enrage Turgenev. Katkov writes that if any changes were made, they were made by the author himself, who at that point "was in the best period of his talent and of his intellectual capacities in general." If changes had been made against his will or without his permission, he would certainly have protested. Instead, he continued to publish his works in the *Russian Herald* for years afterward.[113]

Turgenev's response in a letter to Stasov demonstrates to what extent his attitude toward Katkov had deteriorated: "Katkov's act is worthy of him—he should have been a Bonapartist—to such a degree does he lie self-assuredly and insolently. ... But *in the first place*, he himself is a rather worthless little man—with whom I have no desire to associate; and *in the second place*, I have a positive loathing for all kinds of literary squabbles, explanations, and scandals. The devil take them all!"[114] Turgenev admits that he was wrong not to protest the changes made in both *Fathers and Sons* and *Smoke*, but continues, "One has to know what kind of rogues I was dealing with. It's really true: 'Don't touch shit and it won't smell.'"[115]

One of Turgenev's supporters, V. P. Burenin, published a response to Katkov, signed "Z.," with the colorful title "The Castration of Artistic Works." Burenin revives some of the old accusations of arrogance and high-handed meddling that had marked the Tur polemic, and applies Turgenev's label of "Bonapartist" to Katkov. Burenin concludes: "One must have a truly Bonapartist logic in order to introduce in one's defense arguments like the following: 'You didn't abuse me at the time I deserved it, therefore I'm not guilty but you are.'"[116] In fairness to Katkov it must be noted that Turgenev's letters to him at the period during which *Fathers and Sons* was being edited and printed say nothing about any unwillingness to make suggested changes. Turgenev's main concerns at the time seem to have been, first, the fulfillment of his request that the novel be published as a whole in one issue, not serialized, and second, questions of payment.[117] In April 1862, Turgenev writes to Katkov, "I'm happy to hear that you are satisfied with the success of *Fathers and Sons*—they will abuse it (and it seems have already abused it), that's without doubt; but my main desire was to set in motion two or three ideas—and in this it seems I succeeded."[118]

Fathers and Sons as Comedy

Discussions of whether Turgenev "sympathized with" Bazarov or tried to caricature him often center around the question of Bazarov's death. Some in the radical camp were upset that Bazarov dies without accomplishing anything, a criticism that echoed the charge that Insarov never makes it back to Bulgaria. On the other hand, according to Annenkov, Katkov was not pleased by the "self-sacrificing" nature of Bazarov's death, caused by an illness he incurred in the pursuit of scientific knowledge. But if we turn from the detailed inspection of individual plot events (like Bazarov's losing at cards to the local priest) that marked the contemporary discourse around the novel and consider larger questions of form, the overall form of the novel raises new questions about Turgenev's conception. The novel's form corresponds strikingly to the archetypal plot of comedy, as formulated by Northrop Frye in 1957 based on his study of Greek, Roman, and Shakespearean comedy, a legacy that Turgenev would have been deeply familiar with, as would Katkov, who wrote a dissertation in classics and translated Shakespeare. The traditional form chosen by Turgenev defeats Bazarov in a more subliminal but no less powerful way than any easily perceptible individual moments of the plot, and may explain the negative reaction of most radicals to Turgenev's portrait of the "nihilist."

According to Frye, "the movement of comedy is usually a movement from one kind of society to another."[119] A "blocking character," usually an older father figure, has to be overcome in order for the hero to form a new society at the end of the play. The hero's society "recalls a golden age in the past before the main action of the play begins. Thus we have a stable and harmonious order disrupted by folly, obsession, forgetfulness, 'pride and prejudice,' or events not understood by the characters themselves, and then restored."[120] The hero and heroine are often bland; the hero is left undeveloped because "his real life begins at the end of the play, and we have to believe him to be potentially a more interesting character than he appears to be."[121] The blocking character is obsessed by a humor or ruling passion, "and his function in the play is primarily to repeat his obsession."[122] The comic ending is often brought about by a recognition scene, in which, for example, a heroine who is a slave or courtesan turns out to be "the daughter of somebody respectable, so that the hero can marry her without loss of face."[123] The appearance of the new society that has formed around the hero "is frequently signalized by some kind of party or festive ritual," often a wedding or multiple weddings. "As the final society reached by comedy is the one that the audience has recognized all along to be the proper and desirable state of affairs, an act of communion with the audience is in order."[124]

Fathers and Sons begins with a society that is in dire need of renewal. As Arkadii, his father, and Bazarov ride from the train station through his father's estate, Arkadii looks at the desolate landscape with its emaciated cattle and thinks, "[This land] cannot, cannot stay this way, transformations are necessary ... but how can we carry them out, how should we get started?"[125] The "blocking character," a father figure who does nothing but "repeat his obsession," would seem to be not Arkadii's own father, who never blocks anything, but Bazarov, whose ruling obsession with materialism is repeated ad nauseam. Like the hero and heroine of comedy, Arkadii and his Katia are often criticized for their flatness and lack of complexity, especially when juxtaposed to the "elders" Bazarov and Anna Sergeevna Odintsova. Arkadii's *cognitio* or recognition scene comes not when he realizes that a courtesan is really the daughter of a respectable man, but when he discovers that Katia is not rich like her sister (whose fortune comes from her late husband), and thus he can propose to her without suspicion of fortune-seeking.[126] After the death of Bazarov, the final extended scene in the novel is the "festive ritual" celebrating a double wedding: Arkadii has married Katia, and his father has married Fenechka, his peasant mistress, thus incorporating the hitherto mysterious "*narod*" into the new society, which certainly resembles not something entirely new but the restoration of a golden age. The guests at the wedding feast feel that they have "agreed to perform a kind of simple-hearted comedy." Arkadii's "real life begins at the end," and it is significant that he becomes not a natural scientist or a revolutionary but a "zealous manager [*r'ianyi khoziain*]" of the family estate, a kind of pale precursor of Tolstoy's Konstantin Liovin.[127]

Unlike Dostoevsky, who in his own version of "fathers and sons," the 1871 novel *The Devils* (*Besy*), deploys a chaotic form to reflect the intellectual and moral chaos of the radicals, Turgenev conquers the disruptive force of the nihilists through the most traditional of literary forms. The comedic form of *Fathers and Sons* gives the lie to Turgenev's claims of being a "secret nihilist," more powerfully than any memoir by Feoktistov could have done. Significantly, the form of Katkov's article "On Our Nihilism" has a similar structure. Just as Turgenev leaves Arkadii and his father engaged in the fruitful, positive activities of profitable farming and local self-government, Katkov ends his article by urging that nihilism be combated by concentration on the "normal interests" and "positive strivings" of life. The last word of his article is "death," and it refers to the death of the Bazarov figure. The last words of Turgenev's novel, in the description of the mourning of Bazarov's parents over his grave, are "eternal life."[128]

Almost immediately after *Fathers and Sons* appeared, Turgenev wrote to at least two correspondents that he would never have published the novel if it had not been for Katkov's insistence: "I have never so strongly doubted any of my works as precisely this one; the responses and judgments of people whom I am accustomed to trust were extremely unfavorable; if it hadn't been for the insistent demands of Katkov, *Fathers and Sons* would never have appeared."[129] Turgenev could not have known at the time he wrote this the extent to which precisely this novel would make his reputation, particularly on the level of world literature. Katkov was right in his first article on *Fathers and Sons* that "in later times" it would be read primarily as an illustration of its historical moment; some would say that that is the novel's limitation. It is as if in this work Turgenev took too seriously Katkov's demand "that the artist remain a son of his time, a citizen of his country." Viewed as an artistic production, *Fathers and Sons* feels a bit flat, a bit schematic relative to the later works of Dostoevsky and Tolstoy. In their great novels, Dostoevsky and Tolstoy are more successful in avoiding being hemmed in by Katkov's artistically limited goals. But their drive to get beyond Katkov's program led to major difficulties and disagreements with their editor. Their relationship with Katkov, whom they, like Turgenev, regarded as not just a patron but also an intellectual force, is the subject of the following three chapters.

CHAPTER 4

KATKOV AND DOSTOEVSKY

THEIR POLEMICS OF 1861–63

Of all Katkov's connections with Russian writers, his association with Fyodor Dostoevsky was the most important and lasting relationship of his literary career. Dostoevsky published all his most celebrated novels in Katkov's *Russian Herald*: *Crime and Punishment* (1866), *The Idiot* (1868), *The Devils* (1871–72), and *The Brothers Karamazov* (1879–80); his seminal Pushkin speech was published in Katkov's newspaper *Moscow News* in June 1880, six months before Dostoevsky's death.[1] Dostoevsky's letters from 1865 on make it clear that he relied on Katkov for virtually continuous financial support through payment of advances on his work in progress. Yet their relationship began inauspiciously in 1858–59, with Katkov's rejection of Dostoevsky's novella *The Village of Stepanchikovo and Its Inhabitants* (*Selo Stepanchikovo i ego obitateli*, 1859), and continued in the form of a fairly rancorous polemic between the two men, carried on in the pages of their respective journals in 1861–63.

Dostoevsky and Katkov had very little face-to-face contact, even during the years of their most intense collaboration. We have quite a few letters from Dostoevsky to Katkov, but few from Katkov to Dostoevsky that have survived. So the journalistic polemic offers us a chance to study a kind of dialogue between the two men, a dialogue that preceded a long and productive working relationship. In this chapter we will consider the issues that Katkov and Dostoevsky clashed over, as well as the points of inner, fundamental agreement that can help us understand what made possible their fruitful, if sometimes contentious, partnership. Even more than Turgenev or Tolstoy, Dostoevsky had seriously engaged with Katkov on a range of issues, before Katkov began publishing his works. Thus when he conceived *Crime and Punishment*, Dostoevsky was intimately familiar with Katkov's writings as a journalistic opponent, in a way that neither Turgenev nor Tolstoy was at the time they were working with him, although they had a general familiarity with the articles published in the *Russian Herald*.

The Creation of *Time*

Toward the end of Dostoevsky's nine years of imprisonment and exile in Siberia that began in 1849, as he was trying to reenter Russian literary life from a seemingly unbridgeable distance, he turned to the *Russian Herald*, which he referred to in a letter of 1857 as "indisputably the primary Russian journal at the present time."[2] In 1858 Dostoevsky requested and obtained an advance from Katkov for his work in progress, one of the first works he wrote after prison, *The Village of Stepanchikovo*. But after he had submitted the manuscript and asked for a higher honorarium than he and Katkov had agreed to, the *Russian Herald* rejected the work in 1859. One can hardly be surprised by this: Both *The Village of Stepanchikovo* and "Uncle's Dream," another work written in Siberia, can be seen today as eccentric masterpieces, but in genre and tone they are farcical and unrealistic, more suited to the 1840s than to the atmosphere of social and political ferment represented by the *Russian Herald*.

Dostoevsky was personally stung by the difficulty of his reentry into Russian literary life. In a letter of October 1859 to his brother Mikhail, he despairs about the negotiations with another editor, Nikolai Nekrasov of the *Contemporary*, the man who had been Dostoevsky's first editor in 1846.[3] Dostoevsky suspects that Nekrasov made inquiries at the *Russian Herald* on the sly, that they had told him "the grapes were sour," and that Nekrasov was consequently offering insultingly low terms for publishing his novella (28/1:346). Dostoevsky goes on to speak of himself as a "proletarian," dependent on the good will of editors: "But besides all these intrigues with the *Russian Herald*, Nekrasov is a sensitive animal. After finding out the story with the *Russian Herald* and knowing that I, after returning from Siberia, have spent all my money and am in need, how can he not propose to such a proletarian a reduction in price? 'He'll agree without fail!' they think" (28/1:346). Indeed, according to an associate of Nekrasov, he disliked the novella and said, "Dostoevsky is all used up [*vyshel ves'*]. He won't write anything more" (28/1:507). For the man who was among the first to recognize Dostoevsky's genius to say such a thing was a devastating indicator of how far Dostoevsky had to go to regain his literary position. In the end the novella was published in A. A. Kraevsky's *Notes of the Fatherland* in 1859.

The rejection of *The Village of Stepanchikovo* seemed to tell Dostoevsky something important about how to connect with a Russian audience in the reformist age that followed the death of Nicholas I in 1855. In 1859, in the same letter to his brother in which he lamented the rejection of *Stepanchikovo* by the *Russian Herald* and spoke of the "powerful moral abasement" caused by Nekrasov's haggling (23/1:346), he announced a new project: *Notes from the Dead House*, based on his life in the Siberian prison. "My personality will disappear. It is the notes of an unknown man; but I guarantee its interest. The interest will be of the most capital sort" (28/1:349). This work, published in *Time* (*Vremia*), the journal that Dostoevsky started with his brother upon his return to St. Petersburg, connected powerfully with a reading audience eager for information about previously hidden sides of Russian life. It reestablished Dostoevsky as a major writer.[4] Katkov's rejection was one of the factors that ignited Dostoevsky's desire to write a new kind of novel, one that engaged intimately with current Russian events.

Editing his own journal seemed to offer Dostoevsky the best way out of being a "proletarian," constantly dependent on the whim of editors.[5] In June 1862, when the journal *Time* was well established, Dostoevsky wrote to one of its main contributors, Nikolai Strakhov, "A journal is a great thing [*delo*, also "business," "profession"]; it's the kind of activity that is no risk at all, because, whatever happens, journals as the expression of all the shades of contemporary opinions must remain. And the activity, that is, what precisely is to be done, what one must speak and write about—will always be found" (28/2:26). In announcing the journal in the fall of 1860, Dostoevsky tried to stake out a distinctive position, neither Slavophile nor Westernizer, but rather based on the idea of *pochva*, the native "soil" of Russia:

> We know now that we cannot be Europeans, that we are not capable of squeezing ourselves into one of the Western forms of life, lived through and elaborated by Europe out of its own national [*natsional'nykh*] principles, which are alien and opposite to us—just as we cannot wear someone else's clothing, sewn not to our measurements. We have finally become convinced that we too are a separate nationality [*natsional'nost'*], original [*samobytnaia*] in the highest degree, and that our task is to create a new form for ourselves, our own, native one, taken out of our soil, taken out of the people's [*narodnyi*] spirit and out of the people's principles. (18:36)

This idea of the need for the educated classes of Russia to merge with the common people [*narod*] became the consistent program of the journal and was given the label *pochvennichestvo* (for which no concise and adequate English translation has been coined but which we will call "return to the soil").[6]

Another part of Dostoevsky's program, directed at least in part at Katkov, is his promise not to be dependent on or submissive to "literary authorities." He explains that "golden mediocrity" sometimes is afraid of "opinions established by the pillars of literature, especially if these opinions are boldly, daringly, brazenly expressed." At times it is only this boldness and daring that lends the designation of "pillar and authority" to "a clever writer who knows how to make use of circumstances," and lends him "an extreme, though temporary," influence over the public (18:38). We should recall that this announcement appeared almost simultaneously with Evgeniia Tur's announcement of her new journal *Russian Speech* in fall 1860. That announcement came at the end of the very public polemic between her and Katkov, a polemic to which Dostoevsky made repeated reference in his writings for *Time*. In that polemic Katkov's image was shaped as a man proud of his power in the literary world, arrogant and domineering. Dostoevsky's reference to the arrogant, brazen pillar of authority resonates with the way Katkov was portrayed by Tur and her allies. And Dostoevsky's pledge to keep his journal free of "literary slavery" (18:38) recalls Tur's pledge to avoid doctrinaire attitudes and to honor the right to independent thought.

Dostoevsky's awareness of Katkov's public image as a domineering editor full of selfish pride [*samoliubie*] comes through clearly in the way he reacts to Katkov in print in the early 1860s. As in Tur's polemic with Katkov, there is a strong personal element to Dostoevsky's writings in *Time* that address him. It is clear that Dostoevsky to some extent respects Katkov for the stature his journal has attained, but he also responds almost viscerally to Katkov's perceived arrogance and condescension. This dual attitude can be discerned in Dostoevsky's earliest dealings with Katkov. In May 1858, at the time when Katkov expressed interest in publishing *The Village of Stepanchikovo*, Dostoevsky wrote his brother that he received from Katkov, along with an advance of five hundred silver rubles, "an extremely intelligent and friendly letter" (28/1:311). By July 1859, when negotiations with the *Russian Herald* were clearly breaking down, Dostoevsky wrote that Katkov "considers himself to be Jupiter" (28/1:329) and later complained repeatedly of his impoliteness and lack of consideration. Katkov also at times makes personal attacks on Dostoevsky in the course of the polemic, no doubt conditioned by his desire to put a new upstart competitor in his place. This personal aspect of the polemic has obscured the degree to which Dostoevsky and Katkov actually agree on fundamental issues, as I will show. Dostoevsky is more conciliatory at this stage toward the radicals Chernyshevsky and Dobroliubov than he is toward Katkov, even though their basic position is much less congenial to him, as he later realized.[7]

Dostoevsky and Katkov addressed each other and referred to each other in numerous publications beginning in 1861, and in each case a number of issues were being addressed simultaneously. Rather than following the back-and-forth chronologically, in the following discussion I will consider three broad issues: aesthetics, particularly the question of "art for art's sake" versus the demand that art be "useful"; the role and significance of Pushkin, especially as reflected in the controversy over the public reading of his *Egyptian Nights* by a woman; and Russia's national and imperial role, especially as reflected in the controversy over the Polish uprising of 1863, an issue that led to the official suppression of Dostoevsky's journal.[8] Dostoevsky's and Katkov's articles were unsigned, as was the practice of the time, but they clearly knew whom they were addressing, for the most part.

The Aesthetic Polemic

Dostoevsky's 1861 essay "Mr.—bov and the Problem of Art" is often seen as his aesthetic manifesto. Just as he tried in the announcement of the founding of *Time* to steer a course independent of the Slavophiles and Westernizers, in this essay he attempts to define a position independent of adherents of "pure art," on the one hand, and those now demanding that art serve a "useful" social role, on the other.[9] As the editors of Dostoevsky's complete works note, Dostoevsky's position was adumbrated in his testimony in the Petrashevsky case in 1849, when he said about his literary disputes with other members of the Petrashevsky circle, "I was challenged to this literary argument, the theme of which on my side was that art does not need a [social] tendency, that art is its own aim, that the author must worry only about artistic quality [*khudozhestvennost'*], and the idea will come of itself; for the idea is the necessary condition for artistic quality" (18:128–29).

In "Mr.—bov," Dostoevsky chastises the advocates of "pure art" for rejecting art that has a social tendency. He argues that the exclusion of art that has a social tendency itself constitutes a restriction on art and thus inhibits its freedom in a way that actually goes counter to their stated aims: "Out of hostility to their opponents the adherents of pure art go against themselves, against their own principles, namely—they destroy freedom of choice in inspiration. And it is for that freedom that they are supposed to stand" (18:79). The greater part of his article, however, is directed at Nikolai Dobroliubov ("Mr.—bov") and other utilitarians, who neglect the key issue of artistic quality: "And since a work without artistic quality will never in any form achieve its aim, moreover will rather harm the cause than bring usefulness, that means that in not recognizing artistic quality the utilitarians are themselves harming their own cause more than anyone, and therefore are going directly against themselves, because they seek not harm but usefulness" (18:79). In Dostoevsky's view, only art that is free can be of high quality, and only art that is of high quality can be of use to society. In his reading, the artistically feeble stories of Marko Vovchok (pseudonym of Mariya Vilinska) that Dobroliubov exalts because they represent the correct political position can only bring harm to that very position because of their lack of truthfulness and compelling realism. (Vovchok's stories were published in the *Russian Herald* in 1858-61.)

The key passage in Dostoevsky's essay is his admonition that art will only be useful if it is freed of the demand that it be useful. No kind of preconditions can be set on art if it is to be truly artistic and therefore truly of use to humanity: "The more freely it develops, the more normally it will develop, the more quickly it will find its true and useful path. And since its interest and aim are one with the aims of humanity, whom it serves and with which it is inseparably united, then the freer its development, the more usefulness it will bring to humanity" (18:102). As Robert Louis Jackson has pointed out, this idea is virtually identical to the view of art that Katkov formulated in his 1856 essay on Pushkin: "The lines of Raphael did not solve any practical question from the everyday life contemporary to him; but they brought great good and great usefulness for life with the course of time; they powerfully contributed to the humanization of life."[10] As Dostoevsky says, supposedly paraphrasing the position of the "pure art" adherents but also apparently representing his own views, "The normal historical progress of the usefulness of art in humanity is as yet unknown. It is hard to measure the whole mass of usefulness yielded to all humanity by, for example, the *Iliad* or the Apollo Belvedere, things that are apparently completely unnecessary in our time" (18:77-78). Like Dostoevsky, Katkov in the 1856 essay on Pushkin rejects both socially didactic art and an art that is focused only on elegance of form, since both are equally far from the goal of "true art," whose value cannot be assessed either by purely social or by purely aesthetic criteria. Instead, the goal of true art is "bring[ing] life into human consciousness and consciousness into the most secret convolutions of life."[11]

Katkov responded to "Mr.—bov" in his essay "Our Language and What Are Whistlers." Given the fact that Dostoevsky's basic aesthetic position in that essay is virtually the same as the one Katkov himself expounded in 1856, one might expect him to welcome Dostoevsky's entry into the discussion. He does, but only up to a point. His treatment of the new journal *Time* as a whole is drenched in irony. He quotes a German scholar who recently described Russia as a country that stagnates in oppressive intellectual conditions and has almost lost hope of emerging from them.[12] But, Katkov continues sarcastically, if only this German knew of the new journal *Time*, "where in the tone of the most happy self-satisfaction all the phases of our spiritual life are analyzed."[13] He singles out "Mr.—bov" as an article he took "great pleasure" in: "Some views on art are recounted here that are very sympathetic to us, in a very light style and without 'frowning phrases.'"[14] But he goes on to ridicule the analysis Dostoevsky offered of Afanasii Fet's 1847 poem *Diana* in that article.

Dostoevsky quoted two poems by Fet in his article without giving Fet's name. The first, "Whispers, timid breathing," is presented as the kind of pure aestheticism that, if offered as an appropriate response to a disaster like the Lisbon earthquake, would lead to the enraged citizens' execution of the poet on the spot (18:76). (Dostoevsky goes on to note that they might fifty years later erect a monument to him for the same poem.) The second Fet poem, *Diana*, is introduced as an example of something quite different, a kind of relation to the past and the art of the past that represents not a stale imitation but a "Byronic" enthusiasm. This "Byronic" attitude arises not from "powerlessness before our own life but on the contrary from a fiery thirst for life and longing for an ideal which we are trying to attain in torments" (18:96).

The poem, which Dostoevsky quotes in full, describes a brilliantly white statue of Diana that the lyric speaker almost expects to come to life and begin to walk through the trees, to look upon Rome and its colonnades and squares. The poem concludes, "But the immobile marble / Shone white before me in incomprehensible beauty." Dostoevsky's following words are quoted by Katkov:

> The last two lines of this poem are full of such passionate vitality, such longing, such significance, that we do not know anything more powerful, more vital in all of Russian poetry. This is the obsolete [*otzhivshee*] past, being resurrected after two thousand years in the soul of the poet, being resurrected with such power that he waits and believes, in prayer and enthusiasm, for the goddess to come down now from her pedestal and begin to walk before him, "flashing among the trees with her milky whiteness." But the goddess is not resurrected and she does not have to be

resurrected, she does not have to live; she has already attained the highest moment of life; she is already in eternity, for her time has stopped; this is the highest moment of life, after which it ceases—and Olympian calm sets in. Only the future is endless, eternally calling, eternally new, and there is also its own highest moment, which one must seek and eternally seek, and that eternal seeking is called life, and how much tormenting sadness is hidden in the enthusiasm of the poet! What an endless call, what melancholy about the present in that enthusiasm for the past! (18:97)[15]

Again, one might expect Katkov to welcome Dostoevsky's passionate and moving appreciation of Fet's poem, especially in view of the fact that the *Russian Herald* was one of the major venues for the publication of Fet's poetry after his break with the *Contemporary* in 1859 (although the two poems Dostoevsky quotes were not published there). At this time, two camps were clearly emerging in Russian journalism, one of which, led by Chernyshevsky and Dobroliubov, flaunted its lack of respect for the literary traditions of the past, symbolized mainly by Pushkin. Katkov had recently begun sparring furiously with the "whistlers," an epithet he coined based on the name of the *Whistler* (*Svistok*), the satirical supplement to the *Contemporary*. The "whistlers," in Katkov's parlance, as a kind of precursor term to "nihilist," were Chernyshevsky, Dobroliubov, and their ilk, who "move from one negation to another" and "have thrown mud on all literary authorities, have taken away Pushkin's right to the title of national [*natsional'nogo*] poet."[16] In "Mr.—bov" Dostoevsky was also directing his main fire against Dobroliubov and others who showed insufficient appreciation for the values of art and its historical legacy. Yet instead of embracing Dostoevsky's stance in "Mr.—bov," in particular his tribute to art and its enduring power, and the respect for the past that it inspires, Katkov characterizes Dostoevsky's interpretation of the poem as far-fetched and untrue to the text.

After quoting Dostoevsky's interpretation of *Diana*, Katkov describes it, particularly its explication of the last two lines of Fet's poem, as "that gurgling stream of half-conceptions, half-images, and half-tones, that puts our little Russian thought to sleep so soundly, so stupefies our innocent intellectual movements, and so irresistibly inundates our humble literature."[17] Katkov is being a strict formalist here; in a narrow sense he is correct that the last two lines of Fet's poem do not obviously contain on their surface all the meaning that Dostoevsky has extracted from them. But Katkov is surely being disingenuous when he pretends not to realize that Dostoevsky is creating his own prose poem inspired by Fet's verse, one that, in fact, is true to the sense of Fet's poem as a whole, even if the last two lines do not precisely correspond to Dostoevsky's description.

One must wonder if the personal has again played a role in the supposedly intellectual dispute, as it did in the polemic between Katkov and Tur. In his earlier essay "A Few Words Instead of the Contemporary Chronicle," Katkov had asked, "What is Russian nationality [*narodnost'*]? What is Russian literature, Russian art, Russian thought? Will it be advantageous for Russia that the Russian nationality and the Russian word remain behind every other nationality and ever other word in Europe? Will it be good for Russia for us to remain eternal bad boy whistlers, capable only of petty deeds, of small slanders and scandals?"[18] In his response, "The *Whistle* and the *Russian Herald*," Dostoevsky criticized Katkov for equating all Russian literature to the "whistlers." In the course of his criticism of the *Russian Herald* in this essay, Dostoevsky repeats some of the personal criticisms of Katkov that had been raised in 1860 during the polemic with Tur. Dostoevsky says that the *Russian Herald* (and as in the Tur polemic, "*Russian Herald*" means "Katkov") has attributed far too much significance to the "bad boy whistlers," and places the responsibility for the predominance of literary scandals on the "big-shots and pillars of our literature" who inflate the whistlers' importance by writing about them (19:110). Dostoevsky continues, "Among these pillars there are a very many people who are not insignificant, on the contrary, very intelligent people, who could be very useful. But some kind of selfish pride [*samoliubie*] is eating them up" (19:111). When society turns to them for solutions and instructions, they start preaching humaneness and all the virtues, but have nothing practical to offer.

Dostoevsky's next words are clearly directed at Katkov: "'I'd be glad to act,' says a certain pillar, 'but on the condition that I be considered the center around which the whole universe revolves.' The need for Olympianism, Palmerstonism, is eating away at our literary *caciques* to the point of comedy, of caricature" (19:111). The words "selfish pride" and "Olympianism" will recur repeatedly in Dostoevsky's characterizations of Katkov, and "Palmerstonism" is an allusion to Katkov's well-known reverence for British institutions (Lord Palmerston was prime minister of the United Kingdom in 1855–58 and 1859–65). Katkov's irritable response to Dostoevsky in "Our Language" no doubt reflects his awareness that Dostoevsky was continuing to wage the assault on Katkov's public image that Tur and her associates had begun.

The Polemic over Pushkin

In "A Few Words Instead of the Contemporary Chronicle," the thrust of Katkov's argument when he asks, "What is Russian literature?" seems to be directed against

Russian journalism. Yet the fact that in the parlance of the journals of the day the word "literature" was used to refer both to *belles-lettres* and to journalistic writings makes his attack ambiguous. Dostoevsky chooses to read it as a dismissal of the achievements of Russian writers with Pushkin at their head: "Does the *Russian Herald* really not see in Pushkin's talent a powerful personification of the Russian spirit and Russian meaning?" (19:112). According to the Soviet-era editors of Dostoevsky's complete works, the question of Pushkin and his significance was one of the major points of contention between Katkov and Dostoevsky in their polemic. The editors paint Dostoevsky as defending Pushkin against Katkov's slights. In a typical formulation, they write, "Dostoevsky's surmise about Katkov's far from enraptured personal view of Pushkin was confirmed in the further course of the polemic" (19:297). They claim that Katkov rejected the idea of Pushkin's status as a national [*narodnyi*] poet. Dostoevsky says something similar about Katkov, if obliquely (19:232).[19]

All of this seems strange if we recall not only Katkov's lengthy essay on Pushkin published in the very first issues of the *Russian Herald* in 1856, but also his 1839 introduction to his translation of Varnhagen von Ense's review of Pushkin's works. Here Katkov had claimed that Varnhagen's recognition of Pushkin gave Russians the right to say "that Pushkin is a universal poet who ranks with those few on whom all of humanity looks with reverence." In that same introduction he wrote, "We are firmly convinced and clearly recognize that Pushkin is the poet not of a single epoch, but the poet of all humanity, not of a single country, but of the whole world."[20] Such characterizations of Pushkin as "a universal poet [*vsemirnyi poet*]" and "the poet of all humanity [*poet tselogo chelovechestva*]" are fully in harmony with Dostoevsky's characterizations of Pushkin in his articles in *Time* as a poet of "universal human striving [*obshchechelovecheskoe stremlenie*]" (18:99), a poet with "the capability of universality, universal humanness, universal responsiveness [*sposobnost' vsemirnosti, vsechelovechnosti, vseotklika*]" (19:114). So why is there the feeling throughout the polemic between Katkov and Dostoevsky that Dostoevsky has to defend Pushkin against Katkov, that Katkov does not sufficiently value Pushkin?

The answer could be that Katkov's position had changed since 1839, or even since 1856, when he had published his long essay on Pushkin's significance in the inaugural issues of the *Russian Herald*. But in fact Katkov continued to value Pushkin's contribution to Russian literature very highly, especially when we recall that he continued to express his esteem for Pushkin to the end of his life, in the 1880s. The problem lies in the way that Katkov and Dostoevsky respectively view

Pushkin's accomplishment. Dostoevsky sees it as something integral, completed, whole. Katkov sees it as an impressive but as yet unfulfilled promise of the greatness of Russian culture.

When Dostoevsky read Katkov's essay on Pushkin in 1856, he wrote to a friend that Katkov's ideas were "completely opposite to mine" (28/1:229).[21] Dostoevsky did not elaborate on what it was about Katkov's ideas that made them opposite to his, but it seems likely that he was not happy with Katkov's emphasis in that essay on Pushkin's contribution in shaping the Russian literary language. In 1861, in "The *Whistle* and the *Russian Herald*," Dostoevsky asks Katkov, "Did the phenomenon of Pushkin do nothing more for us than perfect [*vyrabotat'*] the language?" (19:112). The question implies that creating a literary language is somehow an inferior accomplishment, but that was not at all Katkov's view. In both "A Few Words Instead of the Contemporary Chronicle" and "Our Language," Katkov looks with envy on the High German language, which has "acquired immortal significance" and "become the palladium of a great nation [*narodnost'*]" because of the great works of culture and thought that have been produced in it.[22] Pushkin greatly advanced the cause of exalting Russian nationality through Russian language and literature. But for Katkov, one writer does not constitute a literary culture of world significance. Katkov wants to spur Russian literature to go further than Pushkin, to add to his accomplishment, not just sit in awed contemplation of it. It was that mission that he had espoused when he founded the *Russian Herald*; it was that mission that he was to further in his subsequent support of Dostoevsky's own work from 1865 to the latter's death.

In contrast to the claims of worldwide recognition of Pushkin that Katkov had expressed in 1839, in his 1861 essay "Our Language" he stresses that Pushkin has not attained universal significance on the world stage. Part of this is because of what Katkov sees as an unfinished, fragmentary legacy: "Pushkin is a great poet, and we feel that he is second to none in terms of power of creation; but tell us whether everything he achieved corresponds to those powers that one feels in him, and tell us also what Pushkin means for the rest of the world, while everywhere, and here as well, we see the powerful influence of the Byrons and Schillers?"[23] In Katkov's view, Pushkin has not been recognized on the world stage partly because Russian society has not matured to the point that such recognition is deserved: "The strange fate of our talents has long been noted: they disappeared from the stage at the very moment when it was just possible to expect a mature word from them; they appeared in flashes and disappeared at the very moment when they began to become a true force. As if fate wavered about whether to set going those developments that could imprint the Russian word with an immortal significance; as if it had not yet been decided whether the time had come to declare in our life the true principles that are hidden in our calling."[24]

In his 1861 essay "Bookishness and Literacy," Dostoevsky responded angrily to Katkov's claim that Pushkin was not recognized outside Russia, and disputed the idea that writers like Shakespeare, Schiller, and Goethe were well known to nationalities other than their own. In Dostoevsky's view, Katkov is thinking of Russians themselves, who are deeply aware of the literature of other European nations; the actual knowledge of Schiller or Shakespeare in France, for example, is in fact not that deep or broad (for some reason Dostoevsky substitutes Shakespeare for Katkov's Byron) (19:17). But in the end he makes a statement that is not so far from Katkov's own orientation toward the possible future of Russian literature and culture rather than toward its past: "And most importantly, how is Pushkin to blame if he is not yet known in Europe? The point is that Europe doesn't yet know Russia either: it has known it up to now only out of grave necessity. It will be another matter when the Russian element will enter as a fruitful stream into universal human development: then Europe will come to know even Pushkin, and will probably find in him incomparably more than the *Russian Herald* has been able to find up to this time. And then [the *Russian Herald*] will be ashamed in front of the Europeans! Russia is still young and is just now getting ready to live; but that is by no means a cause for blame" (19:18).

The Polemic over *Egyptian Nights*

The significance of Pushkin lay at the heart of the major controversy in which Dostoevsky and Katkov were involved, which was incited by a seemingly insignificant incident in the provincial city of Perm. The journalistic description of the public reading by Mrs. Tolmachova, a civil servant's wife, of Pushkin's unfinished poem *Egyptian Nights* gave rise to a many-sided polemic in which Dostoevsky and Katkov participated actively, mainly sparring with each other. The Tolmachova controversy crystallizes the points of agreement and disagreement between Dostoevsky and Katkov on Pushkin, women's rights, and aesthetics in general. The original newspaper account of Tolmachova's reading has not been translated into English and has not been carefully studied, so I will dwell on it at some length.

In February 1861, an article signed "M. T." appeared in the *St. Petersburg News*, which described an evening of literary readings held to benefit a new Sunday school being opened in Perm, a city at the eastern edge of European Russia, near the Ural Mountains.[25] Sunday schools were a recent development in Russian life: beginning in 1859, members of the liberal intelligentsia were opening schools for the education of workers on their only day off, Sunday (the schools were secular in nature).[26] The author of the article describes his arrival in the depth of winter: "The road was horrible because of the quantity of snow! The frosts made the nearness of Siberia clearly perceptible." After settling in his hotel and learning of the literary evening at the Assembly of the Nobility, he ventures out to the gathering: "I had just seated myself when a tall lady went up to the platform, of a very beautiful, striking, and notably expressive appearance, which seemed even more beautiful and striking because of her unusually simple but very tasteful toilette. There were no bright garish colors or diamonds piled up senselessly, nor an intricate hairdo arousing only amazement at the coiffeur's art—it was all *not in the provincial fashion*, simple and good. Her costume consisted of a black velvet dress, smooth batiste sleeves and the same kind of collar, of masculine cut; on her head was a little black cap with long strips of white gauze sprinkled with black spots. All this looked extremely good with the striking and expressive appearance of the young woman."[27]

Intrigued by this vision of loveliness in the remote provinces, the author consults the program and learns that she is E. E. [Evgeniia Eduardovna] Tolmachova, who is to read a fragment from Pushkin's *Egyptian Nights*: "Aha! I thought. It's not only in her skill at dressing that she's distinguished from the *provincial* public!" Tolmachova's choice of reading is indeed a provocative act, for the poem is a description of how Cleopatra, at a public feast, offered her sexual favors to any man who was willing to sacrifice his life for one night with her, and how three men in the crowd came forward to accept the challenge. Thus as she read Pushkin's poetic monologue, Tolmachova would be promising, in the voice of Cleopatra, to serve the lucky winners "as a simple concubine," to "voluptuously tire out" their desires until dawn.[28] The author of the newspaper report marvels at Tolmachova's "spiritual strength and love for truth" in defying the common wisdom of the "anthill" by openly doing something that "the anthill cannot digest." He notes that "She read simply and also strikingly, with full understanding of the inner meaning of the verse, with the ability to lend the appropriate meaning to each thought and each picture of the poet." And he goes on to describe her reading in emotive detail: "Her large eyes now blazed, now grew dim and were extinguished; her whole face was constantly changing, taking on now a tenderly passionate, now a burning, now an implacably stern, now a proudly challenging expression. The verse following Cleopatra's proposal—to buy one of her nights at the price of one's life—the well-known verse 'and she looks over her admirers with a contemptuous gaze,' was read in actuality with such an expression of offensive contempt and wicked mockery, at this point the young woman looked around at the silent crowd with such a gaze that if this had been in the theater—the hall probably would have shook with applause."

The author approaches the group surrounding Tolmachova after her reading, since he wants a closer look at this woman who has provided "such truly aesthetic enjoyment, and where?—on the border of Siberia, in a distant, cold backwoods!" Although some are enraptured by Tolmachova's reading, others are indignant. A young, highly decorated army officer complains that "some mammas and daughters" feel that their virtue has been insulted. Tolmachova replies, "This is a little strange. If we all, both men and ladies and maidens, read without embarrassment dirty and immoral French novels, watch without blushing obscene and vulgar French vaudevilles, then it would be ridiculous and bizarre in the highest degree not to read in public the beautiful, artistic work of a great poet, *Egyptian Nights*."

Tolmachova goes on to compare Cleopatra's words, offering herself for sale, to the actual deeds of Russian society, where "almost every day we see young women selling themselves—and not just for one night, but for their whole lives, to repulsive, decrepit, but rich old men." She laments the way young girls are brought up in Russia, with no familiarity with science and real life: "In England, for example, a young girl will go boldly into a den of iniquity, will come to know all its dirty and unfortunate aspects, and does not become in the least immoral because of it. On the contrary: she will only come to know life in all its manifestations, will understand it and be a serious woman." Tolmachova also compares herself to the great French actress Rachel, who played the roles of passionate women without being accused of being immodest: "Is this really only the sad privilege of actresses, who are still regarded bizarrely, can I not take on any similar role simply because I'm the wife of a state counselor [Tolmachova's husband was the chairman of the Perm revenue department]? What an absurd view!" The author of the article concludes, "With all my heart I wish that these words that I overheard in the Perm Assembly of the Nobility could be taken into proper consideration even in the enlightened capital cities. He that hath ears to hear, let him hear!"

There seems to be a subtext to the account of the Perm literary evening, one that gives it a feeling of having been at least in part a provocation. The reading was to benefit a new Sunday school. Although the leadership of the Sunday-school movement included people of various shades of political orientation, the government suspected that it was a hotbed of radicalism, kept it under surveillance, and eventually closed it down in 1862. Tolmachova's little speech makes clear that her choice of *Egyptian Nights* was not accidental, but part of her advocacy of the radical solution to the "woman question." According to a report on her by the secret police, "from her early years she was carried away by the theories of Prudhomme and Michelet and set herself the goal of being an emancipated woman."[29]

Among the other readings given that evening were two poems by Apollon Maikov, *Aspasia* (*Aspaziia*, 1853) and *A Midsummer Night's Dream* (*Son v letniuiu noch'*, 1857), both read by M. P. Timmerman. These poems seem to have been chosen to enhance the provocative effect of Tolmachova's reading of *Egyptian Nights*. *Aspasia* is a monologue by the consort of Pericles, like Cleopatra a politically powerful woman who was rumored to be sexually promiscuous. She describes her passionate love for a younger man, and like Cleopatra in Pushkin's monologue, she boasts of her skill at lovemaking: "So what if I'm a woman, and he is still a boy, / Happiness is not for me myself to love / And burn and enjoy fiery feeling; / No, it is to breathe and admire his happiness / And to train his inexperience in bliss."[30] This resonates with Cleopatra's reaction to the young lad who comes forward to take her wager: "Rapture shone in his eyes / The inexperienced power of passions / Boiled in his young heart . . . / And the queen fixed her gaze on him / With tenderness."

In her remarks Tolmachova refers to *A Midsummer Night's Dream* as a poem that "explains my thought [about the upbringing of young girls] very well [and that] will also probably be relegated by our strict moralists to the category of the obscene." This poem is also a monologue by a woman, this time a young girl who lies restless in her bed, intoxicated by the fragrance of flowers. A youth comes through her window, and reveals himself as "the god of visions and daydreams" who has brought her "the bliss of the heavens for the first time": "He spoke—and he quietly pulled my face away / From the pillow with his hands, / And he hotly kissed the edge of my cheek, / And sought my lips with his lips . . . / Under his breathing I became powerless . . ." She awakens at dawn, thinking, "I do not know what happened to me."[31] Since Tolmachova said that this poem expresses her ideas about the proper upbringing of young girls, presumably that program involves a midnight visit by a mysterious phantom youth who kisses them passionately and initiates them into sensual passion. There is some basis for believing that Tolmachova had a hand in the readings of the Maikov poems as well as *Egyptian*

Nights, given that they were read by Timmerman, with whom she moved to Kazan later the same year, abandoning her husband. She also visited Alexander Herzen, the hero of the radicals, in London later that year. By some accounts Timmerman was also the author of the article in the *St. Petersburg News*.[32]

About a week after the appearance of this article, the poet and translator Piotr Isaevich Veinberg (1831–1908), using the pseudonym Kamen'-Vinogorov, published a feuilleton titled "Russian Marvels" in the St. Petersburg journal the *Age*, of which he was one of the editors.[33] Kamen'-Vinogorov, who apparently didn't realize he was walking into a political minefield, tried to derive light humor from the somewhat ridiculous, exalted tone of the article about Tolmachova's reading: "It's joyful to learn that emancipation, that is the liberation of women, has begun in Russia—and where? In distant Perm, on the borders of Siberia."[34] Kamen'-Vinogorov makes fun of the author's enraptured account of Tolmachova's appearance and dress, and reproduces her speech to the officer with interpolated, mocking exclamations like the following: "What an amazing, moral view—to familiarize young girls with *science* and life by means of reading *Egyptian Nights*. Charming! A thousand times charming!"[35]

The key passage of Kamen'-Vinogorov's feuilleton is a response to the article's description of Tolmachova casting on her audience the same contemptuous gaze that Cleopatra cast on her hearers after her challenge. Kamen'-Vinogorov writes that he fails to understand what the relationship was between the audience at the Perm literary gathering and Cleopatra's admirers. If there was no such relationship, then why did Mrs. Tolmachova look at the crowd with a gaze of "contempt and wicked mockery"? He continues, "But I do not know the secrets of Perm, so it's understandable that I didn't understand anything. I call to you, my beautiful female readers, I address you, I appeal to you! Down with all shamefacedness, down with femininity, down with social proprieties; you are invited to this by Mrs. Tolmachova and her respected panegyrist, who has proclaimed to the world about the unbelievable event through the lips of the *St. Petersburg News*."[36] This insinuation about the "secrets of Perm," the idea that by reciting Cleopatra's speech Mrs. Tolmachova was in some way becoming Cleopatra, was one of the most important points in the ensuing polemic.

Kamen'-Vinogorov calls the *St. Petersburg News* "ultra-modern" in its willingness to make fun of "mammas and daughters" who found it strange to hear from the lips of a young woman, in a public assembly, the lines that Cleopatra spoke. He ends by suggesting that next time Mrs. Tolmachova read a different poem by Pushkin, known by its first line, "No, I do not prize the stormy pleasure" ("Net, ia ne dorozhu miatezhnym naslazhden'em," 1830?): "Read it, read it, Mrs. Tolmachova! As you read you'll be able to assume an even more *challenging* expression and make even more expressive gestures! If you're going for emancipation, then go all the way! Why stop halfway?"[37] The Pushkin poem in question is a description of the male lyric speaker's preference for one type of lover (and in particular, one type of orgasm) over another. Thus this "joke" both masculinizes Tolmachova and intensifies the implication that she is sexually debauched.

The first response to Kamen'-Vinogorov's feuilleton was a letter to the editors of the *St. Petersburg News*, published with the title "The Outrageous Action by the *Age*" ("Bezobraznyi postupok 'Veka'"), from Mikhail Larionovich Mikhailov (1829–65), a radical poet who was arrested in 1861 for circulating revolutionary propaganda and died in exile in Siberia after serving a term at hard labor. Mikhailov was one of the most important proponents of the "woman question," the issue of reforming the position and treatment of women in society.[38] Mikhailov focuses on the personal insult to Mrs. Tolmachova represented by Kamen'-Vinogorov's insinuations about the "secrets of Perm," although he does not quote the passage in question ("I do not want to repeat his words. It's enough that they appeared once in print"). Mikhailov's tone is that of an infuriated chevalier riding to the rescue of his lady. He writes that Kamen'-Vinogorov's words "testify to the complete absence in him of any moral feeling, of any consciousness of one's duties to the society in which he lives, of any respect for human dignity, in himself and in others. Such a person cannot be tolerated in literature, and the court of public opinion must forever stigmatize him. There is no name for Kamen'-Vinogorov's action. For all the dark aspects of our literature and journalism, nowhere in it up to now has there been anything so resembling the black slander he has thought up." Mikhailov calls upon the editors of the *Age* to repudiate Kamen'-Vinogorov, who, he says, "has a lump of mud instead of a heart." Mikhailov makes the disclaimer that he is not personally acquainted with Mrs. Tolmachova, "But in her person all women have been insulted—and to be silent would be a crime."

Mikhailov also sent his letter to the *Age*, which printed a note explaining that it had received it only after its journal went to press, that it would deal with the general content of his letter later, but that even before receiving his letter the editors of the *Age* had already expressed to Mrs. Tolmachova their "sincere apology [*chistoserdechnoe izvinenie*]" for the "incautious expressions that had crept into Mr. Vinogorov's article."[39] In the next issue, the *Age* published both a note from the editors and an answer by Kamen'-Vinogorov. The editors summarize Mikhailov's complaint and go on to state that now they have no obligation to publish his letter, especially since its tone is inappropriate.⁴⁰ They repeat that they have expressed their "sincere apology for the admission of certain incautious expressions that crept into Kamen'-Vinogorov's humorous little article," and that the *St. Petersburg News* should have informed its readers about their apology, but: "Some journal editors dedicate their activity exclusively to seeking out *outrageous actions* by other editors."⁴¹ They explain that they do not understand "what the social position of the Russian woman can gain from the public reading of *Egyptian Nights*." In any case the object of the joke was "Mrs. Tolmachova as she was depicted by the feuilleton in the *St. Petersburg News*, or rather the dithyramb in favor of *Egyptian Nights* being read by women, and not the real Mrs. Tolmachova, whose person neither the editors nor, undoubtedly, the humorist himself have any designs on."⁴²

Kamen'-Vinogorov's answer, which follows immediately upon the editors' note, takes a more personal tone towards Mikhailov, calling his article "the fruit of a completely disordered imagination, the result of some kind of pseudo-Don-Quixote strivings that do not wish to see the truth.... While accusing me of slander, he slandered me in the most unceremonious, most unseemly manner."⁴³ Like the editors, he claims that the object of his ridicule was not Mrs. Tolmachova herself but the correspondent of the *St. Petersburg News*, "who described the reading of *Egyptian Nights* by a woman in a public assembly and described it in the most ridiculous, cynical way" [in nineteenth-century Russian parlance, "cynical" was a synonym for "lewd"].⁴⁴ Like the editors, he "sincerely apologizes" for certain expressions that may have inadvertently insulted Mrs. Tolmachova, but that "had an unpleasant effect on me perhaps more than on anyone else."⁴⁵ Kamen'-Vinogorov claims that he did not distort a single word of Mrs. Tolmachova's speech as reported in the *St. Petersburg News*, but simply reprinted those of her expressions "that seemed inappropriate on the lips of a woman." He concludes, "I maintain the firm conviction that a poem like *Egyptian Nights*, for all its great poetic worth, cannot be read by a woman at a public gathering and that the true liberation of women does not consist in finally throwing off all conventions placed on her both by society and by her innate nature."⁴⁶

Up to this point, the controversy centered on Mrs. Tolmachova's act of reading *Egyptian Nights* in public and Kamen'-Vinogorov's insinuations about her character. But with Nikolai Strakhov's article on the topic, the question of the morality of Pushkin's works was brought to the fore. Strakhov, as a major contributor to *Time*, had apparently been asked to respond to the controversy. His article as well as one by Dostoevsky that we will discuss below appeared in the same issue of *Time*. Strakhov's article was written first, before the appearance of the responses to Mikhailov in the *Age*, and Dostoevsky, seemingly dissatisfied with Strakhov's article, published it but added his own entry to the polemic, one that focused on the "sincere apologies" of the editors of the *Age* (19:293–94).

Strakhov's article begins with a review of the ways in which readers and critics have found Pushkin to be "an immoral poet," starting with his earliest published works and continuing into the present, with Kamen'-Vinogorov as the latest to censure Pushkin's works as immoral.[47] Like Mikhailov, Strakhov also assails Kamen'-Vinogorov for his unfounded insinuations about Mrs. Tolmachova's character. But Strakhov is more interested in the question of what it is about Pushkin's verse that Kamen'-Vinogorov finds so improper. Strakhov reminds us that in Pushkin's account, Cleopatra's audience is overcome by horror. But Mr. Vinogorov is apparently filled not with horror but with "other sensations": "He takes Cleopatra's proposition as one of those propositions that are made not out loud but quietly; the sale of her nights reminds him of a well-known type of sale.... Well, is Pushkin to blame because his verse produces such a perverse impression on Mr. Vinogorov? That it does not purify his thoughts, but only sets in ferment all the nastiness that has accumulated in his imagination?"[48] In Strakhov's view, it is not Pushkin's work that is immoral but the perverted way in which it is perceived by certain listeners: "[Vinogorov] judges others by himself and accuses Mrs. Tolmachova of the impurity of his own thoughts."[49] Strakhov concludes by absolving Pushkin of the accusation of immorality: "Pushkin, as a poet and as a great poet, had to embrace all spheres of life.... Therefore Pushkin ... was chaste and pure in the highest degree. His poems can be the most splendid school for the true understanding of love, for the clearing up of coarse ideas, for the elevation of the animal feeling that sometimes arises in a person into a truly human ideal. Here we of course are supposing a correct, deep understanding of the works of Pushkin, and not the kind of which Mr. Vinogorov, for example, is capable."[50] By generalizing the discussion into a consideration of whether Pushkin is or is not an "immoral poet," Strakhov's article diverts attention from Tolmachova's act, provocative for its time, of publicly reading *Egyptian Nights*.

Dostoevsky would also take up the question of the morality of Pushkin's works in his second article on the Tolmachova controversy, but in his first response, published in the same issue of *Time* as Strakhov's article, he focuses more on the insult to Mrs. Tolmachova regarding the "secrets of Perm." In his article, titled "Models of Sincerity [*Obraztsy chistoserdechiia*]," Dostoevsky focuses on the "sincere apology" offered by the editors of the *Age*, comparing it to the apology of a man who has just slapped another man for no apparent reason in the middle of a civilized discussion (19:91–92). Dostoevsky goes line by line through the editors' note in the *Age*, commenting sarcastically on each of their assertions, especially their reference to the "incautious expressions" that "crept into" the "humorous" article by Kamen'-Vinogorov: "The whole article consists of these expressions that have crept in. A humorous article! This is humor, in your opinion!" (19:94). As for the claim by the editors that Kamen'-Vinogorov's target was not Mrs. Tolmachova but the correspondent for the *St. Petersburg News*, Dostoevsky cites the passage about "the secrets of Perm" as an insinuation clearly directed at Mrs. Tolmachova herself (19:97–98). Dostoevsky's indignation is particularly aroused by Kamen'-Vinogorov's advice that Tolmachova declaim with expressive gestures Pushkin's more obviously sensual poem, "No, I do not prize the stormy pleasure": "How disgusting! Doesn't it arouse your indignation?" (19:99). Here he departs from Strakhov's position. Strakhov had claimed that that poem was also an innocent one, since it represents the poet's "complete freedom from the power of pleasures."[51]

Dostoevsky's indignation at Kamen'-Vinogorov's suggestion indicates that he feels that for a lady to publicly read "No, I do not prize the stormy pleasure" would be inappropriate. He also believes that Mrs. Tolmachova acted "rashly and in an untimely way" in reading *Egyptian Nights* in public. Here he differs from Mikhailov and Strakhov, who do not admit that there is anything unseemly about Mrs. Tolmachova's reading. For Dostoevsky the problem with such public behavior by a woman is a matter not of substance but of convention: "To read an artistic work like Pushkin's *Egyptian Nights* out loud, in public, is not at all shameful, just as it is not shameful to stop enraptured before the Medici Venus in an exhibition hall, where visitors of all ages and both sexes throng. But there are many prejudices in society; it is an accepted practice to place naked statues before the public; it is also possible to read *Egyptian Nights*; after all, Pushkin's male improviser read it [in the prose story that precedes the poetic monologue of Cleopatra]. But if a woman reads it, people will protest. Women here do not yet have such rights" (19:102). Dostoevsky looks forward to the day (a future "golden age," 19:103) when society is more established and moral principles are strengthened, so that a woman could with impunity express her rapture over an artistic work in public, without being suspected of "voluptuous intentions [*sladostrastnye pomyshleniia*]" (19:102). Here Dostoevsky implicitly defends Tolmachova by aligning her not with Cleopatra but with Pushkin. She may have been moved by "pure, most lofty artistic rapture [*chistyi, samyi vysokii khudozhestvennyi vostorg*]" and "artistic pleasure [*khudozhestvennoe naslazhdenie*]" (19:102–3).

Dostoevsky departs from Mikhailov and Strakhov in yet another way, when he defends not only Mrs. Tolmachova but the "mammas and daughters" who were ridiculed by the correspondent of the *St. Petersburg News* for being alarmed by Mrs. Tolmachova's reading. Dostoevsky concedes that the opinions of the "old mommies [*starykh mamenek*]" should be respected, because of their concern for their daughters: "Indeed, for those of *adolescent* [*otrocheskogo*] age such a reading *might* even be dangerous. In an adolescent age a person is not formed either physically or morally, and on him even the Medici Venus might not produce a fully artistic impression" (19:103). When he evokes the "adolescent [*otrok*]" in Tolmachova's audience who may be harmed by her reading, one cannot help but think of Cleopatra's third and final victim, the "*otrok*" who comes forward to offer his life, moved by the "rapture of love" and "boundless passion." Thus by endangering the adolescents in her audience, Mrs. Tolmachova takes on the role not of Pushkin, but of Cleopatra. None of the participants in the polemic mention the poems by Maikov (a major contributor to *Time*) that were also read at the evening in Perm. But when Dostoevsky warns of the danger of Tolmachova's reading to adolescents, one thinks of Maikov's Aspasia, who looked forward to initiating an inexperienced young man into sensual bliss, and of the young girl visited by the amorous phantom in *A Midsummer Night's Dream*.

One notable aspect of Dostoevsky's article is the far from sympathetic opinion he expresses about the original account of the Perm evening in the *St. Petersburg News*. He surmises that the piece was written either by "an innocent soul enraptured by progress" or that "the letter from Perm may be a counterfeit, for the purpose of producing a scandal in the literature" (19:101). Although Dostoevsky still sees Kamen'-Vinogorov as the main culprit because of his insinuations about Mrs. Tolmachova, the fact that he acknowledges the possibility of the article's being a provocation is significant. Neither Mikhailov nor Strakhov had admitted the possibility of any ulterior motives on the part of the organizers of the Perm literary evening, or of the author of the report on it. But Dostoevsky, like Katkov later, has his suspicions about the purity of their impulses.

In "Our Language," the same article in which Katkov criticized Dostoevsky's interpretation of Fet's poetry, Katkov also entered the Tolmachova controversy on the side of the *Age* and against Mikhailov, Strakhov, and Dostoevsky. Katkov introduces the Tolmachova affair as an example of the kind of petty squabbles that make Russian journalism resemble a public square that is too dirty to cross. Katkov outlines the history of the incident, which he assumed would have ended with the apologies by the editors of the *Age* and by Kamen'-Vinogorov. But instead, he writes, a whole series of letters have been published in the *St. Petersburg News* repeating Mikhailov's charges, and in one newspaper "there was even an appeal to all editors for each of them to send a copy of their publications to the insulted lady in order to declare their respect and devotion to her and to express sympathy for her great feat and her martyrdom."[52] But the dust had settled, Kamen'-Vinogorov had disappeared without a trace, and one might think that "Russia, our beloved fatherland, unexpectedly alarmed by this storm in the midst of the great reforms that are now being accomplished, could calmly establish justices of the peace and write legislation."[53] But instead we open Dostoevsky's *Time* to discover that "the passions not only have not subsided, but they are bursting open with a new bitterness that had not appeared even in the very heat of battle."[54] Katkov describes the two articles in *Time* as "the double rending of a desecrated corpse."[55]

Katkov characterizes the controversy as being about "the emancipation of woman," an issue first raised by Mikhailov, but then continued by "the whistler of the journal *Time*"—that is, Dostoevsky, who sees such emancipation as an ideal for the future.[56] Katkov professes not to be able to discern any rights that have been taken away from women in Russia, where women have full civil equality: "In the home she is mistress, in the salon she is queen; in literature, in art, even in science, there is a place for her everywhere, if only she has the talent and the desire. It's true, we have no amazon regiments or female civil-service departments. But does woman really want this? Does she really need this?"[57] Women have even served as supreme rulers in Russia, England, and Spain. And "the ages of chivalry" have perfected the relations of man to woman in educated society "to ideal refinement."[58] So, Katkov asks, what does woman want? To be emancipated in all the same ways that a man is emancipated? Here Katkov clearly has in mind sexual emancipation. But for him, such emancipation is undesirable for both men and women: "Only higher moral development, which inculcates in the soul a feeling of duty, saves both man and woman from this gratuitous and easily accessible sort of emancipation."[59] And a woman emancipated in such a way would no longer have the right to demand from a man "that particular respect, that delicacy, to which a woman has a right when she remains in her high and privileged position, which no one disputes, which on the contrary everyone treasures, which everyone preserves, keeping away from woman the emancipators with their dirty hands."[60]

Katkov goes on to admit that Mrs. Tolmachova was subjected to coarse attacks, but perhaps they were "the fruit of the teachings of emancipation": "One does not stand on ceremony with a man, but treats him as a creature with full rights in all respects; why stand on ceremony with a woman, who is also supposed to be a creature with full rights in all respects?"[61] Katkov is taking advantage here of the paradox involved in the Tolmachova incident: on the one hand, Mrs. Tolmachova performed an act that she knew would be provocative in the context of her time, as Dostoevsky acknowledged, and claimed the same freedom as a man to speak of sexual issues in public; on the other, defenders like Mikhailov seemed to be demanding a kind of chivalrous delicacy in her treatment by journalists. For Katkov, Tolmachova had voluntarily stepped onto the dirty public square, and could not expect to be treated any differently from the men who jostled each other there. Katkov goes on to deny the radicals, with their vaunted materialism, the right to speak of human rights at all: "Whoever sees in the human nothing more than chemical alkali, acids, and salts, in the very same significance and force with which they are revealed to us in a test tube, that person should not speak of human rights, of human usefulness, of the improvement of human life."[62]

Katkov professes to be amazed that the "virginal powers of moral indignation" were aroused against Kamen'-Vinogorov's feuilleton and not against the original article in the *St. Petersburg News*, "this outrageous vulgarity that insults the dignity of woman much more than any coarseness." Mr. Mikhailov and the other "noble chevaliers of woman" should have called the writer to account for "the insult to the dignity of Mrs. Tolmachova," if he invented the story, or if not, they should have "mercilessly execute[d] Mrs. Tolmachova for insulting feminine dignity, moral feeling, and common sense."[63]

Katkov focuses on Tolmachova's own words as conveyed by the correspondent for the *St. Petersburg News*. When Tolmachova speaks of how "we all" read dirty French novels, Katkov responds, "Who are these 'we all'? One might assume that not all the people in this hall were fans of immoral novels and dirty vaudevilles. Surely not all of the ladies and young girls in the hall belonged to that category? So why make such an assumption that could insult many of these ladies even more than the sarcasms of Kamen'-Vinogorov could insult Mrs. Tolmachova?"[64] Katkov also criticizes Tolmachova for her choice of *Egyptian Nights*; she could have chosen another work by Pushkin "that could much more successfully contribute to the philanthropic aim of purifying taste and correcting the morals of the Perm public."[65] Tolmachova claims not to find anything immodest in Cleopatra's speech, and why? "Because many young girls marry old men. What strange logic they have in Perm!"[66] Katkov quotes Mrs. Tolmachova about the supposed acceptance in England of the practice of having young girls visit "dens of iniquity" in order to "come to know about the unfortunate aspects of life." He comments, "No, these are not her thoughts, she is not to blame for them; they are those vulgar phrases, unverified either by thought or feeling, that are unfortunately encountered everywhere in Russia."⁶⁷ Here he seems to share Dostoevsky's suspicion that the entire affair has arisen not naturally and spontaneously, but as "a counterfeit for the purpose of causing a scandal in the literature."

Katkov justifies Kamen-Vinogorov's insinuations about the "secrets of Perm" based on the initial description in the *St. Petersburg News*, according to which Mrs. Tolmachova did not just read Cleopatra's words, but acted them out: "What were the Perm matrons supposed to do with their daughters when they saw the eyes of the actress directed at them 'now blaze, now grow dim,' hearing how skillfully she set off 'the significance of every thought and every picture of the poet'? Who doesn't know Pushkin's *Egyptian Nights*? Who doesn't know the kind of lines there are in this piece, full of charm, but with which one must not joke and which must not be cast into the face of the public with the mimicry of passion?"⁶⁸ Again, for Katkov, Tolmachova got what she was asking for, in the form of Kamen'-Vinogorov's suppositions about the "secrets of Perm," because of her inappropriate and provocative reading and the way it was described in detail in the *St. Petersburg News*. By casting a gaze of contempt on her audience as if she were Cleopatra herself, Tolmachova broke the conventional "fourth wall" dividing her from her audience and invited the kind of insinuations made by Kamen'-Vinogorov.

Finally, Katkov turns to the question raised by Strakhov, that of the morality of Pushkin's work. Like Strakhov, Katkov absolves Pushkin of immorality, but he considers *Egyptian Nights* to be dangerous for public reading because of its fragmentary nature: "We agree that there is nothing immoral in Pushkin's fragment. But it is only a fragment, only a hint, only a motif, a few marvelous chords, in which something is darkly felt but nothing has yet been unfolded for clear and full contemplation."⁶⁹ Because the work is unfinished, "the idea of the whole" is not fully clarified, and "Cleopatra's monstrous challenge," not elaborated or surrounded with artistic detail, is all that the audience perceives: "What must have echoed in those present at the sight of the performer who took on the role of Cleopatra, and with her voice, with the play of her face, conveyed to the public all the shades of the speech that she both understood and did not understand?"⁷⁰ He asks what would have happened if Mr. Mikhailov had decided to publicly perform in mixed company a poem about an Eastern potentate exulting over his harem as he chooses one of them, "with his eyes now blazing, now growing dim, looking over the whole company and fixing his gaze on various people? . . . What decent woman would remain in the hall?"⁷¹

Katkov concludes by affirming the need for preserving social proprieties "until they are replaced by something higher," because "they surround with shame and mystery [*taina*, the same word as "secret"] the ultimate expressions of passion" and therefore preserve the human significance of passion, keeping it from descending into animality.[72] In direct response to Dostoevsky's statement that there is nothing indecent about looking at the Medici Venus in a public hall, Katkov continues, "Do the Medici Venus or the Venus de Milo represent those expressions of passion that resound in Cleopatra's words? Don't these Olympian types represent the most chaste images, imbued with that pure elegance that constitutes the living soul of propriety? Are these images not themselves the embodiment of that refined shamefacedness, of that enchanting mystery? Would the chisel not only of Phidias or Praxiteles, but even of the sculptors of the age of decadence, ever extend to depict *the ultimate expressions* of passion [*poslednie vyrazheniia strastnosti*]?"[73]

Katkov takes advantage of the opening Dostoevsky offered him when he conceded that Mrs. Tolmachova's reading might be harmful for adolescents. Katkov depicts Dostoevsky addressing Mrs. Tolmachova "with the elegance of a fop perfumed with patchouli." After pointing out that the opinion of the mammas must be respected because the reading might be dangerous for their daughters, Dostoevsky went on to say, "I hope I did not speak of secrets of Perm or of expressive gestures." Katkov exclaims, "He thinks that Mrs. Tolmachova's feat is a dangerous business; and he speaks of this, smirking and scraping his feet, as if of a trifle that doesn't merit attention, and referring contemptuously to the 'old mommies': he finds that they are only partly right, and therefore are partly not right to protest against something that may be dangerous for their daughters."[74] Katkov skewers Dostoevsky for his inconsistent position: how can he defend Mrs. Tolmachova's reading of *Egyptian Nights* if such a reading is indeed dangerous for the young people in the audience?

In his response, "An Answer to the *Russian Herald*," Dostoevsky appears to have been stung by the personal nature of Katkov's reference to him as a "fop scented with patchouli." He lashes back with all the epithets he can think of for Katkov: "incontinent and quick-tempered"; "limited conceit, unlimited self-satisfaction, a thirst for incense burning and worship"; "petty self-worship, conceit, Jupiter-like grandeur, childish irritability"; "a kind of senility" (19:121, 123). He accuses Katkov of distorting the idea of "emancipation," displaying an inability to recognize the "progressive vital forces" that exist in the radical movement alongside the "bad boys and screamers" (19:124). Dostoevsky depicts Katkov as taking the easy path of spitting on his opponents, inciting a crowd to gather around and jeer, "Ooh! Emancipator! Emancipator! Look, there goes the emancipator! He wants to be pleasing to the fair sex; look, he's perfumed himself with patchouli, the seducer, the Lovelace, the emancipator!" (19:126). Dostoevsky denies that he said anything about emancipation in his article; he simply agreed with Mrs. Tolmachova that "there is a great deal that is dirty, cynically naked, and coarsely perverted in the novels of Dumas-*fils* and in French vaudevilles, and that to read and watch them is incomparably more dangerous than to listen to *Egyptian Nights*" (19:126). Dostoevsky rejects Katkov's implied equation of women's emancipation with sexual emancipation: "If by emancipation you mean the right of any woman to put horns on [cuckold] her husband at any convenient opportunity, then of course you are right to hate emancipation. But we never understood emancipation in this way.... For us, all emancipation amounts to Christian love for humanity, the enlightenment of oneself in the name of love for one another, the love that a woman has the right to demand for herself" (19:126).

For Dostoevsky, the process of showing society the need for more philanthropic attitudes toward women is a valuable process, even though fraught with possible errors, like the potentially dangerous act of Mrs. Tolmachova. He depicts Katkov as "a pedant sitting in his study and waiting for development, progress, and humaneness to fall upon him from the sky all ready-made, without historical life, without efforts, without enthusiasms and mistakes." Such a person is "an indifferent sluggard who has lost his common sense" (19:127). Katkov had denied the right of materialists to speak about human dignity, given that they see the human being as a mere sum of alkali and acids. Dostoevsky responds that such a person still has the right to speak of human rights, of human usefulness and the betterment of the human way of life: "No matter what their convictions may be, they still remain people, they could not destroy their nature.... A person, because he is a person, would sense the need to love his neighbor, the need for self-sacrifice for the benefit of his neighbor, because love is unthinkable without self-sacrifice, and love ... cannot be destroyed" (19:131–32). Katkov took a narrow view of "emancipation," seeing it as a woman's desire to renounce feminine chastity and thus subject herself to the kind of insinuations made by Kamen'-Vinogorov. Dostoevsky takes a broader view of emancipation as having very little to do with sexuality, and everything to do with human dignity and the teachings of Christ.

The most important part of Dostoevsky's essay, however, is his defense of *Egyptian Nights* from Katkov's charge that as a fragment it was unsuitable for public reading, since without being clothed in artistic detail, its potentially salacious aspects stood out more strikingly.[75] Dostoevsky responds that *Egyptian Nights* is not a fragment, but "the most finished work of Russian poetry" (19:132).

This point he asserts rather than argues.[76] There is no question that the poem declaimed by Mrs. Tolmachova was left unfinished at Pushkin's death. But as in the disagreement between Dostoevsky and Katkov over how to interpret Fet's poem *Diana*, here Katkov takes a narrow, formalistic view, while Dostoevsky reacts as a creator, not strictly an interpreter. Rather than seeing the poem's unfinishedness as a defect, he valorizes the very fragmentariness of Pushkin's work:

> Pushkin set himself the task (if it is at all possible that he set a task in advance for his inspiration) to present a moment of Roman life, and only one moment, but in such a way as to produce by it the fullest spiritual impression, in order to convey in a few lines and images the whole spirit and meaning of that moment of the life of that time, so that by this moment, by this little corner, one could guess in advance and understand the whole picture. And Pushkin achieved this and achieved it in such artistic fullness that it appears to us as a miracle of poetic art. (19:133)

We can see here on the micro level the same disagreement the two men had about Pushkin's legacy on the macro level: for Katkov, Pushkin's accomplishment is unfinished, an unfulfilled promise, a fragment in a sense, while for Dostoevsky, it is an integral and complete achievement.

Dostoevsky's second point is that any sexual material in the work has been transformed by a mysterious artistic process: "Here reality has been transformed, *having passed through art*, having passed through the fire of pure, chaste inspiration and through the poet's artistic thought. This is a secret [*taina*] of art, and every artist knows about it" (19:134; emphasis in original). Third, echoing Strakhov, Dostoevsky argues that if any salacious impression is received, it is the fault of the audience, not the artist: "The *chastity* of an image does not save it from a coarse and even perhaps a dirty thought" (19:134; emphasis in original). Finally, again following Strakhov's hint about the "horror" evoked in Cleopatra's audience, he offers his own interpretation of *Egyptian Nights* as a work that produces not a "Marquis de Sade" effect but a powerful moral effect: "This *ultimate expression* [of passion], about which you so often talk, in our opinion can indeed be a temptation, but in our opinion it represents only the perversion of human nature, which has reached such horrible dimensions and is presented *from such a point of view* by the poet (and the point of view is the main thing) that it produces not an obscene but a shattering impression" (19:135; emphasis in original). Pushkin's depiction of the spiritual bankruptcy of decadent Alexandria "makes it clear to what kind of people our divine Redeemer came" (19:137). Dostoevsky is rightly celebrated for the artistically visionary interpretation of *Egyptian Nights* he gives in this essay. But he seems to have entirely lost sight of his own admission in his first essay that Mrs. Tolmachova was putting her adolescent listeners at risk by reading them *Egyptian Nights*, for all its artistic beauty. Perhaps having sensed that Katkov had seized upon this as a weakness, he shifts attention in his second essay away from Mrs. Tolmachova's act of reading and onto Pushkin's creative act of writing *Egyptian Nights*. This represented firmer ground for Dostoevsky.

The Tolmachova controversy provoked the most direct and personal public interaction between Dostoevsky and Katkov. It reveals some of the dynamics that would make possible the later working relationship between the two men. Most important here is that we see Dostoevsky rising to a challenge posed by Katkov. Katkov's questioning of the artistic form of *Egyptian Nights* inspired Dostoevsky to one of his best pieces of literary criticism. This is a foreshadowing of the way in which Dostoevsky was moved to write cogently about his own artistic aims when "pitching" new ideas for novels in his letters to Katkov during the years they worked together. We also see some of Dostoevsky's uneasiness with the radicals whom he seems to have decided to court during his editorship of *Time*. Unlike Mikhailov, Dostoevsky could not defend Mrs. Tolmachova with unalloyed righteous indignation, because he felt too strongly the viewpoint of the "old mommies" whose daughters were subjected to her provocative performance. In this uneasiness we can see that he did not so vehemently disagree with Katkov as it would seem on the surface. But the bare-knuckled nature of nineteenth-century Russian journalism led the two men into making fairly sharp personal attacks on each other. Dostoevsky had the advantage of the clear public image of Katkov that had been developed in the Tur polemic: the selfishly proud, overbearing, intelligent but arrogant editor throwing his weight around. Dostoevsky's public image was not as well defined at this time, but no one who knew him would have described him as a "perfumed fop"; Katkov's barb was much less apt than Dostoevsky's (although it did seem to cause Dostoevsky some pain). In the next stage of the polemic, though, Katkov came closer to identifying some of Dostoevsky's real artistic characteristics, which constitute both his strengths and his failings.

The Charismatic Murderer

Katkov's next attack on Dostoevsky was caused in part by a misunderstanding. Katkov apparently believed that an unsigned feuilleton in *Time* written by P. A.

Kuskov was actually by Dostoevsky. In the feuilleton, Kuskov expresses admiration for the "coarse honesty" of a man who confessed to twenty-three murders.[77] As an example of such honesty, Kuskov offers the man's reply when asked how he could have killed a person for a *chetvertak* [25 kopecks]: "It's all the same: either for a *chetvertak* or for a thousand rubles." Katkov introduces the feuilleton as an example of the "Khlestakovism" reigning in current Russian literature, "not only in beardless youths but in our *soi-disant* scholars and venerable elders."[78] Khlestakov, the hero of Gogol's play *The Government Inspector* (*Revizor*, 1836), is a young, feckless civil servant from St. Petersburg who is mistaken by the officials of a provincial town for an inspector on a secret visit, and who takes advantage of the misunderstanding, accepting bribes from all the townspeople and romancing the mayor's wife and daughter. Katkov's specific reference is to Khlestakov's verbal flights of fancy, in which he gets so carried away by his own lies that he begins to believe them himself. Katkov's next words in his essay make clear that he has Dostoevsky in mind, as a St. Petersburg journalist with the experience of prison and exile behind him: "Often from people who are apparently quite decent, who have even lived in the world and seen a few things, you will suddenly hear such shameless speeches that expose the complete absence of the feeling of truth in the speaker. . . . Even the fact that Khlestakov is a Petersburg civil servant is a very deep and essential feature."[79]

After quoting Kuskov's paean to the murderer, Katkov chastises the Khlestakovism that can be carried away with artistic rapture over a savage slayer, that can "see in him some kind of colossal human image that crushes other petty little people, not one of whom has cut anyone's throat, and who dared to be amazed that this monster resolved on his terrible deed over a flask of vodka—tell me, what kind of pen is capable of writing this!"[80] Katkov could well be seeing in Kuskov's admiration for the murderer an echo of Dostoevsky's vivid portraits of hardened killers in his *Notes from the Dead House*, the first four chapters of which appeared in the same issue of *Time* as Kuskov's feuilleton, although Dostoevsky could never have taken Kuskov's blithe moral stance in relation to such phenomena. Katkov goes on to indict the author of the feuilleton (supposedly Dostoevsky) for his detachment from reality: "He lives in the element of phrases, which forms his own world in which phantom likenesses of moods and thoughts arise. These false likenesses can be developed and formed into various combinations, can create whole narrative poems, critical articles, whole books."[81] Katkov ends with another seeming allusion to Dostoevsky's own literary image: "Among Khlestakovs there is another breed who call themselves demonic natures. You truly can't help but fear such fine lads. They might not slit your throat, but don't leave your *chetvertak* lying around loose."[82]

As the editors of Dostoevsky's complete works indicate, Katkov's description of the Khlestakovian style he perceives in the feuilleton, which he thinks is by Dostoevsky, may be a "tendentious interpretation of Dostoevsky's creative manner with its characteristic turns backwards, to a deeper elaboration of ideas and images that were marked out before" (19:310). His reference to "demonic natures" may also refer to the depictions in *Notes from the Dead House* of terrifyingly amoral criminals whose exploits inspire not just revulsion but awe. In the early chapters of *Notes from the Dead House*, published in the same issue of *Time* as Kuskov's feuilleton, we encounter Gazin, who seemed to be not a man but a "huge spider of gigantic proportions" (4:40; *Time*, 1861, no. 2, 47), and Orlov, who "could master himself without limits, who had contempt for any tortures and punishments and did not fear anything on earth" (4:47; *Time*, 1861, no. 2, 57). Most strikingly, Kuskov's feuilleton arouses Katkov's ire because it empathizes with a cold-blooded murderer and, however ineptly, tries to understand his psychology. Katkov could not have known at this point that the first novel by Dostoevsky that he would publish, *Crime and Punishment*, would do something similar, though with far greater depth and artistic truth.

In his response to Katkov, titled "Literary Hysteria," Dostoevsky hastens to make it clear that the author of the feuilleton was not he but Kuskov. In lashing back at Katkov, Dostoevsky uses a technique that Genrikh Vyzinsky had used against Katkov in the Tur polemic, pathologizing his behavior as a kind of mental disorder (Vyzinsky called it *"mania emendatoria"* ["editor's mania"] or *"lues emendatoria"* ["editor's syphilis"]). Dostoevsky goes Vyzinsky one better, making Katkov's illness the peculiarly feminine one of hysteria: "In the irritation of the *Russian Herald* toward us is expressed more and more something hysterically feminine" (19:146). Vyzinsky may well have been on Dostoevsky's mind in writing this response, because he goes on to allude to the incident during the Tur polemic when in one of his articles Katkov asked Vyzinsky to return some books he had borrowed. Dostoevsky quotes the last lines of Katkov's article on Kuskov, which conclude, "They might not slit your throat, but don't leave your *chetvertak* lying around loose." Dostoevsky exclaims, "As for the concluding words of his article, in which he speaks of demonic natures and of a lost *chetvertak*, we do not understand how a self-respecting person can dare to use such street vulgarity publicly. But we recall that this isn't the first time the *Russian Herald* has dared such a thing: once, in the same manner, it notified the public about a book that had disappeared from someone's desk in connection with one of his previous contributors leaving the journal" (19:146). Dostoevsky concludes by prescribing "medical means" for Katkov's problem, because literary ones won't help (19:146).

Dostoevsky and Katkov continued to spar along basically the same lines, with Katkov gradually withdrawing from the polemic as Dostoevsky got more heated. Dostoevsky's personal attacks on Katkov culminated in his 1862 article "A Ticklish Question." In an entry from his notebook of 1860–62, among literary plans Dostoevsky notes, "Portraits of Men of Letters: Egoism and So-called Tendencies." There follows a list of writers and journals beginning with Katkov, and ending with "personalities and portraits à la Zhemchuzhnikov" (20:153). "Zhemchuzhnikov" is no doubt a reference to the brothers Zhemchuzhnikov, who along with their cousin the poet A. K. Tolstoy created the fictive personality Kozma Prutkov, a bad writer who produced some of the funniest literary parodies of the mid-nineteenth century. Dostoevsky's plan to produce a parodistic portrait of Katkov was realized in "A Ticklish Question," in which Katkov is presented in the guise of a pompous "orator" who boasts of his power on the literary scene and shouts hysterically about the *chetvertak* that disappeared from his desk in the editorial office (20:38). With "A Ticklish Question," Dostoevsky had taken the personalization of his polemic with Katkov to its furthest possible limit, creating out of Katkov a ridiculous fictional character who seems to have stepped out of Turgenev's *Fathers and Sons*. Katkov did not respond to the caricature in any published form.

The Polish Uprising: The Fatal Question

The next major interaction between Katkov's *Russian Herald* and Dostoevsky's *Time* concerned an event that was a watershed for both Katkov and Dostoevsky, the Polish uprising of January 1863. For Katkov, the uprising intensified his feelings of Russian nationalism and greatly enhanced his public profile. As the newly appointed editor of the *Moscow News* (he continued to run the *Russian Herald* as well), in a series of vehement editorials he goaded the government into taking uncompromising measures against the insurgents. The Polish uprising was the catalyst that made Katkov into a political figure above all, and thus muted as part of his public image the literary influence he continued to have through his publication of novels by Turgenev, Dostoevsky, and Tolstoy. For Dostoevsky, the uprising led to the closing of his journal, and although in time he was able to start a new journal, in effect the fallout from the Polish question turned Dostoevsky back into being primarily a fiction writer, not a journalist, at least for the next several years. Soviet scholars have implied that Katkov instigated the closing of *Time*. This is a debatable point. But there is no doubt that the Polish question, like the other questions of the day, added to the acrimony of the dialogue between Dostoevsky and Katkov.

Poland had once been a rival great power to Russia, but the partitions of 1772, 1793, and 1795 had divided the Polish state among Austria, Prussia, and Russia. An earlier rebellion in 1830 had led to a crackdown by Tsar Nicholas I that had destroyed many of Poland's distinctive institutions. As Geoffrey Hosking writes, "When the Russian government resumed the path of reform in Poland, in the 1860s, the result was more or less a repetition of the 1830 rebellion.... Alexander II aroused exaggerated hopes and also provoked bitter disagreements. The result was an armed insurrection in 1863–64, which aimed to restore Polish independence."[83] The uprising was suppressed by the end of 1864.

Katkov's initial response to the uprising came in a forceful article in the *Russian Herald*, "The Polish Question."[84] Katkov rejected European attempts to influence Russia by invoking principles of nonintervention and the rights of nationalities, pointing out what he saw as their hypocrisy: "Don't speak to an Englishman about the rights of nationalities [*narodnosti*] in India: he will consider you to be insane, just as a Frenchman will consider you to be insane if you start to talk to him about the rights of nationalities in Algeria."[85] Katkov's main point is that the question facing Russia *vis-à-vis* Poland is a life-and-death question, or what he calls a "fatal question [*rokovoi vopros*]": "Between these two nationalities [*narodnosti*] of one tribe, history long ago posed a fatal question of life and death. The two states were not simply rivals, but enemies, who could not exist next to each other, enemies to the end. Between them the question was no longer of who was to take precedence or who was to be more powerful: the question between them was which of them was to exist."[86] Poland had threatened to swallow up Russia in the seventeenth century, and in Katkov's view it would not now be content with remaining within its proper borders (i.e., not laying claim to the so-called *zapadnyi krai*, the lands of present-day Ukraine, Lithuania, and Belarus that both sides saw as belonging to them).

According to Katkov, Poland had nourished its feeling of nationality [*narodnost'*] over the centuries, and would not be satisfied with any outcome other than "the restoration of the old Poland, with all its claims": "For him [the Pole] simple independence is insufficient, he wants predominance; it is not enough for him to be liberated from an alien state, he wants the destruction of his triumphant opponent. It is not enough for him to be a Pole; he wants the Russian to also become a Pole, or to clear off to the other side of the Ural mountain range."[87] Katkov speaks darkly of Russia's internal enemies, the radicals who were ready to support Polish aims in order to foment revolution in Russia itself.[88] But the major thrust of Katkov's article is best summarized in the following line: "Our struggle with Poland is not a struggle for political principles, it is a struggle between two nationalities [*narodnosti*], and to yield to Polish patriotism in its claims would mean to sign a death sentence for the Russian people [*narod*]."[89]

It took a while for more liberal journals like *Time* to respond to the Polish uprising. To take a Katkovian line would have been out of character, but to openly support the Polish cause would be extremely dangerous in the heat of the struggle. The atmosphere had changed drastically over the course of 1862: student unrest, mysterious fires in St. Petersburg, and the distribution of revolutionary leaflets had led to a tightening of government restrictions. The *Contemporary* was suspended for eight months in May 1862, and Chernyshevsky was arrested in June 1862, so voices to the left of *Time* had effectively been silenced (Dobroliubov had died in November 1861).

Some articles of an informational nature about the rebellion appeared in *Time* in the first three issues of 1863. But in the April issue there appeared Nikolai Strakhov's article "A Fatal Question," signed with the pseudonym "A Russian." Its title was taken from Katkov but given a very different significance.[90] Strakhov's article is perplexing in many ways. According to his later explanations, he was trying to continue the journal's general policy of elevating current issues to a general and abstract formula: "But life with its concrete feelings and facts was progressing so hotly that this time it would not tolerate abstractions." Thus his basic idea, "that we have to fight the Poles not just with material but with spiritual weapons, and that we have to have a spiritual victory over them," was lost on most readers.[91] Indeed Strakhov's article is written on such a level of abstraction and filled with so many equivocations that scholars are still disputing its general thrust. Many scholars have accepted Strakhov's and Dostoevsky's *ex post facto* explanation that the real but misunderstood message of the article was an anti-Polish, pro-Russian one; others, notably Linda Gerstein, Andrzej Walicki, and Edyta Bojanowska, interpret Strakhov's article much the same way as the Russian government did, as an essay supporting Polish claims to civilizational superiority over Russia.

When Strakhov wrote to Katkov explaining that he was the author of the article, Katkov, who had had friendly dealings with Strakhov as a fellow antinihilist, reacted with amazement: "I was thunderstruck by the news that the article 'A Fatal

Question' was written by you, most respected Nikolai Nikolaevich.... I decidedly do not understand how you could write and publish such an article at the present time."[92] One must share Katkov's amazement when reading the explanation in Strakhov's article of the problem at the root of the "Polish question": "The Poles are incited against us as an educated [or "formed," *obrazovannyi*] people [*narod*] against a less educated or even not at all educated people. No matter what the pretexts for the struggle, the animation of the struggle is apparently inflamed by the fact that on one side is struggling a civilized people, and on the other—barbarians."[93] Although he presents himself as merely ventriloquizing the Polish point of view here, his enthusiastic descriptions of Poland's highly elaborated civilization and its truly European development certainly create the impression that his sympathy for a superior civilization (Poland) dominated by an inferior one (Russia) is real.

As Bojanowska has argued, Strakhov's interpretation is less about Poland than about Russia; it has as its aim the furtherance of the ideology of *pochvennichestvo* ["return to the soil"]. In his view, Russia can only have a true claim to surpass Poland if it develops a civilization that incorporates "the people's principles [*narodnye nachala*]," unlike the aristocratic Polish civilization: "We obviously must turn with greater faith and hope to the people's principles. Only then will we be right in our own eyes, when we believe in the future of still chaotic, still unformed and unclarified elements of the spiritual life of the Russian people."[94] This projection into the future of the maturation of Russian society creates a dangerous trap in Strakhov's argument. As Katkov pointed out in a later article, when the struggle is, as Strakhov argues, between a civilization that exists in the present (Poland) and one that exists only in the future (Russia), the one that is an actually existing force has to win out over the one that is merely "the fantasy of a prophet."[95]

A harsh response to Strakhov's article appeared in Katkov's *Moscow News*, signed by a certain K. Peterson but no doubt commissioned by Katkov himself. In this short note, Peterson excoriated *Time* for publishing such an article under a pseudonym: "Only bandits inflict their blows with a mask on their face."[96] Peterson calls it a "lie" to compare the civilization of the upper classes of Poland with the civilization of the Russian people in general. Most damagingly, Peterson hints that "a perfidious design is secreted in the signature 'A Russian'"—namely, that in fact the article may have been written by a Pole or at least a sympathizer with the Polish cause. Realizing the danger, Dostoevsky immediately wrote a reply, which he tried to get published in the *St. Petersburg News*, but which was forbidden by the censor (20:316).

Two days after Peterson's article appeared, *Time* was closed by order of Tsar Alexander II. The editors of Dostoevsky's complete works, perhaps following up on a hint by Alexander Herzen, at times make it sound as if *Time* was closed only because Katkov's *Moscow News* drew the attention of the government to Strakhov's article (20:252, 316). But as V. S. Nechaeva has described, the attention of the government was already fixed on *Time*, thanks to articles of a supposedly subversive nature that had been written for the journal over the course of 1862. There was a proposal made in the summer of 1862 by the Ministry of Internal Affairs, but not acted on, to suspend the journal for eight months because of its "harmful tendency." As Nechaeva writes, "The swiftness with which the journal was closed in April–May of the following year because of the misunderstood article by Strakhov undoubtedly can be explained by the preceding history and the gaze fixed by the government on the Dostoevskys' journal."[97] Katkov certainly did not help the situation of Dostoevsky's journal, but it would be hard to paint him as the main culprit for its closing.

Dostoevsky's unpublished explanation of Strakhov's article removes all Strakhov's equivocations and reinterprets his essay as an unambiguously pro-Russian statement. Dostoevsky writes, "What is important for us is that the Poles with all their (indisputable) European civilization 'carried death in their very roots.' In our article this is said clearly, too clearly, and it is indicated why it is so" (20:98). In fact, what Strakhov writes is not at all that forceful a statement. He begins with the proposition that Russians are barbarians and Poles are a civilized people. For Russians to refute this means that they must prove either that they are not barbarians but a people full of the forces of civilization, or "that the civilization of the Poles is *a civilization that carries death in its very roots*. It's easy to agree that to prove either the one or the other is very difficult."[98] That deflating last line is typical of Strakhov's exposition throughout his article. Whenever he seems to be making a strong pro-Russian, anti-Polish statement, he follows it with an equivocation or a disclaimer.

Similarly, Dostoevsky wrote to Turgenev, "It was said [in our article] *literally* that this vaunted Polish civilization carried and carries death in its heart. This was said in our article literally" (28/2:34). This is wishful thinking; no one who carefully reads Strakhov's article could come away with any such clear, "literal" message. Another point Dostoevsky makes in his unpublished explanation that is not apparent in Strakhov's article is that Russians do not need to become a part of European civilization. Ostensibly addressing Peterson but actually addressing Katkov, Dostoevsky writes, "You yourselves are reverent before Polish civilization because you are jealous of it, you envy it. You are offended ... because in your imagination there has never been any other standard of Russian dignity and development than European civilization." Dostoevsky claims that his addressees do not recognize "the independence of the people's principles in the Russian tribe, and in the name of your Anglicized patriotism, you are offended that the Poles are more educated than us in the European sense, in other words, that the Russians stubbornly want to remain Russians and not turn by decree into Germans or Frenchmen." But the Russians' desire to remain Russians is a positive phenomenon: "After all, the Poles were ruined by their civilization. Despite all their pride in this civilization, it has ruined them to the point that there will no longer be any resurrection for them, even if they become politically independent" (20:99).

Strakhov, who was afraid he might be exiled, appealed to Katkov for help. Katkov complied, and with difficulty he obtained permission to publish another article on the subject of Strakhov's "A Fatal Question." In this article Katkov absolved Strakhov, and implicitly *Time*, of the accusation of disloyalty, thus making it possible for the Dostoevsky brothers to eventually obtain permission (in January 1864) to open a new journal. But he also set out to demolish *Time*'s ideology of *pochvennichestvo* or "return to the soil," using the word "soil" ironically throughout his article. For Katkov, Strakhov's problem was precisely his attempt to "elevate the [Polish] question to an abstract formula," as Strakhov himself later characterized his aim.

On the first page of his article Katkov writes, "Here is a person who hasn't the slightest bad intention in his soul, but who also does not have soil under his feet, although he constantly repeats the word 'soil'—here this person, intending to perform a civic deed, performs an action that arouses indignation in everyone."[99] For Katkov, the ideology of "return to the soil" is just another set of empty phrases like all the others that predominate in Russian cultural life: "We are more and more convinced that all these fashionable discussions of nationality [*narodnost'*], of root principles, of soil, etc., do not turn thought either to nationality or to root principles, do not lead it to anything sensible, but on the contrary carry it off further into fog and emptiness."[100] Katkov offers advice to the editors of *Time* that seems to be directed primarily not at Strakhov, but at Dostoevsky:

> They will not return to the people and take a stand on the soil about which they talk so much until they stop talking about it and take up some more serious deed.... If

these gentlemen really feel the need to emerge from this emptiness and find themselves amid living reality, then it is not at all so difficult as it seems: for this no strain is needed, no casting up of the eyes and hands, no grimaces, no prophesying, no proclaiming of the good news—on the contrary, all that must be abandoned, all that is the hashish with which they intoxicate themselves; and when they stop doing all that, then they will *eo ipso* find themselves amid living reality, among the people, on firm soil.... The ulcer of our time—an ulcer that rages not just here but everywhere—is the passion for prophesying, for teaching humanity and proclaiming the good news to it.[101]

Katkov identifies here a failing that seems to be an occupational hazard for the Russian writer from Gogol to Solzhenitsyn, and that certainly afflicted Dostoevsky in his later years: the need to be not just a writer but a prophet as well.

In his unpublished explanation of Strakhov's article, Dostoevsky claimed that Russians do not envy the Poles their European civilization because they have their own original path, separate from Europe. Although Katkov could not have read Dostoevsky's explanation, he might have surmised that this was Dostoevsky's position, based on the general ideology propounded in *Time*. In his article about "A Fatal Question," Katkov takes a very different view from Dostoevsky. He rejects Strakhov's implied identification of two camps: on the one hand European civilization, which includes Poland; and on the other Russia's own original civilization, which is still in the process of being created. Katkov complains that Strakhov "gave Poland European civilization and rewarded his fatherland with fantastic prospects for the future."[102] According to Katkov, Russia is indeed part of Europe; in fact it is one of its five great powers, with England, France, Austria, and Prussia. The dichotomy is not between Europe and Russia, but between a single, universal [*vsemirnaia*] Western civilization that unites all peoples [*narody*], and the individual civilizations of each historical people in particular. Russia is part of the universal (pan-European) civilization but also has its own peculiar conditions of life and development: "To develop one's own civilization does not mean to negate or throw off European civilization, to war with it and overcome it. On the contrary, in developing our own civilization, we will more deeply and actually satisfy the demands of universal civilization."[103] Katkov, unlike Dostoevsky, is unwilling to renounce what Europe has contributed to the particular Russian variant of civilization. (Given the extremely important influence of French, German, and English literature on Dostoevsky's own fiction, his general statements about renouncing

Europe ring somewhat hollow.) But like Dostoevsky, Katkov does believe that Russia has its own original character and role in history.

With this article, Katkov had the last word in the polemic with Dostoevsky. With his caustic remarks about "soil" he attempted to relegate the editors of *Time* to the same category as the nihilists, as people caught up in their own dreams and fancies, unable to connect with real life. He reproaches Strakhov and Dostoevsky for their abstract and "transcendental" ideology of "the soil," for "trying to be Russians not in a simple Russian way, but according to German metaphysics."[104] This echoes his "Elegiac Note" of 1861, in which he wrote that in Russian culture one could sense "emptiness and powerlessness, the absence of living soil, an insufficiency of thought that flows out of deeds and leads to deeds."[105] He called in that essay for people to stop trying to reconstruct society according to pure reason and to dedicate themselves to the detailed study of real life: "And when that time comes, all this rot of decomposition that has taken possession of our poor word will disappear all by itself."[106]

Dostoevsky's answer to Katkov's "Elegiac Note" of 1861 is caustic about Katkov acting like a professor, sitting in his study and mocking the real struggles of people trying to make life better. But he also finds common ground with Katkov in the desire for "real life," the need to liberate society from empty phrases: "You know that if there is no soil and if activity is impossible, then a striving spirit will express itself in abnormal and disorderly phenomena, will mistake a phrase for life, will leap at a ready-made alien formula, will even be joyful about it and will substitute it for reality! In a fantastic life all functions are fantastic. But in our opinion these are sufferings, these are inescapable torments. In your opinion, they are all phrasemakers" (19:173). What both men seem to lose sight of in the heat of the polemic, up to the very end in 1863, is that they agree on the basic problem of Russian life: the need to stop philosophizing and start doing something positive and good. They also resemble each other in their inability to clearly define how that is to come about.

By the fall of 1863, with *Time* closed down and a new journal not yet officially approved, Dostoevsky had fallen back into the role of a journeyman writer, or what he called a "proletarian." He wrote to Strakhov asking him to approach the editor of the *Library for Reading* about publishing a new work. He instructed Strakhov to make it clear that he needed to be paid in advance: "I am a proletarian writer, and if someone wants my work, he has to secure my services in advance" (28/2:50). Later in the same letter, Dostoevsky says that if Strakhov is unable to make a deal with the *Library for Reading*, then he should approach the newspapers but avoid the *Notes of the Fatherland*, and "of course not the *Russian Herald*" (28/2:52). After writing "A Ticklish Question" and all his other highly personal attacks on Katkov, Dostoevsky at this point could not contemplate turning to Katkov with his work. But the next two years would be some of the hardest in Dostoevsky's life, and would bring him back, despite everything, to the man he first approached in 1858.

Dostoevsky spent much of 1863 in a difficult love affair with Apollinaria Suslova; his wife, Mariia Dmitrievna, died in April 1864 and his brother Mikhail died in July, leaving Dostoevsky to try to carry on the journal *Epoch*, which never really took off and closed in March 1865. Financially crushed by family needs and gambling debts, in September 1865 he wrote a letter to Katkov "pitching" the idea for *Crime and Punishment*, the first of the four major novels that Dostoevsky would publish in the *Russian Herald*. This letter, which will be discussed in the next chapter, is one of the most important and detailed statements we have on the novel's conception.

CHAPTER 5

KATKOV AND DOSTOEVSKY

PATRONAGE AND INTERFERENCE (*CRIME AND PUNISHMENT* AND *THE DEVILS*)

In early spring 1865, Dostoevsky wrote to his old friend A. E. Vrangel, with whom he had been out of touch for years. Dostoevsky gives Vrangel an account of his life during those years: the establishment of *Time*, its closing, his brother's financial troubles, the establishment and quick failure of *Epoch*, and the deaths of his wife and brother in the space of three months. He sums up: "And so I have remained alone, and I am simply terrified. My whole life has been cracked in two all of a sudden. In one half, the one I have already passed through, was everything for which I lived, and in the other, unknown half, all is alien, all is new, and there is not a single heart that could replace those two for me. Literally—I have nothing left to live for" (28/2:116). Dostoevsky could not see at this point what awaited him: a new marriage, children, and the flowering of his career with the production of five major novels. The first step in his new life was the initiation of his fruitful partnership with Katkov, who had not long before been his primary polemical adversary. Katkov gave Dostoevsky's career a new beginning by publishing *Crime and Punishment*, but he also placed awkward demands on Dostoevsky, insisting that he alter the text in ways that Dostoevsky did not welcome. The struggle over the text of *Crime and Punishment* was minor, however, compared to the rejection by the *Russian Herald* of a key chapter in the third novel Dostoevsky published with Katkov, *The Devils*. The interaction between Dostoevsky and Katkov in relation to these two novels is the subject of this chapter.

Crime and Punishment

Dostoevsky had proposed a new novel to *Notes of the Fatherland* and the *St. Petersburg News* in June 1865, but had been rebuffed by both journals (7:309).

He went abroad hoping to write, but his gambling habit left him constantly on the brink of ruin. By September 1865, destitute in Wiesbaden, he finally broke his earlier resolve and wrote to Katkov.[1] At virtually the same time, Dostoevsky expressed his fears about this step to Vrangel, mentioning the unsuccessful negotiations with Katkov back in 1858–59 for publishing *The Village of Stepanchikovo*. But clearly he was even more troubled by his more recent history with Katkov: "While *Time* was being published, our two journals had some brawls. And Katkov is such a selfishly proud [*samoliubivyi*], vain, and vengeful person that I am very afraid now that, remembering the past, he might haughtily refuse the story I am offering and make a fool of me. All the more since, in offering him this story, I could not make the proposal in any other way but in an independent tone and without any abasement" (28/2:140). Dostoevsky saw before him in his mind's eye the caricatured, vain, and vengeful Katkov of the Tur polemic, which is part of the story of Katkov, but not the whole story. Katkov was never so selfishly proud as to lose sight of the best interests of his journal, and its need for good writers.

Just as Turgenev seems to have tailored the plots of *On the Eve* and *Fathers and Sons* to the interests of Katkov and the *Russian Herald*, Dostoevsky apparently studied the journal's tendency, in particular the writings of Katkov, before making his "pitch" for *Crime and Punishment* in his September 1865 letter to Katkov. Obviously there were many sources, both literary and social, for *Crime and Punishment*, as the critical literature has shown. But virtually no attention has been given to Katkov's writings as one of these sources. Katkov's second essay on *Fathers and Sons*, "On Our Nihilism Apropos of Turgenev's Novel," includes passages that prefigure the creation of Raskolnikov. Katkov speaks of the illusory richness of Russian civilization and intellectual life. Russia lacks what he calls "social forces," "ideas that gather people into groups, connecting them into heterogeneous, more or less strong formations":

> Where these forces do not exist or where they are suppressed, there education [*obrazovanie*, also formation] will always be a phantom, and no matter how apparently rich its content, it will not have any significance, and individual people will always feel the powerlessness of their education. No matter what takes place in their heads, on everything will lie the stamp of the imaginary, the unreal; there will be no harmony between their words and thoughts, there will be no organic connection between their thoughts and actions. Everything in them will be shaky and unsteady [*zybko i shatko*], everything for them will be doubtful, and their own moral personality

will appear dimly to them like a phantom, their own intellectual organization will frighten them like an apparition.[2]

The idea of "*shatost*" or "unsteadiness" will be used by Dostoevsky in his letter to Katkov describing *Crime and Punishment*, and will continue to be a keynote in his depiction of radical youth, as attested by his use of the name Shatov in *The Devils*.

Katkov goes on to contrast Bazarov in *Fathers and Sons* with the more caricatured figures of Kukshina and Sitnikov, and asks, shouldn't we respect Bazarov for his refusal to sink to petty baseness like them? But according to Katkov, even a Bazarov would resort to a base act if he could justify it through some higher objective: "For such people, it is not the immoral that is immoral, but only the impression of the despicable and pitiable. The norm of their morality does not define the quality of the act but only its dimensions and relative significance." If the act seems petty, they won't commit it, but if it looks major and impressive, they will: "The very same act, with the same combination of factors, will, according to their norm, seem both dishonorable and honorable depending on whether it looks petty or major, what impression it will produce— of a despicable trifle or an event to be reckoned with—a vaudeville farce or an epic rhapsody." The moral content of the act is not what determines its moral value for the nihilist, only its dimensions:

> So our hero won't do anything base, but he is repelled by it not because its motives are repellent, not because the meaning of the base act contradicts his moral feeling and consciousness of duty—he negates that moral feeling and consciousness of duty at their foundations—no, he is repelled by baseness only because of its wretched character, its pettiness and the fact that it humiliates his person. Take away this wretched character, enlarge the dimensions of essentially the very same act, exalt this act with some kind of *distant aims*, so that it doesn't seem despicable and petty— and our hero will willingly commit it and will be proud of it. [Emphasis added][3]

The act is justified by "the multiplicity of the expected consequences, the *distant aims* to which it may lead" (emphasis added).[4]

This passage inevitably calls to mind a particular "base act," the murder of the pawnbroker as described by the student whom Raskolnikov overhears in the tavern: "Kill her and take her money, in order with the help of it to then dedicate oneself to the service of all humanity and the common cause: what do you think, wouldn't a single, teensy little crime be expiated by thousands of good deeds? For one life—thousands of lives saved from rotting and decomposition. One death and a hundred lives in exchange—there's arithmetic for you!" (6:54).

Dostoevsky's letter to Katkov offering the work that was to become *Crime and Punishment* is, as Dostoevsky's letters go, unusually detailed and carefully crafted. It is not surprising that it is widely cited and mined for clues to the significance of his conception of the novel. Given his history with Katkov, Dostoevsky clearly wanted to make his description as powerful as he could. (Only a draft of the letter has survived, but it is quite detailed and no doubt close to the final version.) Leonid Grossman describes the letter in terms usually reserved for an artistic work: "'The plan of the *Inferno* alone is already the fruit of a lofty genius,' Pushkin wrote about Dante's creation. One can say the same thing about this letter by Dostoevsky. After reading this brilliant plan, where everything is catastrophic and everything is tragic, the reserved and cautious Katkov immediately sends the author an advance of three hundred rubles."[5]

Although the letter has been quoted countless times in the literature about *Crime and Punishment*, it is worth quoting again at length here in the context of Dostoevsky's relationship with Katkov. With the polemics of the early 1860s fresh in one's mind, the tone and seriousness of the letter are worthy of note. One can only write a letter like this to someone for whom one has a great deal of respect.

The draft, dated September 1865, Wiesbaden, reads in part as follows:

> May I hope to place my story in your journal the *Russian Herald*? ... The idea of the story, as far as I can assume, could not in any way contradict your journal; on the contrary. It is the psychological account of a certain crime. The action is contemporary, taking place in the present year. A young man, expelled from the university, a *meshchanin* [petty bourgeois] by origin, and living in extreme poverty, out of lightmindedness, out of unsteadiness of conceptions [*shatost' v poniatiiakh*], having succumbed to certain strange "half-baked" ideas that are floating in the air, has resolved to get out of his nasty situation all at once. He has resolved to kill a certain old woman, the widow of a titular councillor, who lends money at interest. The old woman is stupid, deaf, ill, greedy, charges Jew-like interest, is wicked and torments other people's lives, torturing her younger sister who works for her as a maid. "She's no good for anything," "Why is she alive?," "Is she useful to anyone at all?," and so on. These questions confuse the young man. He resolves to kill her and rob her; in order to make happy his mother, who lives in the provinces; to save his sister, who is living as a companion in the home of some landowners, from the lascivious importunities of the head of this landowning family—importunities that threaten her with ruin;

to finish his studies, go abroad, and then all his life be honest, firm, steadfast in performing "his humane duty to humanity," by which he will certainly "expiate the crime," if one can even label as a crime this act upon a deaf, stupid, wicked and sick old woman, who doesn't know herself why she is living in the world, and who might die all by herself in a month's time. (28/2:136)

Here we can see clearly the themes, familiar from Katkov's essay, of the "unsteadiness" of ideas floating in the atmosphere that "confuse" a poorly educated young man, as well as the idea of justifying a seemingly base act through the grandiosity of the "distant aims" (in Katkov's words) that the act will make possible.

Dostoevsky goes on to describe how the student manages to commit the crime without being detected but then undergoes "the whole psychological process of the crime" and is tormented by "unresolved questions." The conclusion is to be a triumph of "God's truth": "God's truth, the earthly law make themselves felt, and he ends by being *compelled* to turn himself in" (28/2:137). Dostoevsky stresses that earthly punishment is much less terrifying to the criminal than lawgivers imagine, because the criminal himself morally demands that punishment. He cites recent cases of well-educated criminals, and repeats the idea of the "unsteadiness of convictions" that leads to such crimes: "There are even more traces in our newspapers of the unusual unsteadiness [*shatost'*] of convictions that incite horrible deeds.... In a word, I am convinced that my plot is in part justified by modern life [*sovremennost'*]" (28/2:137).[6] Not only does Dostoevsky draw on Katkov's conception of nihilism for his initial sketch of Raskolnikov's character, he stresses the contemporaneity and news interest of his story, tailoring it for the kind of readership Katkov would desire.

In the draft of Dostoevsky's letter to Katkov, he refers to their past dealings regarding *The Village of Stepanchikovo*, adopting an apologetic tone: "Perhaps I was partly guilty, perhaps I was partly right. Most likely of all is that it was both one and the other. Now I am prepared rather to accuse myself of capriciousness and arrogance." He makes no mention of their polemical skirmishes in their respective journals. But this attempt to preempt any hard feelings Katkov may have toward him is consistent with the letter he sent to Vrangel; Dostoevsky expected the worst from Katkov, another humiliating rejection. He ends by asking for a minimum payment for his projected work of 125 rubles per printer's sheet, half what he received from *Russian World* for the first chapters of *Notes from the Dead House*.[7] Contrary to Dostoevsky's fears, Katkov agreed to work with him and sent him an advance of three hundred rubles (28/2:425).

Something Dostoevsky seems not to have understood at the moment he turned to Katkov is that Katkov needed him perhaps as much as he needed Katkov. He certainly understood it by February 1866, when he wrote to Vrangel, "While I was abroad and crushed by circumstances, I sent Katkov a proposal for the lowest possible payment I could accept, 125 rubles for their printer's sheet, that is 150 rubles for a sheet of the size the *Contemporary* uses. They agreed. Later I found out that they agreed with delight, because for that year they had no *belles lettres*: Turgenev isn't writing anything, and they had quarreled with Lev Tolstoy. I came to their rescue" (28/2:151).

A letter sent to Katkov in March 1863 by the poet Nikolai Fyodorovich Shcherbina illuminates the dynamics that would lie behind the Dostoevsky-Katkov relationship later, in 1865. Shcherbina writes to Katkov to tell him that he has heard A. F. Pisemsky read chapters from his new novel, and that based on these chapters he thinks that the novel is socially useful for Russia's political self-consciousness, especially "at our childish moment" of nihilism and idle talk. He suggests that this novel, *Troubled Seas* [*Vzbalamuchennoe more*, 1863], should be published in the *Russian Herald*, where *Fathers and Sons* was published, the novel "that gave birth to our political understanding and our sovereign and social self-consciousness."[8]

Pisemsky's novel was in fact published in the *Russian Herald*, and is generally classified as part of the series of "antinihilist" novels published by Katkov.[9] In his letter, Shcherbina goes on to lucidly define the importance of high-quality *belles-lettres* for Katkov's journal: "The public, seeing in the *Russian Herald* all the best forces of literature, will become suspicious of nihilist periodicals. They will see that all talents have become attached to the *Russian Herald*—and not for nothing—that means that everything intelligent, honest, and gifted in Russia sympathizes exclusively with it and is on its side—and the Petersburg journals, which indulge the dark instincts of blockheads and the elemental feelings of young ignoramuses—will little by little start to decline and decline."[10] Ironically, Shcherbina goes on to speak of Dostoevsky's *Time*, "the cunning ingratiator, the comedian," as the only possible competitor with the *Russian Herald* for Russia's literary talents. By 1865, when he turned to Katkov, Dostoevsky had become not a competitor but himself a desirable contributor who would advance the cause that Shcherbina urged on Katkov—something that Katkov needed no hints to see.

In 1855, when Katkov petitioned the minister of education for permission to begin what became the *Russian Herald*, he described the vital role that periodical publications could play in this process, offering "capable people" a field for their labor: "A journal cannot create talents but it can call them forth and give them a direction."[11] In accepting Dostoevsky's proposal, despite all the rancor of their journalistic polemic, Katkov was furthering the aim of fostering the development of Russian literature that he had claimed as the mission of the *Russian Herald* only a decade before.

In a draft of a letter written in December 1865, asking for yet another advance, Dostoevsky writes to Katkov in terms that are calculated to flatter the one-time translator of Shakespeare and Heine: "I turn to you as a writer [*literator*] to a writer and ask you to enter into my situation.... you are a writer, you yourself have been involved in artistic literature, you will understand this!" (28/2:145). Dostoevsky may have been trying to flatter Katkov, but he probably could not have known to what extent Katkov could indeed "enter into [*vniknut'*]" his situation. As a young writer in Germany over twenty years before, in 1841 and 1842, Katkov had been in much the same situation as Dostoevsky, destitute and relying on financial support from the editor A. A. Kraevsky. Katkov's description of this period is not far from Dostoevsky's own despairing letters of the 1860s: "Oh, money—that devil's invention—how very much depends on it. Sometimes I have moments of such despair that I need all my strength of will, all the aid of my education, in order not to crown the comedy with a bad ending."[12] The public image of Katkov that had been shaped during the polemic with Tur—the vain, self-satisfied, and overbearing editor exercising despotic power over the writers contributing to his journal—did not take into account the other Katkov, the idealistic, destitute, nearly suicidal young writer of the early 1840s, the young writer who had not been forgotten by Katkov the mature, successful editor.

Dostoevsky's letters from 1865 on make it clear that he relied on Katkov for virtually continuous financial support through payment of advances on his work in progress. The memoirs of Dostoevsky's second wife, Anna Grigorievna Dostoevskaia, are also full of references to their dependence on Katkov, beginning with their marriage itself. She writes of how Dostoevsky went to Moscow in order to offer Katkov his next novel, *The Idiot*, in late 1866: "Our fate depended mainly on whether things could be arranged with the *Russian Herald*.... After learning of Fyodor Mikhailovich's intention to get married, Katkov warmly congratulated him and wished him happiness. He promised to send the two-thousand-ruble advance that had been asked for in two or three installments over the coming January. In this way we found it possible to arrange our wedding for before Lent."[13]

William Mills Todd III has written, "Katkov would regularly send Dostoevsky advances during these years, thereby providing a sort of salary, but at a cost."[14]

The cost was Dostoevsky's justified sense that he was undervalued by the *Russian Herald*. Although it is true that, at least until the publication of *The Brothers Karamazov*, Katkov never paid Dostoevsky as much as he did Tolstoy and Turgenev, and certainly never paid him as much as he wanted to be paid, still Dostoevsky was never able to find another publisher who would support his ongoing work as consistently as Katkov did. He repeatedly speaks of Katkov's "delicacy" and "trustfulness" with him, and at one point refers to him as "providence" (28/2:288; letter of March 23 [April 4], 1868, to A. G. Dostoevskaia). By spring 1867 Dostoevsky seems to have modified his personal view of Katkov to something more nuanced than the caricature that had emerged in the Tur polemic: "As a private person he is the most noble person in the world. I did not know him at all previously [*Ia sovershenno ne znal ego prezhde*]. His boundless selfish pride [*samoliubie*] harms him terribly. But who of us doesn't have boundless selfish pride?" (28/2:183, letter of April 23 [May 5], 1867, to A. P. Suslova). In an article on Dostoevsky's work with the *Russian Herald*, B. L. Modzalevsky provides a measured summation: "The howl of a person in need can be heard in almost every one of [Dostoevsky's] letters to his brother, his stepson, his niece, and other people; the same howl haunts us as we read Dostoevsky's letters to Liubimov [executive editor of the *Russian Herald*] and Katkov. But one must do justice to the editor and publisher of the *Russian Herald*: they treated Dostoevsky with courtesy and with that attention that he so deserved, for so many reasons."[15]

It was not just money that kept Dostoevsky working with the *Russian Herald*, though. He saw it as the major intellectual and artistic center of Russian public life, as he described in an 1869 letter to his niece S. A. Ivanova. "You say that according to rumor [the *Russian Herald*] is declining?" he writes. The letter continues,

> Is that really true? It would seem to me not true—of course, not because I'm a contributor, but because it is definitely the best journal in Russia and the one that firmly knows its own tendency. It's true that it's dry, that the literature in it is not always good (but not worse than other journals; all the most important [*pervye*] things appeared in their journal: *War and Peace*, *Fathers and Sons*, etc., not to speak of the earlier years, and the public remembers that, after all).... The main thing is that reliably every year, every subscriber knows, three or four articles will appear, the most apt, the most characteristic, and necessary at the present time, and the newest, and, the main thing, they will be only in their journal and not in any other—the public knows this. (29/1:23–24)

Although Dostoevsky did not include *Crime and Punishment* in the list of "the most important things" that had been published in the *Russian Herald*, he was well aware that it belonged there. In the same letter he continues, "In 1867 Katkov himself, in the presence of Liubimov and the editorial secretary, told me that they had gotten five hundred new subscribers, and attributed it to *Crime and Punishment*" (29/1:24). *Crime and Punishment* was published serially in the *Russian Herald* in 1866, sharing some issues with Tolstoy's *War and Peace*, and was generally regarded as marking a new level of artistic excellence in Dostoevsky's career, what Grossman has called "the full flowering of his creative powers."[16]

Konstantine Klioutchkine has analyzed the ways in which the plot of *Crime and Punishment* is "constituted by journalistic discourse," as Dostoevsky participates in a "media wave" of writing about crime and the conditions of urban life in the 1860s.[17] He also argues that "the text of the novel was engaged in and constituted by the flow of speech that circulated through the media and permeated all its products—the newspaper and the novel alike."[18]

Dostoevsky's September 1865 letter to Katkov reinforces how closely he followed current events as reported in the newspapers. As Klioutchkine argues, this is not a simple one-way process, since events in the novel as it was being published serially seemed to be reflected in events happening in Russia after its conception, like the murder and robbery of a pawnbroker and his female servant committed by the student A. M. Danilov in January 1866 (7:349). Dostoevsky later referred to this incident as an example of the way in which his "fantastic realism" could foretell events in modern life:

> I have completely different ideas about reality and realism than our realists and critics. My idealism is more real than theirs. Lord! If you were only to narrate what we Russians have lived through in the last ten years of our spiritual development—wouldn't the realists scream that that's a fantasy! But meanwhile it's true, real realism! It's that that is realism, only a deeper one, and theirs swims in the shallows.... With their realism you won't be able to explain a hundredth part of real facts that actually happen. But with my idealism I've prophesied even facts. It has happened. (28/2:329; letter to A. N. Maikov of December 11 [23], 1863)[19]

Crime and Punishment deals not only with murder but with what Strakhov later called "an extreme and characteristic manifestation of nihilism." The attempt on the life of Tsar Alexander II by Dmitrii Karakozov, which happened on April 4, 1866, also during the publication of *Crime and Punishment*, could be seen as yet another instance of Dostoevsky's prophetic powers.[20] Part of the way in which *Crime and Punishment* participated in what Klioutchkine calls the "air of the media" was its engagement with the story of the nihilists, or "new people," that had been inaugurated with Turgenev's *Fathers and Sons* (see 7:336). At the beginning of 1865, Strakhov had listed in *Epoch* the works that had already appeared in this series of novels depicting the "new people": first Turgenev's *Fathers and Sons*, then Pisemsky's *Troubled Seas* and V. P. Kliushnikov's *Mirage* (all published in the *Russian Herald*); finally he lists Chernyshevsky's *What Is To Be Done?*, published in the *Contemporary*. Strakhov writes, "All of this turns around a single main point, namely, images of the new person, and if the business continues further in the same way, apparently we can expect quite a few novels of the same type" (7:336). It is interesting that Strakhov, a staunch antinihilist himself, includes *What Is To Be Done?* in this list, as if all these novels were merely attempting to describe the "new people" objectively, not taking sides for (Chernyshevsky) or against (Pisemsky, Kliushnikov, and in the view of the new people themselves, Turgenev). His later review of *Crime and Punishment*, which he clearly sees as belonging to the same series, also refuses to talk in terms of "for" and "against," and presents Dostoevsky as one who is not attacking the nihilists but trying to take them seriously.

The first chapters of *Crime and Punishment* had evoked an angry response from the radical critic G. Z. Eliseev, whose view of the novel was no doubt influenced in advance by the fact that it was appearing in Katkov's journal, which had already published the "antinihilist" novels of Turgenev, Pisemsky, and Kliushnikov. Eliseev thought that Dostoevsky was mounting an attack on the whole "corporation of students": "What rational goal can justify the depiction of a youth, a student, as a murderer, the motivation of this murder by scientific convictions and finally the extension of these convictions to the whole student corporation? Whom does this serve if not the obscurantists, who see the dissemination of enlightenment as the reason for all the evil in the world?"[21] Strakhov responds that this is an absurd accusation: "How is it possible to accuse students, one and all, not only of attempted murder, but of anything at all?" But unfortunately, he goes on, these days people will believe any absurdity: "We must remember that here a darkness, a deep darkness rules over people's minds; we have no firm, clear points of support for our judgments."[22] Strakhov's defense here echoes Katkov's constant refrain about the lack of firm moral and intellectual standards in the age of nihilism.[23]

Strakhov's further analysis gives Dostoevsky credit for not resorting to cheap ridicule of the "new people" as "ludicrous and nasty creatures, vulgar and repulsive." Dostoevsky has taken on "a more profound and difficult task." For all his faults, Raskolnikov is "a real person." His theory is not a superficial negation, like rejecting the custom of kissing women's hands (a slap at Chernyshevsky's *What Is To Be Done?*). "Instead of comic phenomena, before us the tragic takes place, that is, a phenomenon more human, worthy of sympathy, and not just laughter and indignation." Raskolnikov's terrible crime makes him a figure to be reckoned with: "While other nihilists peacefully enjoy life, not kissing their ladies' hands and not giving them housedresses and taking pride in it, Raskolnikov can't bear the negation of the instincts of the human soul, which led him to crime, and goes to prison. There, after long years of ordeal, he will probably be renewed and become fully a person, that is a warm, living human soul." Strakhov asserts that Dostoevsky has full compassion for his hero: "This is not laughter at the young generation, not reproaches and accusations, it is—a lament for them.... And so, for the first time we have before us the depiction of an unhappy nihilist, a nihilist who is suffering in a deeply human way.... [The author] has depicted nihilism for us not as a pitiful and savage phenomenon, but in a tragic form, as a perversion of the soul, accompanied by cruel suffering." It is the extreme and tragic nature of Raskolnikov's version of nihilism that makes it possible for us to sympathize with him, unlike the haughty, self-satisfied Bazarov.[24]

Strakhov's comparison of Raskolnikov with Bazarov is instructive on a number of levels. As discussed in chapter 3, Bazarov's death represents a kind of defeat of nihilism within the artistic space of the novel. At the end of *Crime and Punishment*, Raskolnikov is very much alive; moreover, we leave him on the brink of "a new story, the story of the gradual renewal of a person, the story of his gradual rebirth, his gradual transition from one world into another, of coming to know a new, hitherto unknown reality" (6:422). If we accept the general assumption of Dostoevsky's contemporaries that Raskolnikov is a representative of nihilism, then Dostoevsky has ensured that, unlike Turgenev's treatment of Bazarov, the final word has not been said about the representatives of that movement; to put it in simplest terms, they have not been condemned but have been granted a complicated, open-ended life.

Again, if we turn to Katkov's own analysis of nihilism in his second article on *Fathers and Sons*, we can see the kernel of Dostoevsky's approach in Katkov's discussion of true doubt, as opposed to simplistic negation. Katkov writes that "doubt neither assumes nor negates; doubt, real, true doubt, admits the possibility of opposite resolutions."[25] The "possibility of opposite resolutions" is a good phrase for the compelling complexity of Raskolnikov's character as elucidated by

Strakhov and others. In a sense, what Dostoevsky has depicted is not a nihilist but a true doubter, in Katkov's terms.

It is not surprising that Dostoevsky was capable of depicting one of the "new people" in a more nuanced way than the other "antinihilist" writers. Not only had some of his collaborators on *Time* been part of the radical youth, but he himself had been drawn to socialist ideas in the 1840s and had been imprisoned for it. Even after the Karakozov assassination attempt, Dostoevsky described radical youth in a far from black-and-white way in a letter to Katkov himself: "Our poor, defenseless Russian boys and girls have their own eternally existing *basic* point, on which socialism will still continue to be founded for a long time, namely, their enthusiasm for good and the purity of their hearts. There are countless numbers of swindlers and creeps among them. But all these little gymnasium students, little university students [*gimnazistiki, studentiki*], of whom I've seen so many, have turned to nihilism so purely, so wholeheartedly in the name of honor, truth, and genuine usefulness!" (28/2:154, letter of April 25, 1866, to M. N. Katkov). Even in his more clearly antinihilist novel *The Devils*, Dostoevsky gave us the figures of Shatov and Kirilov, who in their different ways fit the description in this letter. Nevertheless, the very fact that Dostoevsky placed his novel in the *Russian Herald* made him guilty by association in the eyes of radical critics and readers. Even a review that begins by saying that "Mr. Dostoevsky has carried out [his] task brilliantly, with a truthfulness that shakes the soul," ends by leveling a serious accusation: "He does not say directly that liberal ideas and natural sciences lead young people to murder, and young maidens to prostitution, but in an indirect way he gives us that impression." The review ends by lumping Dostoevsky with the third-rate writer Kliushnikov, whose novel *Mirage* (1864), also published in the *Russian Herald*, is one of the harshest of the antinihilist works published by Katkov.[26]

If one of the hazards of publishing in the *Russian Herald* was to be lumped in with hack writers like Kliushnikov, another was Katkov's insistence on exerting complete control over everything that appeared in his journal, a quality of his that had been well known since the time of the Tur polemic. Although Katkov's involvement with the *Russian Herald* had lessened after he took over the *Moscow News* in 1863, and Liubimov now handled most of the day-to-day decisions, we can see from Dostoevsky's correspondence with Katkov that when it came to major decisions relating to major writers, Katkov was still a hands-on editor. In a draft of a letter to Katkov of December 1865, Dostoevsky makes a bold demand: "If you intend to publish my novel, then I most humbly ask the editors of the

Russian Herald not to make *any* changes in it. I cannot agree to this *under any circumstances*" (28/2:147).

No reply from Katkov to this letter has survived, but by July 1866, it is clear from a letter Dostoevsky sent to his friend the writer A. P. Miliukov that the editors of the *Russian Herald* had not accepted any such ultimatum. Dostoevsky speaks of having been forced to rewrite a chapter based on a decision by Liubimov that was affirmed by Katkov. (The chapter in question is the scene in which the prostitute Sonia reads the story of the raising of Lazarus from the Gospel of John to Raskolnikov, chapter 4 of part 4 in the final edition, 6:241–53.) Dostoevsky's anguish over this interference in his work is clear: "I can't say anything to you about this chapter; I wrote it with true inspiration, but perhaps it is wretched; but their problem is not with literary worth, but with fears about *morality*. In this I was correct—there was nothing against morality and even *extremely the opposite*, but they see something else and, besides that, they see traces of *nihilism*.... This reworking of a large chapter cost me at least three new chapters of work, judging by labor and anguish, but I corrected it and submitted it.... I don't know what will happen next, but this opposition of views between me and the editors that is starting to be discovered is beginning to worry me terribly" (28/2:166).

Despite his worry and indignation, Dostoevsky clearly did not want to irritate Liubimov or Katkov. The ultimatum he had made in December 1865 was not made from a position of strength. In a letter written to Liubimov a few days before the letter to Miliukov, Dostoevsky writes that he has reworked the passage and hopes that it will be satisfactory. Apparently referring to a criticism Liubimov had made, he writes: "*Evil* and *good* have been separated in the highest degree, and there is no longer any possibility of mixing them up or misinterpreting them. I have uniformly made all the other corrections you indicated, and even a bit more, it seems. More than that: I even thank you that you gave me the chance to look over the manuscript again before publication: I can say decisively that I would not have left it without correction myself." But he continues with yet another ultimatum, only this time in a beseeching tone: "And now I have my *greatest* request: *for the love of Christ*—leave all the rest the way it is now. Everything you said, I have carried out, everything has been separated, delimited, and is clear. *The reading of the Gospel* has been given a different coloration. In a word, permit me to rely on you completely: protect my poor work, most kind Nikolai Alekseevich!" (28/2:164). Dostoevsky is similarly conciliatory in a letter to Katkov eleven days later, in which he writes, "I trust you completely as a literary judge—all the more, since I myself have the strange characteristic: after writing something, I completely lose the possibility of having a critical attitude to what I have written, for a certain length of time, at least" (28/2:167). He nevertheless begs for the restoration of a certain passage; apparently Katkov did not honor his request. Dostoevsky's letter appears to be in answer to a letter from Katkov, in which Katkov writes, "I earnestly entreat you not to complain because I permitted myself to eliminate several of your added explanatory lines regarding the character and conduct of Sonia.... I will only say that not a single essential feature in the artistic depiction has suffered. The removal of moralizing passages has only given the depiction a greater objectivity" (28/2:437).[27] These words evoke the Katkov of the Tur polemic, the Katkov who considered his own judgment superior to anyone else's, and who could not help adding his own correctives to the work of his contributors.

The "opposition of views" that Dostoevsky identified in his letter to Miliukov is similar to the opposition of views between him and Katkov in relation to the public reading of *Egyptian Nights* by Mrs. Tolmachova in 1861. The key issues for Katkov in that controversy were the sexual content of Pushkin's poem, and the danger posed to morality by its public reading by a woman, while Dostoevsky tried to move the discussion of "the woman question" to the area of general human rights, not sexual emancipation. From Dostoevsky's point of view, it was as though Katkov could not see beyond the issues of conventional morality to the need, in the face of Kamen'-Vinogorov's attacks, to defend Mrs. Tolmachova as a person worthy of respect, not just a woman overstepping the bounds of propriety.

In his letter to Miliukov about the disputed scene in *Crime and Punishment*, Dostoevsky says, "There was nothing against morality and even *extremely the opposite*." This implies that Liubimov and Katkov were so fixated on Sonia's sexual degradation that they could not acknowledge the higher "morality" that made her worthy of carrying the word of Christ. The "traces of nihilism" that Dostoevsky says Liubimov and Katkov found in the chapter may be due to the fact that the motif of the "good" prostitute is a nihilist trope, most prominently displayed in Chernyshevsky's *What Is To Be Done?* and parodied in Dostoevsky's *Notes from Underground*. Nevertheless, it must be pointed out that, whatever the changes Liubimov and Katkov imposed, the scene of the "harlot [*bludnitsa*]" reading the Gospel to the murderer remains as one of the most powerful scenes in the novel: "The candle-end had long been dying out in the crooked candleholder, dimly illuminating in that beggarly room the murderer and the harlot who had strangely come together over the reading of the eternal book" (6:251–52).

Unfortunately, Dostoevsky's original manuscript for the chapter in question has not survived, so we have no way of knowing exactly what Liubimov and

Katkov objected to. This has not, however, stopped later critics and scholars from speculating. As early as 1889, eight years after Dostoevsky's death and two years after Katkov's, the *Russian Herald* offered its own interpretation of what had happened. In a note accompanying the publication of the letter to Miliukov quoted above, that had just come to light, the editors describe the incident as follows:

> The [chapter] in which is described Raskolnikov's visit to Sonia, an unfortunate woman who supports the existence of her family with her sad trade, and their reading of the Gospel, aroused certain doubts in the editors, and M. N. Katkov could not make up his mind to print the chapter in the form in which the author submitted it. Fyodor Mikhailovich, whose relations with the editors were always amicable and compliant, agreed to rework it, which is talked about in the letter. From the letter it is clear that it was not easy for him to renounce his conception of the exaggerated idealization of Sonia, as a woman who had taken self-sacrifice to the point of such a horrible sacrifice. Fyodor Mikhailovich significantly shortened the conversation accompanying the reading of the Gospel, which in the original version of the chapter was much longer than what remains in the printed text. N. A. Liubimov undertook to arrange this business, inclining Fyodor Mikhailovich to compliance and moderating the demands of Mikhail Nikiforovich.[28]

This note is similar to Katkov's version of the story as presented in his letter to Dostoevsky.

The note in the *Russian Herald* implies that the editors' changes have only improved Dostoevsky's text, eliminating the "exaggerated idealization" of Sonia and shortening a "much longer," and by implication, unnecessarily long, passage. In contemporary criticism, and especially in the discourse surrounding Katkov, it sometimes feels as if it is heretical to suggest that any editorial changes could actually improve the work of writers we now acknowledge to be "great." But there is no question that Dostoevsky is often accused (and accuses himself) of longwindedness, and certainly the figure of Sonia has been seen by some readers as an unbelievably idealized creature. Is it possible that Katkov's interference actually intensified the power of this famous scene?

No such speculation could be allowed during the Soviet period. Leonid Grossman's discussion in his 1965 biography of Dostoevsky is typical: "Such are the fragments and remnants of this chapter, scribbled all over by the red pencils of Katkov and Liubimov, shortened and modified by Dostoevsky himself at their behest to the point of unrecognizability, even to the point of changing the coloration of this dramatic scene."²⁹ He goes on to speculate in great detail about Liubimov's motives (without giving any sources): "The Gospel was the official foundation of the Russian state. Professor Liubimov could not allow any liberal treatment of it. He categorically objected to the depiction in the novel of the reading of this bulwark of Orthodoxy by a street woman who had taken on the role of a spiritual pastor. Can it be allowed for a prostitute to appear in the office of a priest? The author of the novel is placing the dregs of society higher than the greatest institutions of the church and of the supreme power. He is losing moral criteria and falling into nihilism."³⁰ This is an eloquent imagining of what was going through Liubimov's (and by extension, Katkov's) mind, but it fails to take into account one important fact: in the novel as published in the *Russian Herald*, there is still a long, detailed, and powerful scene of a prostitute reading the Gospel and serving as a spiritual guide to Raskolnikov.

Grossman's speculations are mild compared to those of V. Ia. Kirpotin in 1970, who claims that Katkov was looking for any pretext to get back at Dostoevsky for mocking his "obtuse hypocrisy" in the *Egyptian Nights* polemic: "The differences between Dostoevsky and the *Russian Herald* had not been completely overcome, and as soon as the opportunity presented itself, Katkov put his surgeon's knife to work."³¹ Kirpotin bases part of what he imagines to have been in Dostoevsky's original scene on a misquotation of the note in the 1889 *Russian Herald* quoted above. Where the journal note reads that Sonia "had taken self-sacrifice to the point of such a terrible sacrifice," Kirpotin for some reason quotes the text as saying "to the point of the sacrifice of her body." From this he concludes that Dostoevsky must have depicted her giving her body to Raskolnikov in the disputed scene, since it was already clear, from the earlier chapters of the novel that the *Russian Herald* printed, that she had sacrificed her body to passersby; therefore, the scene was censored because in it Sonia became Raskolnikov's lover.³² He goes on, "The text rejected by the *Russian Herald* illuminated the union between Raskolnikov and Sonia, it turned Sonia from a public woman, as the journal so elegantly put it, into the beloved and the wife of Raskolnikov."³³

More important for Kirpotin than the sexual issue is the political one. Liubimov and Katkov committed what Kirpotin calls a "crime," because "in the lost pages the 'secret' of Sonia was revealed." They must have been very busy with their surgeon's knives, because they managed to eliminate the evidence that Sonia is a Christian heretic whose secret "amounts to the interpretation of the Gospel in the spirit of utopian socialism, [amounts] to Christian socialism." Sonia was too naïve to realize this, but Katkov did, and that, even more than the scene's sexual connotations, was why he had to censor it.[34] Like Grossman, however, Kirpotin fails to account for the fact that in the novel as published, Sonia remains one of the most positive characters, and does in fact end up as the beloved and perhaps the wife of Raskolnikov.[35] It is true that she does not appear to be a nihilist or a socialist, but it is hard to follow Kirpotin in believing that that would have been part of Dostoevsky's original conception.

The contemporary review by D. I. Pisarev displays most clearly that, whatever changes Liubimov and Katkov elicited from Dostoevsky, a radical interpretation of Sonia's character could still be made with great power. He writes that Dostoevsky creates a kind of new world in which

> everything is happening inside out and our usual ideas about good and evil cannot have any binding force. What can you say, in fact about Sofia Semionovna's [Sonia's] act? What feeling does that act arouse in you: contempt or reverence? What will you call her for that act: a dirty trollop who has thrown the holiness of her feminine honor into a street puddle, or a magnanimous heroine who has accepted her martyr's crown with calm dignity? What voice was this girl to take as the voice of conscience—the one that said to her, "Sit home and endure to the end; dying from hunger along with your father, your mother, your brother and sisters, but keep your moral purity to the last minute," or the one that said, "do not spare yourself, do not protect yourself, give away all that you have, sell yourself, disgrace and soil yourself, but save, console, support these people, feed and warm them if only for a week, no matter what it takes"? I very much envy those of my readers who can decide such questions on the spot, carelessly and unwaveringly.[36]

Certainly we would like to know what was in the disputed chapter before Dostoevsky revised it, but there is little basis for agreeing with Grossman and Kirpotin that the changes demanded by Katkov amounted to a drastic devaluation of the figure of Sonia.

The Devils

The problems with *Crime and Punishment* were a mild prelude to the serious interference that Dostoevsky experienced with *The Devils*, the third novel he published with Katkov. (There is no documentation of any serious problems with the publication of the novel that followed *Crime and Punishment*, *The Idiot*, but it was not as great a success with the public as *Crime and Punishment*.) As with *Crime and Punishment*, one of the most famous documents of Dostoevsky's conception of this work is to be found in a letter to Katkov, written in October 1870. Dostoevsky outlines the basic plot of the novel, well calculated to please Katkov, as it is an "antinihilist" fictionalization of a notorious case of murder among the young radicals, the killing of the student I. I. Ivanov by five members of the secret society "The People's Summary Justice," led by S. G. Nechaev (29/1:442). But in one of his frequent attempts at staking out a zone of independence from Katkov, Dostoevsky also declares that the antinihilist plot is not what primarily interests him: "In my opinion, these pitiful monstrosities are not worthy of literature"; he dismisses the character of the radical mastermind as having turned out to be a comic figure (29/1:141). The antinihilist element of the plot is only "stage properties and set-up" for the actions of the "main character of the novel," Nikolai Stavrogin: "It seems to me that this character is a tragic one.... I set about writing an epic poem about this character because I have wished for a very long time to depict him. In my opinion, it is both a Russian and a tragic character.... I took him out of my heart.... But wait to judge me until the end of the novel, my dear Mikhail Nikiforovich! Something tells me that I will be able to deal successfully with this character. I won't explain him in detail now; I'm afraid of saying something wrong. I will only note one thing: this whole character has been recorded by me in scenes, actions, and not in discussions; consequently, there is hope that the character will come out successfully" (29/1:142).

One of the most important "actions" through which Dostoevsky attempted to "record" Stavrogin's character appears in the chapter "At Tikhon's." In this scene, Stavrogin visits a monk and has him read a confession he has written, in which Stavrogin describes having sexually abused a very young girl who then hanged herself. The chapter comes near the middle of the novel; serial publication was held up for a year as Liubimov waited for Katkov's final decision as to whether it could be included. Although the chapter had been typeset for the December 1871 issue, and although Dostoevsky actually wrote another, less explicit version in an attempt to placate Katkov, finally the chapter "At Tikhon's" was omitted when this part of the novel was published in the November-December issue of the *Russian Herald* for 1872.[37]

Unlike the disputed chapter in *Crime and Punishment*, in this case we have much more information about what Dostoevsky had wanted to include in the novel. The original version of "At Tikhon's" survives in the form of the proofs for the December 1871 issue of the *Russian Herald*; the other major variant of the text is a partial copy made by Anna Grigorievna Dostoevskaia from an unknown manuscript (12:237–38). The text of the A. G. Dostoevskaia copy seems to represent an attempt by Dostoevsky to revise the chapter in such a way as to make it acceptable to Liubimov and Katkov. In the later version of the chapter, both the explicitness of Stavrogin's crime and his insistence on taking full responsibility for it are removed. The revisions even call into question the fact that a crime took place, suggesting that it might have been a "psychological misunderstanding."[38] Nevertheless, the chapter was not found acceptable by the *Russian Herald*, and was not published in any form until 1922.[39]

There is a vast literature on the omitted chapter and its implications for Stavrogin's character, as well as questions of whether it should be included in modern editions of the novel.[40] The focus of the following discussion, however, is a narrower one, centering on what the omission says about Katkov's relationship with Dostoevsky.

As with the *Egyptian Nights* controversy and the disputed chapter in *Crime and Punishment*, the differences between Dostoevsky and Katkov in this case center on issues of sexuality. Just as in the *Egyptian Nights* controversy Dostoevsky had admitted that Mrs. Tolmachova's reading might be harmful for the young people in the audience, in the case of "At Tikhon's," he had betrayed some uneasiness in a letter to his niece Sofia Aleksandrovna Ivanova in January 1871. Her sister Mariia Aleksandrovna Ivanova, probably inspired by the fact the *The Idiot* had been dedicated to Sofia, had asked for his work in progress to be dedicated to her. Dostoevsky tells Sofia that this is "completely impossible":

> In the novel ... there will be passages which, although they can be read even by a young woman, it would be bad to dedicate to her. One of the main characters in the novel confesses secretly to another character a certain crime he has committed. The moral influence of this crime on this character plays a major role in the novel, but the crime, although I repeat, one can read about it, is not fit to be dedicated. When you dedicate, it is as if you say publicly to the person you are dedicating the work to: "I was thinking of you when I wrote this." (29/1:164)

Dostoevsky's insistence that "one can read" the passage betrays some anxiety on his part; it sounds like "protesting too much." Dostoevsky clearly believed that Liubimov's and Katkov's objections had to do with sexuality; a later letter to Sofia speaks of his having revised the chapter "in order to satisfy the chastity of the editors" (29/1:227). It is not necessarily a matter of Katkov's personal sensibilities, however; he was adept at practicing a kind of voluntary self-censorship to keep the official censors from interfering in his publications. The publication of "At Tikhon's" is a different situation than that of the disputed chapter in *Crime and Punishment* (unless we accept Kirpotin's wilder hypotheses about a sex scene between Sonia and Raskolnikov). It is not simply a matter of describing a prostitute as a positive character, which was not unprecedented in Russian literature of the mid-nineteenth century. Dostoevsky's frank depiction of child molestation would have shocked most Russian readers of the time, including the official censors.

Although the most obvious reason for the rejection is the sexual content of the chapter, what may also be at stake is the fact that the Stavrogin plot was part of Dostoevsky's own artistic program, and from Katkov's point of view could only distract from the main, antinihilist thrust of the work, centered on the character Piotr Verkhovensky, who was based on the infamous radical Nechaev. In Dostoevsky's artistic universe, Stavrogin's confession is the culmination of a decade-long engagement with the theme of "the insulted female child." But for Katkov this sensational and potentially attention-grabbing episode had nothing to do with what he had defined in his articles on Turgenev as the artist's task, to be "a son of his time, a citizen of his country," engaged with the political issues of the day.

A. S. Dolinin advanced a similar hypothesis in his 1922 article on Stavrogin's confession. After cataloguing the novel's "passionate attacks on revolutionary youth," calculated to arouse "a storm of indignation in the camp of [Dostoevsky's] political opponents," Dolinin argues that the inclusion of "At Tikhon's" would have undermined that impact. He imagines Katkov arguing that this "Marquis de Sade" element would weaken, if not completely distort, the sociopolitical message of the novel: "This must be approximately what the politican Katkov said to the politician Dostoevsky, and these arguments might have been effective."[41] Dolinin makes a convincing argument about "the politician Katkov," but whether the "politician Dostoevsky" would have prevailed over the artist Dostoevsky in this matter is more doubtful.

It is impossible to say whether Dostoevsky finally acquiesced to the elimination of the chapter or was simply forced to accept it. In April 1872, seven months before the chapter was definitively excluded, he was still arguing for its vital importance in a letter to Liubimov. After describing the revised version of the chapter, in which "everything that's very scabrous has been thrown out," he writes,

> I swear to you, I could not help but leave in the essence of the matter, this is a whole social type (as I believe), *our* type, a Russian type, the type of the person who is idle

not out of a desire to be idle, but having lost connection with everything that is native to him, and, what is the main thing, having lost faith, debauched *out of anguish* [*iz toski*], but having a conscience and exerting martyr-like, convulsive efforts in order to be renewed and begin to believe anew. Alongside the nihilists this is a serious phenomenon. I swear that it exists in reality. (29/1:232)

For Dostoevsky the phenomenon of Stavrogin deserved to be investigated "alongside the nihilists," and his crime of child molestation was an inseparable part of his characterization. The fact that Dostoevsky did not include the chapter when he published the novel in a separate edition does not prove that he was convinced that it didn't belong there, as some critics have claimed. As Dolinin points out, the separate edition appeared almost simultaneously with the *Russian Herald* edition, and to include the chapter, even assuming it could have passed the official censorship, would have drawn undue attention to his differences with Katkov and to the bombshell nature of the episode. As Dolinin argues, "To introduce a chapter with such a sensational plot (which had perhaps already evoked a lot of gossip, even if only in a limited circle) into the separate edition at the same time that it was absent from the just published edition—would that not mean to make this chapter even more prominent, to draw particular attention to it."[42]

Katkov's censoring of "At Tikhon's" has become a central element in the condemnation of his dealings with Dostoevsky, especially by Soviet critics. A representative example is the 1989 analysis by Iurii Kariakin, which like that of Kirpotin with regard to *Crime and Punishment*, surmises that Katkov interfered in Dostoevsky's text because he was moved by a petty spirit of revenge for having been bested in the *Egyptian Nights* polemic in 1861. Kariakin refers to Dostoevsky's defense of Pushkin's work against charges of unseemliness. He calls Dostoevsky's defense of Pushkin in that polemic, his claim that the depiction of Cleopatra produces "not an obscene but a shattering impression," "a magnificently precise self-evaluation of the chapter 'At Tikhon's.'"[43] In other words, in defending Pushkin in 1861, Dostoevsky was providing a self-defense in advance for his creation of "At Tikhon's" in 1871. Kariakin is correct in identifying a kinship between Dostoevsky's defense of the depiction of sexuality in art as advanced in the *Egyptian Nights* polemic and his later advocacy for the publication of "At Tikhon's," as I have argued elsewhere.[44] But he gives an oversimplified and unfair account of Katkov's role in that polemic, making it sound as if Katkov's target were Pushkin himself, which was not the case. As we have seen, Katkov objected specifically to the public declamation by a woman of a fragmentary and sensational text by Pushkin (Kariakin never mentions the role of Mrs. Tolmachova in the controversy).

Despite this focus on Katkov's supposed sanctimoniousness, Kariakin goes on to dismiss the role of sexuality in Katkov's rejection of the chapter as a red herring. Instead Kariakin claims that what is really at stake is a deeper inability by Katkov to accept the characterization of the holy man Tikhon whom Stavrogin visits. Tikhon is a non-standard spiritual adviser who reads forbidden literature, may be an alcoholic or a heretic, and says to Stavrogin, "Complete atheism is more worthy of respect than the indifference of a member of high society" (11:10). According to Kariakin, it was this supposed flouting of Orthodoxy, and not the sexual content of the chapter, that bothered Katkov. Kariakin writes, "Is it not too naïve to present such arch ideologues and politicians as Katkov and Pobedonostsev as meek guardians of 'chastity' and nothing more? It was advantageous for them to reduce the whole question to that, while in fact the matter consisted of a deep antagonism of worldviews between them and Dostoevsky, Pushkin, and art in general."[45]

Kariakin introduces here, alongside Katkov, Konstantin Petrovich Pobedonostsev, adviser to the tsar and later Ober-Procurator of the Holy Synod, although there is no evidence that he played a direct role in rejecting "At Tikhon's." He was, however, one of the people to whom Dostoevsky read the chapter and who advised against including it in the novel. To return to Kariakin's major conclusion, one must ask why, if there was a "deep antagonism of worldviews" between Katkov and Dostoevsky, Katkov nevertheless published four of Dostoevsky's five major novels and maintained a professional relationship with him up to the time of the writer's death. In Soviet scholarship, the fact that Katkov gave Dostoevsky the platform for the most important and substantial part of his oeuvre has seemingly been outweighed by his interference in the text of *The Devils* and, to a lesser extent, *Crime and Punishment*. As Kirpotin did in the case of *Crime and Punishment*, but with more justice, Kariakin refers to Katkov's rejection of "At Tikhon's," and the resulting impossibility of creating a text of *The Devils* that fully reflects Dostoevsky's artistic conception, as a "crime": "We are to this day paying for Katkov's crime against our culture and we do not realize it, we deceive ourselves."[46]

The absence of "At Tikhon's" from the published text of *The Devils* ensured that the novel would be perceived as part of the antinihilist canon. In a typical contemporary response, D. I. Minaev lumped Dostoevsky together with Pisemsky, Kliushnikov, and Leskov (author of yet another antinihilist novel published in the *Russian Herald, At Daggers Drawn* [*Na nozhakh*, 1870]), seeing this as a sad comedown for the author of *Notes from the Dead House*. Minaev describes Dostoevsky and Leskov as participating fully in the Katkov program, as advanced in the *Russian Herald* and the *Moscow News*: "Educated [*vospitannye*] according to the program of the *Russian Herald*, [they] have put their free creative work at the complete disposal of the clever Moscow leader of a den of thieves [*pristanoderzhatel'*] and write in stages, as if for a competition, multivolume novels and all kinds of stories on assigned topics." Like Leskov, Dostoevsky is perceived as a mere creature of Katkov: "[They have] become *Katkovized* [*okatkovilis'*] to such a degree that in their latest novels *The Devils* and *At Daggers Drawn* they have merged into a single type, a homunculus that was born in the famous inkwell of the editor of the *Moscow News*." Minaev concludes that *The Devils* and *At Daggers Drawn* constitute not independent artistic works, but mere illustrations for the editorials of the *Moscow News*, "seasoned with the nervous-sickly analysis of F. Dostoevsky and the Vidocq-like penetration of [Leskov]."[47]

As we have seen from Dostoevsky's letter to Katkov when he was beginning the publication of *The Devils*, the psychological portrait of Stavrogin, of which "At Tikhon's" was the cornerstone, was the part of the novel that belonged more to Dostoevsky's own artistic program than to the political program of Katkov, and was of more importance to Dostoevsky than his satire of the nihilists. The reaction of Minaev, who sees Dostoevsky turning out major novels on the "assigned topics" of the "Katkov progam," was Dostoevsky's worst nightmare. Katkov's interference had had a serious impact on the reception of the novel. If "At Tikhon's" had been included in *The Devils*, it would have complicated the novel's major thrust, would no doubt have inspired vigorous discussion only tangentially related to politics, and would have made it harder to pigeonhole the novel as a standard antinihilist piece of hackwork.

Another contemporary review, by the radical theorist P. N. Tkachov, gives some sense of the problem. Tkachov sees Stavrogin as a highly unsuccessful attempt by Dostoevsky at illustrating his theory about the Russian man as one who constantly wants to commit daring acts but then strives toward meek repentance and self-flagellation: "It is this person, daring to do anything and then repenting, that Mr. Dostoevsky endeavors to depict in the eccentric little son of Varvara Petrovna [Stavrogina]. But the element of repentance is shaded in [*ottenen*] extremely weakly. Although Stavrogin patiently endures slaps in the face 'for his sins,' in general he doesn't repent very assiduously."[48] The "element of repentance" in Stavrogin's character of course emerges most vividly in "At Tikhon's," which did not appear in the novel as published, thus distorting the general outlines of his personality and making such criticisms seem quite valid.

Dostoevsky Takes a Break from the *Russian Herald*

Dostoevsky published his next novel, *A Raw Youth*, in the more liberal *Notes of the Fatherland* in 1875, after Katkov refused to offer financial terms that were acceptable to him (29/1:318, 528). After his experience with *The Devils*, it is not terribly surprising that Dostoevsky only half-heartedly tried to place this novel with Katkov, and, although hurt and offended, was on one level relieved that Katkov did not meet his terms so that he could accept the offer for it from the *Notes of the Fatherland*.[49]

When *Crime and Punishment* was published, one reviewer noted that the profundity of Dostoevsky's analysis of the psychology of a murderer had given rise to rumors that he himself had "cut someone's throat or something like that."[50] This tendency of the public to think that an artist is incapable of imagining the psychology of a crime unless he has committed it himself was even more damaging to Dostoevsky's reputation in the case of *The Devils*. Even though "At Tikhon's" was not published, Dostoevsky had read it to several people in order to get their opinion about the justice of Katkov's objections. In 1978 V. N. Zakharov demonstrated that the persistent rumors that Dostoevsky had himself molested a child can be traced back to the conflict with the *Russian Herald* over "At Tikhon's": "Someone or other talked about the exceptionally scabrous plot of the rejected chapter, someone or other found the scene of the corruption of Matriosha suspicious. Dostoevsky suspected certain contributors to the *Russian Herald* of spreading these rumors."[51] Dostoevsky's close colleague N. N. Strakhov was responsible for giving the rumor wider currency after Dostoevsky's death, when he wrote to Tolstoy, in an 1883 letter that was published in 1913, that Dostoevsky had boasted of raping a little girl in a bathhouse.[52]

Zakharov bases his assertion that Dostoevsky "suspected certain contributors to the *Russian Herald*" of spreading rumors about him on a notebook entry Dostoevsky made in 1876, apparently as notes for a reply to an article by V. G. Avseenko: "Filth. Av[seen]ko found filth in *A Raw Youth*. . . . He proclaimed that the *Russian Herald* corrected my filth. I didn't answer. There was no such thing. From what sources." (24:235). The reference to the *Russian Herald* "correct[ing] my filth" alludes to Avseenko's review of *A Raw Youth*. After describing *A Raw Youth* as taking place in "a stifling and gloomy underground," Avseenko characterizes the novel as unseemly and immoral, directing particular attention to Dostoevsky's depiction of the young narrator's struggles with his own sexuality (a depiction that can now be recognized as brilliantly ahead of its time). Avseenko claims that the defect of unseemliness had not been as prominent in Dostoevsky's earlier works, thanks to the "significant omissions" made in the texts by "the editors of the *Russian Herald*, where Mr. Dostoevsky used to publish." Avseenko continues, "His new editors probably turned out to be less exacting, and now Mr. Dostoevsky appears in his own, uncorrected form. One cannot help but regret this."[53]

Although the review of *A Raw Youth* referenced above was published in the *Russian World*, Avseenko had been a contributor to the *Russian Herald* since 1873, and his negative reviews of the novel must have been keenly painful for Dostoevsky, as they were in effect a slap at him from the journal to which he had been contributing major artistic works for a decade. Dostoevsky's letter to his wife of December 20, 1874, reveals the degree to which he was hurt and alienated by Katkov's refusal to meet his terms for *A Raw Youth* at virtually the same time that he was offering Tolstoy a far higher rate for *Anna Karenina*. Dostoevsky had read in the *Citizen* that Tolstoy had sold his novel to the *Russian Herald* for five hundred rubles per printer's sheet, while Katkov had refused to give him 250 rubles per sheet: "No, I am valued far too cheaply, because I live by my work" (29/1:370).

A Raw Youth, the one major novel that Dostoevsky did not publish in the *Russian Herald*, is generally considered the weakest of the series of novels that began with *Crime and Punishment* and ended with *The Brothers Karamazov*, which marked Dostoevsky's return to working with Katkov. Although *A Raw Youth* is a complex and intriguing work in which Dostoevsky experiments both with form and with new psychological subject matter, it lacks the narrative drive and political energy that has made his other works compulsively readable to this day. It is hard to say to what extent the different character of *A Raw Youth* can be attributed to Dostoevsky's temporary departure from a partnership with Katkov that was fruitful and challenging, in both a positive and negative sense. It cannot be denied, however, that Dostoevsky's return to the *Russian Herald* was marked by his weightiest and perhaps most enduring contribution to the canon of Russian and world literature, *The Brothers Karamazov*. It is this novel that, as Frederick Griffiths and Stanley Rabinowitz have shown us, "created within the form of the novel a monumental surpassing of the novel that leaves off where the epic tradition takes up."[54]

Another essay by Avseenko, which appeared in the *Russian Herald* itself in January 1876, shows even more clearly the extent to which Dostoevsky's relationship with the *Russian Herald* had deteriorated.[55] In this essay Avseenko repeats his criticisms of *A Raw Youth*, calls it one of Dostoevsky's weakest works and basically a rehash of *The Devils*, and accuses Dostoevsky of exceeding "certain boundaries set by the established demands of seemliness and taste": "We think that in depicting filth and the horror of moral degradation, a novelist must not overstep the lines beyond which an artistic impression ends and the dirty anatomy of an infected organism begins.... In *A Raw Youth* there are details that outrage an educated feeling, there are filthinesses that in our opinion are decisively impermissible in a literary work."[56]

What is most offensive, however, in view of Dostoevsky's dismay at hearing the price Tolstoy had received from Katkov for *Anna Karenina*, is that the first half of Avseenko's essay is devoted to effusive praise of Tolstoy's novel as the best and most important work to have appeared in the past year: "Everyone is carried away by the author's artistic talent, everyone has felt the inexpressible charm of the story, everyone, according to their aesthetic capabilities, has enjoyed the marvelous richness of colors which are bright and soft at the same time, stimulating the eye with their rich multifariousness and plunging the soul into a contemplative calm, thanks to the secret art with which the author has managed to reconcile this rainbow-like, festive array of colors into the unity of general tone."[57] Avseenko goes on to make a statement that was calculated to cut Dostoevsky to the heart: "[Tolstoy's] success is so great that in this respect he stands apart from any competition."[58] Immediately after this apotheosis of Tolstoy, Avseenko moves on to the dismissal of *A Raw Youth* quoted above.

Avseenko's over-the-top praise of *Anna Karenina* appeared in January 1876, while the novel was in the process of serial publication in the *Russian Herald*. By the spring of 1877, however, Tolstoy was to endure a similar experience to the one Dostoevsky had had with *The Devils*, as Katkov refused to publish the eighth and final part of *Anna Karenina* in the *Russian Herald*. The problems surrounding *The Devils* were known to a limited circle of writers and critics who were personally acquainted with Dostoevsky and Katkov, but the average reader would have remained unaware of what was going on behind the scenes. The scandal of *Anna Karenina*, however, was a public one. It will be discussed in the next chapter, which will deal with Katkov's literary relationship with Tolstoy.

CHAPTER 6

KATKOV AND TOLSTOY

ANNA KARENINA AGAINST THE *RUSSIAN HERALD*

In their initial dealings with Katkov, both Turgenev and Dostoevsky made efforts to tailor the conception of their novels to conform to the program of the *Russian Herald*. *On the Eve* centered on the struggle of Bulgarians, as Slavs and Christians, against their Ottoman overlords; and *Fathers and Sons*, at least as originally conceived, participated in Katkov's campaign against the nihilists. In pitching *Crime and Punishment* to Katkov, Dostoevsky used Katkov's own discourse about nihilists from his essay on *Fathers and Sons* to describe the novel's conception, and *The Devils* was perceived by contemporaries as one of the series of antinihilist novels published and promoted by the *Russian Herald*. The case of Tolstoy, who began publishing in the *Russian Herald* in 1859, after his break with the *Contemporary*, is quite different. Eduard Babaev has called Tolstoy "the model of the independent thinker," who found it virtually impossible to submit to the program of any journal.[1] But as William Mills Todd III has explained, journal publication was far more lucrative than publication of separate editions, so Tolstoy could not afford to dispense entirely with venues like the *Contemporary* and the *Russian Herald*.[2]

Tolstoy's attitude toward Katkov in his letters once they begin collaborating is polite and proper, but he never approaches Katkov as a petitioner, the way Dostoevsky and to a lesser extent Turgenev do. He also never addresses him "as one writer to another," as Dostoevsky did, apparently sincerely. There are no letters from Tolstoy to Katkov at all similar to Dostoevsky's long and detailed outlines of *Crime and Punishment* and *The Devils*. The first three works that Tolstoy published in the *Russian Herald*, *Family Happiness* [*Semeinoe schast'e*, 1859], *The Cossacks* [*Kazaki*, 1863], and *Polikushka* (1863), do not seem to be conceived with the *Russian Herald* particularly in mind, either in a conciliatory or a polemical sense.[3] *War and Peace*, the first parts of which were published in the *Russian Herald* in

1865 and 1866 under the title *1805*, does at first glance appear to suit the Russian national program of Katkov. Vast and imposing in size and scope, it is beautifully designed to promote the national "self-consciousness" that Katkov called for in his earliest articles on Pushkin (although the *Russian Herald* was sharply critical of the philosophy of history expounded in the novel's later parts).[4] *Anna Karenina*, the work that led to Tolstoy's violent break with Katkov, is something different. While Dostoevsky clashed with Katkov over a single chapter in *The Devils* that departed from Katkov's program, a close look at *Anna Karenina* reveals that the entire novel is ideologically opposed to many of Katkov's most cherished plans and ideals.

In 1864, when considering whether to publish *War and Peace* in a journal as opposed to a separate edition, Tolstoy wrote to Katkov, "Of all the journals, I would prefer to publish it in the *Russian Herald* for the reason that it is the only one I read and subscribe to" (61:58). As a reader and subscriber, Tolstoy had absorbed the various aspects of the program of the *Russian Herald*, and in *Anna Karenina* he called them all into question: England as a model for Russia, the promotion of railroads, the development of industry alongside agriculture, the growth of credit institutions, the Russification of the western provinces, classical education, the education of women, spiritualism, and, most prominently, the participation of Russian volunteers in the Serbian war with the Ottoman Empire. In this chapter we will consider the ways in which *Anna Karenina* derives narrative energy from attacking the program of the *Russian Herald* in the pages of the *Russian Herald*. A close reading of articles from the *Russian Herald* casts new light on the context of the novel's conception, and the directed nature of Tolstoy's response to Katkov's editorial program.

A "Non-Contemporary" Writer

Katkov's letters to Tolstoy in the early years of their collaboration take a very different tone from that of the proud, imperious editor known to the public from the time of the polemic with Tur. Tolstoy's social position, wealth, and literary talent seemed to cow Katkov, who had the reputation of a social climber overawed by the high nobility. Tolstoy dictated his financial terms to Katkov, and Katkov almost always agreed to them. In response to an 1865 letter from his cousin Aleksandra Andreevna Tolstaia (1817–1904) in which she asked in dismay why he had quarrelled with Katkov, Tolstoy wrote, "Why do you say I have quarrelled with Katkov. I never dreamed of it. In the first place, because there was no reason, and in the second place, because between me and him there is just as much in common as between you and your water carrier" (61:115). Yet for Katkov, Tolstoy was the greatest hope of Russian literature. In letters of 1861–62, before the publication of Tolstoy's most famous works, Katkov tried to persuade Tolstoy to abandon his activities connected with theories of pedagogy and educating the Russian peasant and to return to his true calling, literature: "With all my heart I wish life to 'Yasnaya Polyana' [Tolstoy's journal on education]; but of the success of your strictly literary activity, of its fruitful and important significance, of the truth of your calling, I am deeply convinced—and there is no need for wishing"; "Don't forget your true calling, and whoever is familiar with what you have already done cannot doubt your true calling"; "Having read [your pedagogical article], I became completely convinced that you are sinning against your calling.... I write you frankly, precisely by virtue of my respect for you, for your talent, for that significance that you have and should have in our literature."[5] In accordance with his faith in Tolstoy, Katkov was willing to pay him vastly more than any other writer.[6]

In the same letter to A. A. Tolstaia, Tolstoy went on to express his disdain not only for Katkov but for journalistic discourse as a whole: "I neither sympathize with a person who forbids the Poles to speak Polish, nor do I get angry with them for it, and I do not indict the Muraviovs and Cherkasskys, and it is completely the same to me who slaughters the Poles or took Schleswig-Holstein or pronounced a speech at the meeting of the *zemstvo* institutions. And butchers kill the bulls we eat, and I am not obligated to indict them or sympathize with them" (61:115). Here Tolstoy adopts a stance of indifference regarding some of the burning issues of the day, such as the intensification of the imposition of the Russian language in Poland and the western provinces after the 1863 Polish uprising, a "Russification" strongly supported by Katkov in the ensuing decades. Mikhail Nikolaevich Muraviov (1796–1866) served as the governor-general of Vilna and became known as the "hangman" because of the cruel measures he took to suppress the insurrection. Edward Thaden notes that Muraviov, "a very unpopular figure who had once been considered an enemy of progress and justice for the peasants, was suddenly transformed into a sort of national hero—especially in the pages of M. N. Katkov's *Moskovskie vedomosti* (*Moscow News*)." As reforms were being planned for Poland, Muraviov and Vladimir Aleksandrovich Cherkassky (1824–78) belonged to the "patriotic party" promoted by Katkov's *Moscow News*. The dispute between Denmark on the one hand and Prussia and Austria on the other over Schleswig-Holstein merited its own rubric in many issues of the *Moscow News*. S. V. Beriozkina has shown that Katkov saw the Schleswig-Holstein issue in relation to questions of Russia's own territorial integrity.[7]

A similar attitude toward current events is expressed in a letter Tolstoy wrote to the historian M. P. Pogodin in November 1868, jocularly proposing that they start a journal called the *Non-Contemporary* (*Nesovremennik*), which would devote itself to "everything that could count on lack of success in the nineteenth century and on, if not success, then on readers in the twentieth and later centuries." The publication would concern itself with history, the philosophy of history and the raw materials of history; the philosophy of natural sciences and the raw materials of these sciences; mathematics and applied sciences; and art—"non-contemporary" art. What would be excluded would be "only that which now fills 99 percent of all the printing plants of the world with work, that is, criticism, polemics, compilations, that is, unproductive nonsense and cheap and rotten goods for consumers who are poor in intellect" (61:207–8).

Most famously, Tolstoy wrote to P. D. Golokhvastov in September 1874 that "there is no such thing as a not-vile journal, and *Notes of the Fatherland* is vile in its own vile way, and the *Russian Herald* is vile in its vile way that is opposite to the vile way of the former, and there is no middle ground" (62:114). This letter was written, however, several months after Tolstoy had written to Katkov to state that his terms for publishing *Anna Karenina*, should he decide to publish it in a journal, would be five hundred rubles per printer's sheet (62:70). He had also considered placing the novel in the other "vile" journal, N. A. Nekrasov's *Notes of the Fatherland* (62:124–25). As Boris Eichenbaum has wittily noted, there is a clear link between Tolstoy's unsuccessful attempt, in October 1874, to borrow ten thousand rubles from A. A. Fet for a land purchase and his definitive agreement with Katkov for an advance of that sum as a condition of selling *Anna Karenina* to the *Russian Herald*, as we know from a dismayed letter to Tolstoy from N. N. Strakhov in November 1874.[8]

Tolstoy may have planned to maintain his stance of disdain for everything "contemporary" as he wrote and published *Anna Karenina*, but as several critics have noted, the novel became more and more engaged with the contemporary scene and with current events as its serial publication proceeded.[9] The first parts of *Anna Karenina*, covering the events corresponding to parts 1 and 2 and the first twelve chapters of part 3 in modern editions, were published in the *Russian Herald* in the January, February, March, and April issues of 1875.[10] These chapters set in motion the stories of the novel's upper-class characters: marital discord in the home of Stiva and Dolly Oblonsky, the adulterous romance of Anna and Vronsky, Liovin's unsuccessful proposal to Kitty Shcherbatskaia, and Liovin's life on his country estate.

In May 1875, the *Russian Herald* published a review by V. G. Avseenko in which he defended the novel-in-progress against critics who were unhappy with its lack of engagement with contemporary social issues. Avseenko reproaches readers for demanding novel characters. According to him, it is only in the "ephemeral stratum of society" that "new people" appear, "formed on the pattern of the latest journal idea" and influenced by "everything that is carried on the wind." The traditional nobility offers something different: "But in our society, despite all its shakiness [*rasshatannost'*] and dissoluteness [*raspushchennost'*], there exists something more rich in content and stable than this ephemeral stratum. The milieu traced in *War and Peace* and *Anna Karenina* (it is the same old-nobility, Moscow milieu) has its own life, its own historical and life traditions that present a significant resistance to the new currents."[11] In January 1876, Avseenko published yet another essay in the *Russian Herald* that touched on *Anna Karenina*, praising it extravagantly: "[With his huge artistic talent] Count Tolstoy has crushed all objections that have arisen upon the reading of his novel." Again Avseenko refers to Tolstoy's choice of a high-society milieu, seemingly detached from the burning questions of the contemporary moment. After noting that some novelists in this transitional time feel more comfortable with historical subjects, where they deal with "generations that have already finally expressed and explained their ideals," he includes Tolstoy's latest novel in the category of "historical," because "in the foreground of the action is the old society, while figures of a new pattern appear only as accessories, still poorly elucidated."[12]

This is the same essay by Avseenko that contrasted the brilliant artistic success of Tolstoy's novel-in-progress with Dostoevsky's *A Raw Youth*, the publication of which in the *Notes of the Fatherland* had concluded in December 1875. Avseenko labeled *A Raw Youth* one of Dostoevsky's weakest efforts, which depicted the kind of "filth" ["*griaznosti*"] that should not be allowed in a literary work. But in referring in January 1876 to *Anna Karenina* as a historical novel because of its focus on the hereditary nobility, Avseenko was echoing the ending of Dostoevsky's novel itself. *A Raw Youth*, which for most of its length is narrated by a callow nineteen-year-old, Arkadii Dolgoruky, ends with the voice of the young man's tutor Nikolai Semionovich, who has read the manuscript of the novel we too have just read and offers his assessment of it in a letter to Arkadii. As has often been noted, Nikolai Semionovich voices some of Dostoevsky's own feelings about his rival Tolstoy, setting up an opposition between the novelist who chooses to remain safely in the "historical" milieu of the hereditary gentry and the one who plunges into chaotic contemporary society, with its decomposition of social forms.[13]

Nikolai Semionovich writes, "If I were a Russian novelist and had talent, then I would certainly take my characters out of the Russian hereditary nobility, because only in that cultural type of Russian people alone is there possible even an appearance of beautiful order and a beautiful impression, so necessary in a novel for an elegant effect on the reader."[14] Nikolai Semionovich goes on to say that such a writer would have no choice but to write in a historical genre, because

> such a beautiful type no longer exists in our time.... Such a work, even by a great talent, would belong not so much to Russian literature as to Russian history.... The grandson of those characters who were portrayed in a picture that portrayed a Russian family of the middle-high cultural circle over the course of three generations in a row and in connection with Russian history—this descendant of his ancestors could no longer be portrayed in a contemporary type in any other way than in a somewhat misanthropic, solitary, and undoubtedly sad form.

The work that depicted a Russian family "in connection with Russian history" is *War and Peace*; and the "misanthropic grandson" is Liovin in *Anna Karenina*.[15]

No reactions by Tolstoy to either Avseenko's articles or Dostoevsky's ending to *A Raw Youth* have come down to us. But as publication of *Anna Karenina* resumed in early 1876, contemporary issues of the kind that were to be banned from the *Non-Contemporary* began to occupy a much more prominent place in the novel, most strikingly in the scene of the dinner party at Stiva Oblonsky's (February 1876), in the extensive summary of Liovin's book on agriculture (April 1876), and continuing to the novel's controversial end. It is as if Tolstoy was demonstratively rejecting any idea that *Anna Karenina* is a historical novel, untouched by what Nikolai Semionovich calls "nostalgia for the present moment [*toska po tekushchemu*]" (Dostoevskii, *PSS*, 13:455). It is this engagement with current events that led to Tolstoy's violent break with Katkov in the spring of 1877.

It is well known that Katkov refused to publish the eighth and final part of *Anna Karenina*, probably because of its harsh treatment of the movement of Russian volunteers traveling to Serbia to assist the "brother Slavs" in their struggle with the Ottomans, and that Tolstoy had to resort to publishing it as a separate brochure. What is less obvious is that part 8 of *Anna Karenina* is only the most blatant and explicit attack on some of Katkov's most favored policies and programs to be found in it. In his extensive, illuminating work on *Anna Karenina* and its context in print culture, Todd has pointed out that the *Russian Herald* published articles on many of the current topics discussed by the characters in *Anna Karenina*.[16] But the *directedness* of Tolstoy's novelistic discussions *against* the policies of Katkov and the *Russian Herald* merits further study. The attack on the Russian volunteer movement in part 8 was not a sudden, unanticipated burst of negativity towards one of Katkov's pet causes; it was only the last in a series of such attacks within the novel, and no doubt had the effect of a last straw. To understand the context of Katkov's rejection of part 8, it will help to consider in some detail the ways in which *Anna Karenina*, both in its initial general conception and in its intensified engagement with current events beginning in February 1876, is permeated by opposition to the program of Katkov's journal, that program that Katkov had been vigorously defending since the journal's inception twenty years before.

England as a Model for Russia

As discussed above, Katkov was well known for his Anglophilia, and he had promoted English institutions and culture beginning with the first issues of the *Russian Herald*. Articles on Parliament, the English jury system, English courts, and figures such as Sir Robert Peel, Lord Palmerston, and William Gladstone are a constant feature of the journal. Novels by Wilkie Collins, Charles Dickens, and Anthony Trollope appear in Russian translation, often in the same issues as the installments of *Anna Karenina*.[17] In "A Ticklish Question," Dostoevsky lampooned Katkov's slavish admiration for English institutions, conflating him with Turgenev's character Pavel Petrovich in *Fathers and Sons*. Katkov's associate E. M. Feoktistov attested that Katkov would carefully excise all unfavorable opinions about England from articles destined for the *Russian Herald*, which Herzen had nicknamed the "Westminster Herald."[18]

Tolstoy made subtle, varied, and satirical use of the French language in *War and Peace*. French continues to be a major linguistic and cultural presence in *Anna Karenina*, but alongside it, English language, culture, amusements, and consumer products play a central role. As with the use of French in *War and Peace*, sometimes English is a benign or neutral presence, such as the English nicknames of Dolly and Kitty. But England is most closely associated with the tragic and violent story of Anna and Vronsky: the English novel, seemingly by Trollope, that Anna tries to read in the train returning home after her initial infatuation with Vronsky;

Vronsky's English jockey Cord, who trains the mare Frou-Frou, destroyed by Vronsky's blunder during the steeplechase; Cord's daughter Hannah, whom Anna, not long before her death, takes in as her ward, at a time when she is neglecting her own daughter; the frivolous atmosphere of Princess Betsy's dacha, where her guests play croquet and she has a "cosy chat" with Anna (the words are given in English in the original); and the faddish lawn tennis, perambulators, baby toys, and luxury goods at Vronsky's estate. As Dolly thinks in looking around her room there, "Everything produced in her an impression of abundance and foppery [*shchegol'stvo*] and that new European luxury about which she had read only in English novels, but had never seen yet in Russia and in the country."[19] But the most pervasive and most ominous manifestation of English influence in the novel is the railroad. It was in England that the development of the steam locomotive made the railroad a means of mass transportation in the mid-nineteenth century, a revolution that soon spread throughout Europe.

The Railroad

From its beginnings in 1856, the *Russian Herald* published numerous articles on the need to establish and expand railroad lines in Russia, as part of the modernization that Russia's defeat in the Crimean War had revealed the need for. Articles on the railroad appear alongside articles on land reform, industrialization, and the development of credit operations, as part of the general discussion of Russia's economy in preparation for the emancipation of the serfs and the other great reforms of the 1860s. The discussion of railroads in the journal is at its most intense in 1856 and 1857, but significant articles continue to appear in the 1860s. The general thrust of these articles is well represented by one of them in particular, "On Railroads in Russia," by D. I. Zhuravsky (1821–91), in the May 1856 issue. The contribution by Zhuravsky is a measure of the quality of writers the *Russian Herald* was able to attract. He was a brilliant engineer who had taken part in the design and construction of the bridges for the first major railway line in Russia, the Nicholas Line from St. Petersburg to Moscow (1842–51), and had won the prestigious Demidov Prize from the Academy of Sciences in 1855. At the time he contributed to the *Russian Herald* he was working on a railroad line from Moscow to Oriol. In 1857–58, he engineered a metal spire to replace the wooden spire of the Peter and Paul Cathedral in St. Petersburg. From 1877 to 1889 he was the director of the Department of Railroads in the Ministry of Transport.

In his forty-page article, Zhuravsky argues that railroads are needed to improve the material, intellectual, and moral life of Russia, increasing the productive forces of the state and developing Russia's material wealth. He points out that all European peoples have become convinced of the necessity of railroads, which are a marker of the degree of a country's enlightenment: "Material well-being gives man independence; independence engenders a feeling of one's own worth, respect for oneself as a person, which constitutes a reliable principle of moral improvement. So we can say that railroads, which in the highest degree promote the rapid development of industrial powers and the increase of the material wealth of the people, also serve as a powerful mover for the intellectual and moral development of humanity."[20] Zhuravsky even claims that railroads will promote peace among nations, causing the interests of private persons in various states to become interwoven, so that "the declaration of war between two peoples will encounter the more obstacles the greater the mass of the population loses its capital from the cessation of peaceful relations." Railroads "increase the means of defense of enlightenment against barbarism."[21] Zhuravsky quotes French railroad engineer Auguste Perdonnet as having said that if Russia had had a railroad to transport troops to the Crimea, it could have successfully defended Sevastopol. Zhuravsky's quotation of Perdonnet concludes, "'Let us congratulate ourselves that Russia does not have at its disposal this terrible weapon, and let us say that *railroads present the state with a powerful means of defense!*'"[22]

Zhuravsky sees another advantage of railroads: they make it possible for people to live within easy traveling distance to the capitals. He notes that, thanks to the Nicholas Line railroad (which he helped to build),

> inhabitants of St. Petersburg now rent dachas seventy to a hundred versts away and even further, for example in Vyshnii Volochok, 350 versts away, where life is cheaper in many ways than near the capital. Making it cheaper to travel to St. Petersburg and making it possible to arrive there in a short time permits a greater mass of people than previously to take advantage of proximity to the capital, where capital [in the monetary sense—S.F.] and social pleasures are concentrated. This is in part how the civilizing influence of railroads is expressed.[23]

Zhuravsky's utopian message is clear:

> Railroads, which make movement quick and cheap, will not only give greater value to the natural riches that cover and fill the Russian land, will not only call to life the

material powers of the country, but will serve the development of its intellectual and moral powers, and also will give the state the possibility of preserving its independence with less expense than before.[24]

In 1863, well before he conceived *Anna Karenina*, Tolstoy had reacted against the optimistic view of railroads presented in the *Russian Herald*, in the course of responding to the journal's assessment of his pedagogical activities. Although Katkov had promised in a letter of April 15, 1862, that he was going to write about Tolstoy's pedagogical journal *Yasnaya Polyana* in the *Russian Herald*, instead there appeared an article by Evgenii Markov, "Theory and Practice of the Yasnaya Polyana School: Pedagogical Remarks by a Tula Teacher," in the May 1862 issue.[25] Markov's article is respectful but ultimately dismissive of Tolstoy's pedagogical theories and his definition of education. Markov describes the tone of *Yasnaya Polyana* in terms that may be familiar to anyone who has read Tolstoy: "The deficiencies of our schools have struck him to such a degree that he has fallen into a strange extreme. He acts as if before him the earth had been moving in a false orbit, and he was the first to whom it fell to turn it back into its true path. You would think that pedagogical experience began only today."[26] In rejecting the theoretical bases of Tolstoy's pedagogy, Markov, like Katkov in his letters to Tolstoy, seems to be trying to push Tolstoy back into the role of artist, constantly praising him for the poetic, picturesque, artistic pictures he paints of his school: "Whoever does not draw from this reading useful psychological and pedagogical conclusions *will at least receive aesthetic enjoyment*."[27]

In his response to Markov's article, published in the last issue of *Yasnaya Polyana* (no. 12, 1863), Tolstoy reacted not only to Markov's criticism but to the entire program of "progress" promoted in the pages of the *Russian Herald* from its inception, in particular to "the so highly praised steamships, steam locomotives, and machines."[28] Tolstoy rejects the idea that "the application of steam to travel and to factory production" will increase the well-being of the people at large. He writes of "a Tula muzhik who is very close and well known to me," and says the man

> has no need to make rapid journeys from Tula to Moscow, to the Rhine, to Paris, and back. The possibility of such journeys does not add to his well-being in the slightest. He satisfies all his needs by his own labor, and from food to clothing, he produces

everything himself: money does not constitute wealth for him. This is so true that when he has money, he buries it in the ground and does not find it necessary to make any use of it. Therefore, if the railroads make objects of manufacture and trade more accessible to him, he remains completely indifferent to this greater accessibility. He needs neither tricot, nor satins, nor clocks, nor French wine, nor sardines. Everything he needs and that in his eyes constitutes wealth and the improvement of well-being is acquired by his labor on his land. (8:343)

Tolstoy goes on to say that European political economy wants to prescribe its laws for Russia, while in fact railroads do not bring any benefits to the mass of the population, based on their own ideas of their needs and not the benefits "that the progress of civilization wants to forcibly thrust on them" (8:344). Far from increasing well-being, railroads destroy forests and increase "urban temptations" (8:344). This critique of the railroad would become a central issue in *Anna Karenina* over a decade later.

The centrality of the railroad to *Anna Karenina* is well known and well studied. Liza Knapp gives an excellent overview, tracing the ways in which the railroad "infiltrates the plot and form" of the novel: "The mobility that is so essential to the structure of the novel on the formal level, moving the plots along and allowing them to intersect, reflects changes in the fabric of life that were greatly disturbing to Tolstoy as he wrote *Anna Karenina*."[29] Anna meets Vronsky by accident at the St. Petersburg station in Moscow, as she arrives to visit her brother Stiva and happens to be in the same compartment as Vronsky's mother, whom he is meeting. On that same occasion, a railroad worker is accidentally run over by a train, an incident that Anna reads as a "bad omen"; Vronsky travels in the same train with Anna back to St. Petersburg, emphatically not by accident, and declares his love to her on the train platform during a stop along the way; Anna commits suicide near the end of the novel by throwing herself under a "goods train" ["*tovarnyi poezd*"]; and in part 8, we see Vronsky at a provincial railroad station, on the way to Serbia in the hope of finding death. At both the beginning and the end of the novel, a person is crushed by a train, and in the epilogue, trains are carrying the Russian volunteers, including Vronsky, to Serbia for the purpose of "vengeance and murder," in Liovin's words.[30] The *Russian Herald*'s vision of the railroad as an agent for material well-being, moral improvement, and peace-making is directly contradicted in *Anna Karenina*, where the railroad facilitates frivolous luxury, adultery, suicide, and war.

Credit, Industry, Agriculture

Although the railroad is associated mainly with the story of Anna, it is Liovin who provides a larger socioeconomic context for the meaning of the railroad and its interrelationship with agriculture, credit operations, and industrialization, in the long description of the argument of his book in progress that appeared in the April 1876 installment of the novel. This passage crystallizes many of the issues that had been discussed in the *Russian Herald* in the late 1850s, so it is useful to quote it in full. After his marriage to Kitty, Liovin has returned to work on his book "in which were to be set forth the bases of a new kind of economy [*khoziaistvo*; can also mean *farming*]":

> He was now writing a new chapter about the reasons for the disadvantageous position of agriculture in Russia. He was arguing that the poverty of Russia stemmed not only from an incorrect distribution of land property [*pozemel'naia sobstvennost'*] and from a false orientation of policy, but that this was fostered in recent times by an external civilization that had been abnormally grafted onto Russia, in particular means of communication [*puti soobshcheniia*], railroads, which brought with them centralization in cities, the development of luxury, and as a result of that, to the detriment of agriculture, the development of factory industry, credit, and its fellow-traveler stock-market gambling [*birzhevaia igra*]. It seemed to him that with the normal development of wealth in a state all these phenomena come only when significant labor has already been put into agriculture, when it has achieved correct, or at least defined conditions; that the wealth of a country must grow uniformly and in particular in such a way that the other branches of wealth do not overtake agriculture; that in conformity with the known state of agriculture there must be means of communication corresponding to it; and that with our incorrect use of the land, railroads, called forth not by economic but by political necessity, were premature and instead of the fostering of agriculture that was expected of them, having overtaken agriculture and called forth the development of industry and credit, had stopped it; and that therefore, just as the one-sided and premature development of one organ in an animal would hinder its general development, so for the general development of wealth in Russia, credit, means of communication, intensification of factory activity, which are undoubtedly necessary in Europe, where they are timely, here only caused harm, having pushed aside the main next-in-line question of the organization of agriculture.[31]

The argument of Liovin's book is embodied in multifarious ways in the dramatic action of the novel; it is also a refutation of the economic program promoted by the *Russian Herald*.

Soon after the passage quoted above, Liovin and Kitty are called to the aid of Liovin's brother Nikolai, who lies dying in a hotel. As Knapp has noted, the hotel is yet another example of the degradation of Russian life by the railroad: The hotel "was one of those provincial hotels built on new perfected models, with the best intentions of cleanliness, comfort, and even elegance, but which because of the public that patronizes them, turn with extreme rapidity into dirty inns with pretensions to modern perfections, and are made by virtue of that very pretension worse than the old, simply dirty hotels." Among the unpleasant details is "the cast-iron, ornamental, gloomy and unpleasant staircase." The hotel is marked by "dirt, dust, slovenliness everywhere, and together with it some kind of new modern railroad self-satisfied preoccupation."[32] In England, the development of railroad travel had given rise to new types of buildings, not only the railroad station but also the railroad hotel. Such hotels used cast iron and wrought iron for visible interior details, as a sign of modernity. A typical example would be the heroically scaled open staircase with ornamental railings in London's Midland Grand Hotel at St. Pancras Station, designed by George Gilbert Scott and opened in 1873.[33] In *Anna Karenina*, the detail of the "cast-iron staircase" is meant to evoke the railroad, not as a positive sign of progress and modernity, but as another omen of death. It is not by accident that the "cast-iron staircase" appears again at Vronsky's estate, in the hospital he is building. We see clearly through Dolly's eyes that the hospital, full of new technology (huge sheet-glass windows, "ventilation organized according to a new system," beds with unusual springs, new kinds of gurneys and wheelchairs), is being built not for the needs of the peasants (there are no maternity facilities) but as yet another empty display of Vronsky's wealth and imported luxury goods.[34]

The connection between railroads and the growth of credit operations noted in Liovin's book was a constant theme in the articles in the *Russian Herald* promoting the modernization of Russia after the Crimean War. A typical article is a summary of a speech given by I. K. Babst (1823–81), professor of political economy at the University of Kazan (at Moscow University from 1857), that appeared in August 1856 (the summary is probably by Katkov).[35] In a prologue, the summarizer speaks of "the convenience and inexpensiveness of railroads," and asserts that "most of the objections to social improvements arise from an incomplete understanding of the usefulness of these transformations."[36] He says that Babst sees the main motive force of national wealth in capital, and discounts fears of the influx of foreign capital: "But let us look more closely and attentively at this comforting and highly significant phenomenon of the migration of capital, let us look directly, and not through the poor spectacles of old theories and views, and the phenomenon will appear to us in a completely different guise. The more cheaply we can satisfy any economic need, the more advantageous for us, because it costs us fewer efforts.... We are rich in land, rich in natural products, but poor in capital that is necessary for the strengthening of our production, for the exploitation of the rich and varied products of our motherland, and that means it is obvious that it is much more advantageous for us to make use of cheap foreign capital."[37]

In the January 1857 issue, an article signed "E. L." speaks of the necessity of credit institutions for the development of railroads and industry: "In Europe and America the accumulation of capital has been helped by credit institutions, or so-called banks.... Banks do not establish railroads themselves, but by their mediating influence, bringing capital into movement, banks foster the animation of the spirit of enterprise, accustom people to using credit, and consolidate confidence in the benefits of the self-sufficient use of capital, without external support." According to this writer, as Zhuravsky had asserted about the railroad, credit institutions are a beneficial moral influence: "Credit institutions or banks, which fertilize productivity, also disseminate moral fruits in the state, developing feelings of honesty and the strict fulfillment of the obligations that the trading parties have taken upon themselves."[38]

A Soviet historian has summarized the economic program of the *Russian Herald* in the late 1850s: "A broad program of bourgeois reorganization of the country, and first of all its economy, is unfolded in the journal. Demands are advanced for the abolition of serfdom relationships, the acceleration of industrial development, the rationalization of agriculture, the establishment of free trade, and the expansion of credit." The education of the Russian public about credit institutions, banks, and the stock market continued in the pages of the *Russian Herald* into the 1860s, particularly in articles by the Belgian political economist Gustave de Molinari (1819–1912).[39]

Both Liovin in *Anna Karenina* and Katkov recognize the moral and social need for emancipation, but they disagree about the economic consequences and about the effects of industrialization on the healthy development of agriculture. Like Liovin, the writers in the *Russian Herald* link railroads and credit to agriculture, but they see modernization as having a beneficial effect. A typical view is expressed in the January 1857 issue by Iu. A. Gagemeister (1806–78), a senior official in the Ministry of Finance who helped develop the system of state banks in Russia. Gagemeister claims that agriculture can be perfected only with the help of capital and the knowledge acquired through industry and trade: "A surplus of capital and technical powers is always turned to the land. Land serves as the point of departure for the well-being of the nation [*narod*], and the brilliance of the nation finally reflects on the land. On this basis, agriculture has reached its highest state of perfection in states in which manufacturing is most developed, namely in Great Britain and in Belgium." Gagemeister explains that manufacturing industries open the way to improvements, and agriculture follows behind them with slow steps, borrowing from them working capital and technical aid, so that "neither Russia nor any other extensive country can renounce the establishment of factories and manufacturing industries if it wishes for the success of agriculture."[40]

Far from seeing a moral improvement in Russian society as a result of the introduction of railroads, banks, and stock markets, as promised by the contributors to the *Russian Herald*, Liovin sees moral corruption. This is dramatized in a conversation he has with his brother-in-law Stiva and the visitor Veslovsky as the three men spend the night in a barn during a hunting expedition. Stiva tells Liovin and Veslovsky about the hunting party he attended the summer before at the estate of Malthus, a "famous railroad magnate who was ingratiating himself with society and whom Stepan Arkadievich sincerely considered a fine fellow." Liovin reacts angrily, invoking the recently abolished practice of "tax-farming," which gave concessions to private individuals to collect taxes, usually on liquor, leading to huge profits:

> "I don't understand you," said Liovin, rising up on his mound of hay. "How are you not repulsed by these people? I understand that a lunch with Lafite is very pleasant, but is this luxury really not repulsive to you? All these people, like our tax-farmers earlier, acquire money, so that while making money they earn the contempt of people, they disregard this contempt, and then with what they dishonorably gained they buy themselves off of the former contempt. . . . Note that this evil, the acquisition of huge fortunes without labor, as it was with tax-farming, has just changed its form. *Le roi est mort, vive le roi!* They just managed to destroy tax-farming when the railroads and banks appeared: also acquisition without labor."[41]

Liovin is echoing a criticism of the system of railroad concessions that appeared in the *Herald of Europe* in June 1873: "At first concessions were given for this or the other railroad line without preliminary consideration of which was more necessary, and without any competition. Then the Strusbergs appeared here, concessionaires who, without their own capital, by entrepreneurship and speculation experience alone, in several years acquired huge fortunes. The former tax-farmers were resurrected in the person of the concessionaires of railroads, with the difference that the enrichment of the concessionaires was incomparably more rapid and less risky than the profits of the tax-farmers."[42] It is appropriate that Stiva, who in this scene defends the quick and easy profits of the new railroad barons and the banks, ends the novel as a "member of the commission of the united agency of the credit–mutual balance of southern railroads and bank institutions [*mesto chlena ot kommissii soedinennogo agenstva kreditno–vzaimnogo balansa iuzhno–zheleznykh dorog i bankovykh uchrezhdenii*]," a job title that sounds like a parody of the titles of articles in the *Russian Herald*.[43]

Russification

Besides large-scale economic questions, *Anna Karenina* deals with questions of politics and education that are also a central part of the program of the *Russian Herald*. The scene of Stiva Oblonsky's dinner party, which appeared in the February 1876 issue of the *Russian Herald*, has been called the "keystone" of the novel's structure by Elisabeth Stenbock-Fermor.[44] It is also the scene in which two of Katkov's most important causes, the Russification of the western provinces of the Russian Empire and the privileging of classical education in the Russian gymnasium (secondary school), are discussed, along with the question of women's education, a topic that also concerned Katkov, if to a lesser degree.

As discussed above, the Polish uprising of 1863 marked Katkov's emergence as a major political figure whose commentaries in the *Moscow News* were influential on both public opinion and government policies. As Thaden writes,

> Katkov pushed for vigorous measures to defend Russia's vital interests in the southwestern provinces. He advocated . . . the expropriation of Polish landowners involved in the revolt, increasing the number of Russian clergymen in the southwestern region, the expansion of Russian schools, tax relief for Russian peasants, the introduction of the Russian language into Roman Catholic services in the region, diminishing the influence of the Catholic clergy, the construction of railroads to speed up Russification, and the like. In so doing he gave full support to the brutal policies of General M. N. Murav'ev [Muraviov] in the Vilna region and

campaigned against the liberal or humanitarian policies favored by many bureaucrats, intellectuals, and journalists.[45]

The process of Russification continued into the 1870s under the direction of Minister of Education D. A. Tolstoy, "an anti-Catholic, anti-Polish bureaucrat trained in the school of Nicholas I, to Russify all levels of education in Poland."[46] D. A. Tolstoy (not a close relative of L. N. Tolstoy) also worked in tandem with Katkov on the reform of education in Russia as a whole, as will be discussed below.

The conversation about "Russification" in *Anna Karenina* is not as pointed as Liovin's attack on railroads, credit, and modernization, or the attack on the Russian volunteer movement that led to Katkov's refusal to publish part 8. Tolstoy may have wished to be cautious in view of the extreme sensitivity of this topic, which had been the cause of the closing of Dostoevsky's journal *Time*. As the men at Stiva's party enjoy vodka and hors d'oeuvres, they begin their political discussion: "Aleksei Aleksandrovich [Karenin] was arguing that the Russification of Poland could be accomplished only as a result of higher principles which must be introduced by the Russian administration. Pestsov was insisting that one people [*narod*] assimilates another only when it is densely populated."[47] Liovin's half-brother Koznyshev turns this into a witticism about bachelors and married men, saying that Stiva is the most patriotic of all because of his production of children.

The conversation is taken up again at the dinner table, over the soup, as Pestsov says to Karenin that he did not mean density of population alone, but also "fundamentals." Karenin replies, "'In my opinion, only a people that has a higher development can have an effect on another people, that ...' 'But that is the question,' Pestsov, who always rushed to speak and seemed always to put his whole soul into what he was talking about, interrupted in his bass voice, 'what we can assume as higher development. Englishmen, Frenchmen, Germans, who stands on a higher level of development? Who will nationalize whom?'" Karenin replies that "influence is always on the side of true education." This leads the conversation to the topic of education in Russia.[48] The question of "who will nationalize whom" based on which nation stands at a higher level of development is reminiscent of Strakhov's fatal 1863 article in *Time* on "the fatal question," in which he seemed to be arguing that Polish culture was far ahead of Russian culture in its level of civilization.

Although the substance of the discussion at Stiva's does not openly run counter to Katkov's advocacy of Russification, the phrase "Russification of Poland [*obrusenie Pol'shi*]" strikes a discordant note. In Katkov's editorials in the *Moscow*

News and articles in the *Russian Herald* on this topic, he is most concerned not with "Poland [*Pol'sha*]," but with the Western Territory [*zapadnyi krai*], the provinces on the Russian Empire's northwestern and southwestern edges, corresponding roughly to present-day Ukraine, Belarus, and Lithuania. Through the partitions of Poland by Russia, Prussia, and Austria over the course of the eighteenth century, sovereign Poland had ceased to exist. In Katkov's view, only the idea of Poland survived as a seditious and disruptive revolutionary element within the Russian Empire. He writes in an editorial of 1866, "Polish nationality is a political term. Where Polish nationality is recognized, there in principle a Polish state is recognized. But the Polish state lost its existence almost a hundred years ago, and history attests that it was a dead body long before its partition. Polish nationality [*natsional'nost'*] at the present time can be nothing other than a revolutionary principle, a protest against the existing state. The word Pole means nothing, or it means the citizen of a state that once existed, now does not exist and must be resurrected."[49] According to Katkov, the Western Territory was primordially Russian but has been polonized [*opoliachit'*] by an accident of history. For Katkov, people whom we would call today Belarussians and Ukrainians are pure Russians who have been subjected to the alien influence of Poland for centuries. So in the Western Territory, it is not a matter of Russification but of *re*-Russification, of eliminating the foreign Polish influence that has been imposed on the native Russian inhabitants of the Western Territory.

The intransitive verb *obruset'* means "to become Russian." The transitive verb *obrusit'* means "to make someone Russian." The former has the connotation of a natural, unforced process, what Thaden calls "unplanned Russification"; the latter involves coercion, and corresponds both to what Thaden has termed "administrative Russification," a "gradual introduction of Russian institutions and laws and extension of the use of Russian in the local bureaucracy and as a subject of instruction in schools," and to what he calls "cultural Russification," by which borderland minorities are made to accept "the language and cultural and religious values of the Russian people."[50] But in Katkov's writings, it is not clear that such a clear demarcation between natural, unforced Russification and forcible Russification exists.

One of Katkov's major themes is that the "Russian" inhabitants of the Western Territory who profess the Roman Catholic faith have been forcibly Polonized because the prayers, songs, and sermons in their church services are in Polish. Katkov, unlike other Russian conservatives such as I. S. Aksakov, advocated for the introduction of Russian into Catholic services in place of Polish.[51] Theodore

R. Weeks writes, "As a modern nationalist, Katkov believed in the possibility of 'Catholic Russians' and thus supported the use of the Russian language in Catholic churches in the northwest provinces.... Aksakov could not accept the concept of a 'Russian Catholic.'... In essence this was an argument over the predominance of either religion or language in determining ethnicity."[52]

Katkov agrees that Orthodoxy is the distinguishing feature of the Russian people [*narod*] as a historical phenomenon, as a nation [*natsiia*]. But he also believes that there should be religious tolerance and diversity within the Russian empire. If Catholicism is to be tolerated for Russian subjects, they should be able to use the official language of the Russian state in their observances, and this in itself may bring them back naturally to Orthodoxy: "If Orthodoxy is the basic elemental nature [*stikhiia*] of Russian nationality [*narodnost'*], then why does [an opponent of introducing Russian into Catholic services] fear Russifying [*obrusit'*] Catholics by means of the Russian language? Let these peasants feel that they are Russians, and they, even while preserving their rite, will feel themselves much closer to this basic element [*stikhiia*] of Russian nationality [*narodnost'*] than now, when they must recognize themselves as Poles."[53] The word *stikhiia* can refer to one's natural surroundings, the air one breathes, the water one floats in. For Katkov, Russification in the Western Territory is not a forcible imposition of something alien but a restoration of the natural elements in which the "purely Russian" inhabitants need to live and move and have their being. When Tolstoy uses the phrase "the Russification of Poland" in *Anna Karenina*, one can hear an echo of the 1865 letter in which he told his cousin he did not sympathize "with a person who forbids the Poles to speak Polish." Strangely enough, in his earlier drafts for the scene at Stiva's, the discussion was not about the Russification of Poland but about "the Russification of Russia [*obrusenie Rossii*]."[54] I have not encountered this strange phrase in any of the writings of the time, but it is consonant with Katkov's view of the process going on in the Western Territory.

Classical Education

Katkov was deeply concerned with education, and for him gymnasium study focused on classical languages and literature as well as mathematics was the only legitimate path to the university, where the leaders of Russia were formed. He had written a doctoral dissertation on pre-Socratic Greek philosophy, *Sketches of the Most Ancient Period of Greek Philosophy*, first published in P. M. Leontiev's series

Propylaea in 1851 and 1853.[55] Leontiev (1822–75) was a professor of classics at Moscow University who collaborated closely with Katkov on the *Russian Herald* and the *Moscow News* until his death in 1875. In 1868 the two men founded a lycée, the Moscow Imperial Lycée in Memory of Tsesarevich Nicholas (known casually as the "Katkov Lycée"), as a kind of laboratory for their ideas on classical education (Tolstoy's son Mikhail studied there in the 1890s [83:287n7]).

Katkov and Leontiev, whose personal and professional ties were so close that they were sometimes called "twins," were deeply involved in the development of the Gymnasium Statute of 1871, a process in which they used the megaphone of the *Moscow News* both to support and to goad Minister of Education D. A. Tolstoy. As Allen Sinel has written, "It was a volatile but mutually beneficial alliance. [D. A.] Tolstoi needed Katkov's and Leont'ev's [Leontiev's] expertise and their favorable press; they in turn depended on the minister's authority within the government to carry through educational reform and protect their journalistic enterprises."[56]

Joseph Backor has traced Katkov's interest in education to his Hegelian formation: "He learned from Hegel that the state should provide education necessary for everyday life and a higher humanistic education for future scholars. This higher humanistic education was to be based on familiarity with classical languages and civilizations, knowledge indispensable for 'training the mind in logical thinking' and for passing on values which shaped European culture and civilization—values 'which it would be perilous to bypass.'"[57] Katkov spoke in similarly idealistic terms to the journalist G. K. Gradovsky, in explaining the reasons for his zealous promotion of classical education as the only path to the university: "'I do not understand,' Katkov concluded, 'how a true scholar or writer could fail to appreciate all the intellectual and artistic riches that have been bequeathed to us by Greece and Rome. If we want to attain that state of society [*obshchestvennost'*], those political institutions that the leading Western peoples enjoy; if we wish to have enlightened men of state, outstanding scholars and writers, we must create the school that produces such minds, that lies at the basis of innovation, culture, the development of knowledge.'"[58] Gradovsky reports that he asked why Katkov did not introduce such arguments in his editorials in the *Moscow News*, where the constant theme was that the study of classical languages had to be forced on youth as a way of preventing the development of nihilistic ideas, associated in the 1860s with the study of natural sciences, as illustrated in Turgenev's *Fathers and Sons*. Gradovsky suggested that Katkov's more idealistic arguments would be more convincing to the intelligent public. According to Gradovsky, Katkov replied, "The point is not society. The intelligent part of society must understand, and no one asks the stupid people and ignoramuses. The reform is decided not in society, but in the Ministry, in government spheres. ... Can you really get through to these spheres by arguments about scholarship, enlightenment, tasks of political significance?" Gradovsky continues, "And Katkov burst out laughing ironically. 'What are our men of state,' he continued. 'For the most part they are parquet-scrapers, masters of drill marching and obsequiousness. What is scholarship to them and what are they to it? Even the jurists and lycée graduates are nothing more than coached, trained [as animals are trained, *dressage*] civil servants. These gentlemen have to be convinced by arguments that enlightenment does not present the slightest danger, and that the classics will not lead to a republic, will not disturb the well-being of the police and will be a support for the existing order.'"[59]

One of these "trained civil servants" was A. I. Georgievsky (1829–1911), a student and protégé of Katkov and Leontiev who was appointed by D. A. Tolstoy to an important post in the Ministry of Education. He was their man in the ministry, who helped to push for the Gymnasium Statute of 1871, which privileged classical education, as the only path to the university, over the study of modern languages and natural sciences.[60] When Leontiev died in 1875, the *Russian Herald* published a thirty-page obituary for him in April, in the same issue as an installment of *Anna Karenina* (part 2, chapter 30, to part 3, chapter 12 in modern editions).[61] The obituary quotes a eulogy given by Georgievsky, including the following passage: "[Leontiev] saw the sole healing means [*tselebnoe sredstvo*] against the ulcer of materialism [*protiv iazvy materializma*] in the restoration of serious classical education, together with an upsurge of religious and patriotic feeling."[62]

Georgievsky's eulogy is evoked quite specifically in the scene of Stiva's dinner party, but in a new tonality very far from the solemnity of the commemoration of Leontiev. After Karenin states that only peoples with true education (or "formation," *obrazovanie*) can influence other peoples, Pestsov challenges him to identify the signs of true education. Karenin claims that such signs are well known, but Koznyshev expresses doubt. He suggests that despite the fact that the Gymnasium Statute of 1871 (which he does not mention specifically) would seem to have settled the question in favor of the classics, there are powerful arguments on the side of modern education: "I am a classicist by education, but in this argument I personally cannot find my place. I do not see clear arguments why classical studies are given precedence over the real [in the sense of *Realschule*, modern languages and natural sciences]." Pestsov takes up the argument, pointing out that natural sciences are just as beneficial as ancient languages for the development of logical thinking: "Take only astronomy, take botany, zoology with its system of general laws." Karenin responds that "the very process of studying the forms of languages has a particularly beneficial influence on spiritual development. Besides, one cannot deny either that the influence of classical writers is moral in the highest degree, while unfortunately with the teaching of natural sciences is connected those harmful and false doctrines that constitute the ulcer [*iazva*] of our time." As with the initial discussion of Russification, Koznyshev derails the conversation with a witticism. Karenin seemed to be quoting Georgievsky about the "ulcer of our time," and Koznyshev also quotes Georgievsky, but in a mocking, jocular vein: "'If there were not that advantage of the antinihilist influence on the side of classical sciences, we would have thought more, weighed the arguments on both sides,' Sergei Ivanovich said with a subtle smile, 'we would have given free scope to both trends, but now we know that in these pills of classical education lies the healing power [*tselebnaia sila*] of antinihilism, and we boldly offer them to our patients.... And what if there is no healing power?'"[63] The other guests burst into loud laughter at Koznyshev's joke about the "pills." In the context of the *Russian Herald*, they are laughing at the most cherished project of Katkov and his dear, recently deceased friend and colleague Leontiev.[64]

Education of Women

The conversation at Stiva's moves from education in general to the education of women, which brings it much closer to the central concerns of the novel. This too was a subject on which Katkov had expressed definitive views, perhaps most strikingly in an article in the *Moscow News* in 1873. In this editorial, Katkov argues that women should be educated in exactly the same way as men, since even if a woman remains within the sphere of the family, it would be beneficial for her to "rise to the heights of scholarship," because she will then bring "high intellectual development" into the education of her children: "If the world of domestic life is the sphere that is primarily appropriate for a woman, that does not mean that a woman is obligated to limit herself to the circle of cares prescribed to her by the old *Domostroi*."[65] But Katkov moves beyond the traditional wisdom that women should stay in the home, and argues a position that might surprise those who write him off as a hidebound conservative: "There is no basis for excluding woman from higher social professions." He asks, "Does every woman become the mistress of her own home, the mother of a family? Is there not everywhere and always a multitude of women who are not privy to the happiness and cares of family life? Must these women, often deprived of their lot in family life by accidental reasons, remain, like pariahs, deprived of any lot? There are always many women born in the best circumstances who have received an education for life in the highest social spheres, but who have remained without a crust of bread. Must they inevitably have to become cooks or seamstresses in order to earn their bread, finding all higher professions closed to them?"[66]

Katkov goes on to argue that women, while perhaps not best suited to government service, could be of great use in the professions of teaching and medicine. Once again, however, for women as well as men the only correct type of gymnasium education is a classical education of the kind being offered by Katkov's protégée Mrs. S. N. Fisher in her women's classical gymnasium, opened in 1872. For Katkov, higher education for women should not be equated with nihilism, as it had been in the 1860s: "Woman can prove her right to higher education not by cutting her hair, putting on glasses, taking a common-law husband [*grazhdanskii muzh*] and learning the creed of the new faith that consists in the fact that man is a beast and God does not exist."[67] In the classical gymnasium, women would derive the same advantages as men, presumably including the antinihilism influence: "The harmonious development of all mental [also spiritual] capabilities, a wealth of historical material taken directly from the sources, a treasure of ideas and images derived from the greatest works of human understanding and creation, direct familiarity with the basic elements of world civilization, thought cultivated in a practical way by the logic of the most perfect verbal organisms, thought that is capable of distinguishing the tiniest shades of meaning and of rising to the broadest generalizations, while maintaining constant control of itself, finally a noble skill for intellectual labor that turns into a need and becomes a source of highest enjoyments— these are the fruits which they will bring out of their instructional course."[68] Such a woman will find her "clear and firm understanding" to be a "reliable support amid temptations and trials."[69] Katkov's view of the moral nature of an intellectually developed woman is far from Tolstoy's depiction of Anna, whose intellectual interests grow as her moral degradation increases. Katkov writes, "A truly educated woman, with well-developed intellectual interests, with an independent thought that is capable of supplementing men's work not only in manual, unskilled labor but in intellectual labor, cannot help but become a true blessing for the social milieu where she appears in significant numbers, in various characters and callings."[70]

Tolstoy's character Koznyshev discusses classical education with flippant wit. Similarly, Katkov's heartfelt ideas about women's education are echoed in the conversation at Stiva's and ultimately dismissed with mocking humor. As the men consider the wisdom of educating women and allowing them to work in various professions, such as office assistant or telegraph clerk, they touch on the subject raised by Katkov, the woman who has to make her way in life without being in the secure position of wife and mother. On this topic the person who, like Katkov, speaks up for women without a family is Stiva, who is doing so not out of altruism but because he is thinking of his mistress, a pretty dancer.[71] There is a disturbing echo here of Tolstoy's March 1870 (unsent) letter to N. N. Strakhov, in which he took a very different position than Katkov did on the possible occupations of women without families of their own:

> There is no need at all to think up a way out for women who have finished having children and women who have not found a husband: for these women without offices, university positions, and telegraph agencies there always is and has been a demand that exceeds supply—midwives, nannies, housekeepers, debauched women.... You will probably be amazed that among these respected callings I include the unfortunate whores.... The fact that we need such a type of woman is proved to us by the fact that we have ordered them from Europe. (61:232)

Unlike Katkov, who asserts that women have intellectual capacities that are equal to if not better than those of men, in the scene at Stiva's the old prince Shcherbatsky, who often represents the voice of common sense and reason, interjects into the conversation the proverb "Woman's hair is long, but her wits are short."[72] The prince also gets the final, facetious word in the conversation about women's education. After the liberal Pestsov says, "A woman wants the right to be independent, educated. She is constrained, oppressed by the consciousness of the impossibility of that," the prince says, "And I am constrained and oppressed by the fact that they won't accept me as a wet-nurse at the Foundling Hospital."[73]

There is a coda to the men's conversation, however, in which Tolstoy's callous position expressed in his 1870 letter to Strakhov is refuted. After dinner, Liovin says to Kitty "that not a single family can do without a female helper, that in every poor and rich family there are and must be nannies, either hired or relatives." (He leaves out the debauched women mentioned in Tolstoy's letter to Strakhov.) Kitty responds, "A young girl may be so placed that she cannot enter a family without humiliation." Liovin's eyes are opened, "and he understood all that Pestsov had been arguing over dinner about the freedom of women only by the fact that he saw in Kitty's heart the terror of being an old maid and of humiliation and, loving her, he felt that terror and humiliation and immediately renounced his arguments."[74] Liovin's new position is more in line with Katkov's sympathetic question, "'Must these women, often deprived of their lot in family life by accidental reasons, remain, like pariahs, deprived of any lot?"

Spiritualism

Yet another burning issue of the 1870s that Tolstoy treats in *Anna Karenina* is spiritualism, but in this case he broached the subject before Katkov did. Once again, the positions of the two men prove to be at odds. In the first installment of *Anna Karenina* published in the *Russian Herald* in January 1875, Kitty's friend Countess Nordston starts a conversation about "table-turning and spirits" at the home of Kitty's parents, just after Liovin has proposed to Kitty and been rejected. Liovin fails to maintain his politeness when goaded by the countess to express his opinion: "'My opinion is only this,' Liovin answered, 'that these turning tables prove that so-called educated society is no higher than the peasants. They believe in the evil eye and spells and love potions, and we . . .'" When Vronsky attempts to argue that the appearance of spirits is "a new force as yet unknown to us," Liovin demolishes him:

> "When electricity was discovered," Liovin quickly interrupted, "then only the phenomenon was discovered, and it was not known where it came from and what it produces, and centuries passed after that before they even thought of applying it. But spiritualists, on the contrary, began with little tables writing to them and spirits coming to see them, and only then they began to say that it was an unknown force … with electricity every time you rub resin on wool a certain phenomenon is revealed, and here it doesn't happen every time, so that means it is not a natural force."[75]

At the time this installment appeared, the *Russian Herald* had not published anything connected to spiritualism, but by the time Tolstoy returned to the subject in part 7 of *Anna Karenina*, Katkov had brought his journal into the thick of the discussion. Although he refrained from taking the kind of unambiguous, forceful stand he normally did, there is evidence that his sympathies lay with the spiritualists.

As Ilya Vinitsky has described in *Ghostly Paradoxes*, his study of "the paradoxical refraction of various spiritualist ideas and doctrines in [Russian] realist literature," many Russian writers and cultural figures were interested and involved in spiritualism in the nineteenth century.[76] The report by the zoologist N. P. Vagner (1829–1907) that appeared in the *Herald of Europe* in April 1875 had a particularly strong impact.[77] As Vinitsky explains, "Vagner, a famous St. Petersburg naturalist, was calling on Russian society to take mediumistic phenomena seriously; to construct, through spiritualist séances, a solid scientific bridge between the material and spiritual worlds; and to resolve, through the summoning of souls and their scientific investigation, the long-standing debate between materialsm and spiritualism."[78]

The initial response in the *Russian Herald* was a skeptical article by the botanist and mathematician S. A. Rachinsky (1833–1902), who attempted to provide physiological and material explanations for the phenomena described by Vagner in his letter to the *Herald of Europe*. Katkov apparently was torn about publishing Rachinsky's article, and prefaced it with the following footnote: "We do not think that the opinions and explanations set forth by the respected author of this article would satisfy Mr. Vagner and other researchers who have conveyed their observations of these phenomena that have so unexpectedly intruded into scientific spheres that would seem to be most inaccessible to them. Therefore, leaving this question open, we are not averse to giving a place here for communications also from the other side."[79]

According to the managing editor of the *Russian Herald*, the physicist N. A. Liubimov, this footnote was the result of a certain amount of "bargaining" between him and Katkov, as Katkov apparently wished to come out more definitely in favor of taking spiritualism seriously. Liubimov reports that he had many arguments with Katkov about spiritualism: "Mikhail Nikiforovich defended the authenticity of the descriptions [by the adherents of spiritualism] with a certain exaggeration, and almost got angry at my skepticism." As Liubimov writes, "The description of spiritualist experiments, made by scientists who were carried away by spiritualism, seemed to Mikhail Nikiforovich to be the intrusion into the sphere of science of new facts that demanded explanations. That there must be facts of such a sort— this was not subject to any doubt for him. That which had seemed the fairytale narrative of an old nanny had suddenly found a place in scientific knowledge." But Liubimov also claimed that Katkov's "lucid sobriety of mind stopped him, despite his enthusiasm, from taking a stand on the side of the scientific adherents of spiritualism."[80]

Rachinsky's article is reminiscent of the position taken by Liovin in the first installment of *Anna Karenina*. Rachinsky writes that there are two categories of people who participate in mediumistic events.

> Some, happily the majority, take away an impression similar to that which they produced on me, that is, the movements of the table and the accompanying sounds seem to them to be the result of involuntary muscle movements of the people who are touching the table. The others, and these are mostly women, people inclined to mysticism or suffering from a more or less powerful nervous disturbance, come to the conviction that between the movement of the table and the muscle movements of those touching it there is no connection, and that the phenomena they see depend on some special unknown power.[81]

In October 1875, Katkov provided an opportunity in the *Russian Herald* for Vagner to counter Rachinsky's rationalist, Liovin-like argument. Katkov prefaced Vagner's article with a note explaining that "we give space to an article by such a well-known natural scientist, whose name, just as his position in science, give a particular significance to the strange information that he conveys."[82] Vagner's article is eighty-five pages long and contains detailed descriptions of the appearance of various spirits at séances in America and in Russia. The very length and prominence of the article seem to lend it credibility. Vagner's article is followed up in the November 1875 issue by another lengthy article by his spiritualist collaborator, the chemist A. M. Butlerov (1828–86). For almost fifty pages Butlerov presents arguments in favor of spiritualism, and concludes, quoting the British mathematician Augustus De Morgan: "The physical explanations which I have seen are easy, but miserably insufficient: the spiritualist hypothesis is sufficient, but ponderously difficult.... The spiritualists, beyond a doubt, are in the track that has led to all advancement in physical science; their opponents are the representatives of those who have striven against progress."[83]

Katkov also offered space to a third major adherent of spiritualism in 1870s Russia, A. N. Aksakov (1832–1902), in his memoir of P. D. Iurkevich, published in the *Russian Herald* in January 1876, in the same issue as an installment of *Anna Karenina* (part 3, chapters 13 through 32 in modern editions).[84] Iurkevich (1826–74), a professor of philosophy who became an ardent spiritualist, had done battle with the materialist philosophy of Chernyshevsky in the pages of the *Russian Herald* in 1861, in articles titled "From the Science of the Human Spirit."[85] The link with Iurkevich perhaps explains the interest of the normally hardheaded

Katkov in the phenomena of spiritualism, as yet another weapon in the battle with materialism and nihilism.

Aksakov writes, "For Iurkevich, as a true philosopher, educated in the succession of historical evidence, it was not even enigmatic; for him the possibility of phenomena of so-called spiritualism was completely clear; he saw in them only a new, intensified expression of the action of such properties of human nature as had been felt in all times, among all peoples, and now, making use of new conditions by the law of general progress, are manifesting themselves in more precise, concrete forms."[86] This allusion to "all times and all peoples" may well have resonated with Katkov. Vagner claimed that when he visited Katkov to see about publishing his response to the attacks on him, they had a long conversation about mediumistic phenomena, and Katkov "cited for me facts from the [twelfth-century] chronicle of Nestor that corroborated the appearance of people from the other world."[87]

In his letters Tolstoy seldom mentions articles in the *Russian Herald*, but the articles by Vagner and Butlerov elicited a vigorous response from him, in a letter to Strakhov of January 1876: "The articles in the *Russian Herald* upset me terribly." He says that he is struck by "the fact that muzhiks constantly see devils, and no one finds that that is a phenomenon worthy of attention, that these are facts; but Butler and Wurst [Tolstoy's contemptuous nicknames for Butlerov and Vagner] saw them, and I am supposed to believe them—those are facts. I would like to show that the stories of the muzhiks' devils are just as authentic as theirs, but that it is not Butler and Wurst, who have gone stupid sitting over a microscope or test-tubes, who deserve to be trusted, but the clear-headed [*svezhii*] muzhik, who knows a lot less (his analysis, in your terms, is less developed) but for whom the bases of any knowledge—beliefs, a religious view of the world (synthesis, if you will) is incomparably more correct than that of Wurst" (62:235–36). Tolstoy claimed in this letter that he had written an article in response to spiritualism; no such article exists, but he did return to the theme of spiritualism in part 7 of *Anna Karenina*.[88]

In the second half of part 7, published in the April 1877 issue of the *Russian Herald*, Stiva travels to St. Petersburg to try to obtain his railroad-bank-credit position and to get an answer from Karenin about a divorce for Anna. By this time, Karenin is completely under the influence of Countess Lidiia Ivanovna, who is susceptible to all high-society fads, spiritualism included. When Stiva appears at her house for his interview with her and Karenin, he finds them with Landau, a French shop clerk who has been adopted by a Russian countess after displaying his mediumistic powers. Landau goes into a hypnotic sleep and commands Stiva to leave. The next day "he received from [Karenin] a positive refusal of a divorce for Anna and understood that this decision was based on what the Frenchman had said yesterday in his real or feigned sleep."[89] Landau appears to be based mainly on Daniel Dunglas Home (1833–86), who gave a séance attended by Tolstoy in Paris in March 1857 and who visited Russia in 1870 at the invitation of A. N. Aksakov.[90] The description of Landau owes a great deal to the description of Home and of another medium, Camille Brédif, in the articles by Aksakov and Vagner in the *Russian Herald*.[91]

Before Stiva goes to the home of Countess Lidiia Ivanovna, Princess Miagkaia warns him about Landau: "'What, you don't know Jules Landau, *le fameux, Jules Landau le clairvoyant*, he's also half-witted, but the fate of your sister depends on him. Here is what comes from living in the provinces, you don't know anything. Landau, you see, was a clerk in a store in Paris and came to the doctor. In the doctor's waiting room he fell asleep and in his sleep started to give advice to all the patients. And amazing advice. Then you know Iurii Meledinsky, the sick man? His wife found out about this Landau and brought him to her husband. He is treating her husband. And he hasn't done him any good, in my opinion, because he is just as sickly, but they believe in him and take him around with them.'"[92] Aksakov described a similar trance-with-medical-advice in his article on Iurkevich. At a séance in 1872 at the home of Butlerov,

> Home fell into a somnambulistic state and, walking around the room with closed eyes, went up to Iurkevich, felt his body with his hands, and finally, putting them on his stomach, said, "There is illness here," and prescribed him some simple remedy. At that time Iurkevich was quite healthy, but two and a half years later, an illness *of the stomach*, developing with amazing rapidity, as a result of moral and physical shocks, carried him away to the grave.... The sleeping man started walking around the room, began to feel us with his hands, and among other things, gave me a prescription for curing my stomach: hot salt compresses.[93]

The physical description of Landau in *Anna Karenina* is as follows: "A short, lean man with a woman's pelvis, knock-kneed, very pale, handsome, with gleaming, beautiful eyes and long hair lying on the collar of his frock-coat, was standing at the other end of the room, looking at the wall hung with portraits."[94] He has sweaty hands and "a childish, naïve smile."[95] Stiva is puzzled by the strangeness of the man and his relations to Karenin and Lidiia Ivanovna: "Hearing Countess

Lidiia Ivanovna and feeling the beautiful, naïve or knavish—he himself did not know—eyes of Landau directed at him, Stepan Arkadievich began to experience a kind of special heaviness in his head."[96] In his *Russian Herald* article, Vagner describes Brédif in the following way:

> On one of my acquaintances he produced at first meeting the impression of "a naïve calf who has been brought to the slaughter." But that impression is not quite true. Brédif is not crystal clear. He is not averse to being sly when an opportunity offers: his eyes do not always look straight, in his voice can be heard rather strong false notes, but in general both at the first and at the twentieth meeting with him anyone would say that in this person there is more simplicity than slyness.... He would not at all be averse to supplementing a phenomenon in some modest séance or even faking it, but if he were to be caught in this fakery, he would probably be endlessly upset.... He is strikingly trivial and all his [mediumistic] accessories are childishly naïve and coarsely tasteless.[97]

Both Vagner and Butlerov admit the possibility that Brédif fakes phenomena on occasion, but nevertheless assert that he is capable of making contact with the spirit world on other occasions. Liovin might say that their medium's resin does not always produce the same effect when rubbed on wool.

It may not be true, as Princess Miagkaia asserts, that Anna's fate depends on Landau; she never receives from Stiva the news of the definitive refusal of her divorce that was apparently ordered by the medium "in his real or feigned sleep." But for the readers of the *Russian Herald*, the juxtaposition of the Landau episode with Anna's shocking suicide, which comes about thirty pages later in the same installment, would have fixed the association of spiritualism, presented by Tolstoy as charlatanism and inane cruelty, with her destruction.

The War in Serbia

Despite the many ways in which Tolstoy questions and undermines Katkov's social, political, educational, and economic programs in *Anna Karenina*, there is no hint in the surviving documents that Katkov made any attempt to change the novel's text regarding these issues. There is a letter from Tolstoy to Katkov of February 1875 in which Tolstoy writes, "In the last chapter [the scene in which Anna and Vronsky consummate their relationship] I cannot touch anything.

Vivid realism, as you put it, is my only tool, since I can use neither pathos nor discussions. And this is one of the passages on which the whole novel stands. If it is false, then everything is false" (62:139). Katkov's letter about this has not survived, but he appears to have backed down from making Tolstoy change the scene.[98] As far as we know, Katkov allowed all of Tolstoy's attacks on his favored projects to pass without objection or amendment. Just as he gave Tolstoy special treatment in financial matters, during most of the publication of *Anna Karenina* he refrained from the intrusive editorial practices that had plagued Tur, Turgenev, and Dostoevsky. But when Tolstoy submitted what he then referred to as the epilogue to the novel (later part 8), with its savage attack on the movement of Russian volunteers to Serbia to aid the Slavic Christians in their fight against the Ottomans, it was apparently the last straw. Katkov demanded changes to which Tolstoy would not submit; Tolstoy published part 8 as a separate brochure and broke off relations with Katkov for good.

As we have seen, articles supporting the Slavic Christians of the Ottoman Empire had been appearing in the *Russian Herald* since 1858. Such articles continued to appear with increasing frequency into the 1870s, especially after June 1876, when the principality of Serbia declared war on the Ottoman Empire, and private citizens began traveling from Russia to fight alongside the Serbs. One notable earlier publication in the *Russian Herald* is a translation of excerpts from *The Christians in Turkey*, by W. Denton, an Anglican priest, which appeared in the January 1864 issue.[99]

The article is supplied with an introductory footnote, probably by Katkov, that says, "Never yet has there arisen such a powerful denunciatory voice against the policy of the British government on this question."[100] Denton reports on a recent visit to Serbia, which "first enabled me, on the spot, to collect materials illustrative of the unhappy condition of those races who are subject to the caprice of Turkish officials."[101] Denton's object is to persuade the British government to stop supporting the Ottoman government in the interests of the balance of power: "My object, let me state at the outset, is not to ask the rulers of England to interfere in the behalf of these cruelly oppressed people, but rather that our governors should cease from that strange interference against the people of Turkey which is the present policy of the English Government, and that they should no longer actively aid a despotism the most grinding on the face of the earth, and which, not content like the fanatical cruelty which led to the Diocletian, and other early persecutions, with cruel pains and martyrdoms, poisons and pollutes the whole domestic life of the vast majority of the subjects of Turkey."[102] Katkov clearly found Denton's catalogue of the persecutions and immoralities of the Ottoman administration useful to publish, even though it included Denton's argument that England, not Russia, would be the natural ally of the Christians of the East, since "Russia they dread as a gigantic power on their frontier, which would absorb them, to the loss of all national existence, and they turn away from her with dread, proportionate to her nearness and her strength."[103]

Later articles on the "Eastern question" continue the theme of the oppression of the Slavic Christians subject to Ottoman rule, but in these articles Russia is unambiguously presented as the natural protector and savior of the Christians of the East. A typical passage appears in a review by Feoktistov of a German book on the history of Turkey from 1826 to 1856: "There is not the slightest doubt that the main guilt of Russia before Europe in relation to the Eastern question is the spiritual and blood tie that unites it with the Christian tribes, and its immutable calling to be the intercessor and protector of these tribes. When Catherine II openly took upon herself this holy obligation, one could immediately foresee that on this path there would be no agreement between us and Europe."[104] In the summer of 1876, the frequency of articles on the Eastern question increases, and by December of that year they appear in the same issue as installments of *Anna Karenina*, as noted by Todd. In December 1876 and January, February, and April 1877, installments of *Anna Karenina* appear alongside articles such as "Turkey, Russia, and Europe from the Point of View of International Law," which remarks, "Unbiased people cannot regard without sympathy the Slavs who are rebelling against the Turks, who have proved with their whole history an inability to adopt for their state policies those basic elements of civilization whose presence in the state organization alone gives a state the right to be considered a member of the international family."[105] The last installment of *Anna Karenina* published in the *Russian Herald*, ending with Anna's suicide, is followed in the April 1877 issue by V. S. Nekliudov's heralding of Russia's declaration of war on Turkey: "*Alea jacta est*. The limit has come to Russia's long-suffering: that fatal hour has come about which, six months ago, the Russian tsar foretold to his people in the Moscow Kremlin. Everything that could be thought of to preserve peace, everything was exhausted, everything was put into effect.... Finally the matter has touched the very honor of Russia, and the Sovereign's word was spoken: with God, forward! To the holy battle, for the holy cause!"[106]

Besides the articles in the *Russian Herald* that promoted Katkov's view of Russia as the protector and defender of the Slavic Christians in the East, Katkov himself wrote numerous editorials on the subject in the *Moscow News*. There is not room here to give an adequate digest of these editorials, but in considering

Tolstoy's shaping of part 8 of *Anna Karenina*, it will be helpful to look closely at a few key editorials. In August 1876, Katkov reports on the progress of the war between Serbia and Turkey:

> Today's telegrams are being received with joy in all corners of Russia; in the entire Slavic world. The main forces of the Serbs gained a brilliant victory over the main forces of the Turks.... [The Turks] are fortifying on the left bank of the Morava. This means new battles are to come, new victims.... The news of the victory, which we conveyed in a special supplement, spread like lightning today about the city. A load fell from everyone's shoulders—over recent days the tense expectation of the outcome of the battle had reached an extreme degree. The same thing is happening throughout all of Russia [*Rus*].[107]

Two days later he reports, "[At Aleksinac] the Turkish assault columns were overrun and made to flee, the Serbs went on the attack and chased the Turks to the border. Everyone in Russia responded with a joyful greeting to this news of the victories of our brothers in faith and tribe."[108] Katkov anxiously follows the fate of Russian volunteers traveling to Serbia, noting that Russian newspapers "are filled with reports about the volunteers who are leaving every day for Serbia and about the material aid to the Slavs that is flowing from all ends of Russia, from all classes of the population.... All the worse for [the European Turcophiles] if they cannot rise to the comprehension of the historical significance of that powerful force which has been expressed in this ardent impulse of a people [*narod*] of eighty million."[109]

Another key editorial is from January 6, 1877, titled "The Russian People's [*narodnoe*] Movement of the Past Year." Katkov begins by claiming that "in Russia not only the attention of society, but the whole soul of the people [*narod*] has been seized by the struggle that has arisen in the East." The Russian people, moved by their feeling of "mercy and living faith," have moved to the aid of their "brothers in Christ suffering from horrible brutalities."[110] Katkov recounts a spontaneous upsurge of support from the Russian common people, taking the form of monetary contributions, sympathy, and compassion. He quotes the head of the Moscow Slavic Committee, I. S. Aksakov: "'When the Serbian troops experienced their first failure, when onto the soil of aroused popular [*narodnoe*] sympathy fell the first drop of Russian blood, when the first heroic feat of love was accomplished and the first pure sacrifice was made in the name of Russia from a Russian for the sake of faith and brothers, then the conscience of the whole Russian land shuddered.'"[111]

Katkov continues to quote Aksakov, who describes simple people praying to be sent to the field of battle "to die for the faith": "'One felt that before us in humble form, without proud and self-satisfied bearing stood heroes—I will say more: people of the same temper out of which came the martyrs of the first centuries of Christianity. Yes, we had the honor of seeing the very soul of the people!'"[112]

The earliest versions of Tolstoy's epilogue to *Anna Karenina* begin with a direct attack on the volunteer movement, in the voice of the narrator (20:548–56). These long disquisitions on matters distant from the main line of the plot are reminiscent of the ruminations on the theory of history in the later parts of *War and Peace*. Tolstoy apparently revised this version in the course of his negotiations with Katkov, presenting the criticisms of the volunteer movement in the voices of the characters, particularly Liovin and Prince Shcherbatsky, rather than in the more didactic voice of the narrator (20:638–39).[113] The substance of the criticisms remains in the final version of part 8, however, so for ease of analysis we will focus on that text, although it is not identical to the text that Katkov rejected.

In part 8, Katkov's holy cause of aiding the Slavic Christian brethren is presented as yet another in a series of high-society fads: "All that the idle crowd usually does when killing time was now done for the benefit of the Slavs. Balls, concerts, dinners, speeches, ladies' outfits, beer, taverns—everything attested to sympathy for the Slavs" (19:352). Liovin's half-brother Koznyshev recognizes that "many people with mercenary, vain goals" are involved in puffing up the Slavic question, and that "the newspapers were printing much that was unnecessary and exaggerated, with a single goal—to draw attention to themselves and to out-shout the others" (19:352). He does, however, see the essence of the matter in Katkovian terms: "The slaughter of coreligionists and brother Slavs called forth sympathy for the sufferers and indignation for the oppressors. And the heroism of the Serbs and Montenegrins who were fighting for a great cause engendered in the whole people [*narod*] the desire to help their brothers no longer with word but with deed" (19:353). Just as Aksakov, quoted in Katkov's editorial, had claimed to have seen "the very soul of the people," so does Koznyshev: "The people's [*narodnaia*] soul had found expression" (19:353).

Koznyshev's motives for throwing himself into the Slavic movement are suspect, since he has been disappointed by the reception of his recently published book, and so can be classed along with the "commanders-in-chief without armies, ministers without ministries, journalists without journals, heads of parties without partisans" who are seizing upon the Serbian war as a distraction from their own failures (19:352–53). Vronsky, abandoning his own daughter to

Karenin and joining the volunteers in a form of slow-motion suicide, belongs to the same category. As Stenbock-Fermor notes, Tolstoy may have been drawing on his personal knowledge of the story of A. A. Fet's brother Piotr Afanasievich Shenshin.[114] Shenshin had been disappointed in love and had gone to Herzegovina for the uprising of the Slavs and then as a volunteer to Serbia, where he had "fantastic adventures," according to Fet. He could never find a place for himself in Russia, and ended up working in an arboretum somewhere in Ohio, and then disappearing without a trace. In his letters to Fet of 1876–77, Tolstoy constantly asks for news of Shenshin. In contrast to his depiction of the ne'er-do-well volunteers in part 8, according to Fet, Tolstoy dearly loved Shenshin and considered him "a high moral ideal."[115]

On his way to visit his half-brother Liovin in the country, at the Kursk station in Moscow, Koznyshev sees the Russian volunteers leaving for Serbia and being accompanied by enthusiastic crowds offering bouquets. Everyone he meets is talking about "today's telegram," with the news that "again they smashed the Turks" (19:354). Katkov's triumphant editorials about the telegrams bringing news of Serbian victories, alongside the promise that new battles lie ahead, are wickedly satirized a few pages later, when Koznyshev's traveling companion Katavasov goes into a train compartment to talk to some of the volunteers. Far from the "martyrs of the first centuries of Christianity" of whom Aksakov spoke, they all turn out to be empty braggarts of one sort or another. After the volunteers leave the compartment to have a drink, Katavasov and an old soldier in the compartment "began to talk about the latest military news, and they both hid from each other their bewilderment about whom the battle was expected to be with the next day, when the Turks, according to the latest news, had been smashed at all points" (19:358).

Just as the crowds cheering the volunteers grow smaller and less enthusiastic as the train gets farther from Moscow, Koznyshev's confident ideas about the justness of the volunteer movement are called into question by Liovin and the old prince, and even Dolly, when he reaches Liovin's country estate. Liovin questions the right of any private person to "take on the responsibility for the beginning of a war" (19:387). Koznyshev responds in terms that echo the articles in the *Russian Herald* and Katkov's editorials in the *Moscow News* on the subject: "There is no declaration of war here, but simply the expression of human, Christian feeling. They are killing our brothers, of one blood and one faith with us.... The people [*narod*] has heard about the sufferings of its brethren and has spoken" (19:387–88).

Liovin responds that he himself is one of the people and he does not feel anything of the kind. As in the earlier conversation at Stiva's, the old prince steps in to express the common-sense view, one that is contrary to everything Katkov stands for: "I was living abroad, reading the newspapers, and I admit even before the Bulgarian horrors I did not at all understand why all Russians had so suddenly come to love their brother Slavs, but I felt no love at all for them? I was very distressed, I thought that I was a monster or that Carlsbad had had that effect on me. But after coming here, I calmed down, I see that besides me there are people who are interested only in Russia, and not in the brother Slavs" (19:388). After an inconclusive attempt to find out what one representative of the people, the old beekeeper Mikhailych, thinks of the matter, Liovin sums up: "'The word "people" is so indefinite,' Liovin said. 'District scribes, teachers, and out of the muzhiks perhaps one in a thousand knows what is going on. The rest of the eighty million, like Mikhailych, not only are not expressing their will, but do not have the slightest conception of what they are supposed to express their will about. What right do we have to say what the will of the people is?'" (19:389).

Koznyshev attempts to turn the conversation by referring to the fact that "all the social organs are saying the very same thing," to which the prince replies, "It's the newspapers that are all saying one thing.... But that's the same thing as when frogs make noise before a storm." After pointing out that newspaper editors profit financially from war, he continues, "'Alphonse Karr wrote this splendidly before the war with Prussia. "You consider that war is necessary? Fine. Whoever preaches war—into a special front legion and to the siege, to the attack, in front of everyone!"' 'The editors would be fine,' said Katavasov, laughing loudly, imagining the editors he knew in this select legion. 'Oh, they would run away,' Dolly said, 'They'd only be in the way.' 'And if they run, then shoot them with buckshot from behind or put Cossacks after them with whips,' the Prince said" (19:391). Although Tolstoy uses the plural "editors," Katkov was the editor "in front of everyone" in calling for the liberation of the Slavs from the Ottoman yoke. To say first that he was promoting war for his own financial gain, and then that he would be too cowardly to fight himself, was a grave insult to the person who had given *Anna Karenina* such a prominent place in his journal.

Koznyshev attempts a defense of the press, saying, "Every member of society is called to do the deed that is characteristic of it . . . and people of ideas carry out their deed in expressing public opinion. And unanimity and the full expression of public opinion is the service of the press and is a joyful phenomenon as well. Twenty years ago we would have been silent, but now the voice of the Russian people is heard, which is ready to rise as one person and ready to sacrifice itself for its oppressed brothers" (19:391). Liovin responds, "But not only to sacrifice, but to kill Turks.... The people sacrifice and are ready to sacrifice for the sake of their soul, but not for murder" (19:391). This is a direct rebuke to Katkov's claim that the motives of the people in joining the volunteer movement stem from "mercy and living faith," not, as Liovin would have it, "vengeance and murder."

The End of an Unhappy Family

Instead of the long-awaited ending to *Anna Karenina*, in the May 1877 issue of the *Russian Herald*, on the very last page, tacked to the bottom of a survey of the war in progress with Turkey, complete with maps and troop movements, there appeared the following note: "In the previous issue under the novel *Anna Karenina* there was the note: 'To be continued.' But with the death of the heroine the novel essentially was ended. According to the author's plan, there would follow a short epilogue, about two printer's sheets, from which the readers could learn that Vronsky, in confusion and sorrow after the death of Anna, is setting off as a volunteer to Serbia and that all the others are alive and well, and Liovin remains at his country estate and is angry at the Slavic committees and the volunteers. The author will perhaps develop these chapters for a separate edition of his novel."[116]

Tolstoy was enraged by this note and drafted an angry letter to the newspaper *New Time*, but later calmed down and did not send it. In the unsent letter Tolstoy refers to "a note that modestly hid itself in a strange place in the *Russian Herald*" (62:331). In a version of the letter found among Strakhov's papers, Katkov's note is referred to as "modestly hiding from the eyes of the reader, like a fragrant violet."[117] Tolstoy's letter also parodies Katkov's summary of part 8, suggesting that Katkov could have saved everyone a lot of trouble if instead of torturing its readers for three years with the publication of a long novel, he had simply given its contents as, "There was a certain lady who abandoned her husband. Having fallen in love with Count Vronsky, she got angry in Moscow at various things and threw herself under a railroad car" (62:331).

As Stenbock-Fermor notes, Tolstoy was angered by Katkov's "breach of publishing ethics" in summarizing the end of *Anna Karenina* that he had refused to publish in full.[118] Tolstoy may also have been struck by an article that appeared in the same issue as Katkov's note, "Memoirs of a Volunteer." Near the beginning of this account of a young volunteer's experiences in the Serbian campaign, there is a scene at the Kursk railroad station in Moscow that is extremely similar to the scene at the same station in the epilogue to *Anna Karenina*. The narrator describes being greeted by the excited crowd, and seeing a gentleman who gets up on a table and reads a dispatch: "A unanimous shout of 'Hurrah' ended the reading. 'What is it? What were they reading?' 'We have smashed the Turks!' 'Listen, the Turks are smashed, several guns have been seized.'"[119] The account is not devoid of some satire of the volunteers, and even echoes Tolstoy's text in saying, "The sympathy of the public for us was expressed noticeably more weakly as we moved away from Mother Moscow."[120] Given that Tolstoy had already written the epilogue (including the railroad scene) before this article appeared, the only conclusion is that its author was given access to Tolstoy's text. The similarities are too striking to be mere coincidence.

"Memoirs of a Volunteer" begins by reprising Tolstoy's railroad scene, but rather than abandoning the volunteers at that point, as Tolstoy does, leaving the unpleasant impression of them with the reader, the narrator takes us along with him to Serbia. The narrator himself is a sensible, experienced soldier who refrains from the drinking bouts that some of his fellow volunteers indulge in, and he shows the Russian volunteers being greeted by well-wishing crowds in Romania and Serbia. When he first sees the lights of Serbian outposts, he says, "In my soul there was a whole sea of love for my suffering brothers, and the thirst for vengeance on the Turks simply suffocated me; it seems that the majority of Russians shared my feeling."[121] The picture he paints is much more nuanced than what is presented in Katkov's editorials: not all the volunteers are saints, there are mistakes and setbacks in the military operations, "vengeance" plays a part in his motivations, as Liovin argues. But this "alternative part 8" is also more nuanced than Tolstoy's portrait of the volunteers in *Anna Karenina*: some of the volunteers are true heroes, and the narrator himself is honest, self-critical, and genuinely concerned about the fate of the Slavic Christians of the Ottoman Empire. "Memoirs of a Volunteer" appears to be yet another salvo in Katkov's battle with Tolstoy over part 8.

In his letter to Strakhov telling him that he was probably going to have to publish part 8 as a separate book, Tolstoy wrote, "It turns out that Katkov does not *share my views*, and it could not be otherwise, since I condemn precisely such people as him" (62:326, emphasis in original). To say "it turns out that Katkov does not share my views" is strangely disingenuous, since Tolstoy must have realized from the start that the condemnation of "precisely such people as him" extends throughout the novel, and that given Katkov's towering stature, "such people as him" really means "him."

In an article titled "What Happened after the Death of Anna Karenina," presented as a review of Tolstoy's separate publication of part 8, Katkov offers aesthetic arguments for having refused to publish the end of the novel, when in fact the reasons were political. Katkov gives long excerpts from the last part, as if trying to make sure that the end of *Anna Karenina* did in fact appear in the *Russian Herald*, in a properly abbreviated form. He makes the keen-eyed observation that Anna's name is never mentioned in part 8, and that the characters seem strangely unaffected by her terrible death. Katkov inserts his journal into the fictional world of the characters: "Quite a few people have gathered at the family home of the Liovins, Sergei Ivanovich is there, and Katavasov, and the old prince, and Dolly with her children, they talk about a lot of things, but for this whole company it is as if the terrible episode which so struck even readers who knew Anna only from stories, and not from personal acquaintance like these people, had not happened. As if the fourth issue of the *Russian Herald* had not yet reached Liovin's estate."[122]

But in general in this essay Katkov fails to show his usual acumen as a reader. He pretends not to understand why, after the death of Anna, Tolstoy returns to Liovin's story, even though the two stories have run in parallel throughout the novel: "If the work was not finished [*ne dorabotalos'*], if no natural resolution appeared, then it seems better to have broken off the novel on the death of the heroine than to conclude it with talk about the volunteers, who are not at all to blame for the events of the novel. A broad river flowed smoothly, but did not fall into the sea, but got lost in the sands. It was better to get out ahead of time onto the shore than to sail out onto a sandbank."[123] Katkov's usual directness and ruthlessness as a polemicist are absent in this feeble attempt at self-justification. Katkov was apparently unable to grapple with the fact that Tolstoy, the writer in whom he placed his highest hopes, had in this novel rejected and ridiculed virtually every one of his most cherished projects for Russian society.

Just as Turgenev had said that he never would have finished *Fathers and Sons* if it had not been for Katkov's insistence, so Tolstoy at several points was ready to give up on *Anna Karenina*, but was constantly pushed to continue it by Katkov (and the monetary rewards he promised). In November 1875 Tolstoy wrote to Strakhov, "My God, if only someone would finish *Anna Karenina* for me!" (62:215).[124] Strakhov was Tolstoy's confidant throughout the writing of *Anna Karenina*, and in one of his letters to Tolstoy he has left us a vivid portrait of Katkov that testifies to the extent of Katkov's investment in publishing the novel. In fall 1875, Strakhov writes Tolstoy that he had seen Katkov in St. Petersburg. Strakhov wanted to talk to Katkov about his own articles for the *Russian Herald*, but, he writes, "he kept talking about you." Katkov was worried about when *Anna Karenina* would be finished, and also about rumors that Tolstoy might decide not to publish the second half of the novel in the *Russian Herald*. Katkov feverishly insisted to Strakhov that he was making all kinds of concessions to Tolstoy, and that Tolstoy "would have no possibility of extracting more profit" from the novel than by publishing it with Katkov. Then Strakhov offers a striking image of Katkov: "I confess, in general this time I felt a certain pity for Katkov, mixed with respect. His emaciated face, gray hair, thin as a cobweb, his heavy manner of speaking and the very form of his skull, which for some reason arrested my attention, produced a painful impression; this person is never calm for a moment—some kind of inner work is constantly and tensely going on in him."[125] Given that Strakhov makes this observation as he is being exhorted by Katkov to help push along the production of *Anna Karenina*, the "inner work" was the same work that made Katkov pester Turgenev to finish *Fathers and Sons* and support Dostoevsky as he produced four of his five major novels: the work of creating the canon of Russian literature as a part of world literature. Katkov did not "finish *Anna Karenina* for" Tolstoy, but it would probably not have been finished without him. Tolstoy's mental battles with every aspect of Katkov's national program enabled him to generate a novel that, even while escaping the total control of both men, helped to promote that program in the most meaningful way.[126]

The last direct communication between Tolstoy and Katkov was a telegram Tolstoy sent him demanding that he send back the manuscript of the epilogue and breaking off any further contact (62:332n1). But there is a coda to their relationship, one that fittingly takes place at a railroad station in Moscow. In the summer of 1877 Strakhov, who was acting as Tolstoy's agent in publishing part 8 as a separate brochure, was on his way back to St. Petersburg after visiting Tolstoy at Yasnaya Polyana and going to the Optina Pustyn Monastery with him. At the Kursk station in Moscow Strakhov met with Fyodor Fyodorovich Ris, the owner of the printing plant in which part 8 was to be published (he had also printed *War and Peace* and was to print the separate edition of *Anna Karenina* in 1878). Strakhov and Ris go from the Kursk station to the St. Petersburg station in Ris's carriage, and when they arrive, Strakhov realizes that his baggage has not been transferred. Ris returns to the Kursk station to try to find it. In his impatience, Strakhov goes to wait for Ris near the station entrance:

> A new misfortune! I see Katkov riding up with someone to the station. No sooner had I noticed him when he got out of the carriage. I pretended that I did not see him.

He passed by, as if on purpose coming close to me, but also did not acknowledge me.... I admit, this meeting was very unpleasant for me. It is stupid to pretend not to recognize someone, but the task of talking to him seemed so difficult to me that even now I am delighted at the swiftness with which I made the decision not to see him.[127]

As if to add to the irony of the situation, the person Katkov was seeing off to St. Petersburg was Minister of Education D. A. Tolstoy, his ally in the struggle for the supremacy of classical education. The railroad as the locus for chance meetings is a major theme of *Anna Karenina*. Here Strakhov, Tolstoy's surrogate, has a last, accidental non-meeting with Katkov. Even if Tolstoy was arguing with Katkov throughout *Anna Karenina*, arguing is still dialogue. In the very last moment of their connection, there is no dialogue, only intentional non-recognition and non-communication.

CHAPTER 7

KATKOV AND PUSHKIN

THE END OF KATKOV'S LITERARY CAREER

Tolstoy had nothing more to do with Katkov after the debacle of 1877 concerning *Anna Karenina*. Turgenev had stopped publishing his works in the *Russian Herald* in 1869, and in 1874 had angered Katkov by sanctioning the public airing of the contention that Katkov had altered the text of *Fathers and Sons* without his permission. Dostoevsky, who had published *A Raw Youth* in *Notes of the Fatherland* in 1875, returned to the *Russian Herald* to publish his final, most acclaimed novel, *The Brothers Karamazov*, in 1879–80.[1] While the publication of *The Brothers Karamazov* was the culmination of Katkov's achievement in fostering the development of the Russian novel, it also marked the end of Katkov's literary career, as Dostoevsky died in January 1881 and no more significant works of literature were published in the *Russian Herald* before Katkov's death in 1887. More than halfway through the publication of *The Brothers Karamazov*, Turgenev, Dostoevsky, and Katkov encountered each other at the June 1880 celebration marking the erection of a monument to Pushkin in Moscow, which Tolstoy refused to attend. There had been numerous assassinations and attempted assassinations of government officials, including attempts on the life of Alexander II, throughout 1879 and into 1880. This wave of antigovernment violence had spurred Katkov to a frenzy of editorial writing, with the constant theme that the Russian intelligentsia had spawned and encouraged the birth of nihilism and its development into terrorism. The man who had hailed Pushkin's world stature in 1839, and who had devoted prominent space in the first issues of his journal in 1856 to the evaluation of Pushkin's significance, was now the avowed enemy of the liberal intelligentsia who were the moving force in the Pushkin celebration and who, led by Turgenev, attempted to exclude him from the event. The story of the Pushkin celebration has been told in magisterial detail by Marcus C. Levitt in his book *Russian Literary Politics and the Pushkin Celebration of 1880*.[2] My discussion will focus on the event as the last chapter in Katkov's relationship with Turgenev and Dostoevsky, and in his lifelong engagement with Russian literature and its national significance.

The structure of this chapter is complex. It begins by reviewing where Dostoevsky and Turgenev were in their relationships with Katkov as the Pushkin Celebration approached. Dostoevsky had returned to the *Russian Herald* for the publication of *The Brothers Karamazov*, in which he placed great hopes for his own reputation; thus he arrived at the Pushkin Celebration as an ally of Katkov, although he was uneasy about being publicly linked with him. Turgenev, in contrast, had just been attacked in the *Russian Herald* for his supposedly too-cozy ties with the nihilists, a dangerous accusation in an atmosphere of assassination of government officials. An angry Turgenev actively participated in marginalizing Katkov at the Pushkin festivities, depriving him of an opportunity to deliver a major speech. As we will discuss, however, Katkov was present at the feast in two major ways: Dostoevsky's own Pushkin speech shows traces of the conception of Pushkin that had been advanced in Varnhagen von Ense's review of his works, translated by Katkov in 1839; and Katkov published his own "Pushkin speech" in the *Moscow News* and the *Russian Herald*, simultaneously with the 1880 celebration. I will consider the four approaches to Pushkin—Katkov's translation of Varnhagen of 1839, as well as Turgenev's, Dostoevsky's, and Katkov's 1880 meditations on Pushkin—in relation to each other and to Katkov's editorial program. Finally, in this chapter we will consider Katkov's verdicts on both Dostoevsky and Turgenev after their deaths, and the question of a monument to Katkov himself.

Before the Celebration: Publication of Dostoevsky and Polemic with Turgenev

Dostoevsky's return to the *Russian Herald* was marked by the same kind of trepidation as his approach to Katkov with the idea for *Crime and Punishment* in September 1865. When he visited Katkov's office in June 1878, Dostoevsky feared either an outright rejection or a refusal to meet his financial terms.[3] As often happens in Dostoevsky's accounts of his encounters with Katkov in 1878–80, a striking personal detail crystallizes Dostoevsky's emotions. He writes to his wife that after a sleepless night he went to the editorial offices: "Katkov received me cordially but also rather *carefully*. We began to talk about general matters, and suddenly a terrible thunderstorm started up. I think: I'll start talking about my business, he'll refuse, and the storm won't pass, and I'll have to sit here refused and disgraced [literally "spit upon"], until the downpour stops."[4] Dostoevsky's discomfort at the prospect of having to wait out a rainstorm in Katkov's presence demonstrates that despite their thirteen years of collaboration, the personal awkwardness between the two men persisted. Dostoevsky reports that although Katkov responded in a generally positive way, his face contorted when Dostoevsky mentioned his price of three hundred rubles per printer's sheet, and he also refused to give a conclusive answer since, as he claimed, he was considering closing down the *Russian Herald* for the coming year because he did not have time to run it along with the *Moscow News* (30/1:32). But by November 1878, Katkov had agreed to Dostoevsky's terms, the *Russian Herald* had suffered no hiatus, and Dostoevsky had brought Katkov the first two parts of *The Brothers Karamazov*. The novel began publication in the *Russian Herald* in January 1879.

During his visit to Moscow in November 1878, Dostoevsky's complicated relationship with Katkov was expressed through yet another telling personal detail. Dostoevsky happened to be visiting Katkov at his home the day before Katkov's name day, November 8. But although Katkov's daughters came in ostensibly to say goodnight to their father but really to have a look at Dostoevsky and chat with him, Katkov did not invite him to dinner the next day. Offended by being left out of what he assumed was a grand banquet, Dostoevsky wrote to his wife that evening that he had "definitively" decided not to pay a congratulatory visit to Katkov on his name day (30/1:47). Nevertheless, he changed his mind and went to Katkov's house the next day, where a large crowd of well-wishers was gathered. Katkov received him warmly and, Dostoevsky notes with gratification, continued to be attentive to Dostoevsky even after they were joined in conversation by the governor-general of Moscow, Prince V. A. Dolgorukov (mistakenly called Dolgoruky by Dostoevsky, perhaps thinking of the hero of *A Raw Youth*, Arkadii Dolgoruky). As Dostoevsky left the house, he went out not through the drawing room, as he had come, but through the dining room, where he noted "that the table was set for no more than twenty or even eighteen places. And since Katkov's family alone would seat at the table no fewer than twelve people, I concluded that there was to be no banquet at all, but only the closest relatives would be dining" (30/1:48–49). The image of the writer of *Crime and Punishment* and *The Devils* slipping through the dining room to determine whether he has been personally slighted by his publisher is a poignant one indeed.[5]

Throughout the publication of *The Brothers Karamazov*, Dostoevsky corresponds not with Katkov himself but with the executive editor of the *Russian*

Herald, N. A. Liubimov. But at all times Dostoevsky is aware of the extent to which the publication of the novel depends on Katkov personally. He often sends "messages" to Katkov via Liubimov, knowing that the contents of his letters would be shared with the all-powerful editor. Soon after the name-day party, on November 11, 1878, Dostoevsky writes his wife that Katkov has not been able to meet with him because he has fallen seriously ill. At the very end of the letter Dostoevsky returns to this news in an anxious postscript: "What if Katkov in fact gets very seriously ill? It could affect everything to come [*Mozhet povliiat' i na vse dal'neishee*]" (30/1:52). The phrase "everything to come" refers to the completion of publication of *The Brothers Karamazov*, as well as Dostoevsky's future literary work, both of which depend on the continued good health and activity of Katkov.

On March 12, 1879, Dostoevsky wrote to the journalist V. F. Putsykovich, "*The Brothers Karamazov* is producing a furor here—in the palace, and in the public, and in public readings, which you will see from the newspapers" (30/1:57). At this point, books 1, 2, and 3 of *The Brothers Karamazov* had appeared in the January and February issues of the *Russian Herald*. These sections introduce the Karamazov family: the lecherous and rapacious father Fyodor Pavlovich; his son with his first wife, the wild military officer Dmitri; and his two sons with his saintly second wife, the intellectual Ivan and the novice monk Alyosha. Book 2 describes a family meeting in the cell of the holy elder Zosima, during which the sacred space is defiled by the violent sexual competition between father Fyodor and son Dmitri over the "loose woman" Grushenka. In book 3, titled "Sensualists," several dramatic clashes occur, including Dmitri's savage beating of Fyodor and an emotional, sexually charged verbal duel between Grushenka and Dmitri's noble fiancée Katerina Ivanovna, witnessed by the embarrassed virgin Alyosha. Even in these first sections, the narrative energy of the novel and its irresistible juxtaposition of pulp-fiction devices with the most profound religious searching have become evident. Reading these passages today and trying to imagine the impact they would have had on a reading public that had never seen anything like it, one is not surprised that they caused a "furor." Yet the very next day after writing this letter, in conversation at a dinner in honor of Turgenev, who was visiting from Paris, Dostoevsky repudiated Katkov, the man who was providing his novel its prominent platform. The familiar conflict arose once again: to publish in the *Russian Herald* was to be read by all of educated Russia, but it also meant being associated with, and compromised by, Katkov, whose editorials in the *Moscow News* at this time were raging against the liberal intelligentsia and blaming it for heinous political violence.

Although Dostoevsky was closer to Katkov in his political views than Turgenev and Tolstoy were, he was always concerned to distance himself from Katkov and maintain as much independence of thought as possible.[6] At the dinner in honor of Turgenev, two young journalists challenged Dostoevsky to explain why he was publishing *The Brothers Karamazov* in the *Russian Herald* and thus "contributing to the dissemination of a journal whose tendency, of course, he cannot share." Dostoevsky chose the "financial" excuse, explaining passionately "that he needed to live and to feed his family, and meanwhile journals with a more sympathetic tendency have refused to publish him."[7]

Dostoevsky's friend A. N. Maikov was stunned by this speech, and the very same evening wrote Dostoevsky a passionate letter (which he apparently never sent), saying that Dostoevsky had struck a blow "into the holy of holies of my soul." Maikov's account of the interchange at the dinner is somewhat more detailed than that of the other eyewitness, quoted above:

> Someone from among the young generation asks you, "Why ever do you publish in the *Russian Herald*?" You answer: in the first place, because they pay more and more reliably, and they pay in advance; in the second place, the censorship is lighter, it almost doesn't exist; in the third place, in Petersburg they would not accept your works. I kept waiting for the fourth point and made an effort to suggest it to you—but you evaded it. I expected that you as an independent person would have to say, [that you work with the *Russian Herald*] out of sympathy with Katkov and out of respect for him, even out of like-mindedness on many of the main points, if only on those that were being discussed here at the dinner,—you evaded, you didn't say it. What? You publish with Katkov because of money? But that's not serious, that's not true. What is this? Denial? As Peter denied? For the sake of what? For fear of the Jews? [*Radi strakha iudeiska*?] For the sake of popularity?[8]

The phrase "for fear of the Jews" should not be taken literally. It is an idiom taken from the Gospel of John, chapter 19, verse 38: "After these things, Joseph of Arimathea, who was a disciple of Jesus, though a secret one *because of his fear of the Jews*, asked Pilate to let him take away the body of Jesus" (New Revised Standard Version; emphasis added). It is used in Russian to mean "for fear of the authorities" or "for fear of the powerful." But the fact remains that Maikov is comparing Dostoevsky in his renunciation of Katkov to two men, Peter and Joseph of Arimathea, who publicly renounced Jesus Christ. Maikov ends by lamenting,

"Poor Katkov—I mean the ideal, moral Katkov—or Katkov in the ideal! Who would be afraid to proclaim his solidarity with him!"⁹

Maikov never sent his letter, so we have no idea how Dostoevsky would have answered him. But Maikov was one of his oldest friends, so one should not dismiss his shock and surprise that Dostoevsky refused to express solidarity with Katkov and attributed their relationship to purely financial motives. Dostoevsky's answer was in tune with the interpretation of his long collaboration with Katkov that has become canonical, thanks to Soviet scholars: Dostoevsky held his nose and published with Katkov because he was financially desperate. But as with the polemics of the early 1860s, there is a feeling that Dostoevsky is protesting too much. There is a core of inner kinship between him and Katkov that he is sometimes embarrassed by, but has trouble concealing.

Dostoevsky's renunciation of Katkov in March 1879 was bound up with his sense of his legacy and the need to redeem himself in the eyes of the younger generation. That summer, Dostoevsky wrote to his wife from the German health spa Ems, where he was being treated for the emphysema that was to kill him a year and a half later, "I keep thinking, my dearest, about my death (I've been thinking seriously here) and about what I will be leaving you and the children with. Everyone thinks we have money, but we have nothing. Now [*The Brothers*] *Karamazov* is burdening me, I have to finish it well, to give it a jeweler's finishing, but it is a difficult and risky piece, lots of strength will be used up on it. But it is also a fatal piece: *it must establish my name*, otherwise there will be no hope" (30/1:109, emphasis added).

In a letter the same month to Konstantin Petrovich Pobedonostsev, the powerful government official who was soon to become Ober-Procurator of the Holy Synod, Dostoevsky wrote of how with *The Brothers Karamazov* he was staking a claim to significance independently of the Westernizing intelligentsia, but without abandoning a connection to forward-looking youth. He wrote,

> My literary position (I never told you about this) I consider to be almost phenomenal: How can a person who as a rule writes against European principles, **who has compromised himself forever with *The Devils*, that is with retrogradism and obscurantism** [*obskurantizm*]—how can this person, separate from all the Europeanizers, their journals, newspapers, critics—how can he nevertheless be recognized by our youth, by that very unstable [*rasshatannaia*] youth, the nasty little nihilists [*nigiliatina*], etc.? They have declared this to me, from many places, by individual declarations and in whole corporations. They have even announced that it is from

me *alone* that they expect a sincere and sympathetic word and that **it is me alone they consider their *guiding writer*.** These declarations by youth are known to our literary figures, **the bandits of the pen and swindlers of the press,** and they are very struck by this, otherwise would they really allow me to write freely! They would eat me up like dogs, but they are afraid and are watching in bewilderment to see what will happen next. (Letter of August 24 [September 5 N.S.], 1879, 30/1:121; boldface added)

The phrase "bandits of the pen and swindlers of the press," often attributed to B. M. Markevich, was also used by Katkov and had become a catchphrase used by Markevich in the *Moscow News* to refer to liberal journalists, sometimes with the insertion "fornicators of thought [*preliubodei mysli*]," which Dostoevsky would use as the title of chapter 13, book 12 of *The Brothers Karamazov* in reference to the sophistic reasoning of the defense attorney Fetiukovich.[10] Thus even as Dostoevsky claims the role of a guide to the young generation, he expresses solidarity with the conservative project of Katkov and the *Moscow News* (to which his correspondent Pobedonostsev would have been sympathetic). Dostoevsky had "compromised [himself] forever with *The Devils*," which, especially after the exclusion of "At Tikhon's," had been received as one of Katkov's made-to-order antinihilist potboilers. But he was dependent on Katkov again to bring forward the work that was to "establish [his] name" and make him the "guiding writer" even of radical youth.

Turgenev too had been "forever compromised" with radical youth by the publication of *Fathers and Sons* in Katkov's *Russian Herald*, and like Dostoevsky he was seeking in 1879 to establish himself as a leader among them. He had begun the process in 1869 with "Apropos of *Fathers and Sons*," in which he claimed that his sympathies lay entirely with the nihilist Bazarov. In 1874 he had authorized V. V. Stasov to publicly state that Katkov had made changes to *Fathers and Sons* without Turgenev's permission. Now, in the fall of 1879, his efforts to liberate himself from the "antinihilist" label led to another public clash with Katkov.

In October 1879 Turgenev sent a letter to Adrien Hébrard, editor of the Paris newspaper *Le Temps*. The letter was published in November as an introduction to "En cellule: Impressions d'un nihiliste [In solitary confinement: Impressions of a nihilist]," by I. Ia. Pavlovsky. Turgenev's introductory letter was translated into Russian in the *Moscow News* by Katkov's associate Markevich, as a way of drawing attention to its potentially subversive nature. I will quote this translation in full, including Markevich's insertions of phrases from the French original and his italicizations of certain passages. Turgenev writes (in Markevich's translation):

Here is a fragment from autobiographical notes that seemed to me to be worthy of being communicated to the readers of your newspaper. The author is one of those young Russians, too numerous at the present time [*trop nombreux par le temps qui court*], whose convictions have been deemed dangerous and subject to punishment [*punissables*] by the government of my country. Without at all approving of his convictions, I consider that the simple [*naïf*] and sincere narrative of that which he had to suffer may, *in arousing at the same time interest in his person*, serve as proof of how little preliminary solitary confinement is justified in the eyes of a healthy legislation [*combien la prison cellulaire préventive est peu justifiable aux yeux d'une saine législation*]. I hope that you will be struck as I was by the tone of truth [*l'accent de vérité*] that reigns in these pages, as well as by the absence of complaints and reproaches that are useless if not inappropriate [*inutiles sinon déplacés*]. You will see that *these nihilists*, about which much has been said in recent times, are *neither as black nor as inveterate as people have wished to represent them* [*ne sont ni si noirs ni si endurcis qu'on veut bien les représenter*].[11]

To publish such a letter in November 1879, after, to name just two events, the assassination of the governor-general of Kharkov in February 1879 and the attempted assassination of Tsar Alexander II in April 1879, showed a certain tone-deafness on Turgenev's part, which Katkov's *Moscow News* did not hesitate to exploit.

Responding in November 1879 to fears expressed by a friend that after the publication of Pavlovsky's memoir Turgenev might have trouble returning to Russia, Turgenev stresses the innocuous content of the nihilist's narrative: "The article published in *Le Temps* is not at all a protest, but a simple, very naïve and touching story about a prisoner's detention in prison *without any political hints or reproaches*."[12] But the feuilleton published in the *Moscow News* in December 1879 by Markevich (under the pseudonym "Inhabitant of Another Town," namely St. Petersburg) directs attention not to the "naïve" content of Pavlovsky's memoir but to Turgenev's introductory letter, which it quotes in its entirety, as given above.

Markevich (1822–84) had been closely associated with Katkov since the mid-1860s, and had served him in two ways: as a writer of antinihilist novels and articles in the *Russian Herald* and the *Moscow News*, and as a conduit for information from the Ministry of Education, where he held a responsible position beginning in 1866. In his article on Turgenev, Markevich incessantly and mockingly repeats Turgenev's statement that the nihilists are "neither as black nor as inveterate" as they have been portrayed. He hints that Turgenev had a hand in writing or at least translating Pavlovsky's text, which is written "so skillfully and beautifully in French" and "testifies to the close acquaintance of the writer with the devices and ways of the literary masters."[13] He also alludes to Turgenev's 1870 essay "The Execution of Troppmann," which is in some respects comparable to "En Cellule," in that the essay focuses on the inhumaneness of public execution rather than on Troppmann's crime, the murder of an entire family. Markevich remarks that there is no explanation in the publication of Pavlovsky's memoir of what he did to deserve imprisonment. The prisoner has a right to the interest of "honest and right-thinking people" only in relation to the severity of his crime: "Lacenaire and Troppmann cannot in any case arouse human sympathy to the same degree that it is given to Savonarola, Thomas More, or even those unhappy hostages who were shot by the Paris Commune."[14]

Markevich accuses Turgenev of being "the friend, the confidant, the servant, the slave, the buffoon" of the younger generation, ready to dance on any tightrope "if only he is not deprived of the good will of these 'Russian nihilists.'"[15] Markevich concludes brutally, claiming that Turgenev is controlled by the need to ingratiate himself with the "force" of nihilism:

> Neither the evil deeds committed by this "force"—evil deeds that are unprecedented, unheard-of in Russia over the whole course of its thousand-year history, nor the horror and indignation they arouse in all levels of the Russian people, nor the revulsion from blood and destruction that is innate to his own nature, can overcome in him this shameful itch for trying to be popular. Under this influence, he is not at all capable of realizing the significance of his actions; he does not understand that through the attestation he has given to Russian "nihilists" he has acknowledged their foul cause to be just, that they, of course, are laughing at his careful shielding of his own person, and understand his letter published in *Le Temps* as nothing other than a document that encourages them.[16]

Turgenev referred to Markevich's article as a "foul [political] denunciation" and as "slander" in a letter to M. M. Stasiulevich, the publisher of the *Herald of Europe*. To Tolstoy, he wrote, "When I left the *Russian Herald*, Katkov told them to warn me that, he supposedly said, I do not know what it means to have him as an enemy: now he is trying to prove it to me. Let him! My soul is not in his power."[17]

Turgenev responded to Markevich in a letter published in the newspaper *Rumor* [*Molva*] and the journal *Herald of Europe*.[18] In the letter he rejects Markevich's accusations of servility and ingratiation, since such servility would imply a departure from one's own convictions and a pretense at adopting someone else's:

> Without boasting or hesitating, but simply stating a fact, I have the right to assert that the convictions that I have expressed both in print and orally have not changed one iota over the past forty years; I have never hidden them from anyone. In the eyes of our youth—since we are speaking about them—in their eyes, no matter what party they belong to, I always was and to this day have remained a "gradualist," a liberal of the old style in the English, dynastic sense, a person who awaits reform *only from above*,—a principled opponent of revolution, not to speak of the outrages of recent times.[19]

Finally, Turgenev turns Markevich's accusation against him, alluding to Markevich's publicly perceived subordinate position to Katkov: "And when you think from whose mouth these slanders, these accusations come?! From the mouth of a person who from the cradle has earned the reputation of a virtuoso in the business of ingratiating and 'turning somersaults,' first voluntarily, and finally involuntarily!"[20]

Markevich responded to Turgenev by publishing a letter he received from Turgenev in 1863 in which Turgenev expressed warm gratitude to him for using his connections in government circles to save him from a Senate trial for "supposedly criminal dealings with Herzen."[21] More important than Markevich's publication, however, was the introduction to it, written by Katkov himself. In his open letter, Turgenev had said that Markevich had attributed to him "nearly criminal intentions."[22] Katkov mocks Turgenev for accusing Markevich of making political denunciations when all he did was draw attention to Turgenev's own published letter. Katkov explicitly states that Turgenev himself is not a nihilist, but at the same time he condemns Turgenev's relations with radical youth, making reference to the "ovations" that greeted Turgenev during his spring 1879 visit to Russia:

> It would indeed be ridiculous to suspect Mr. Turgenev of sympathy for the nihilists. But all the worse for him that, without sincerely sympathizing with them, he flirts with them, at a time when any serious and firm person must to the best of his ability offer them a stern resistance. What constitutes the strength of this ulcer if not the complaisance with which our public milieu relates to it? That is why it is a sin for people with the authority and name of Mr. Turgenev to be carried away by vain popularity-seeking in spheres that do not deserve respect, it is shameful to fear contemptible abuse, when duty orders them to say a truthful and strong word, and such people should abhor ovations that make them a tool of goals that are alien to them.[23]

Katkov gets to the real heart of his problems with Turgenev, however, when he returns to the perennial sore point of the previous seventeen years, the publication of *Fathers and Sons*. Katkov writes, "Mr. Turgenev created Bazarov and he himself imprinted this type with the name of nihilist. The author, of course, does not share the views of his hero. In his mind and heart he belongs to the type of the *fathers*, the sybarite-aesthetes and *gradualists* of the 1840s. The type of Bazarov is hateful to the author, but also terrifying." Katkov continues, "When he depicted the type of the nihilist, he gave him the character of integrity and strength that is so captivating for young minds. Without some tiny features that the author introduced into this figure on the advice of the publisher [Katkov] of the journal where *Fathers and Sons* first saw the light, it perhaps would have completely lurched in the direction of being favorable to nihilism, and the fatuous, embittered, coarse *studiosus medicinae* [medical student—that is, Bazarov] would have emerged as a high ideal for the young generation."

Katkov then recalls the "schism" in the ranks of the nihilists over how to regard Bazarov, whether as a superb ideal or as evidence of Turgenev's hatred for the young generation, and claims that Turgenev kept silent at that time. But with the passing of the years, nihilists multiplied and took over "our literature," and their voices made noise all over Russia: "Then Mr. Turgenev, incessantly abused and reviled by them, came before the public with the expression of his true respect and complete devotion to Mr. Bazarov, and as proof of his feelings for him he betrayed [*vydal*] the publisher of the journal [Katkov], referring to his disagreements with him during publication."[24] Here Katkov gives us his view of the relationship: Turgenev betrayed Katkov in order to prove his feelings for Bazarov.

The Contest over Pushkin in June 1880

The Pushkin Celebration was scheduled to take place on Pushkin's birthday, May 26, but it had to be postponed until June because of the death of Alexander II's wife Mariia on May 22. The latest attempt on the life of the tsar, an explosion in the Winter Palace on February 5, had inspired a spate of editorials by Katkov in which he continued to point the finger at the intelligentsia as having fostered the violence. He also returned to the theme of his glory days, the perfidy of Poland, both in insinuating connections between the Russian radicals and Polish insurrectionists and in calling for the application to the Russian revolutionaries of the same severe measures that had been used against the Polish uprising. In an editorial dated February 6, Katkov calls for a dictatorial power to be set up to carry on the struggle with sedition: "The more powerful and decisive such a dictatorship, the more rapid will be its action. One needs in essence the same kind of action, concentrated and plenipotentiary, that was so successful in the struggle with the Polish revolutionary organization. The experience of that time cannot help but convince us that half-measures only intensify and exacerbate evil."[25] And in an editorial dated February 13, he claims that "as at the time of the Polish rebellion," the agents of sedition are more obedient to their cause than the servants of government are to the execution of their duties: "Besides its direct agents, the sedition now, as at the time of the Polish rebellion, has many people who tolerate it thanks to the political demoralization that is widespread in the intelligentsia spheres of our society, and the chaos of immature ideas that fermented in it then and even more so today."[26]

Perhaps Katkov's most notorious editorial is the one dated February 20, 1880, in response to an attempt to assassinate Count M. T. Loris-Melikov, who on February 14 had been appointed head of the Supreme Executive Commission for the Preservation of Civic Order and Social Calm with Extreme Authority (as Katkov says, "a too-long title for a power that must act quickly, energetically, and surely [*metko*]!").[27] Katkov makes a serious accusation: that the government cannot rely on the intelligentsia for support. He writes, "It is not in the Petersburg intelligentsia but in the Russian people [*narod*] that one must seek support in this as in any government matter.... People say that the authorities should turn to society and find support for itself there. But what society? Where are the elements in the intelligentsia spheres of our society on which the government of a great power, which bears responsibility for the national good and fate of Russia, could rely? Tell me, where are such elements to be found at this time? In Petersburg salons? In the feuilletons of Petersburg newspapers?" He continues, "At the present time the government can successfully carry out its task only through strict discipline from top to bottom in its own ranks. Can one really think at such a time about representative government as a useful force? Is it really possible to think of something like that in solidarity with the most repulsive conspiracy, guided by a hostile hand?"[28]

In an editorial dated April 3, 1880, Katkov draws a stark line, not between liberal and conservative, but between the "national and antinational," or "Russian and anti-Russian," parties: "The national party can wish only that which is useful for Russia, which is for its good, and not that which is liberal or conservative. Conversely, for people of the antinational party, what is good is what weakens

Russia in its state composition, that introduces discord [*smuta*] into its social life: the motto of this party is the worse, the better."²⁹ Katkov explains that the two parties are not easy to distinguish, because not everyone with a Russian name belongs to the national party, and "any politically honest Russian subject of any tribal origin belongs to the national party." Unfortunately, the intelligentsia, in Katkov's analysis, tends to gravitate toward the antinational party, because it "has a superficial, imitative, and cosmopolitan character; it does not belong to its people and, leaving it in shadow, itself remains without grounding [*pochva*, literally *soil*]."³⁰

In this editorial Katkov returns to his favorite topic, the Polish threat. He argues that autocracy, "that necessary condition for a people predestined for independent state life," was never firmly established for the Polish people [*narod*]. Thus the Polish nationality exists only in the *szlachta*, the hereditary nobility, and is "like a soul deprived of a body, but possessed by the lust to be materialized, to find a body for itself." It seeks to restore its dead state "on the historical soil of the Russian people [*narod*], which once fell under Polish power and was Polonicized in the higher strata of its population."³¹ (The "historical soil of the Russian people" apparently refers here to the contested regions of present-day Ukraine, Lithuania, and Belarus.) Katkov echoes the theme of his 1863 editorials on the "fatal question," that an independent Polish nation cannot exist side by side with an independent Russian nation: "Although the Polish party does not have the people [*narod*] behind it, it nevertheless represents a definite national principle. *Its anti-Russian character is nothing other than its Polish character*, but it has found sympathy and support in our cosmopolitan intelligentsia, deprived of a national character, although nominally belonging to the Russian nationality."³² It is no surprise that the members of the intelligentsia who were planning the Pushkin Celebration, in particular Turgenev, were deeply offended by Katkov's rhetoric and sought to exclude him from the festivities.

In the months leading up to the celebration, Turgenev worked to ensure that Katkov would play no prominent role in the proceedings, referring to him in his letters as a "bad element."³³ Turgenev had an effective ally in S. A. Iuriev, editor of the journal *Russian Thought* (*Russkaia mysl'*) and the president of the Society of Lovers of the Russian Word, which was organizing the celebration. Iuriev had responded vigorously to Katkov's spring 1880 editorials in his newly established journal (for which he had tried to acquire *The Brothers Karamazov*, 30/1:33). On unnumbered pages apparently inserted into the March 1880 issue at the last minute, Iuriev writes of the insult inflicted by the editor of the *Moscow News* on the Russian press and Russian society: "Will there really be no consequences to this, and will this insulting scream of a fantasy inflamed by inquisitorial ardor not be reined in? [mixed metaphors in original] Can this voice, which declares publicly that the Russian intelligentsia, and the Russian press, and the Russian government, are tools of the enemies of the people, really play and spread over Russia unhindered? ... Is this not a malicious summons to anarchy, only coming from the other direction? Is this not anarchical nihilism hiding under the mask of conservatism?" He asks for Katkov to show the positive path to salvation, rather than calling only for executions and terror.[34]

Turgenev, Iuriev, and the majority of the organizing committee agreed not to invite Katkov. Levitt writes, "Despite his recent crusade against the intelligentsia, Katkov certainly had as much right as anyone to attend the unveiling of Pushkin's monument. In the 1860s he had defended Pushkin and the autonomy of art against the radicals' attacks, and, more recently, had occasionally taken part in planning for the monument itself."[35] The clumsy rescinding of the Society's invitation to the editor of the *Moscow News*, as Levitt writes, "raised numerous questions—about the society's handling of the celebration, about methods of dealing with one's ideological opponents, and about the importance of the Pushkin Celebration in general."[36]

Dostoevsky had come to Moscow for the celebration at the originally scheduled time in late May. (His letters to his wife are a marvelous diary of his feelings and impressions throughout the Pushkin Celebration.) When the ceremonies were postponed and for a time seemed to be threatened with cancellation, he wavered about whether to stay or to go home to his wife and family. Having gotten wind of the "clique" that he feared was plotting to turn the celebration into a triumph for the radicals, he was torn between his desire to avoid unpleasantness and his equally strong desire to speak his mind and affirm his own beliefs, as he had explained to Pobedonostsev earlier in May (30/1:156). Once in Moscow, he was gratified by the reception he received at a dinner arranged for him by Iuriev, at which speeches were given that attested to his great significance as a "universally responsive" artist (30/1:160). His good relations with Katkov were affirmed by the remarkable fact that at the end of a visit to the editorial offices of the *Russian Herald* and *Moscow News* Katkov left his desk and accompanied him to the door: "He came out into the entryway to see me off, and thus amazed the entire editorial staff, which saw everything from another room, because Katkov never comes out to see anyone off" (30/1:167–68). (Again, as with the name-day dinner party, it seems pitiful that

Dostoevsky considers this display of normal courtesy on Katkov's part worthy of note.) Nevertheless, Dostoevsky's nervous impatience with the logistical details of being away from home, and the uncertainty about what might happen at the celebration, brought him several times to the brink of leaving. Iuriev, Ivan Aksakov, and others urged him to stay.

Dostoevsky writes to his wife on May 29 that the decisive factor is Katkov's insistence that he should stay:

> The main point is that I am needed ... by our whole party, our whole idea, for which we have been struggling for thirty years, because the hostile party (Turgenev, Kovalevsky [liberal professor M. M. Kovalevsky], and almost the whole university) decisively wishes to belittle the significance of Pushkin as the exponent of Russian national character [*narodnost'*], negating his very national character. The only opponent they have from our side is Ivan Sergeevich Aksakov (Iuriev and the others do not have any weight), but Ivan Aksakov has gotten old and also they have gotten tired of him in Moscow. Moscow has not seen or heard me, but they are interested only in me. My voice will have weight, and therefore our side will triumph. I have fought for this my whole life, I cannot run from the field of battle now. And when Katkov said, "You must not leave, you cannot leave,"—a person who is not at all a Slavophile,—then of course, I *must not* leave. (30/1:169)

Despite the efforts of Turgenev and the other liberals, Katkov did have an opportunity to participate in the public celebrations on the evening of the first day, June 6, at the dinner sponsored by the Moscow City Duma, of which he was a member. Contrary to Turgenev's expectation that Katkov would say something insulting, and his plans to walk out if Katkov "permitted himself anything," Katkov's brief speech was one of conciliation, devoid of the fire-breathing rhetoric of his editorials—in other words, it was completely uncharacteristic of Katkov. He seemed to be attempting to reenlist in the ranks of the intelligentsia that he had been excoriating for the past year: "I am speaking under the shelter [*pod seniiu*] of the monument to Pushkin and therefore I hope that my sincere word will be received in a friendly way by everyone without exception. No matter who we are, and where we have come from, and no matter how we have differed in everything else, on this day, at this celebration we all, I hope, are like-minded people [*edinomyshlenniki*] and allies."[37] The phrase "under the shelter of the monument to Pushkin" sounds like Katkov's attempt to use Pushkin to protect him from retaliation for his recent assaults on the intelligentsia.

The aftermath of Katkov's speech has been told in various ways and from various points of view, but what is undisputed is that when Katkov extended his wineglass to Turgenev for a toast, Turgenev twice refused to clink glasses with him. This was either a seismic act of civic courage (in the versions of the liberal press and of Turgenev himself) or a petty act of petulance that was drowned out in the general good will (in the version offered by Dostoevsky to a correspondent later that summer). Two years later, Turgenev was still boasting of his refusal to publicly reconcile with Katkov.[38] In his memoir of Turgenev, N. Ia. Stechkin recalls, "I remember that I could not restrain myself and with the sincere bitterness of youth I said to Turgenev, 'Why did you do that?' 'Why should I,' Turgenev answered irritably, 'reconcile with him on a holiday in order to quarrel with him again when it's over [*v budni*].'"[39]

The version of the incident offered in the newspaper the *Voice* (*Golos*) was one of general rejection of Katkov's message of reconciliation: "Publically at the dinner, Katkov, in the presence of everyone, asked forgiveness of everyone, prayed for them to forget, extended his hand, but no one would shake that hand."[40] This was the widely disseminated version that Dostoevsky was asked about by his friend Elena Andreevna Shtakenshneider in June 1880. She wrote: "Gaevsky [critic V. P. Gaevsky] related how things were, and that Turgenev did not at all want to go to the dinner so as not to have to encounter Katkov, and went only when his friends promised him that at the first unpleasantness that Katkov caused him, they would all leave the hall together with him" (30/1:365). On July 17, Dostoevsky wrote her his version of what had been called in the press "*l'incident Katkoff*": "I don't know how Gaevsky conveyed it to you, but the business with Katkov did not happen that way. The Society of Lovers of the Russian Word insulted Katkov when they were organizing the celebration by taking back the ticket they had sent him; and Katkov gave a speech at the Duma dinner, as a representative of the Duma and at the Duma's request." His letter continues,

> Turgenev could not *at all* have feared insults from Katkov or pretend that he feared them, but on the contrary, Katkov could be afraid of some kind of nastiness directed at him. Turgenev had prepared (with Kovalevsky and the University) such a colossal party, that he had nothing to fear. But Turgenev was the first to insult Katkov. After Katkov gave his speech and when such people as Ivan Aksakov went up to him to clink glasses (even his enemies were clinking with him), Katkov *himself* extended his glass to Turgenev in order to clink with him, but Turgenev moved his hand away and would not clink. That is how *Turgenev himself* told me the story. (30/1:198–99)[41]

Four Views of Pushkin:

1. Varnhagen von Ense

The centerpiece of the Pushkin celebration, the part that has lasted in literary history, were the speeches given by prominent literary figures, particularly Turgenev's speech on June 7 and Dostoevsky's on June 8. Katkov was not invited to give a major speech; his speech at the Duma dinner was extremely brief and did not include any substantive remarks on Pushkin's *oeuvre*. He did, however, publish an extensive appreciation of Pushkin in the *Moscow News* on June 6, thus in a sense joining in what certainly felt like a competition over Pushkin's legacy.[42] Levitt, Joseph Frank, Igor Volgin, and others have provided an extensive analysis of Turgenev's and Dostoevsky's speeches, which I will not attempt to retrace here. My focus will be on the points of contact and dissent between these speeches, delivered orally at the celebration, and Katkov's published evaluation of Pushkin.

Marina Kanevskaya has argued that Dostoevsky's famous speech expressed the same Hegelian approach to art that is evident in the essay on Pushkin published by Varnhagen von Ense in 1838 in the journal founded by Hegel.[43] Varnhagen's essay first appeared in Russian in Nikolai Polevoi's *Son of the Fatherland* (*Syn otechestva*) in 1839. Katkov was unhappy with the translation and, in his first act of correcting someone else's work in public, he published his own translation with an extensive introduction in *Notes of the Fatherland* later in 1839.[44] Kanevskaya cites the original translation, relegating Katkov's version to a footnote. She surmises that Dostoevsky may have learned of Varnhagen's article from Strakhov, who quoted it in an article in *Notes of the Fatherland* in 1867. But Strakhov's article quotes *Katkov's* translation of Varnhagen (as well as his 1856 article on Pushkin).[45] Kanevskaya also omits the extensive polemic that Dostoevsky carried on with Katkov in the early 1860s, during which he would have had ample opportunity to become familiar with Katkov's views, even as he sparred with him. Given that Turgenev was subject to the same philosophical influences as Katkov at the beginning of his career, before discussing the views on Pushkin that the three men expressed in 1880, it will be helpful to return to Varnhagen von Ense's 1839 essay and Katkov's introduction to it.

Katkov's introduction is prefaced by his letter to Kraevsky, the editor of *Notes of the Fatherland*, in which he defines the "main, essential obligation of a journal" as "revealing to the public the treasures of the fatherland and being a conduit of new contemporary interests, making the public familiar with the phenomena of its native life and with the life of other formed [or educated; *obrazovannye*] peoples."[46] He notes that Varnhagen von Ense's article has already appeared in Russia, but the public is still unfamiliar with it, because "some kind of pitiful, unfaithful translation has without authorization called itself Varnhagen's article on Pushkin and has set off, together with the journal that accepted it into its embraces, to wander about the world and mislead honest people."[47]

As discussed above, Katkov's introduction hails the importance of Varnhagen's article in its establishment of the world significance of Pushkin: "It would seem ludicrous to many if we said that Pushkin is a universal poet [*poet vsemirnyi*], who ranks with those few on whom all humanity looks with reverence.... What if we say to them what we have just said, in the voice of a foreigner who is alien to all bias, a foreigner who judges Russia and its phenomena not as a member of the nation [*narod*] but as a member of all humanity—what will they say then?"[48] This assertion of Pushkin's universality [*vsemirnost'*] would become the keynote of Dostoevsky's 1880 speech. Katkov ends his introduction by claiming that Varnhagen's article, published in the journal founded by Hegel, represents the entry of Russian literature onto the world scene: "In the person of Hegel, Germany extends its hand to us, in the person of Germany—all of Europe, all of humanity extends its hand to us."[49]

In discussing Varnhagen's essay in Katkov's translation, I will translate the word *obrazovanie* and its derivatives as "formation," although it can also mean "education," as does the German word *Bildung,* for which it is a translation. For Katkov, it is the "formation" that is the key concept. Varnhagen begins by discussing the reasons for Russian literature having been neglected in Germany: the prejudice that the Russian language is "unformed [*neobrazovan*; *ungebildet*] and coarse" and that as a beginning literature it is limited to imitation of foreign models and so does not reward the labor necessary for studying it.[50] He writes that after the Napoleonic wars, "which awakened in Russia all its national power [*narodnaia sila*; *Nationalkraft*]," a new spiritual striving toward formation [*obrazovanie*; *Bildungstrieb*] has arisen, and "the Russians have learned to value themselves as a nation [*natsiiu*; *Nation*]."[51] He argues that the task of learning Russian is well worth the labor: "The Russian language, the richest and most powerful of all the Slavic dialects, can compete with the most formed [*obrazovannymi*; *gebildetsten*] languages of present-day Europe."[52] Varnhagen reminds the German reader that German poetry is a recent phenomenon, and that before Goethe and Schiller the Germans did not have a poet who could express their formation in its totality: "The nature poetry [*Naturpoesie*] of a people is united in these works with an artistically assimilated content of general, universal progress [*vseobshchego, vsemirnogo progressa*; *des allgemeinen Weltfortschrittes*], to which each nation [*natsiia*; *Nation*] has a right, a part of which it develops by its life and which in the poet interpenetrates with his nationality [*narodnostiiu*; *Volksthümlichkeit*]. Such a poetry has at the present time broken through in Russia, and its purest, most powerful expression is Pushkin."[53]

In speaking of Pushkin, Varnhagen makes a distinction, glossed by Katkov in a footnote, between "folk" (*narodnyi*; *Volksmässige*) and "national" (*natsional'nyi*; *national*): "In fact, he is the expression of all the fullness of Russian life, and therefore he is national [*natsionalen*; *national*] in the higher meaning of the word." Katkov's footnote explains, "We must distinguish the folk [*narodnoe*] from the national [*natsional'nogo*]. We must call folk everything that flows out of the natural state of the people [*narod*], the state in which the spirit is indifferently merged with nation; the national is everything that is stamped with the self-aware, developing spirit of a people [*narod*] as an organic part of all of humanity, as a nation [*natsiia*]. We say 'Russian folk songs,' we will say 'national poet.'"[54] In fact, by 1880 the word *narodnyi* had become far more accepted as expressing the concept "national" than the word *natsional'nyi*, and the debate over Pushkin was whether he was a *narodnyi* poet. But as we shall see, Turgenev in his speech revived the distinction made here by Varnhagen and Katkov between *narodnyi* and *natsional'nyi*.

Like Dostoevsky in 1880, Varnhagen rejects the accusation that Pushkin is an imitator, and reinterprets his indebtedness to other writers in a positive light: "That Pushkin is an original poet, a distinctive poet—this is directly obvious from the impression produced by his poetry. He might borrow external forms and walk along paths that existed before him; but the life he calls forth is a completely new one."[55] Also like Dostoevsky, he stresses the multifarious nature of Pushkin's art, which he sees as conditioned by the vastness and multifariousness of Russia itself:

> South and North, Europe and Asia, savagery and refinement, the ancient and the modern, are all equally accessible and kindred to him; in depicting the most various objects, he is depicting those of his fatherland. The grandeur and power of Russia, the expanse and contents of the Russian empire, have the most beneficial influence in this respect; we can see from here the inner correlation between poetry and the state. Consisting of the same basic elements that make the state powerful, poetry develops from within outwards [*von innen her*]. Pushkin, possessing powerful forces, took full advantage of his nationality [*natsional'nost'*; the word is not repeated

in Varnhagen], completely realized it. In contemplating the most opposite situations that he depicts, you feel that they all belong to the poet equally, that he has equal rights to all of them; they are his, they are Russian.[56]

As Kanevskaya writes, "Here Varnhagen applied the Hegelian concept of the subordination of the 'subjective principle' (the individual) to the 'objective principle' (relating broadly to the state). Thus, the power of the state, which in the case of the Russian Empire happened to be multinational, gave a protean nature to the genius of its poet."[57]

Varnhagen offers analyses of several of Pushkin's works, which we will not discuss here. But one aspect of his article is relevant to Katkov's 1880 article on Pushkin: the prominent position he gives Pushkin's poems in response to the Polish uprising of 1830–31. Varnhagen writes that Pushkin's views on contemporary political issues "are filled with grandeur and nobility, with an all-encompassing farsightedness, mature consciousness, gentle warmth at the thought of the general good, lofty love for his homeland."[58] After praising Pushkin's poem on the death of Napoleon, he continues, "Even more remarkable, even more significant are two other poems by Pushkin, which belong to the time of the last Polish war."[59] The poems he is referring to are *To the Slanderers of Russia* (*Klevetnikam Rossii*) (1831) and *The Anniversary of Borodino* (*Borodinskaia godovshchina*) (1831).

To the Slanderers of Russia has been characterized by Michael Wachtel as "one of Pushkin's most jingoistic poems, a defense of Russia's brutal response to the recent Polish uprising and a saber-rattling rant against the French, whose free thinkers (e.g., Lafayette) had spoken out on behalf of the Poles."[60] In it the speaker warns European critics to stay out of this "quarrel of the Slavs among themselves," a "domestic, old quarrel," a "family enmity" the historical roots of which they do not understand. Like Katkov in 1863, Pushkin in 1831 poses the "fatal question" between Poland and Russia as a zero-sum game: "These tribes have been in hostilities / For a long time now; / More than once now their side, now ours / Has bent beneath the storm. / Who will prevail in the unequal quarrel: / The haughty Pole [*kichlivyi liakh*] or the faithful Russian? / Will the Slavic streams merge in the Russian sea? Or will that sea dry up? That is the question."[61] He goes on to recall Napoleon's invasion in 1812, when "on the ruins of burning Moscow / We did not acknowledge the insolent will / Of the one before whom you trembled." The poetic speaker asserts that "we redeemed with our blood / The freedom, honor, and peace of Europe." He then challenges the Europeans to make good on their threats, and promises that they will meet resistance from the entire Russian land, "from Perm to Tauris, / From the cold Finnish cliffs to fiery Colchis, / From the shaken Kremlin / To the walls of unmoving China" (a passage quoted by Varnhagen earlier in his essay, when speaking of the multifarious nature of the Russian empire). The poem ends with a reminder to the French that in the fields of Russia they will find a place "amid graves that are not alien to them"—that is, the graves of the French who perished after invading Russia in 1812.

In the second "remarkable" poem alluded to by Varnhagen, *The Anniversary of Borodino*, Pushkin commemorates the fact that Praga, a suburb of Warsaw, was subdued by the Russians on August 26 (September 7 N.S.), 1831, the anniversary of the Battle of Borodino, which marked the turning point of the war with Napoleon in 1812. Wachtel notes, "To compare Russia's war of self-defense against Napoleon to its brutal treatment of the Polish uprising was offensive to many liberal thinkers of the time (and of later times)."[62] In the poem Pushkin recalls that "all of Europe" came in 1812 to threaten Russia, but that Russia resisted so valiantly that the unequal battle became an equal one. He renews the threat spoken in *To the Slanderers of Russia* that the foreign invaders will find "a cramped, cold housewarming / Under the grass of the northern fields."[63] This time, however, the Poles (who served under Napoleon) will not lead the charge, because their "crushed rebellion has fallen silent." The lyric speaker magnanimously promises that "we will not burn down their Warsaw." Again addressing the "light-tongued orators" of Western Europe, he asks ironically how far they want Russia to go in giving up its territory in Ukraine and Lithuania—all the way to "our ancient, golden-domed Kiev, / That ancestor of Russian cities"? Instead, he asserts that Russia still stands, and that "the fate of Poland has been decided." He ends by invoking Aleksandr Suvorov, who subdued the Poles in 1794 at the Battle of Praga (and killed many civilians in doing so).

These two poems have embarrassed many of Pushkin's admirers from the time of their appearance to the present.[64] They do, however, reflect Pushkin's sincere opinions, as Wachtel argues based on Pushkin's letters: "There is every indication . . . that Pushkin was not writing these verses to curry favor with the authorities, but was expressing his own political convictions."[65] In a letter of December 9, 1830, to E. M. Khitrovo, daughter of the hero of 1812, General Mikhail Kutuzov, Pushkin writes, "The news of the Polish insurrection has bowled me over. So our old enemies, then, will be exterminated. . . . Do you know the scathing words of the Marshal [Kutuzov] your father? Upon his entry into Vilna, the Poles came to throw themselves at his feet. *Vstan'te*, he told them, *pomnite chto vy russkie* [Get up, remember that you are Russians]."[66] In June 1831 he wrote to Prince P. A.

Viazemsky, "But all the same they must be throttled, and our slowness is tormenting. For us Poland's rebellion is a family affair, an ancient, hereditary dissension; we cannot judge it by the impressions of Europeans, no matter what our own mode of thinking may be."[67] Contemporaries like Viazemsky were embarrassed by the 1831 poems, but after Pushkin's death Viazemsky wrote, "These poems are not triumphal, occasional odes: they are the effusion of intimate feelings and deeply rooted opinions and convictions."[68]

Varnhagen, himself a veteran of the Napoleonic wars, including service in the Russian forces, writes, "In these poems the poet subordinates the question of the (in any case) dubious freedom of an individual tribe to another, higher question— of the general mission of the Slavic peoples. Here he is entirely Russian, burning with passion for his fatherland, celebrating victory, demanding submission, not as shame and slavery, but as the realization of the law of a higher power, for general glory and prosperity."[69] As Kanevskaya writes, "With the help of Hegelian teaching on the creative genius, Varnhagen managed to interpret Pushkin's pronounced imperialism and nationalism positively."[70] Varnhagen writes, "The poet always belongs to his homeland, and when his compatriots are fighting and shedding their blood, he has the full right to wish them victory and glory.... Casting aside all these reasonings, we must say about these poems that, from the artistic point of view, they belong to the very best poems by Pushkin."[71]

2. Turgenev

Not surprisingly, in his Pushkin speech on June 7, 1880, Turgenev did not follow Varnhagen in singling out the 1831 poems as among Pushkin's best; he alludes to them only indirectly, in deploring Pushkin's "ardent sympathy for our sometimes official glory."[72] But he does resemble Varnhagen (and Katkov) in his use of the distinction *narodnyi/natsional'nyi* (which I have been calling folk/national).[73] He applauds what he sees as Pushkin's growing beyond not only the imitation of European models but also "the temptation of counterfeiting a folk tone."[74] He goes on to argue that the German simple folk [*narod*] do not read Goethe, the French folk do not read Molière, and the English folk do not read Shakespeare; "they are read by their nation [*nattsia*]."[75] He explains, "All art is the elevation of life to an ideal: those who stand on the soil [*pochva*] of usual, everyday life remain lower than that level. It is a summit to which one must approach. And all the same Goethe, Molière, and Shakespeare are folk [*narodnye*] poets in the true meaning of the word, that is, national [*natsional'nye*]. Allow us a comparison: Beethoven, for example, or Mozart, are without doubt national German composers, and their music is primarily German music; meanwhile, you will not find in a single one of their compositions a trace, not only of borrowings from the music of the simple folk, but even a similarity to it, precisely because this folk music, still elemental, has passed into their flesh and blood, has animated them and been hidden in them in the same way as the very theory of their art,—just as, for example, the rules of grammar are hidden in the living work of a writer."[76] (The factual foundation for the assertion that there is no trace of folk music in Beethoven or Mozart is highly dubious.)

Turgenev continues, "Let us return to Pushkin. The question: whether he can be called a national poet in the sense of Shakespeare, Goethe, etc., we will leave open for the time being."[77] A bit later he restates the same question, using the title "universal poet" that had been affirmed by Varnhagen and Katkov in 1838–39: "Can we rightfully call Pushkin a national poet in the sense of a universal [*vsemirnyi*] poet (these two expressions often coincide), as we call Shakespeare, Goethe, Homer?" Instead of answering, he says, "Pushkin could not do everything"—that is, he could not both create a literary language and create a literature.[78] After explaining and justifying the rejection of Pushkin by critics in the 1860s, when politics came to displace artistic literature, Turgenev jumps over any direct answer to his own central question and looks to the future: "Who knows? Perhaps there will appear a new, 'as yet unknown chosen one,' who will surpass his teacher and completely earn the title of national-universal [*natsional'no-vsemirnyi*] poet, which we cannot make up our minds to give to Pushkin, although we do not dare to take it away from him."[79] This waffling conclusion was not enthusiastically received. As Levitt writes, "After all the talk about a 'showdown' between the Slavophile and liberal Westernizer camps, the euphoria of the unveiling, Turgenev's ecstatic reception at the university and his public snub of Katkov, the speech itself came as somewhat of an anticlimax."[80] Dostoevsky wrote to his wife, "[Turgenev] degraded Pushkin, taking from him the title of national [*natsional'nyi*] poet" (30/1:182).

Although Turgenev was definitely in the anti-Katkov camp in 1880, his feeling that Pushkin was not yet the national-universal poet echoes both Katkov's 1856 article on Pushkin and his polemics with Dostoevsky in 1861. In 1856, after quoting the fragmentary ending to Pushkin's poem *Autumn* [*Osen'*], Katkov writes, "It seems that all the conditions for extensive and powerful creation were given, but something arrested its development. The moment of inspiration came, everything began to speak vividly in the poet's soul; but hardly had his thought managed to move forward before the moment passed."[81] As discussed above, in 1861, Katkov had written even more explicitly of Pushkin's unfulfilled promise. According to Katkov, Pushkin has not been recognized on the world stage partly because Russian society has not matured to the point that such recognition is deserved:

> The strange fate of our talents has long been noted: they disappeared from the stage at the very moment when it was just possible to expect a mature word from them; they appeared in flashes and disappeared at the very moment when they began to become a true force. As if fate wavered about whether to set going those developments that could imprint the Russian word with an immortal significance; as if it had not yet been decided whether the time had come to declare in our life the true principles that are hidden in our calling. Truly, that time has not yet come, and the life of the best minds in our milieu was and remains a life of hopes and aspirations alone.[82]

Between the time when Katkov wrote this, in 1861, and the time of the Pushkin Celebration in 1880, however, *Fathers and Sons*, *Crime and Punishment*, and *Anna Karenina* had appeared in the *Russian Herald*, and *The Brothers Karamazov* was in the process of unfolding. Whether Katkov, who had been absorbed largely with politics since 1863, recognized what he had helped to achieve in literature since 1861 is far from clear.

3. Dostoevsky

Dostoevsky's letter to his wife the evening of June 8, after his speech, is a vivid description of the triumph he had enjoyed, an account that is corroborated by many other witnesses. At midnight the night before the speech, he had written to her of the rumor that "a whole cabal" had been prepared against him and Ivan Aksakov (30/1:183). He seemed to fear something resembling the hilariously scandalous literary festival he had described in *The Devils*, in which the young radicals orchestrate a buffoonish sabotage of the performances of the oldsters Karmazinov and Stepan Verkhovensky. But on the actual day, no sabotage occurred. Before he even spoke, Dostoevsky was met by a long ovation, which he saw as being conditioned by the success that *The Brothers Karamazov* was having: "I bowed, made gestures, asking them to let me read—nothing helped: ecstasy, enthusiasm (it's all from the *Karamazovs*!)" (30/1:184). Finally the audience allowed him to read, but he was interrupted constantly by bursts of applause. The enthusiastic reception of his ideas about Tatiana in *Eugene Onegin* was "a great victory of our idea over twenty-five years of delusion" (30/1:184). This refers in part to his polemical dialogue with Belinsky, who in his ninth essay on Pushkin in 1845 had criticized Tatiana's decision not to leave her husband.[83]

The conclusion of Dostoevsky's speech was met with fevered enthusiasm: "When I concluded by proclaiming the *universal unification* [*vsemirnoe edinenie*] of people, the hall seemed to be in hysterics, when I finished—I cannot tell you about the roar, about the howl of ecstasy: people in the audience who were strangers were weeping, sobbing, embracing each other and *swearing to each other to be better, not to hate each other any more but to love*" (30/1:184; emphasis in original). Turgenev embraced him tearfully, and Aksakov ran to the stage and announced "that my speech *is not simply a speech but an historical event!*" (30/1:184; emphasis in original). Dostoevsky interprets the reception of his speech as the opening of a chapter even as he fears that it is an ending: "You must agree, Anya, that it was worth staying for this: this is a pledge of the future, a pledge of *everything*, even if I die" (30/1:185; emphasis in original).

One eyewitness, M. A. Venevitinov (1844–1900), recorded in his diary the passionate reception of Dostoevsky's speech and summarized its significance in this way:

> The views expressed in [Dostoevsky's speech] produced an especially powerful impression, the most striking of all the speeches at the Pushkin Celebration. I explain this impression by the fact that Dostoevsky was able to clearly and positively formulate all those vague and ardent dreams and strivings of the last two decades from the time of the peasant emancipation, all those ardent hopes and expectations, all those dark wanderings in the question of merging with the people [*narodnost'*], which had long constituted the sore spot of our literature and for the expression of which it had vainly attempted to find the appropriate images and words.[84]

The reaction to the speech once it was published in the *Moscow News* was far from the ecstatic reception of the same text when it was delivered orally by Dostoevsky at the Pushkin Celebration, and it is easy to see why. The speech is beautifully written and offers what must have been felt as a fresh view of Pushkin, but it also resembles the flights of fancy that Dostoevsky wrote about Fet's *Diana* and Pushkin's *Egyptian Nights* in his journal *Time* in 1861, poetically inspired meditations that do not bear too much close inspection or formalistic comparison with the original texts.

There is an extensive literature on Dostoevsky's Pushkin speech, and I will not offer a comprehensive analysis of it here, but will give its main outlines and particularly the points that connect both to Katkov's translation of Varnhagen von Ense and his own 1880 article on Pushkin.[85] Dostoevsky presents Pushkin as a "prophetic" phenomenon of the Russian spirit (26:136). He divides Pushkin's career into three periods. The first is emblematized by the narrative poem *The Gypsies* [*Tsygany*] (published 1827), with its hero, the nobleman Aleko, who attempts to assuage his disillusionment with civilization by finding refuge in a gypsy camp but only brings violence into the peaceful world of the gypsies. Dostoevsky interprets Aleko as "that unfortunate wanderer in his native land, that historical Russian sufferer, who with such historical necessity appeared in our society, torn away from the people [*narod*]" (26:137). According to Dostoevsky, such wanderers still exist in Russia, but they escape to socialism rather than to a gypsy camp, believing like Aleko that they will find not only their own happiness but universal happiness: "For the Russian wanderer needs precisely universal [*vsemirnoe*] happiness in order to calm down" (26:137).

In Dostoevsky's analysis, *Eugene Onegin* is the key work of Pushkin's second period, in which he continues the ideas of *The Gypsies* in a more realistic mode, with Onegin as the wanderer who is not at home in his native land. But for Dostoevsky, the hero of the novel is not Onegin but Tatiana: "Perhaps Pushkin would have done better if he had named his *poema* for Tatiana and not Onegin, because she is indisputably the main heroine of the *poema*. She is a positive type, not a negative one, a type of positive beauty, the apotheosis of the Russian woman, and the poet predestined her to express the idea of the *poema* in the famous scene of the last meeting of Tatiana with Onegin" (26:140). In 1845 Belinsky had interpreted Tatiana's refusal to leave her unloved husband and run away with Onegin, whom she admits she still loves, as "a profanation of the feeling and purity of femininity, because certain relationships that are not consecrated by love are in the highest degree immoral."[86] For Dostoevsky, Tatiana expresses the idea that one cannot build one's happiness on the unhappiness of another person: "Happiness is not only in the pleasures of love, but also in the higher harmony of the spirit. How can you calm down your spirit, when behind you stands a dishonorable, pitiless, inhuman act?" (26:142). Unlike Onegin, Tatiana maintains, through her recollection at the fatal moment of the cross over her peasant nanny's grave, her connection "with her motherland, with her native people [*narod*], with its holiness" (26:143). And so, Dostoevsky continues, "In Onegin, in this immortal and unattainable *poema*, Pushkin has appeared as a great national [*narodnyi*] writer, like no one ever before him" (26:143). It is clear from the context that Dostoevsky uses the word *narodnyi* not in the sense of something simpler and cruder than *natsional'nyi*, as Varnhagen-Katkov and Turgenev do; for him it means national, not folk.

Before moving to the third section of his speech, Dostoevsky makes a statement that reads as an echo of Katkov's 1839 introduction to Varnhagen von Ense's article, which had ended, "May God grant that we finally feel in ourselves the strength for original and independent intellectual activity."[87] Dostoevsky proclaims: "If Pushkin had not existed, perhaps our faith in our Russian independence, our conscious hope in our national [*narodnye*] powers, and consequently our faith in our future independent mission in the family of European peoples [*narody*] would not have been defined with such unshakable strength" (26:145).

According to Dostoevsky's periodization, it is in Pushkin's third period that there began to shine in his works "universal [*vsemirnye*] ideas, and the poetic images of other peoples were reflected and their geniuses were embodied" (26:145). Varnhagen von Ense had claimed that Pushkin's ability to capture the multifariousness of experience was conditioned by his Russianness. Dostoevsky makes a similar claim, asserting that Pushkin's "universal responsiveness" is a uniquely Russian trait. According to Dostoevsky, neither Shakespeare, Cervantes, nor Schiller had the power of being completely reincarnated into an alien nationality [*natsional'nost'*]. Pushkin shares this capability with the Russian people: "What is the power of the spirit of the Russian nationality [*narodnost'*] if not the striving in its ultimate aims toward universality and universal humanity [*vsechelovechnost'*]?" (26:147). The Petrine reform was not just about the adoption of European costumes, inventions, and science, but also the striving toward "universal human unification": "Without hostility (as, it seems, it would have to happen), but with friendship, with complete love we accepted into our soul the geniuses of other nations [*natsii*]" (26:147). Dostoevsky continues: "Later, I believe, we, that is, of course, not we, but future coming Russian people, will understand to the last person that to become a true Russian will mean precisely: to strive to decisively introduce reconciliation into European contradictions, to show the way out for European anguish in our Russian soul, which is universally human and all-unifying, to find room in it with brotherly love for all our brothers, and finally, perhaps, to utter the decisive word of great, general harmony, of brotherly decisive harmony of all tribes according to Christ's evangelical law!" (26:148).

As Kanevskaya notes, Dostoevsky does not mention Pushkin's Poland poems in his speech "given [their] somewhat scandalous reputation ... as servile and conservative."[88] She sees a hint at them, though, in Dostoevsky's statement that if Pushkin had lived longer, he might have helped "our European brethren" to understand "the whole truth of our aspirations" (26:148). Kanevskaya concludes that the central idea for both Varnhagen and Dostoevsky is Pushkin's universality: "This term—universality—which most of Dostoevsky's critics found meaningless in 1880, was Hegelian in essence. First of all, when applied to a poet, 'universality' suggests that the poet so evaluated is a truly 'national' poet. This means that the poet's art represents the highest stage of his nation's cultural or—as Dostoevsky would have it—spiritual development, and the highest level of a nation's self-perception."[89] I would add that Pushkin's universality lay at the heart of Katkov's conception of him beginning with his translation of Varnhagen in 1839, although for Katkov it was devoid of the messianic coloration it was given by Dostoevsky.

4. Katkov

As we have seen, Katkov was not given the kind of public platform at the Pushkin Celebration that was given to Turgenev, Dostoevsky, and other writers by the Society of Lovers of the Russian Word, although he had been a member of the Society for many years. But he did have the platform of the *Moscow News*, in which he published a special supplement on June 6 that contained his essay "Pushkin's Achievement (*Zasluga Pushkina*)."[90] The supplement, which was republished in the June 1880 issue of the *Russian Herald*, also included Katkov's Duma speech, a selection of Pushkin's poems, including *To the Slanderers of Russia* and *The Anniversary of Borodino*, a large excerpt from Katkov's 1856 articles on Pushkin, and a brief excerpt from Dostoevsky's Pushkin speech, a kind of teaser for the full publication that was to ensue on June 13.[91]

In Katkov's essay "Pushkin's Achievement," he leaves behind the reservations and qualifications that had marked his evaluation of Pushkin's significance in his 1856 articles and in his polemics with Dostoevsky in 1861. Unlike Turgenev, he forthrightly grants Pushkin the title of "national poet," now using, as Dostoevsky does, the adjective *narodnyi*, not *natsional'nyi*: "Pushkin stands on the heights of universal [*vsemirnogo*] significance. A Russian national [*narodnyi*] poet, he has full right to an honored place in the pantheon of all times and peoples."[92] This apparent promotion of Pushkin is made in the context of Katkov's enlistment of Pushkin in his struggle with sedition. In this essay Pushkin is not merely an artist, but also a fighter for the Russian national cause—like Katkov.

The essay begins not with the monument to Pushkin but with the monument to Minin and Pozharsky on Red Square in Moscow, opened in 1818. Kuzma Minin and Dmitri Pozharsky were a merchant and a prince credited with repelling the invasion of the Poles in 1612 by raising an all-volunteer Russian force. As Katya Hokanson argues, Pushkin was alluding to this invasion of Moscow by the Poles when he warned the "slanderers of Russia" to stay out of a long-standing family quarrel.[93] Katkov writes, referring to the beginnings of the Romanov dynasty, "A great, unparalleled people's [*narodnoe*] movement, full of strength and spirit and at the same time humble in spirit, simple and not haughty [*nekichlivyi*] in its grandeur! The foreign enemy was shamed and banished, sedition was crushed, the state was saved, and supreme power was carefully and without detriment passed to the chosen one of the entire Russian land, the progenitor of a new ruling house, which opened a new era in the history of our fatherland."[94] The somewhat unusual adjective Katkov uses to describe the spirit of the Russian people, *nekichlivyi*, "not-haughty," is the negation of the adjective *kichlivyi*, used by Pushkin to describe the Poles in *To the Slanderers of Russia*. Katkov continues, "Now [this monument] will be joined by another, dedicated to a person who did not lead national [*narodnyi*] militias into battle, but also a national [*narodnyi*] motive force, the great Russian national [*narodnyi*] poet, as the common voice lauds our Pushkin."[95]

As he had at the very beginning of his career, Katkov links the role of art to the maturation and strengthening of a nation's world-historical significance: "The life of a people [*narod*] and its calling are not exhausted by deeds of state necessity. When the body has been formed and strengthened, the soul is liberated for independent life. The existence of a people is not yet guaranteed by the development of external power and armed force, its right to existence has not yet been proved. There were colossi fortified by external force that, having carried out their temporary mission, crumbled into dust and disappeared. A great people that is called to life possesses the force of inner unity and manifests its spirit not in the cares of self-preservation alone, but also in the development of the gifts of human nature." Katkov points out that Pushkin "did not have the opportunity to save his fatherland from enemies, but he was given the opportunity to beautify, elevate, and glorify his nationality [*narodnost'*]."[96] At the end of his literary career, Katkov is reasserting the importance of a great literature for the establishment of a great nation.

As in 1856, Katkov praises Pushkin's work on the Russian literary language, which caused not only his compatriots but also foreigners to love the Russian language. But as with the opening comparison to Minin and Pozharsky, Katkov shifts the emphasis from art to national identity: "No one brought so much true benefit [*pol'za*] to the Russian nationality [*narodnost'*] as Pushkin during the time that God granted him to live, and his works are worth many battles won."[97] Later in the essay Katkov discusses works by Pushkin that are "sources of the purest patriotism": *Poltava*, *Boris Godunov*, all the poems addressed to Peter the Great, and, of course, *To the Slanderers of Russia* and *The Anniversary of Borodino*. Katkov writes, "These patriotic songs were called forth by the events of 1831 and deal with a question of the greatest importance for Russia.... Thirty years passed, and the very same question arose—but in what state did it find our journalism [*literatura*], which back then had already found its voice and taken up politics? Our journalism then occupied itself with the desecration of Pushkin himself and of everything that is dear to the Russian feeling and the enlightened mind, it tried to surpass even our enemies with its slander of our country."[98] He implicitly links the supposedly pro-Polish sympathies of the intelligentsia in 1863 with the same sentiments he detects in the intelligentsia of 1880.

Katkov expands on the question of Pushkin's politics, asking what party he belonged to. This recalls his April 1880 editorial that asserted that there was no liberal or conservative party in Russia, only the national and antinational party, or the Russian and anti-Russian party. Not surprisingly, he counts Pushkin as belonging to the Russian party, and even traces the coinage of the term to Pushkin. He writes, "Presenting in his journal the *Contemporary* the memoirs of Moreau de Brasey, a foreigner who served in the troops of Peter the Great, Pushkin pauses on the complaints of this adventurer, who reproached the Russian tsar for being partial to Russians. And he makes the following note: 'We thank our author for his precious testimony. It is pleasant for us to see an attestation by a foreigner that Peter the Great and Field-Marshal Sheremetiev belonged to the *Russian* party.'"[99]

Throughout his 1880 essay, Katkov connects what he sees as Pushkin's great patriotic contribution with the embattled condition of the Russian state in 1880. So it is not unexpected that as he writes about Pushkin he seems to be also writing about himself. In describing the cooling of the public toward Pushkin as he matured, Katkov writes, using rhetorical turns from Pushkin's own poems,

> He felt the growing coldness of the public towards him, he was annoyed by the gossip of fools; but not once did he fall into temptation or degrade himself by seeking popularity. He remained in solitude on his summit, disturbed neither by praise nor abuse. Blessed is he who has experienced this holy solitude! Blessed is he who at the summit of his deeds, upon carrying out his duty, remains alone with his conscience!

... Whoever has not experienced this lofty feeling of independence of thought, not submissive to anything other than duty, does not know the best that a person can experience and that cannot be replaced by any intoxication of vanity.... Only that cause is firm, and holy, and fruitful, that is conceived and carried out by a person alone with his conscience.[100]

Katkov, excluded from the communal celebration of Pushkin, denied the chance to speak publicly alongside the writers whose works he had published in the *Russian Herald*, turned rejection by his peers into a proud assertion of kinship with Russia's great national poet.

The End of Dostoevsky

Although they had disagreed about Pushkin's significance during their polemic in 1861, in 1880 Dostoevsky and Katkov both asserted Pushkin's status as national poet. Dostoevsky's speech, which he had tentatively offered to both Iuriev and to A. S. Suvorin, the editor of *New Time* [*Novoe vremia*], was published in Katkov's *Moscow News* on June 13, 1880.[101] According to Dostoevsky in a letter to his wife, his choice was determined by the fact that in order to participate in the Pushkin Celebration, he had had to take a break from the publication of *The Brothers Karamazov*, and if he were to give the article to Iuriev, "it would turn out that I am asking for an extension from Katkov precisely with the goal of using that extension in order to work for his enemy Iuriev.... Katkov will be offended" (30/1:163).

The line taken by Soviet-era scholars is that Katkov did not really like Dostoevsky's speech and was merely using it as "a trump card in his political game" (26:470). Volgin makes much of an uncorroborated report by K. N. Leontiev that Katkov had laughed at the speech behind Dostoevsky's back, saying, "What kind of event was *this*?"[102] But this is flimsy evidence on which to base the idea that Katkov rejected the basic thrust of Dostoevsky's speech, in particular its assertion of the special mission of Russia in the world. Turgenev, who had tearfully embraced Dostoevsky after the speech, offered a sharply critical response in a letter to Stasiulevich, the editor of the *Herald of Europe*, written the very day that the speech appeared in the *Moscow News*: "This very intelligent, brilliant, and cunningly-skillful speech, for all its passion, is entirely based on a falsehood, but a falsehood that is pleasant for Russian self-love.... 'We will say the final words to Europe, we will give her herself as a gift—because Pushkin brilliantly recreated

Shakespeare, Goethe, etc.'? But he *recreated* them, and did not *create* them—and we will not create a new Europe—as he did not create Shakespeare and the others."[103] We do not have Katkov's direct response to Dostoevsky's speech, but it would be hard to imagine him offering this kind of criticism. For Katkov it was impossible to go too far in exalting the mission of Russia.

Volgin writes, "The appearance of the Speech in Katkov's newspaper was perceived as a political gesture, as an act of ideological solidarity. The reputation of the publication could not help but reflect on the reputation of the Speech."[104] There is no question that the widespread criticism of a speech that had received such a heartfelt positive response when delivered orally was conditioned by the "compromise" once again entailed by publishing in one of Katkov's organs. Dostoevsky was so affected by the criticism that he devoted an entire issue of his *Diary of a Writer* to explaining himself, mainly in response to the liberal critic A. D. Gradovsky.[105]

Despite the compromises and criticisms that went along with publishing in the *Russian Herald* and the *Moscow News*, as he finished *The Brothers Karamazov*, Dostoevsky was clearly planning to continue to work with the journal that had brought almost all of his great works to light and had "established his name." In November 1880, in a letter transmitting the epilogue of *The Brothers Karamazov*, Dostoevsky wrote to Liubimov, "Well, now the novel is finished! I worked on it for three years, spent two years publishing it—a significant moment for me.... Allow me not to say goodbye. After all, I intend to live and write for another twenty years" (30/1:227). At the end of November, in another letter to Liubimov, Dostoevsky as usual sent his regards to Katkov, but now in words he had never used before: "When you see Mikhail Nikiforovich, kindly convey to him my esteem, respect, and constant sincere devotion now, in the future, and forever and ever [*vo veki vekov*]" (30/1:231).

The night of January 25–26, 1881, Dostoevsky suffered a pulmonary hemorrhage. On January 26 he wrote a letter, the last in his own hand, to Liubimov asking for the last four thousand rubles owed him for *The Brothers Karamazov*: "Since you have for so long now and so often been constantly gracious to all my requests, may I hope one more time for your attention and assistance with my present, perhaps *last* request" (30/1:241; emphasis in original).[106] It did in fact turn out to be the last of Dostoevsky's many requests for payment from the *Russian Herald*; he had a more serious hemorrhage the next day and died on January 28. The day after Dostoevsky's death, Pobedonostsev wrote to Katkov, "Before his death Fyodor Mikhailovich was worried about the money he was expecting from the *Russian Herald*. He was worried that the money would come after his death and his wife would have difficulty getting it. That is how it turned out."[107] The money was sent to a bank in the name of Dostoevsky, and Pobedonostsev was asking for the name to be changed to that of Anna Grigorievna or his own name. Literally to his last moment, Dostoevsky was enmeshed with the *Russian Herald*.

The obituary, apparently written by Katkov, that appeared in the *Moscow News* made reference to Dostoevsky's final letter to Liubimov:

> Last night we were thunderstruck by the news of the demise of Fyodor Mikhailovich Dostoevsky. Just the day before, January 27, we received from him a letter in his own hand, written in a firm handwriting and not arousing any apprehensions. There was, however, an ominous word in this letter, which at the time slipped by unnoticed by us. In asking us about a certain matter, he added: "This is perhaps my *last* request." Only now has the sorrowful meaning of this word *last* become clear to us. It expressed the premonition of death even before the fatal hemorrhage that so quickly extinguished the dear life of our friend.[108]

The obituary continues with some rather conventional words: "Goodbye, good laborer in the Russian fields! We expected much more from you, but that which you have done is enough to preserve your name forever in the Russian national [*narodnyi*] memory. The earth will take its own, dust will be to dust; but your spiritual legacy will remain forever the precious property of your fatherland."

Much less well known and much more remarkable is an essay on Dostoevsky that Katkov published a few days later, "A Characterization of the Inner World of Dostoevsky (On the Occasion of His Demise)."[109] Katkov begins the essay by praising Dostoevsky's spiritual depth, his constant search for God: "It is there, in that searching for God, that true progress for both a person and for humanity is found!"[110] Referring to Dostoevsky's imprisonment when he was "in the very flower of his life," Katkov writes, "Perhaps he would not have become what he became in his activity if God had not decreed this trial for him."[111] Dostoevsky struggled with himself, and chastised in himself, not in others, all the bad aspects of human nature, "and the more he purified and mastered himself, the more deeply he became a son of his people [*narod*] and a Christian who believed with the simplicity of his heart."[112] He found Christ "in Russian national feeling [*v russkom narodnom chuvstve*]": "In him we see the Russian mind, which seeks and finds its ideals not in emptiness, not in abstractions, not in a foreign land, but in the living soul of its people [*narod*]."¹¹³ What Dostoevsky found in the people above all was the spirit of mercy [*miloserdie*], "the most Christian principle in Christianity, which we feel lives in the depths of our nationality [*narodnost'*] and in which is hidden its true strength."¹¹⁴

Katkov goes on to make a virtue of the very quality of Dostoevsky's art that had given rise to their differences, his drive to depict humanity in all its manifestations, even the most repulsive and offensive. I will quote this passage at length, because it provides remarkable testimony that, whatever motivated Katkov's interference in the texts of Dostoevsky's novels, it was not caused by lack of comprehension of the originality and power of Dostoevsky's artistic talent:

> In his works Dostoevsky often depicts people who are morally sick, leprous people. He was not disgusted by any hideousness [*bezobrazie*], he was not afraid of any horror, he was not embarrassed by any nakedness. His analysis extended to the tiniest details of moral ailments, and one must be amazed at the calmness, the seemingly merciless subtlety with which his dissecting scalpel operated. Is this what is called an exposé? No. Is it what is called realism in art? No. Was it the dispassionate observer pursuing some art or science? No. Or, finally, was he like a doctor who treats his patients conscientiously, but sees in them nothing more than pathological cases? No, if he resembled anyone, it would be the nurse, the sister of mercy [*sestra miloserdiia*], selflessly devoted to God, who has doomed herself, who is endlessly permeated with a feeling of her service, who is not repelled by any ulcer, who is not squeamish about any pus, and is entirely concerned only with easing the sufferings of the sick person. In his analyses he seeks the truth and goes more and more deeply, goes to the end, not embarrassed by anything, until under this filth, under this nastiness one feels, one senses the sick, trembling, oblivious, desolate human soul itself. And we begin to understand this minute analysis; in these details that had aroused a feeling of disgust in us we perceive the work of love, which seeks God in the human being and does not despair of finding the human being in a wild and lost creature.¹¹⁵

This is a singularly perceptive and penetrating description of the artistry that created Stavrogin's confession. More broadly, if one thinks back to Katkov's assessment that Pushkin, for all his poetic gifts and skill, did not quite achieve the stature of a world figure in literature, then effectively Katkov sees Dostoevsky as having reached that level of distinction as a universal writer. In other words, with Dostoevsky, the Russian canon merged with the world's.

The End of Turgenev

Katkov also responded in print to the death of Turgenev in September 1883, but with much less greatness of spirit than he displayed in the meditation on Dostoevsky, who had never broken with him. Katkov took the opportunity of Turgenev's death to renew his accusations that Turgenev had flirted with the revolutionaries, supporting a radical publication edited by P. L. Lavrov. Katkov characterized Turgenev's support for Lavrov not as "alms" but as ransoming himself from persecution: "With his impressionability, authorial vanity, and weak character he could not stand the insults that were being showered on him by many of those who are now celebrating him, and he surrendered."[116] Katkov claims the authority of one who has known Turgenev since youth in order to deny the sincerity of his sympathy with the radicals: "The coarse radicalism that began to take possession of our literature from the end of the 1840s was hateful to his artistic nature, the elegance of his taste, and his educated mind."[117] Turgenev had run away from the *Contemporary* without looking back as soon as Dobroliubov and Chernyshevsky took over: "We remember with what irritation, with what bitterness he then spoke about the nihilism that was then arising, about that very Bazarov to whom he later publicly bowed."[118] But everything changed in the late 1860s and the 1870s; the government was weakened, civic spirit declined, and revolutionary propaganda became a force with which it was difficult to argue.

Katkov goes on to offer an evaluation of Turgenev's artistic gift and achievement: "Turgenev was primarily an artist. Each person has his calling. He was not much interested in politics, and he did not have a firm civic cast of thought. All the merit of his works is contained in pure artistry. He was not called to the struggle, and he ran away or ransomed himself off from what was hateful to him. At first he had to force himself, he tried to cajole his opponents. But when insults were replaced by ovations, then the path of cajolery became easier and more alluring."[119] Finally he became the symbol of a sort of indefinite liberalism. No one cared about his literary works; "he was celebrated as a political figure, which he never was, although he was quite willing to appear to be one so that the dogs would not bite but would fawn on him."[120]

Katkov's final judgment on Turgenev makes clear that, despite the achievement of *Fathers and Sons*, Katkov saw the activity of Turgenev as a failure in terms of advancing the cause of a Russian national literature: "If Turgenev's talent was not distinguished by depth and breadth of conceptions, still his works shine with the charm of the narration, the poetry of the descriptions, the subtlety of the finishing, a mastery if not of characters then of types and situations, that artist's power of observation that elevates into clear outlines that which in life is scattered, lost, and hidden by chance happenings.... But no matter how significant the merits of Turgenev's best works, everyone will recognize that they are far from being of the character that would raise him to the level of universal [*vsemirnyi*] genius."[121] Katkov's "eulogy" for Turgenev denies him major significance either as an artist or as a political figure, and ends with a horrifying image: "Gentlemen, you made fun of Turgenev while he was alive: have the shame not to continue the same game on his grave. Have at least some respect for the memory of the deceased. Leave Turgenev his true achievements and merits; at least do not dress up a dead body in the same costume in which you led him about the streets when he was alive. At least allow him to be buried honorably."[122]

The End of Katkov

With *The Brothers Karamazov*, Katkov's literary achievement was at an end. Tsar Alexander II was assassinated on March 1, 1881. In the reign of his son Alexander III, Katkov's meddling in government policy, especially foreign policy, got out of hand, to the point that in March 1887 the tsar threatened to give him a public warning a few months before Katkov's death in July. The tsar had written on a copy of one of Katkov's editorials promoting an alliance with France, "An article that is unseemly in the highest degree. In general Katkov is forgetting himself and playing the role of some kind of dictator, forgetting that foreign policy depends on me and that I answer for the consequences, not Mr. Katkov."[123]

Pobedonostsev, by now ober-procurator of the Holy Synod, felt it necessary to write to the tsar to urge him not to issue a public warning, which would lead to Katkov's closing the *Moscow News* and would be received as a blow to the conservative cause. In his letter Pobedonostsev agrees that Katkov has gotten out of hand, but he blames government officials for having spoiled him by hanging on his every word in the *Moscow News*. In the course of pleading (successfully) with the tsar not to carry out his intention, Pobedonostsev gives an interesting evaluation of Katkov's significance:

> Katkov is a highly talented journalist, intelligent, sensitive to true Russian interests and to firm conservative principles. As a journalist he has performed valuable services to Russia and the government in difficult times. He became the object of the

fanatical hatred of all enemies of order and an object of adoration and authority among many Russian people who strive toward the establishment of order. Both one and the other are extremes, but both one and the other are a *fact* of considerable political significance. A fact with which one must reckon. All of Katkov's power is in the nerve of his journalistic activity as a Russian publicist, and moreover the *only* one, because everything else is triviality or trash, or a merchant's shop. I will add that for all his deficiencies and enthusiasms, Katkov and his newspaper are very valuable precisely now, at a time of troubles, because when he is no more, there will decidedly be *no one* to replace him in our debauched press, poor in serious talents; and, finally, because that moment, which one must fear, is probably not far off, because Katkov will hardly hold out much longer.[124]

Katkov died of cancer in July.

Katkov's Monument

At the time of the Pushkin Celebration, after "*l'incident Katkoff*," the conservative theorist K. N. Leontiev suggested, only half-facetiously, that a monument be erected to Katkov opposite that of Pushkin: "If we Russians had even a spark of moral courage and what is called intellectual creativity, we could do an unheard-of thing: *politically canonize Katkov while he is alive*. Open a subscription for a monument to him, right here, *near Pushkin, on Strastnoi Boulevard* [where the offices of the *Russian Herald* and *Moscow News* were located].... Who can be considered equal in power, in talent, and in influence in the field of *political literature* to Pushkin in the field of *artistic literature*? Of course, Katkov!"[125]

Another sort of monument was suggested by Dostoevsky to the art patron P. M. Tretyakov in 1872. Tretyakov, whose collection later became the foundation of what is now the world-famous State Tretyakov Gallery, was commissioning portraits of Russia's most important cultural figures from some of the best artists. He had commissioned V. G. Perov to paint the portrait of Dostoevsky that is the most powerful image we have of the writer. On May 10, 1872, Perov wrote Tretyakov, "Dostoevsky and Maikov consider that you absolutely have to have for your gallery a portrait of old man Tiutchev, as the most important poet-philosopher, who had no equal other than Pushkin, and who stands higher than Heine,—and of Katkov, as the most important mind in Russia. Dostoevsky even said that without their portraits, you could say to yourself: 'I didn't notice the elephants' [idiom for "I missed the point"]—in a word, they consider Katkov a *genius*."[126] Two months after Dostoevsky's death in 1881, Tretyakov asked Ilia Repin to paint a portrait of Katkov. Repin categorically refused, arguing that only people who were dear to the nation should be immortalized in such a way, not a retrograde like Katkov, who "attacked every bright thought, stamped every free word with shame." When Tretyakov was explaining to I. N. Kramskoi in 1886 which portraits were still missing, he mentioned Katkov and explained, "No one wanted to paint him."[127]

But Katkov had erected a monument to himself not made by hands. By nurturing, nagging, financing, inspiring, and sometimes infuriating the writers of *Fathers and Sons*, *Anna Karenina*, and *The Brothers Karamazov*, he had played a vital role in creating the Russian novels that would enter the world's literary canon.

CONCLUSION

THE EDITOR AS PATRON

Although Turgenev, Dostoevsky, and Tolstoy responded in their great novels to Katkov's program, the works they published in the *Russian Herald* transcend Katkov's artistically limited goals in the interest of these writers' own aesthetic goals. The moments of Katkov's most glaring interference in the texts of these writers' novels are the moments where they are clearly trying to escape and get beyond Katkov's program, even as they participate most powerfully in his drive to create the canon of Russian literature as the sign of a historically significant nationality.

In his study of the "worlds" of people working together who make the creation of art possible, sociologist Howard S. Becker says that he "looks for trouble" in the process, "supposing that by so doing ... I will find the basic forms of cooperation that make the art possible."[1] It was "trouble" that brought Mikhail Katkov to my attention, when after years of teaching Dostoevsky's *Devils* and Tolstoy's *Anna Karenina*, I suddenly realized that the (to my mind) supernumerary, insignificant editor who had stepped in to exclude a key chapter from *The Devils*, and the equally insignificant meddler who had refused to publish part 8 of *Anna Karenina*, were the same person. This "trouble" was what alerted me to the fact that perhaps this person was not so secondary after all.

Katkov's reputation in Russian literary history has been deeply damaged by his intrusive revisions of the work of Turgenev, Dostoevsky, and Tolstoy. The writer Nikolai Leskov, who saw the *Russian Herald* as his only possible venue but who also suffered terribly from Katkov's editorial interventions, wrote in a letter of 1875 that, although he admired Katkov, he regarded him as "the murderer of my native literature."[2] My task in this book has been to grasp the other side of Katkov's activity, his role not as the murderer but as the inciter and inspirer of Russian literature. In his 1880 article on Pushkin, Katkov asserted that for the true poet, words "are not simply signs of general conceptions that can be reproduced in any other language with no residue; but each is felt by him as something in itself, as a living being that has its own fate and carries the impress of the combinations it has passed through.... That is why a work of a truly creative talent can only approximately be reproduced in another language."[3] Perhaps ironically, given his emphasis on the Russian language, Katkov's program for Russian literature gave rise to a type of novel that is eminently "translatable," because of its rich historical, psychological, and political content, and that consequently spread beyond Russia's boundaries to be considered part of world literature.

J. A. Sutherland has shown how writers like Charles Dickens and William Makepeace Thackeray were able to negotiate the world of Victorian publishing in such a way as to gain greater artistic control over their works. He writes, "Holding onto this independence was often difficult. Those who managed to do so showed considerable skill and sense of tactics. Usually it required not becoming too attached, by friendship or financial ties, to any one publisher."[4] For both financial and political reasons, the world of the thick journal in Russia in the 1860s–80s did not offer the possibility for this kind of mobility. Among journals publishing serious fiction, the *Russian Herald* could not be equaled in stability and prestige.

There is no fixed, immutable "truth" about the proper role of an editor. At one extreme stands Milan Kundera, who has written, "If a work of art emanates from an individual and his uniqueness, it is logical that this unique being, the author, should possess all rights over the thing that emanates exclusively from him."[5] At the other stands the practice of editors like Max Perkins and Gordon Lish, who played transformative (and also at times controversial) roles in shaping, and reshaping, the work of writers like Thomas Wolfe and Raymond Carver.[6]

Interestingly, both Kundera and Katkov use the metaphor of the house to express their opposing views. For Kundera, the house belongs to the artist. He quotes Igor Stravinsky as telling the conductor Ernest Ansermet about his cuts in one of Stravinsky's works, "I would like to say: 'But you're not in your own house, my dear fellow'; I never told you: 'Here, take my score and do whatever you please with it.'"[7] Kundera comments, "It's clear what was at stake in the dispute that wrecked the friendship: Stravinsky's author's rights, his *moral* rights; the anger of an author who will not stand for anyone tampering with his work; and, on the other side, the annoyance of a performer who cannot tolerate the author's proud behavior and tries to limit his power."[8]

In an 1860 letter to A. V. Druzhinin, Katkov complains about a young upstart writer who asked him, as Dostoevsky would do a few years later in connection with *Crime and Punishment*, not to make any corrections to his story. Katkov writes, "Setting this kind of condition upon submitting an article is the same as someone who wishes to make a person's acquaintance and enter his house, and who sets a condition in advance that [the host] would not do something nasty, curse him or beat him. It is both indelicate and absurd. If you do not trust a person, don't make his acquaintance and don't send him your articles."[9] For Kundera, the house is the inviolable creation that belongs solely to the artist. For Katkov, the house belongs to the editor. Those who enter it are expected to trust the host to treat them properly, according to his discretion.

In the Tur polemic, Vyzinsky had compared Katkov to a rich English landlord, whose contributors are unskilled laborers "who work for him but also enjoy his powerful patronage."[10] Indeed Katkov seems to combine elements of both the editor and the patron. He presented through his writings a clear program for Russian literature, which was to affirm the political and historical importance of the Russian nationality as expressed through its language, and he paid for the works that were to embody that program.[11] Becker writes, "a patronage system makes an immediate connection between what the patron wants and understands and what the artist does. Patrons pay, and they dictate—not every note or brush stroke, but the broad outlines and the matters that concern them. They choose artists who provide what they want."[12] When we consider the ways that Katkov interacted with writers like Turgenev and Dostoevsky, this description seems apt. In the case of Tolstoy, the system broke down spectacularly.

Michael Baxandall, speaking of the patronage of painting in fifteenth-century Italy, has written:

> A fifteenth-century painting is the deposit of a social relationship. On one side there was a painter who made the picture, or at least supervised its making. On the other side there was somebody else who asked him to make it, provided funds for him to make it and, after he had made it, reckoned on using it in some way or other.... The man who asked for, paid for, and found a use for the painting might be called the *patron*. ... This second party is an active, determining and not necessarily benevolent agent in the transaction of which the painting is the result.[13]

The analogy is not exact, given the vast differences between Renaissance Italy and reform-age Russia, but it can be helpful in thinking about Katkov, who could aptly be described as playing an "active, determining and not necessarily benevolent" role in the creation of the great Russian novel. Baxandall goes on, "In the fifteenth century painting was still too important to be left to the painters. The picture trade was a quite different thing from that in our own late romantic condition, in which painters paint what they think best and then look round for a buyer."[14]

In Russia in the second half of the nineteenth century, at least in Katkov's universe, novel writing was still too important to be left entirely to the novelists. If we think that Russian literature of the golden age of the novel is the product of a collection of geniuses writing "what they think best and then looking round for a buyer," if we do not reckon with the influence of the powerful patron/editor Katkov in shaping what they wrote, we are falling victim to a romantic fallacy. Today we may be indifferent or antagonistic to Katkov's nationalist project, but we need to recognize the role it played in the formation of the canon of Russian literature. This does not mean to reduce the great works of Russian literature to Katkov's program, but to restore an awareness of the context in which they arose.

Notes

INTRODUCTION

1. The patronymic of Katkov's mother is sometimes given as "Ekimovna." An excellent recent source on Katkov's early life is S. M. San'kova, *Mikhail Nikiforovich Katkov: V poiskakh mesta (1818–1856)* (Moscow: APK and PPRO, 2008). See also Timofei Prokopov, "Introduction to M. N. Katkov," in M. N. Katkov, *Sobranie sochinenii*, 6 vols., ed. A. N. Nikoliukin (St. Petersburg: Rostok, 2010–12), 1:10–15 (hereafter cited as *SS*); and E. V. Perevalova, *Zhurnal M. N. Katkova Russkii vestnik v pervye gody izdaniia (1856–1862): Literaturnaia pozitsiia* (Moscow: Moskovskii gosudarstvennyi universitet pechati, 2010), 17–23. The major sources in English are Martin Katz, *Mikhail N. Katkov: A Political Biography, 1818–1887* (The Hague: Mouton, 1966); and Catharine Theimer Nepomnyashchy, "Katkov and the Emergence of the *Russian Messenger*," *Ulbandus Review* 1, no. 1 (1977): 59–89. Neither is primarily biographical; Katz focuses on Katkov's political discourse, and Nepomnyashchy describes his literary activity. See also Elizabeth Mary Mullen, "M. N. Katkov as Editor of *Russkii vestnik* from 1856–1862," MA thesis, Brown University, 1965.

2. On the notices in the *Damskii zhurnal*, see E. Kalmanovskii, "Pobezhdennyi pobeditel': Istoricheskoe esse," *Novaia Rossiia*, no. 3 (1995): 131. The journal was edited by Prince P. I. Shalikov, whose daughter, Sofia Petrovna, Katkov later married. An eyewitness source on Katkov's childhood, T. P. Passek, recalls that Mefodii lived with an aunt, not in the prison. She also refers to Tulaeva's post as "*glavnaia nadziratel'nitsa*" [chief female warden], not "*kasteliansha*" [linen-keeper], as other sources have it. See Passek, *Iz dal'nykh let: Vospominaniia*, vol. 3 (St. Petersburg: A. F. Marks, 1906), 288.

3. Passek, *Iz dal'nykh let*, 290.

4. Perevalova, *Zhurnal M. N. Katkova*, 23.

5. N. A. Liubimov, *Mikhail Nikiforovich Katkov i ego istoricheskaia zasluga* (St. Petersburg: Tovarishchestvo "Obshchestvennaia Pol'za," 1889), 20.

6. M. N. Katkov, *Sobranie peredovykh statei Moskovskikh vedomostei*, 25 vols. (Moscow: V. V. Chicherin, 1863–87) (hereafter cited according to year, e.g., *1863 god.*).

7. Act 1 of *Romeo and Juliet* was published in *Syn otechestva* in 1838; more scenes were published in *Moskovskii nabliudatel'* in 1838; the full version appeared in *Panteon russkogo i vsekh evropeiskikh teatrov*, pt. 1, bk. 1 (1841): 1–54. The master's dissertation is *Ob elementakh i formakh slaviano-russkogo iazyka. Rassuzhdenie, napisannoe na stepen' magistra Kandidatom M. Katkovym* (Moscow: V universitetskoi tipografii, 1845); reprinted in *SS* 4:12–160.

8. Katkov was also heavily influenced by the thought of Schelling, whose lectures he attended in Berlin, but Russian sources, following statements in the letters of Belinsky, tend to overemphasize Katkov's abandonment of Hegel. Two dissertations provide convincing arguments for the continuing importance of Hegel's thought for Katkov: Joseph Backor, "M. N. Katkov: Introduction to His Life and His Russian National Policy Program, 1818–1870," PhD diss., Indiana University, 1966; and Stephen M. Woodburn, "The Origins of Russian Intellectual Conservatism, 1825–1881: Danilevsky, Dostoevsky, Katkov, and the Legacy of Nicholas I," PhD diss., Miami University (Oxford, OH), 2001. Woodburn writes, "The important subtlety to grasp in this discussion of Katkov's philosophical allegiances is that he had established a devotion to Hegel that did not simply disappear when he began to study under Schelling. Although the two philosophic traditions have their differences, they are not mutually exclusive, nor should Katkov have considered them to be so" ("The Origins of Russian Intellectual Conservatism," 115).

9. William Mills Todd III, "Dostoevskii as a Professional Writer," in *The Cambridge Companion to Dostoevskii*, ed. W. J. Leatherbarrow (Cambridge: Cambridge University Press, 2002), 77. Todd has extensively studied the poetics and pragmatics of serialization in the nineteenth-century Russian novel. See notes to chapters 4, 5, and 6 for references to more of his articles dealing with Katkov, Dostoevsky, and Tolstoy.

10. Mikhail Katkov, "Pushkin," *Russkii vestnik* 1 (January 1856): 155-72; 1 (February 1856): 306-23; and 2 (March 1856): 282-310; reprinted in Katkov, *SS* 1:273-74 (1:320-21 in original). Throughout this study I will give the Russian equivalent of the word *nation* and its derivatives in each specific case, since there are multiple ways of rendering the word in Russian.

11. Katkov, *SS* 1:275 (1:322 in original).

12. Perevalova, *Zhurnal M. N. Katkova*, 211.

13. Mikhail Katkov, "Neskol'ko slov vmesto sovremennoi letopisi," *Russkii vestnik* 31 (January 1861): 478-84, reprinted in Katkov, *SS* 1:311-12.

14. Katkov, *SS* 1:312-13.

15. Mikhail Katkov, "Zasluga Pushkina" (dated June 5, 1880), *Russkii vestnik* 261 (June 1899): 403-09, reprinted in Katkov, *SS* 1:699-701.

16. Andreas Renner, "Defining a Russian Nation: Mikhail Katkov and the 'Invention' of National Politics," *Slavonic and East European Review* 81, no. 4 (October 2003): 659, 670. See also his *Russischer Nationalismus und Öffentlichkeit im Zarenreich: 1855-1875* (Cologne: Böhlau, 2000), 196-273. Olga Maiorova cites Renner's argument but implies that he overstates Katkov's importance: "Katkov was not alone, during these years, in this attempt to single out the Russian people as the culturally and politically dominant group within the empire." (Olga Maiorova, *From the Shadow of Empire: Defining the Russian Nation through Cultural Mythology, 1855-1870* [Madison: University of Wisconsin Press, 2010], 21). Part of Renner's argument, though, is that through his publications Katkov had a unique and peerlessly powerful role in shaping public opinion about the place of the Russian ethnos within the empire. The literature on Katkov's nationalism is vast and growing, particularly in post-Soviet Russia, and a thorough treatment of the topic is beyond the scope of my study. Notable recent works, besides those by Renner and Maiorova, are Geoffrey Hosking [Dzhefri Khosking], "Mikhail Katkov i imperskii natsionalizm," in *Katkovskii vestnik: Religiozno-filosofskie chteniia. K 190-letiiu so dniia rozhdeniia M. N. Katkova* (Moscow: Progress-Pleiada, 2008), 83-89; A. V. Repnikov, *Konservativnye modeli rossiiskoi gosudarstvennosti* (Moscow: Rosspen, 2014); and S. M. San'kova, *Gosudarstvennyi deiatel' bez gosudarstvennoi dolzhnosti: M. N. Katkov kak ideolog gosudarstvennogo natsionalizma* (St. Petersburg: Nestor, 2007). See Repnikov, *Konservativnye modeli*, 223n180, for further bibliography.

17. Petition to Minister of Education A. S. Norov, quoted in Liubimov, *Katkov i ego istoricheskaia zasluga*, 47-52, 61-62. See also "M. N. Katkov kak redaktor 'Moskovskikh Vedomostei' i vozobnovitel' 'Russkogo Vestnika,'" *Russkaia starina* 92 (November and December 1897): 355-73 and 571-89. An excellent overview of Katkov's tenure as editor of the *Moscow News* (*Moskovskie vedomosti*) in the early 1850s is I. K. Kremenskaia, "'Moskovskie vedomosti' 1850-kh gg.—Redaktorskii debiut M. N. Katkova," in *Iz veka v vek: Iz istorii russkoe zhurnalistiki 1702-2002*, ed. B. I. Esin (Moscow: No publisher given, 2002), 68-83. See also Perevalova, *Zhurnal M. N. Katkova*, 30-31. Perevalova is more inclined than Kremenskaia to argue that Katkov significantly improved the journal during his tenure, despite the constraints placed on him. See also "M. N. Katkov kak redaktor."

18. The question of the financing of the *Russian Herald* is not explored in depth in any source that I am aware of. Its subscriptions were healthy by the end of the 1850s, and Katkov's collaborator P. M. Leontiev was by most accounts a thrifty financial manager. Rumors that Katkov received subsidies from the government or from wealthy railroad tycoons and merchants appear in some sources, but without documentation, as far as I can determine. A recent article by Maksim Artemiev claims that Katkov received subsidies from railroad contractors and other "Moscow financial big shots" to found the Tsesarevich Nicholas Lycée, in which he implemented his theories on the benefits of classical education, but Artemiev dismisses the idea that Katkov received direct subsidies from the government to support his publications. He provides no supporting documentation for either of these statements.

NOTES TO INTRODUCTION

(Maksim Artem'ev, "Starinnaia russkaia traditsiia: Kak SMI vliiali na vlast' i obshchestvo v Rossii," Forbes.ru, March 21, 2014.) Katkov publicly denied receiving subsidies for his publications.

19. An excellent discussion of the phenomenon of the "thick journal" in Russia of the second half of the nineteenth century, particularly questions of readership, can be found in A. Reitblat, *Ot Bovy k Bal'montu: Ocherki po istorii chteniia v Rossii vo vtoroi polovine XIX veka* (Moscow: MPI, 1991), 32–47. But perhaps in a hangover from the Soviet era, Reitblat never mentions Katkov in his study. All his examples of editing practice are drawn from the radical press. See also the discussion of literary honoraria (78–96), which again does not mention Katkov. For more information on journalism in this period, see Deborah A. Martinsen, ed., *Literary Journals in Imperial Russia* (Cambridge: Cambridge University Press, 1997).

20. F. M. Dostoevskii, *Polnoe sobranie sochinenii*, 30 vols. (hereafter cited as *PSS*) (Leningrad: Nauka, 1972–90) 29/1:23–24 (letter of 8 [20] March 1869, to S. A. Ivanova).

21. Katkov, "Pushkin," *SS* 1:289.

22. Liubimov, *Katkov i ego istoricheskaia zasluga*. Nepomnyashchy, "Katkov and the Emergence," 71n6.

23. Katz, *A Political Biography*, 13; "Pamiati Mikhaila Nikiforovicha Katkova. 1887–20 iulia–1897," *Russkii vestnik* 250 (August 1897): 1–182.

24. V. P. Meshcherskii, "Vospominaniia o M. N. Katkove (Pis'ma v Tveritino)," *Russkii vestnik* 250 (August 1897): 10. This and other memoirs of Katkov are reprinted in SS 6 (*Mikhail Nikiforovich Katkov: Pro et contra*), and in *Vospominaniia o Mikhaile Katkove*, ed. G. N. Lebedeva and O. A. Platonov (Moscow: Institut russkoi tsivilizatsii, 2014).

25. B. N. Chicherin, *Moskva sorokovykh godov*, ed. T. F. Pirozhkovaia (Moscow: Izdatel'stvo Moskovskogo universiteta, 1997), 159, 163.

26. S. Nevedenskii [S. G. Shcheglovitov], *Katkov i ego vremia* (St. Petersburg: Tipografiia A. S. Suvorina, 1888). Katz, *A Political Biography*, 12. Like Nepomnyashchy and most older sources, Katz attributes the work to S. S. Tatishchev, but recent Russian sources attribute it to S. G. Shcheglovitov.

27. R. I. Sementkovskii, *M. N. Katkov: Ego zhizn' i literaturnaia deiatel'nost'* (St. Petersburg: Iu. N. Erlikh, 1892). Katz, *A Political Biography*, 13.

28. See, for example, the discussion by San'kova, *V poiskakh mesta*.

29. Sementkovskii, *M. N. Katkov*, 72–73.

30. Vladimir Solov'ev, "'... Dlia blaga Rossii i vsego mira,'" ed. Tat'iana Lapteva, *Nashe nasledie* no. 5 (1992): 77.

31. Solov'ev, "Dlia blaga Rossii," 77.

32. V. A. Kitaev, *Ot frondy k okhranitel'stvu: Iz istorii russkoi liberal'noi mysli 50–60kh godov XIX veka* (Moscow: Mysl', 1972); V. A. Tvardovskaia, *Ideologiia poreformennogo samoderzhaviia (M. N. Katkov i ego izdaniia)* (Moscow: Nauka, 1978).

33. Kitaev, *Ot frondy k okhranitel'stvu*, 282; Tvardovskaia, *Ideologiia*, 270.

34. V. Kantor, "M. N. Katkov i krushenie estetiki liberalizma," *Voprosy literatury* no. 5 (1973): 181, 212. Kantor has published extensively on Katkov and on Russian conservatism in the post-Soviet era. In 2007 he published a new version of his classic 1973 article, stripped of the quotations from Lenin and presenting a less bleak conclusion about Katkov's life work, pointing out that those Russian writers, whose funerals his funeral outshone, nevertheless published their best novels in his journal. Far from consigning Katkov to oblivion as he did in 1973, in 2007 Kantor argues for his continuing significance: "As for the position of Katkov the politician, it has remained a serious problem for Russian thought, which has more than once stood before this insoluble dilemma: revolutionary radicalism or autocratic authoritarianism. This problem is alive even today; therefore, one cannot escape the experience and ideas of this outstanding Russian thinker." (V. K. Kantor, "O sud'be imperskogo liberalizma v Rossii (M. N. Katkov)," *Filosofskie nauki* no. 2 [2007]: 91.) See also his *Sankt-Peterburg: Rossiiskaia imperiia protiv rossiiskogo khaosa: K probleme imperskogo soznaniia v Rossii* (Moscow: Rosspen, 2008). For a description of Katkov's funeral, see *Russkii vestnik* 190 (July 1887).

35. V. V. Vinogradov, *Istoriia slov* (Moscow: Tolk, 1994), 322–31.

36. Katkov, *Sobranie sochinenii*.

37. "Ot redaktsii," in Katkov, *SS* 1:7.
38. Ėduard Popov and Irina Veligonova, "Spasitel' otechestva," *Moskva* no. 11 (2013): 148–58.
39. "V Ameriku ne vpustiat," interview with Aleksandr Nikoliukin conducted by Sergei Dmitrenko, *Novaia gazeta*, *Ex libris* no. 14 (April 18, 2013).
40. "V Ameriku ne vpustiat."
41. Protoierei Artemii Vladimirov, "Slovo o Katkove," in *Katkovskii vestnik*, 9.
42. Protoierei Artemii Vladimirov, "Zakliuchitel'noe slovo," *Katkovskii vestnik*, 121, 122–23.
43. The program is available on YouTube, accessed June 28, 2015.
44. Katkov's relationships with Alexander Herzen, Mikhail Saltykov-Shchedrin, and Nikolai Leskov are worthy of further study, but they are beyond the scope of my book. See Nepomnyashchy, "Katkov and the Emergence of the *Russian Messenger*," for an overview of Katkov's treatment of Leskov.

CHAPTER 1

1. "Death of M. Katkoff," the *Times*, Tuesday, August 2, 1887, 6.
2. John Randolph, *The House in the Garden: The Bakunin Family and the Romance of Russian Idealism* (Ithaca: Cornell University Press, 2007).
3. Randolph, *House in the Garden*, 12–13. The classic study of these figures is Isaiah Berlin, *Russian Thinkers*, ed. Henry Hardy and Aileen Kelly (New York: Viking, 1978). For sheer readability, nothing has surprassed Edward Hallett Carr, *The Romantic Exiles: A Nineteenth-Century Portrait Gallery* (Boston: Beacon Press, 1933), and *Michael Bakunin* (London: Macmillan, 1937).
4. Nevedenskii, *Katkov i ego vremia*, 2. On Katkov's involvement in the Stankevich circle, see 9–16.
5. Much of Katkov's own correspondence has been lost, but a letter from Belinsky to N. V. Stankevich, dated by editors to September 29–October 8, 1839, mentions a visit by Katkov to Bakunin's estate, Priamukhino, where the personal dramas involving Bakunin's sisters, described in great detail by Randolph, were played out. (V. G. Belinskii, *Polnoe sobranie sochinenii*, 13 vols. [hereafter cited as *PSS*] [Moscow: AN SSSR, 1953–59], 11:392.)
6. Herbert E. Bowman, *Vissarion Belinski 1811–1848: A Study in the Origins of Social Criticism in Russia* (New York: Russell & Russell [Harvard Studies in Comparative Literature], 1954), 40–41. See also Backor, "M. N. Katkov," 59–60.
7. Randolph, *House in the Garden*, 235.
8. Aileen Kelly, *Mikhail Bakunin: A Study in the Psychology and Politics of Utopianism* (Oxford: Oxford University Press, 1982), 47. For an alternative view, see Ilya Kliger, "Genre and Actuality in Belinskii, Herzen, and Goncharov: Toward a Genealogy of the Tragic Pattern in Russian Realism," *Slavic Review* 70, no. 1 (Spring 2011): 45–66.
9. Kelly, *Mikhail Bakunin*, 47.
10. Kelly, *Mikhail Bakunin*, 47.
11. Belinskii, *PSS* 11:391, letter to Stankevich of September 29–October 8, 1839. This letter contains Belinsky's most detailed description of the affair. See also *Literaturnoe nasledstvo* 56: *V. G. Belinskii II* (Moscow: AN SSSR, 1950), 90–91, 123–24. Woodburn discusses Katkov's personal entanglements with Belinsky in detail ("The Origins of Russian Intellectual Conservatism," 98–113). See also San'kova, *V poiskakh mesta*, 28–38, 53–61.
12. Belinskii, *PSS* 11:391.
13. Belinskii, *PSS* 11:391.
14. Belinskii, *PSS* 11:405.
15. Belinskii, *PSS* 12:95, letter of April 6, 1842, to M. N. Katkov and A. P. Efremov. It is not clear from the existing sources why Katkov broke with Shchepkina, but it is likely that his poverty kept him from considering marriage with anyone at this time. A 1911 memoir by A. I. Sokolova, who worked as a drama critic for Katkov's newspaper *Moskovskie vedomosti* in the 1860s, seems to be referring to Shchepkina in the following passage:

> Katkov's morality was impeccable, almost unheard-of, and everyone who was close to him knew that during his early youth, when he was still a completely indigent student, for a long

time he lived in harmony with a young girl, the close relative of one of our world-class actors—he lived in one room with her and, while adoring her, was able to preserve chaste, brotherly relations with her. He could not marry her because he was a completely poor person, without any definite future ahead, and he did not want to abuse her love and trust and make her his mistress (A. I. Sokolova, "Vstrechi i znakomstva," *Istoricheskii vestnik* 124 [1911]: 840).

I have not found any support for the notion that Katkov lived in one room with Shchepkina, but Sokolova's explanation for the end of their affair seems likely. On the other hand, a letter from Belinsky to Botkin of April 16–21, 1840, implies that it was Shchepkina who broke off the relationship. He speaks of Katkov "taking revenge" on her for his "offended self-esteem [*samoliubie*]," *PSS* 11:513. Belinsky's announcement of Shchepkina's death is followed immediately by a dig at Katkov for supposedly forsaking Hegel for Schelling. Katkov referred sarcastically to Belinsky's letter in his own letter to the editor Andrei Aleksandrovich Kraevsky, June 29, 1842: "A little and very dear dissertation on the theme: all people are mortal, we are people, ergo we are mortal" (S. Nevedenskii, *Katkov i ego vremia*, 90).

16. *Literaturnoe nasledstvo* 56:91. Katkov appears offstage in another work of drama, Tom Stoppard's 2002 trilogy *The Coast of Utopia*, which is set among the Stankevich and Herzen-Ogariov circles. In the first play, *Voyage*, he is mentioned as one of the people chipping in to provide funds for Belinsky to take a restorative trip to the Caucasus in February 1837. In the third play, *Salvage*, in a scene set in May 1859, Turgenev announces to Herzen that he is planning to publish his new novel with Katkov. Herzen responds, "Everyone will think you've joined the reactionary camp." (Tom Stoppard, *The Coast of Utopia: A Trilogy. Voyage. Shipwreck. Salvage* [New York: Grove Press, 2007], 102, 297.)

17. Belinskii, *PSS* 3:557.
18. Belinskii, *PSS* 3:559.
19. Belinskii, *PSS* 11:398.
20. Belinskii, *PSS* 3:581.
21. Belinskii, *PSS* 3:588.
22. Belinskii, *PSS* 3:533.
23. Belinskii, *PSS* 3:558.
24. Belinskii, *PSS* 3:584.
25. *Literaturnoe nasledstvo* 56:118; letter from I. V. Stankevich to N. V. Stankevich, end of November 1838.
26. Belinskii, *PSS* 11:358; letter to V. P. Botkin, February 10–16, 1839, Moscow. Karl Werder (1806–93) was a professor at the University of Berlin who befriended young Russians studying there.
27. E. M. Feoktistov, *Vospominaniia: Za kulisami politiki i literatury, 1848–1896*, ed. Iu. G. Oksman, introductions by A. E. Presniakov and Iu. G. Oksman; reprint introduction by Hans J. Torke (Leningrad: Priboi, 1929; reprint ed. Oriental Research Partners, 1975), 84–85. Feoktistov became a close associate of Katkov's, writing for both the *Russian Herald* and the *Moscow News*. Varying accounts of the Katkov-Ogariova affair can be found in Carr, *Michael Bakunin*, 81, 86–87; A. A. Kornilov, *Semeistvo Bakuninykh*, vol. 1: *Molodye gody Mikhaila Bakunina: Iz istorii russkogo romantizma* (Moscow: Izdanie M. i S. Sabashnikovykh, 1915), 677–79; and in the commentary to M. A. Bakunin, *Sobranie sochinenii i pisem, 1828–1876*, ed. Iu. M. Steklov, 4 vols. (Moscow: Izdatel'stvo Vsesoiuznogo obshchestva politkatorzhan i ssyl'no-poselentsev, 1934–35), 2:481–85. See also Nevedenskii, *Katkov i ego vremia*, 59–62; and Backor, "M. N. Katkov," 79–90. Irina Paperno has analyzed the love entanglements of the Herzen-Ogariov circle, but does not include Katkov in her discussion: *Chernyshevsky and the Age of Realism: A Study in the Semiotics of Behavior* (Stanford, CA: Stanford University Press, 1988), 42–44, 60–65.
28. Belinskii, *PSS* 11:424; letter to V. P. Botkin, December 16, 1839–February 10, 1840, St. Petersburg.
29. Kornilov, *Molodye gody Bakunina*, 15–16.
30. Bakunin, *Sobranie sochinenii i pisem*, 2:482.
31. Belinskii, *PSS* 11:542; letter to V. P. Botkin, August 12–16, 1840, St. Petersburg. Katkov and Bakunin were both on the point of leaving for Germany and agreed to fight their duel in Berlin. The duel never took place. Belinsky attributed cowardice to Bakunin, but there is no documentation of what actually happened to forestall the duel. See Belinskii, *PSS* 11:557.

32. Belinskii, *PSS* 11:542.

33. Belinskii, *PSS* 11:543.

34. Belinskii, *PSS* 12:13; letter to V. P. Botkin, December 30, 1840–January 22, 1841, St. Petersburg. Ogariov had evoked George Sand in a letter to his wife that preceded the Katkov affair (and other more serious and well-documented affairs she had with other men). In a letter of March 22, 1839, Ogariov writes, "Do you remember how we read *Jacques*? Oh! If only it were necessary for your happiness for me to be Jacques, I would be Jacques; I am ready for any sacrifice. But no! What am I saying! Could you really love another? Could you really find happiness with anyone other than Kolia [Ogariov]? Never, never!" (Mikhail Gershenzon, *Obrazy proshlogo* [Moscow: A. A. Levenson, 1912], 356.) George Sand's 1834 novel *Jacques*, in which a man commits suicide so that his wife can be united with her lover, was wildly popular in Russia and had both a literary and a personal influence. Gershenzon writes, "At that time educated people in Russia were carried away by George Sand; Mariia Lvovna avidly adopted these radical views on family life, dreams of the emancipation of women from their age-old slavery, in which the egoism of men held them. She had been prepared for these ideas by everything—her life before marriage, her character, and finally by the radical views that reigned in that circle into which she was introduced from the day of her marriage to Ogariov himself" (Gershenzon, *Obrazy proshlogo*, 366–67). A letter from Katkov to Ogariov, presumably from late 1839, absolves Mariia Lvovna of guilt and gives the impression that there was no affair but perhaps a misunderstanding prompted by some kind of liberties taken by Katkov: "I have so deeply offended you, Nikolai—before her I am as sinful as a criminal and lower than the most despised animal. My heart is turning over, so vilely, so basely did I repay her for her angelic kindness, for her friendliness, which I did not know how to appreciate." *Pis'ma M. A. Bakunina k A. I. Gertsenu i N. P. Ogarevu*, ed. M. P. Dragomanov (St. Petersburg: Izdanie V. Vrublevskogo, 1906), 15. The definitive study of Chernyshevsky's experimentation with the family is Paperno, *Chernyshevsky and the Age of Realism*.

35. Gershenzon, *Obrazy proshlogo*, 458.

36. Gershenzon, *Obrazy proshlogo*, 476.

37. Marshall S. Shatz, "Michael Bakunin and His Biographers: The Question of Bakunin's Sexual Impotence," in *Imperial Russia 1700–1917: State—Society—Opposition; Essays in Honor of Marc Raeff*, ed. Ezra Mendelsohn and Marshall S. Shatz (DeKalb: Northern Illinois University Press, 1988), 224.

38. Shatz, "Michael Bakunin and His Biographers," 224.

39. See Susanne Fusso, *Discovering Sexuality in Dostoevsky* (Evanston: Northwestern University Press, 2006), 77, 185–86.

40. V. Sazhin, "Ruka pobeditelia: Vybrannye mesta iz perepiski V. Belinskogo i M. Bakunina," *Literaturnoe obozrenie*, special edition: *Erotika v russkoi literature ot Barkova do nashikh dnei: Teksty i kommentarii* (Moscow, 1992), 39. See Fusso, *Discovering Sexuality*, 98–99.

41. Belinskii, *PSS* 11:425; letter to V. P. Botkin of December 16, 1839–February 10, 1840, St. Petersburg.

42. Belinskii, *PSS* 11:405.

43. On *Songs of the Russian People*, Belinskii, *PSS* 11:370; on Varnhagen von Ense, Belinskii, *PSS* 3:182–83; on Maksimovich, Belinskii, *PSS* 11:509 and 11:525; and on *Romeo and Juliet*, Belinskii, *PSS* 11:380. Belinsky had commissioned the translation of Varnhagen von Ense for the journal he edited, *Moskovskii nabliudatel'*, where Katkov's translation of Heinrich Theodor Rötscher's study of art appeared (see below), but it eventually appeared in *Otechestvennye zapiski*. A. D. Galakhov, who worked with Katkov on *Notes of the Fatherland* in 1839 and later became an important contributor to the *Russian Herald*, offers an analysis of some of Katkov's early works in his memoir, *Zapiski cheloveka*, ed. V. M. Bokovaia (Moscow: Novoe literaturnoe obozrenie, 1999), 166–81. See also 371–72n25 for Galakhov's list of unsigned works published in journals in 1839 that were by Katkov. For a much less sympathetic review of Katkov's articles, see V. I. Kuleshov, *"Otechestvennye zapiski" i literatura 40-kh godov XIX veka* (Moscow: Izdatel'stvo Moskovskogo universiteta, 1959), 28, 90–92, 295–96.

44. Belinskii, *PSS* 11:509; letter to V. P. Botkin of April 16–21, 1840, St. Petersburg.

45. "O filosofskoi kritike khudozhestvennogo proizvedeniia (Stat'ia Rëtshera)," *Moskovskii nabliudatel'* 17, May 1838, bk. 2, 159-95, and June 1838, bk. 1, 303-34 and bk. 2, 431-57. Katkov's introduction to this translation has been reprinted in *SS* 4:7-11.
46. "O filosofskoi kritike," May, bk. 2, 160, 161; *SS* 4:8-9.
47. See Backor, "M. N. Katkov," on the importance of Katkov's translations of Hegelian terminology.
48. "O filosofskoi kritike," May, bk. 2, 191.
49. "O filosofskoi kritike," June, bk. 1, 309.
50. "O filosofskoi kritike," May, bk. 2, 164; *SS* 4:10.
51. "O filosofskoi kritike," May, bk. 2, 186, 187-89.
52. "O filosofskoi kritike," May, bk. 2, 190.
53. "O filosofskoi kritike," May, bk. 2, 193.
54. "O filosofskoi kritike," June, bk. 2, 433.
55. "O filosofskoi kritike," June, bk. 1, 333-34.
56. "O filosofskoi kritike," June, bk. 2, 443, 447, and 453.
57. "O filosofskoi kritike," June, bk. 2, 448-49.
58. G. W. F. Hegel, *Elements of the Philosophy of Right*, ed. Allen W. Wood, trans. H. B. Nisbet (Cambridge: Cambridge University Press, 1991), secs. 346-347, 374. See Nevedenskii, *Katkov i ego vremia*, 26.
59. Review of "*Pesni russkogo naroda, izdannye I. Sakharovym: Piat' chastei*. Sanktpeterburg. 1838-1839," in *Otechestvennye zapiski* 4 (1839), bk. 6, sec. 6, 1-24; bk. 7, sec. 6, 25-92; this passage is bk. 6, 8; *SS* 1:91.
60. Review of "*Istoriia drevnei russkoi slovesnosti: Sochinenie Mikhaila Maksimovicha*. Kniga pervaia. Kiev, 1839," *Otechestvennye zapiski* 9 (1840), bk. 4, sec. 5, 37-68; this passage is 40-41. Reprinted in *SS* 1:171-213, p. 175-76. Emphasis added.
61. "*Pesni russkogo naroda*," bk. 6, 16; *SS* 1:98.
62. "*Pesni russkogo naroda*," bk. 7, 34; *SS* 1:113-14.
63. "*Pesni russkogo naroda*," bk. 7, 88; *SS* 1:161. Despite this public endorsement, however, Katkov was privately very unhappy with Nicholas I and the policy of official nationality. See Nevedenskii, *Katkov i ego vremia*, 95; Backor, "M. N. Katkov," 103, 124.
64. "*Istoriia drevnei russkoi slovesnosti*," bk. 4, 43; *SS* 1:178-79.
65. "*Istoriia drevnei russkoi slovesnosti*," bk. 4, 47, 48; *SS* 1:185-86.
66. Shlomo Avineri, "Hegel and Nationalism," in *The Hegel Myths and Legends*, ed. Jon Stewart (Evanston: Northwestern University Press, 1996), 125. Stewart's collection is useful for any student of the Russian reception of Hegel in the nineteenth century, given that the imperfect transmission of Hegel's ideas led to numerous "myths and legends."
67. Belinskii, *PSS* 3:618. The original translation is "Sochineniia A. Pushkina," *Syn otechestva* 7, pt. 4 (1839): 1-37.
68. Belinskii, "Russkie zhurnaly," *PSS* 3:182.
69. Katkov, "Otzyv inostrantsa o Pushkine," *Otechestvennye zapiski*, 1839, vol. 3, no. 5, *Prilozhenie*, 1-36; reprinted in Katkov, *SS* 1:53-54. For further discussion of this article in relation to the 1880 Pushkin Celebration, see chapter 7.
70. "Otzyv inostrantsa o Pushkine," *SS* 1:54-55.
71. "Otzyv inostrantsa o Pushkine," *SS* 1:56.
72. "Otzyv inostrantsa o Pushkine," *SS* 1:55.
73. See, for example, Belinsky's "Literaturnye mechtaniia" for 1834: "Pushkin reigned for ten years: *Boris Godunov* [1825] was his last great feat; in the third part of the complete collection of his poems the sounds of his harmonious lyre have died down [*zamerli*]. Now we do not recognize Pushkin: he has died [*umer*], or perhaps has only swooned [*obmer*] for a while. Perhaps he no longer exists, but perhaps he will be resurrected, that is the question, that 'to be or not to be' of Hamlet is hidden in the mist of the future." *PSS* 1:73.
74. Belinskii, "Russkie zhurnaly," *PSS* 3:183.

75. Belinskii, *PSS* 11:540; letter to V. P. Botkin of August 12–16, 1840, St. Petersburg. Belinskii, *PSS* 12:11; letter to V. P. Botkin of December 30, 1840–January 22, 1841, St. Petersburg.

76. Belinskii, *PSS* 12:24; letter to V. P. Botkin of March 1, 1841; Bowman, *Vissarion Belinski*, 102; and Victor Terras, *Belinskij and Russian Literary Criticism: The Heritage of Organic Aesthetics* (Madison: University of Wisconsin Press, 1974), 45.

77. Belinskii, *PSS* 11:581; letter to V. P. Botkin of December 10–11, 1840, St. Petersburg. The Katkov article he is referring to is his review of the poetry of Sarra Tolstaia, "Sochineniia v stikhakh i proze grafini S. F. Tolstoi: Perevod s nemetskogo i angliiskogo. Moskva. Dve chasti," *Otechestvennye zapiski* 12 (1840), bk. 10, sec. 5, 15–50; partly reprinted in *Sobranie sochinenii*, 1:169–70.

78. Belinskii, *PSS* 11:584; letter to V. P. Botkin of December 11–12, 1840, St. Petersburg.

79. Belinskii, *PSS* 12:11; letter to V. P. Botkin of December 30, 1840–January 22, 1841, St. Petersburg.

80. Belinskii, *PSS* 12:12.

81. Belinskii, *PSS* 12:131; letter to V. P. Botkin of February 6, 1843, St. Petersburg; censored word restored.

82. Belinskii, *PSS* 12:22; letter to V. P. Botkin of March 1, 1841, St. Petersburg. Bowman writes, "[Belinsky's] formal rejection of Hegel only succeeded, in fact, in making him into a better Hegelian than he had ever been. In his vociferous defense of the concrete individual as the sole effective bearer of the universal in history, he supposed that he was repudiating Hegel; in reality, he had only just achieved a valid comprehension of Hegel. By his negation of the world of actuality in favor of a rational reality which exists behind the world of appearance and which unfolds itself through the history of humanity, he had finally come to grasp the major theme of the Hegelian philosophy of history. By combining an original Schilleresque idealism with a subsequent realization of social and historical actuality, Belinski arrived at a position which Hegel might have been the first to certify: a dynamic conception of the concrete individual as the incarnation of the universal" (Bowman, *Vissarion Belinski*, 147–48).

83. Belinskii, letter to N. V. Gogol', July 15, 1847, Salzbrunn, in V. Veresaev, *Gogol' v zhizni: Sistematicheskii svod podlinnykh svidetel'stv sovremennikov* (Moscow: Moskovskii rabochii, 1990), 412.

84. Belinskii, *PSS* 12:20–21; letter to V. P. Botkin of December 30, 1840–January 22, 1841, St. Petersburg.

85. See, for example, "Literaturnye mechtaniia" for 1834, *PSS* 1:24.

CHAPTER 2

1. Nevedenskii, *Katkov i ego vremia*, 66–67. See also Liubimov, *Katkov i ego istoricheskaia zasluga*, 41; Backor, "M. N. Katkov," 91–108; and Katkov, *SS* 1:15–20. On the period of Katkov's life treated in this chapter, see also San'kova, *V poiskakh mesta*, and Perevalova, *Zhurnal M. N. Katkova*.

2. Letter to Kraevsky of May 30, 1842, cited in Nevedenskii, *Katkov i ego vremia*, 68.

3. Letter to Kraevsky of March 30, 1842, cited in Nevedenskii, *Katkov i ego vremia*, 89.

4. Undated letter to mother and brother, "Materialy dlia zhizneopisaniia M. N. Katkova: Iz pisem M. N. Katkova k materi i bratu," *Russkii vestnik* 250 (August 1897): 160.

5. Cited in Nevedenskii, *Katkov i ego vremia*, 80.

6. Nevedenskii, *Katkov i ego vremia*, 79.

7. See Backor, "M. N. Katkov," 96–98, 108.

8. "Iz pisem Katkova k materi i bratu," undated letter, 165.

9. Liubimov, *Katkov i ego istoricheskaia zasluga*, 41; Nevedenskii, *Katkov i ego vremia*, 96.

10. *Ob elementakh i formakh slaviano-russkago iazyka*, in Katkov, *SS* 4:12–160. See the commentary in *SS* 4:737–49; Liubimov, *Katkov i ego istoricheskaia zasluga*, 41; Nevedenskii, *Katkov i ego vremia*, 96–97. The important historian M. P. Pogodin wrote in his diary, "June 9, 1845. In the morning in the university at Katkov's defense. A consoling phenomenon. About ten people were debating—and wonderfully, eruditely and sensibly. And the Grimms, and the Bopps, and the Burnoufs—all had been read and studied thoroughly, evaluated! The question was examined from all angles." Cited in "Materialy dlia zhizneopisaniia M. N. Katkova," 172. Katkov also wrote a doctoral dissertation on pre-Socratic

Greek philosophy, published as *Ocherki drevneishego perioda grecheskoi filosofii*, first published in P. M. Leont'ev's series *Propilei*, Moscow, 1851, bk. 1, 305–59, and Moscow, 1853, bk. 3, 61–144, and then as a separate edition (Moscow: Tipografiia Moskovskogo Universiteta, 1854). Reprinted in Katkov, *SS* 4:161–328; commentary, 4:749–68. Both Backor and Stephen M. Woodburn describe Katkov's choice of philological topics as "safe," but from the very beginning of his career Katkov displayed a deep and enduring interest in literature and language. See Backor, "M. N. Katkov," 121; and Woodburn, "The Origins of Russian Intellectual Conservatism," 119. D. I. Chizhevskii is dismissive of Katkov's efforts in philosophy and linguistics (*Gegel' v Rossii* [Paris: Dom knigi, 1939], 218, 234).

11. "Materialy dlia zhizneopisaniia," 172.
12. "Materialy dlia zhizneopisaniia," 172–73.
13. Nevedenskii, *Katkov i ego vremia*, 97.
14. G. P. Izmest'eva, "Istoricheskie portrety: Mikhail Nikiforovich Katkov," *Voprosy istorii* no. 4 (2004): 74.
15. A. V. Nikitenko, *Dnevnik*, 3 vols., ed. N. L. Brodskii et al. (Moscow: Khudozhestvennaia literatura, 1955), 1:334.
16. Nikitenko, *Dnevnik*, notes, 1:524, and diary entry for January 11, 1852, 1:341.
17. Nevedenskii, *Katkov i ego vremia*, 98. The previous editor, Vladimir Khlopov, lost his position as a result of his excessive enthusiasm for the Austrian ballerina Fanny Elssler; inspired by one of her performances in Moscow, he got up onto the box of her carriage with a huge bouquet and accompanied her to her hotel. This appeared to the administration of the educational district to be "incompatible" and "too youthful" for the editor of a university newspaper. "Materialy dlia zhizneopisaniia," 174. A vivid sense of Katkov's struggles after losing his university post is given in "Pis'ma M. N. Katkova k A. N. Popovu," *Russkii arkhiv*, no. 8 (1888): 480–99.
18. E. M. Feoktistov, *Vospominaniia*, 90. Perevalova argues that Katkov greatly improved the quality of the *Moscow News* during his first tenure as editor (*Zhurnal M. N. Katkova*, 24–37). Kremenskaia is more measured in her claims ("Redaktorskii debiut M. N. Katkova"). For Katkov's own assessment of his tenure, which stresses the fact that he doubled the number of subscribers, see "M. N. Katkov kak redaktor," 582–83; and I. Bozherianov, "Pamiati M. N. Katkova," *Russkii vestnik* 304 (August 1906): 535.
19. Katkov, "Otzyv inostrantsa o Pushkine," *SS* 1:56.
20. Katkov's report to Minister of Education A. S. Norov, May 29, 1855, petitioning for the emperor's permission to publish a new journal under the name of *Russkii Letopisets* [*Russian Chronicler*; the name was eventually changed to *Russian Herald* because permission was withheld to publish a daily supplement], cited by Liubimov, *Katkov i ego istoricheskaia zasluga*, 47–48. See also "M. N. Katkov kak redaktor."
21. Petition to Norov, cited in Liubimov, *Katkov i ego istoricheskaia zasluga*, 48–52.
22. Nevedenskii, *Katkov i ego vremia*, 23.
23. Letter of May 1839, cited in Nevedenskii, *Katkov i ego vremia*, 24.
24. Todd, "Dostoevskii as a Professional Writer," 77.
25. Liubimov, *Katkov i ego istoricheskaia zasluga*, 64, 66. See also San'kova, *V poiskakh mesta*, 143–49; and Perevalova, *Zhurnal M. N. Katkova*, 35ff.
26. Katkov, "Pushkin," *SS* 1:260 (*RV* January 1856, 171).
27. Katkov, "Pushkin," *SS* 1:266 (*RV* February 1856, 312).
28. Katkov, "Pushkin," *SS* 1:269 (*RV* February 1856, 315).
29. Katkov, "Pushkin," *SS* 1:274 (*RV* February 1856, 321).
30. Katkov, "Pushkin," *SS* 1:275 (*RV* February 1856, 322).
31. Mikhail Katkov, "Nash iazyk i chto takoe svistuny," *Russkii vestnik* 32 (March 1861): 11; *SS* 1:339–40. See also "Neskol'ko slov vmesto sovremennoi letopisi," *SS* 1:311–13.
32. Perevalova, *Zhurnal M. N. Katkova*, 59. See also San'kova, *V poiskakh mesta*, 143–49. Perevalova provides detailed commentary, based on archival sources, on Katkov's difficulties with the censorship in the early years of the *Russian Herald*. See also Charles A. Ruud, *Fighting Words: Imperial Censorship and the Russian Press, 1804–1906* (Toronto: University of Toronto Press, 1982).

33. See Kitaev, *Ot frondy k okhranitel'stvu*, 143–44.

34. The most extensive sources on Tur in English or Russian are Jehanne Gheith's dissertation and book: "In Her Own Voice: Evgeniia Tur, Author, Critic, Journalist," PhD diss., Stanford University, 1992; and *Finding the Middle Ground: Krestovskii, Tur, and the Power of Ambivalence in Nineteenth-Century Russian Women's Prose* (Evanston: Northwestern University Press, 2004). The dissertation includes more detailed discussion of the Tur–Katkov polemic than the book. I am indebted to Gheith's work for pointing me to some of the entries in the polemic, and for her detailed research on Tur's life. Although our discussions of the polemic intersect on some points, my orientation in considering it is for the understanding of Katkov's career trajectory, while Gheith's emphasis is of course on Tur's own role. For Tur's work on the *Russian Herald*, see also D. Iazykov, "Literaturnaia deiatel'nost' grafini E. V. Sal'ias (Evgeniia Tur): Bibliograficheskii ocherk," *Istoricheskii vestnik* (May 1892): 489–90. For a lively but no doubt biased account of Tur's life and career, see Feoktistov, *Vospominaniia*, 365–72. See also Perevalova, *Zhurnal M. N. Katkova*, 70–72, 250–51.

35. Iazykov, "Literaturnaia deiatel'nost'," 489.

36. Gheith, "In Her Own Voice," 134; *Middle Ground*, 43.

37. A partial list includes "Ty, utselevshii v serdtse nishchem" (March 1856); poems from the cycle *Fantasmagorii* (September 1858, December 1858, September 1859); *Kadril'* (January 1859, February 1859); "Kogda odin, sredi stepi Siriiskoi" (June 1859); and *Sputnitsa Feiia* (December 1859). An interesting side note is that several of the poems Pavlova published in the *Russian Herald* are either dedicated to Boris Utin or invoke her recent love affair with him, at a time when he was also contributing to the journal. Katkov had warmly praised Pavlova's translations of Russian poetry in a footnote to his 1839 translation of Varnhagen von Ense's essay on Pushkin ("Otzyv inostrantsa o Pushkine," *SS* 1:59).

38. Gheith, *Middle Ground*, 40–41.

39. Katkov, "Sochineniia S. F. Tolstoi," 24. The *Sobranie sochinenii* gives only a brief excerpt from this article. The excerpt does not include this passage.

40. For a complete list of Tur's articles in the *Russian Herald*, see Gheith, *Middle Ground*, 272. Tur also published a collection of fiction in Katkov's own press: *Povesti i rasskazy* (Moscow: V tipografii Katkova i Ko., 1859).

41. Gheith, *Middle Ground*, 92–98; and "In Her Own Voice," 62–76.

42. Feoktistov, *Vospominaniia*, 93.

43. Evgeniia Tur, "Nravoopisatel'nyi roman vo Frantsii: *Madame Bovary, moeurs de province, par Gustave Flaubert*," *Russkii vestnik* 10 (July 1857): 245.

44. Tur, "Nravoopisatel'nyi roman," 280, 282–83.

45. Tur, "*La Jeunesse, comédie en cinq actes et en vers*, par Emile Augier, Paris, 1858," *Russkii vestnik* 14 (April 1858): 210.

46. Tur, "*Le fils naturel, comédie en cinq actes, dont un prologue*, par Alexandre Dumas fils," *Russkii vestnik* 15 (May 1858): 121.

47. "Gospozha Svechina: *Madame Swetchine, sa vie et ses oeuvres publiés*, par le C-te de Falloux, de l'Académie française, 1860," *Russkii vestnik* 26 (April 1860): 362–92. The publication in question is *Madame Swetchine, sa vie et ses oeuvres, publiés par le Cte de Falloux*, 2 vols. (Paris: Didier et Ce, 1860).

48. Dennis J. Dunn, *The Catholic Church and Russia: Popes, Patriarchs, Tsars and Commissars* (Aldershot: Ashgate, 2004), 44.

49. See Dunn, *Catholic Church*, 54.

50. Tur, "Gospozha Svechina," 380–81.

51. Tur, "Gospozha Svechina," 365.

52. Tur, "Gospozha Svechina," 370.

53. Tur, "Gospozha Svechina," 372.

54. Tur, "Gospozha Svechina," 387.

55. Tur, "Gospozha Svechina," 390.

56. Katkov's note appears at the end of Tur's "Gospozha Svechina," 392. Katkov's contributions to this polemic are not signed, but it is agreed in the scholarly literature that he is their author.

57. On the Tur-Katkov polemic with an emphasis on Tur's point of view, see Gheith, *Middle Ground*, 43, and especially the detailed discussion in "In Her Own Words," 135–48.

58. Liubimov, *Katkov i ego istoricheskaia zasluga*, 122–23.

59. Tur, "Pis'mo k redaktoru" ["Letter to the Editor"], *Russkii vestnik, Sovremennaia letopis'* 26 (April 1860): 406–11; Katkov, "Po povodu pis'ma G-zhi Evgenii Tur" ["Apropos of Mrs. Evgeniia Tur's Letter"], *Russkii vestnik, Sovremennaia letopis'* 26 (April 1860): 468–88.

60. Tur, "Pis'mo k redaktoru," 410. The reference to the "dark doctrine" is on 409.

61. Katkov, "Po povodu pis'ma," 469.

62. Katkov, "Po povodu pis'ma," 468, 472.

63. Katkov accuses Tur of having translated Svechina "with the most charming feminine inaccuracy," 480. Consultation of the original and of Tur's and Katkov's translations does not reveal any inaccuracy in Tur's translation, with the exception of a single word ("compare with" as a translation for "surpass"), but it does confirm that Tur misrepresents the general import of Svechina's discussion in the way that Katkov describes. See Tur, "Pis'mo k redaktoru," 408–10; Katkov, "Po povodu pis'ma," 481–83; and *Madame Swetchine*, 2:225–26. See Gheith, "In Her Own Words," on how insulting the accusation of inaccurate translation must have been for Tur (138).

64. Katkov, "Po povodu pis'ma," 485. A few years later, an English translation of the first volume of de Falloux's work was reviewed by Henry James, whose response to Svechina was closer to that of Katkov than to that of Tur. After describing the process of Svechina's conversion, James writes, "We may differ from her conclusions, but we are obliged to admit that they are indeed conclusions, and that they were purchased at the expense of her dearest treasure,—the essential energies of her mind and heart. Mme. Swetchine had staked her happiness upon the truth which she finally embraced. It is not uncommon for people to die for their faith: Mme. Swetchine lived emphatically for hers." Review of *Life and Letters of Madame Swetchine*, *The North American Review* 107, no. 220 (July 1868): 332.

65. Katkov, "Po povodu pis'ma," 470.

66. Cited in N. F. Budanova, "'Nov'": O prototipe Khavron'i Pryshchovoi v romane Turgeneva," *Turgenevskii sbornik: Materialy k polnomu sobraniiu sochinenii i pisem I. S. Turgeneva*, vol. 3, ed. N. V. Izmailov and L. N. Nazarova (Leningrad: Nauka, 1967), 157.

67. See Dunn, *Catholic Church*; and James H. Billington, *The Icon and the Axe: An Interpretive History of Russian Culture* (New York: Knopf, 1966), 297.

68. G. V. Vyzinskii [I. Mai], "Kratkoe skazanie o poslednikh deianiiakh Russkogo vestnika" ["A Short Tale about the Recent Acts of the *Russian Herald*"], *Moskovskie vedomosti*, no. 109, May 19, 1860, 858–62. The word Vyzinsky uses for "acts" is an archaic one, as in "Acts of the Apostles," in keeping with the facetious tone of most of his article.

69. Feoktistov, *Vospominaniia*, 367–69. See Gheith, "In Her Own Words," 140, who disputes Feoktistov's assertion. Perevalova suggests that there was a touch of "Polonophilia" in the early *Russian Herald*, based partly on the participation of Vyzinsky (*Zhurnal M. N. Katkova*, 64–65).

70. Vyzinskii, "Kratkoe skazanie," 859. Blagoveshchensky was unhappy that portions of two lectures on Juvenal he had submitted were excised and the lectures combined into one article. Utin had submitted an article on the history of the jury trial in England on the condition that not a single word be omitted or changed. Katkov abided by the letter of the agreement, but inserted footnotes disagreeing with specific points of the article, particularly a criticism of the institution of justices of the peace. See B. Utin, "Svidetel'skoe pokazanie" ["A Witness's Testimony"], *Moskovskie vedomosti*, no. 136, June 21, 1860, 1077–78; and N. Blagoveshchenskii, "Otvet na 'Ob"iasnenie' pomeshchennoe v No. 10 'Russkogo Vestnika'" ["An Answer to the 'Explanation' Published in no. 10 of the *Russian Herald*"], *Moskovskie vedomosti*, no. 138, June 23, 1860, 1093–94.

71. Vyzinskii, "Kratkoe skazanie," 859.

72. Vyzinskii, "Kratkoe skazanie," 859.

73. Vyzinskii, "Kratkoe skazanie," 860.

74. Vyzinskii, "Kratkoe skazanie," 860.

75. Vyzinskii, "Kratkoe skazanie," 860.

76. Katkov, "Ob"iasnenie" ["Explanation"], *Russkii vestnik, Sovremennaia letopis'* 27 (May 1860): 146.

77. Katkov, "Ob"iasnenie," 146.

78. On Vyzinsky's youth, Katkov, "Ob"iasnenie," 155, 157; on Tur, 155, 164.

79. Katkov, "Ob"iasnenie," 163. Vyzinsky's reference to Tur's letter is in "Kratkoe skazanie," 861.

80. Katkov, "Ob"iasnenie," 167. "Gneist" is Heinrich Rudolf Hermann Friedrich von Gneist (1816–95), German jurist and politician. The work in question is probably *Das heutige englische Verfassungs- und Verwaltungsrecht*, 2 vols. (Berlin, 1857–60). József Eötvös (1813–71) was a Hungarian statesman who wrote *Der Einfluss der Herrschenden Ideen des neunzehnten Jahrhunderts auf den Staat*, 2 vols. (Vienna, 1851; Pest, 1854).

81. "Iz pis'ma k redaktoru," *Moskovskie vedomosti*, no. 140, June 25, 1860, 1110.

82. Utin, "Svidetel'skoe pokazanie"; Blagoveshchenskii, "Otvet na 'Ob"iasnenie'"; Katkov, "Nevladeiushchie klassy i mirovaia iustitsiia," *Russkii vestnik, Sovremennaia letopis'* 27 (June 1860): 429–62; Katkov, "Dopolnitel'noe ob"iasnenie po povodu stat'i g. Blagoveshchenskogo," *Russkii vestnik, Sovremennaia letopis'* 27 (June 1860): 462–63; and Blagoveshchenskii, "Redaktsii Russkogo Vestnika," *Moskovskie vedomosti*, no. 151, July 10, 1860.

83. Vyzinskii, "Ob"iasnenie 'Ob"iasneniia' Russkogo vestnika" ["An Explanation of the 'Explanation' by the *Russian Herald*"], *Moskovskie vedomosti*, no. 137, June 22, 1860, 1082–85.

84. Vyzinskii, "Ob"iasnenie 'Ob"iasneniia,'" 1083–84.

85. Vyzinskii, "Ob"iasnenie 'Ob"iasneniia,'" 1085.

86. N. G. Chernyshevskii, "Istoriia iz-za G-zhi Svechinoi," *Sovremennik*, bk. 10, (June 1860): 249–78. My citations will be from the more accessible edition of the article as published in Chernyshevskii, *Polnoe sobranie sochinenii*, 7:303.

87. Chernyshevsky also echoes Vyzinsky's accusation that in his published answer to Tur, Katkov had indulged in some kind of coarse personal remarks about her ("Istoriia iz-za G-zhi Svechinoi," *PSS* 7:308; see Vyzinskii, "Kratkoe skazanie," 862). After close scrutiny of Katkov's article, the only passage I can find that remotely fits this description is the one in which Katkov counters Tur's accusation that Svechina was "coldhearted." He adduces Svechina's warmth in pursuing charitable works and her religion, then adds, "It's true, Svechina did not engage in love affairs. But is that really the only way to manifest ardor?" (Katkov, "Po povodu pis'ma," 473). Vyzinsky and Chernyshevsky seem to be reading this as a hint that Tur herself engaged in love affairs (she had been separated from her husband for many years). Feoktistov's insinuations in his memoirs about her intimate relations with Vyzinsky (he was "the closest of her friends," who supposedly influenced her to break with Katkov, *Vospominaniia*, 367) suggest that rumors of this kind were associated with her. But one would have to be primed to read this into Katkov's actual words; as he says, "The impression left by a word depends not only on the speaker but on the listener" ("Ob"iasnenie," 166).

88. Chernyshevskii, "Istoriia iz-za G-zhi Svechinoi," *PSS* 7:317.

89. Chernyshevskii, "Istoriia iz-za G-zhi Svechinoi," *PSS* 7:318.

90. Katkov, "Nevladeiushchie klassy," 431.

91. Chernyshevskii, "Istoriia iz-za G-zhi Svechinoi," *PSS* 7:317–18.

92. The version I had access to is "Ob izdanii G-zheiu Evgenieiu Tur v 1861 godu gazety Russkaia Rech'. Obozrenie literatury, istorii, iskusstva i obshchestvennoi zhizni na zapade i v Rossii" ["About the Publication by Mrs. Evgeniia Tur in 1861 of the Newspaper *Russian Speech*. A Review of Literature, History, Art, and Public Life in the West and in Russia"], *Moskovskie vedomosti*, no. 258, November 27, 1860, 2051–53. See the discussion of *Russkaia rech'* by Gheith, "In Her Own Words," 141–65; and *Middle Ground*, 36–37, 42, 43, 101.

93. Tur, "Ob izdanii," 2052.

94. Tur, "Ob izdanii," 2052.

95. Tur, "Ob izdanii," 2053.

96. Katkov, "Ob"iasnenie," *Russkii vestnik, Sovremennaia letopis'* 29 (October 1860): 432. I cannot explain how Katkov was able to respond in October to an announcement published in November, but it is possible that the *Russian Herald* appeared later than the printed date.

97. Tur, "Ob"iasnenie," *Moskovskie vedomosti*, no. 252, November 19, 1860, 2000–2001.
98. Tur, "Ob"iasnenie," 2001; Gheith, "In Her Own Voice," 141.
99. Katkov, "Zametka" ["Note"], *Russkii vestnik, Sovremennaia letopis'* 30 (November 1860): 104.
100. Katkov, "Zametka," *Russkii vestnik, Sovremennaia letopis'* 30 (November 1860): 210. This is a separate entry from the "Note" that responds to Tur cited above, footnote 99.
101. Katkov, "Ob"iasnenie" (October 1860), 433.
102. Tur, "Ob"iasnenie" (November 1860), 2001. Tur's publication lasted only a year. Gheith believes, as did Tur herself, that Katkov damaged the prospects of the paper by his public disparagement of Tur and through the control he exerted over important contributors like Turgenev. (See Gheith, "In Her Own Words," 145–49.) Turgenev had promised Tur that he would contribute an article, which never materialized. Then he offered to let her publish a chapter from *Fathers and Sons*, but asked Katkov's permission, which came with conditions that Tur could not accept. See Gheith, "In Her Own Words," 160–61; L. N. Nazarova, "I. S. Turgenev i E. V. Salias-de-Turnemir v nachale 60-kh godov," in *Teoriia i istoriia literatury (k 100-letiiu so dnia rozhdeniia akademika A. I. Beletskogo)*" (Kiev: Naukova dumka, 1985), 118–19, 120–21; and Turgenev, *Polnoe sobranie sochinenii i pisem*, 28 vols. (hereafter cited as *PSS 1960-68*) (Moscow-Leningrad: AN SSSR, 1960–68), *Pis'ma* 4:110, 159, 195–96, 208, 548n. Tur, feeling the pressure of police surveillance in Moscow, moved to Paris in November 1861. N. F. Budanova traces Tur's evolution from the anti-Catholic campaigner of 1860 to the woman Feoktistov depicts as flirting with Catholicism and supporting the restoration of the Bourbon dynasty in France. (Budanova, "O prototipe Khavron'i Pryshchovoi," 153–63; Feoktistov, *Vospominaniia*, 366–67.)

CHAPTER 3

1. Mikhail Katkov, "Pushkin," *SS* 1:294 (March, 294, in original).
2. Katkov, "Roman Turgeneva i ego kritiki [Turgenev's Novel and Its Critics]," *Russkii vestnik* 39 (May 1862): 393; *SS* 1:459. The other essay is "O nashem nigilizme po povodu romana Turgeneva [On Our Nihilism Apropos of Turgenev's Novel]," *Russkii vestnik* 40 (July 1862): 402–26; *SS* 1:507–27.
3. Katkov, "Roman Turgeneva," 402; *SS* 1:466–67.
4. See Mikhail Katkov, "Ob"iasnenie mezhdu g. Turgenevym i redaktorom 'Russkogo vestnika,'" *Russkii vestnik, Sovremennaia letopis'* 7 (January 1857): 152–58; Turgenev, *Polnoe sobranie sochinenii i pisem*, 30 vols., 2nd ed. (Moscow: Nauka, 1978–86), *Pis'ma*, 3:123–24, 126, 155–56, 158, 175–76, 200, 490–92, 508–9, 520, 533 (hereafter cited as *PSS*); E. V. Perevalova, "I. S. Turgenev i M. N. Katkov," *Spasskii vestnik* 14 (2007): 178–79. "Prizraki" was finally published in 1864 in Dostoevsky's journal *Epoch (Epokha)*.
5. Katkov's letter has not survived, but Turgenev refers to it as "a proposal from the *Russian Herald* with various compliments" ["*predlozhenie ot 'Russkogo vestnika's raznymi liubeznostiami i t.d.*"] (letter of October 11 [23], 1858, to N. A. Nekrasov, *PSS, Pis'ma* 3:342).
6. Turgenev, *PSS, Pis'ma* 3:350–51, 615.
7. Turgenev, *Nakanune, Russkii vestnik* 25 (January 1860): 69–212. Citations will be to the *PSS* edition. The review is P. Basistov, "*Nakanune* I. S. Turgeneva. Moskva 1860," *Otechestvennye zapiski* 130, no. 5, sec. 3 (May 1860), 5.
8. See the polemic between "A Russian Woman" (pseudonym of N. P. Grot) and Evgeniia Tur over Elena's moral character: Russkaia zhenshchina, "Elena Nikolaevna Stakhova," *Nashe vremia*, no. 13 (April 10, 1860): 207–10; Evgeniia Tur, "Neskol'ko slov po povodu stat'i 'Russkoi Zhenshchiny,'" *Moskovskie vedomosti*, April 17, 1860, 665–67; N. F. Pavlov, "Pis'mo iz Peterburga po povodu vozrazheniia Evgenii Tur, na stat'iu Russkoi zhenshchiny," *Nashe vremia*, no. 17 (April 8–20, 1860): 262–68; Russkaia zhenshchina, "Otvet russkoi zhenshchiny gospozhe Tur," *Nashe vremia*, no. 18 (May 15, 1860): 284–87. The polemic is analyzed by Gheith, *Finding the Middle Ground*, 88–92.
9. D. I. Pisarev, "Zhenskie tipy v romanakh i povestiakh Pisemskogo, Turgeneva i Goncharova," *Russkoe slovo*, 1861, bk. 12; cited according to Pisarev, *Sochineniia*, 4 vols. (Moscow: Khudozhestvennaia literatura, 1955–56), 1:267. Similar references to Turgenev's incomprehensible choice of a Bulgarian hero appear in N. P. Nekrasov, "Neskol'ko slov o povesti g. Turgeneva: 'Nakanune,'" *Moskovskie*

vedomosti, no. 99, May 5, 1860, 762, and *Moskovskie vedomosti,* no. 100, May 6, 1860 (page nos. illegible in the copy available to me); Basistov, "*Nakanune,*" 13; and Anonymous [K. N. Leont'ev], "Pis'mo provintsiala k g. Turgenevu," *Otechestvennye zapiski* 130, no. 5, sec. 3 (1860): 23–24, 25, 26.

10. Dobroliubov's article was first published without signature in *Sovremennik,* bk. 3, sec. 3 (March 1860): 31–72, under the title "Novaia povest' g. Turgeneva ('Nakanune,' povest' I. S. Turgeneva, *Russkii vestnik,* 1860 g., nos. 1–2)" ["Mr. Turgenev's New Tale (*On the Eve,* a tale by I. S. Turgenev, *Russian Herald,* 1860, no. 1–2)"]. The original title was restored ("Kogda zhe pridet nastoiashchii den'?" ["When, When Will the Real Day Come?"]) when it was republished with important changes in the 1862 edition of his works, N. A. Dobroliubov, *Sochineniia,* 4 vols. (St. Petersburg: Ogrizko, 1862), 3:275–321. The article is cited here according to N. A. Dobroliubov, *Polnoe sobranie sochinenii,* 6 vols., ed. P. I. Lebedev-Polianskii (Moscow: Khudozhestvennaia literatura, 1934–39), 2:226.

11. Dobroliubov, "Kogda zhe pridet," *PSS* 2:227–28.

12. Dobroliubov, *PSS* 2:653.

13. Dobroliubov, "Kogda zhe pridet," *PSS* 2:229.

14. Dobroliubov, "Kogda zhe pridet," *PSS* 2:209.

15. Dobroliubov, "Kogda zhe pridet," *PSS* 2:239, emphasis added. On the connections between *What Is To Be Done?* and *On the Eve,* see Turgenev, *PSS* 6:468.

16. Turgenev, *PSS* 6:451, 467–68. Jane T. Costlow, who provides a reading of *On the Eve* that seeks to restore the novel's timelessness through a focus on aesthetic considerations, succinctly notes the more widespread conventional approach: "Insarov the revolutionary hero (Bulgarian, not Russian, for reasons that have long absorbed critics) and Elena (an equally revolutionary heroine, whose radical behavior elicited both condemnation and imitation) are representatives of the 'new people' so eagerly awaited by mid-century radicals." *Worlds Within Worlds: The Novels of Ivan Turgenev* (Princeton: Princeton University Press, 1990), 83. For a compelling analysis of Insarov's character in psychological terms, see Elizabeth Cheresh Allen, *Beyond Realism: Turgenev's Poetics of Secular Salvation* (Stanford: Stanford University Press, 1992), 181–85. On Elena and "The Threshold," see Allen, *Beyond Realism,* 246–47n19.

17. Turgenev, *PSS, Pis'ma* 4:110 (letter of November 13 [25], 1859 to I. S. Aksakov). Turgenev follows up by saying, "therefore we're not talking about the common people [*narod*] here." In other words, the "consciously" in "consciously heroic" implies an educated, probably noble-class heroism.

18. Turgenev, *PSS, Pis'ma* 4:163 (letter of February 19 [March 2], 1860 to N. A. Nekrasov).

19. Turgenev, *PSS* 6:461–62.

20. I. Berezin (Beriozin), "Stseny v pustyne: Mezhdu Basroi i Bagdadom," *Russkii vestnik* 13 (January 1858): 322, 332.

21. K. Ugrinovich, "Kratkii obzor voennykh deistvii na Kavkaze v minuvshem 1857 godu," *Russkii vestnik, Sovremennaia letopis'* 13 (February 1858): 165–82; "Kratkii obzor voennykh deistvii na Kavkaze v minuvshem 1857 godu (Okonchanie)," *Russkii vestnik, Sovremennaia letopis'* 13 (February 1858): 266–81; and K. U., "Izvestiia s Kavkaza," *Russkii vestnik, Sovremennaia letopis'* 14 (March 1858): 64–69.

22. M. Kapustin, "Budushchee Turtsii," review of *Le passé et l'avenir de l'Empire Byzantin,* by J. Pitsipios-Bay, *Russkii vestnik, Sovremennaia letopis'* 14 (March 1858): 127.

23. Anonymous, "Letter from Bolgrad," *Russkii vestnik, Sovremennaia letopis'* 14 (April 1858): 439. Bolgrad, now Bolhrad, is in southwest Ukraine. On Phanariotes, see Dennis P. Hupchick, *The Balkans: From Constantinople to Communism* (New York: Palgrave Macmillan, 2004), 206–11.

24. "Letter from Bolgrad," 440.

25. P. Sret'kovich, "Istoriia odnoi serbskoi derevni," *Russkii vestnik* 14 (April 1858): 572–73, 576.

26. D., "Turetskie dela," *Russkii vestnik, Sovremennaia letopis'* 13 (February 1858): 245–65; 14 (March 1858): 35–53; and 15 (May 1858): 33–51. Liubimov identifies the author as "the Bulgarian Daskalov"; Perevalova identifies him as Khristo Dostalov (Liubimov, *Katkov i ego istoricheskaia zasluga,* 72; Perevalova, *Zhurnal M. N. Katkova,* 192).

27. "Turetskie dela," February, 245.

28. "Turetskie dela," February, 250.

29. "Turetskie dela," February, 261.

30. "Turetskie dela," May, 34–35.
31. "Turetskie dela," May, 46–47.
32. "Turetskie dela," May, 34. These articles drew the unfavorable attention of the Holy Synod because of their harsh criticism of the Phanariote clergy. On July 29, 1858, Katkov submitted a lengthy explanation to the Moscow Censorship Committee and the Minister of Education, in which he successfully argued that the religious authorities should not be involved, since the articles did not concern doctrinal issues of the Orthodox church. He wrote, "In these articles the readers' attention is concentrated primarily upon the sufferings of a people [*narod*] that is close to us in faith and blood, the descendants of those same Bulgarians from whom our fatherland received its church language—the first weapon of its spiritual enlightenment and the foundation stone of its secular education." Katkov affirms that his journal was merely doing its duty to the public and to the truth by publishing these articles. He speaks of the Bulgarians who are agitating for freedom as "humble schoolteachers, educated primarily in our universities, and taking from them a love for their Slavic nationality [*narodnost'*], for their native language." This description sounds strikingly like a description of Turgenev's Insarov. (Liubimov, *Katkov i ego istoricheskaia zasluga*, 72–96, quotations on 77, 95; Perevalova, *Zhurnal M. N. Katkova*, 80–81, 192–93).

33. M. Klevenskii, "Literaturnye sovetniki Turgeneva," in *Tvorcheskii put' Turgeneva: Sbornik statei*, ed. N. L. Brodskii (Petrograd: Seiatel', 1923), 242.

34. Turgenev, *PSS* 6:430. Despite the implication in some sources that Karateev died in the war, a letter by Turgenev indicates that he died at home in March 1859 (Turgenev, *PSS, Pis'ma* 4:28, letter to E. E. Lambert, March 27 [April 8], 1859).

35. P. V. Annenkov, *Literaturnye vospominaniia*, ed. S. N. Golubov et al. ([Moscow]: Khudozhestvennaia literatura, 1960), 427; André Mazon, *Manuscrits parisiens d'Ivan Tourguénev: Notices et extraits* (Paris: Librairie ancienne Honoré Champion, 1930), 16, 59–60.

36. Turgenev, *PSS* 6:430. For biographical information on Nikolai Katranov and on Turgenev's ties to Bulgaria, see *PSS* 6:442–46. The Soviet editors are at pains to associate Katranov's liberational activity not with Russian imperialism but with the aspirations of the Russian "revolutionary-democrats."

37. Henri Granjard notes the timeliness of the topic of Bulgaria, and mentions that articles on the oppression of the Bulgarian church had appeared in the *Russian Herald* in 1853, which must be a typographical error for 1858, since the *Russian Herald* was founded in 1856. *Ivan Tourguénev et les courants politiques et sociaux de son temps* (Paris: Institut d'études slaves de l'Université de Paris, 1966), 283.

38. Turgenev, *PSS* 6:214.
39. Turgenev, *PSS* 6:213.
40. Turgenev, *PSS* 6:213–14, 437–38.
41. N. F. Pavlov, "Pis'mo iz Peterburga," 264.
42. Turgenev, *PSS, Pis'ma* 4:142 (letter of January 16 [28], 1860, to P. V. Annenkov).
43. Turgenev, *PSS, Pis'ma* 4:142 (letter of January 16 [28], 1860, to P. V. Annenkov).
44. Unpublished letter to Turgenev of February 14 (26), 1861, cited in Turgenev, *PSS, Pis'ma* 4:623.
45. Turgenev, *PSS* 6:468. *Fathers and Sons* was published in *Russkii vestnik* 37 (February 1862): 473–663.

46. The most important articles by Katkov are "Starye bogi i novye bogi [Old Gods and New Gods]," *Russkii vestnik, Sovremennaia letopis'* 31 (February 1861): 891–904, and 32 (April 1861): 891–904 (*SS* 1:314–28); "Nash iazyk i chto takoe svistuny [Our Language and What Are Whistlers]," *Russkii vestnik, Sovremennaia letopis'* 32 (March 1861); "Po povodu 'Polemicheskikh krasot' v *Sovremennike* [Apropos of 'Polemical Beauties' in the *Contemporary*]," *Russkii vestnik, Sovremennaia letopis'* 33 (June 1861): 138–58; "Elegicheskaia zametka [An Elegiac Note]," *Russkii vestnik, Sovremennaia letopis'* 34 (August 1861): 162–66 (*SS* 4:453–57); and "Koe-chto o progresse" ["A Little Something about Progress"], *Russkii vestnik, Sovremennaia letopis'* 35 (October 1861): 107–27 (*SS* 2:7–28). Some of these articles will be analyzed in more detail in the next chapter on Dostoevsky, because the polemic was a complex one that also involved Dostoevsky and his journal *Time* (*Vremia*).

47. P. Iurkevich, "Iz nauki o chelovecheskom dukhe. P. Iurkevicha. Trudy Kievskoi dukhovnoi Akademii. 1860 knizhka chetvertaia," *Russkii vestnik, Sovremennaia letopis'* 32 (April 1861): 79–105; 33 (May 1861): 26–59. Katkov provided introductions to both excerpts that showcased his command of the philosophical issues involved.

48. I. S. Turgenev, *Ottsy i deti*, ed. S. A. Batiuto and N. S. Nikitina (St. Petersburg: Nauka, 2008), 203.

49. See Turgenev, *Ottsy i deti*, 605, 607. G. F. Perminov discusses a set of parodic verses published by Turgenev in the humor journal *Iskra* in 1859 that had Dobroliubov as their satirical target, in the person of a "six-year-old unmasker," a scrofulous child marked by "cold, bilious calmness interrupted from time to time by outbursts of energetic sarcasm." "Turgenev o N. A. Dobroliubove: Neizvestnyi fel'eton-parodiia Turgeneva v 'Iskre,'" in *Turgenevskii sbornik: Materialy k Polnomu sobraniiu sochinenii i pisem I. S. Turgeneva*, vol. 3, ed. I. V. Izmailov and L. N. Nazarova (Leningrad: Nauka, 1967), 108.

50. B. P. Koz'min, "Dva slova o slove 'nigilizm,'" *Izvestiia AN SSSR, Otdelenie literatury i iazyka* 10, no. 4 (1951): 378–85. Katkov had first used the word "nihilist" in his 1840 article on Sarra Tolstaia, in the sense of one adhering to materialism as opposed to mysticism (see Koz'min, "Dva slova," 382).

51. A. I. Batiuto, "K voprosu o proiskhozhdenii slova 'nigilizm' v romane I. S. Turgeneva 'Ottsy i deti' (Po povodu stat'i B. P. Koz'mina 'Dva slova o slove "nigilizm"')," *Izvestiia AN SSSR, Otdelenie literatury i iazyka* 12, no. 6 (1953): 520–22.

52. B. P. Koz'min, "Eshche o slove 'nigilizm' (Po povodu stat'i A. I. Batiuto)," *Izvestiia AN SSSR, Otdelenie literatury i iazyka* 12, no. 6 (1953): 527.

53. M. P. Alekseev, "K istorii slova 'nigilizm,'" in *Sbornik statei v chest' akademika Alekseiia Ivanovicha Sobolevskogo*, ed. V. N. Peretts (Leningrad: AN SSSR, 1928), 414–15.

54. Katkov, "Starye bogi i novye bogi," February 1861, 896; *SS* 1:319.

55. Turgenev, *Ottsy i deti*, 25. See also Allen, *Beyond Realism*: "As a nihilist, [Bazarov] considers the past filled with outmoded and unconstructive conventions which must be abandoned, and as an idealist—which nihilists so often are—he regards the present as nothing but a workshop in which to labor toward future achievements" (96).

56. Katkov, "Koe-chto o progresse," 108; *SS* 2:8.

57. Katkov, "Koe-chto o progresse," 127; *SS* 2:27. See also the earlier "Elegicheskaia zametka": "We will be on the path to something better only when we renounce pretensions to reconstructing society according to pure reason, and devote ourselves to the precise, thorough, and conscious study of real life" (166; *SS* 4:457).

58. V. Arkhipov, "K tvorcheskoi istorii romana I. S. Turgeneva 'Ottsy i deti,'" *Russkaia literatura* no. 1 (1958): 143.

59. See for example G. Bialyi, "V. Arkhipov protiv I. Turgeneva," *Novyi mir*, no. 8 (August 1958), 255–59; P. Pustovoit, "V pogone za sensatsiei (Po povodu stat'i V. Arkhipova o romane 'Ottsy i deti')," *Voprosy literatury*, no. 9 (1958): 79–88; and A. Batiuto, "Parizhskaia rukopis' romana I. S. Turgeneva 'Ottsy i deti,'" *Russkaia literatura*, no. 4 (1961): 57–78.

60. V. M. Markovich, "Roman I. S. Turgeneva 'Ottsy i deti' v otechestvennom literaturovedenii 1952–2006 godov," in Turgenev, *Ottsy i deti*, 516–17.

61. Markovich, "Roman Turgeneva v otechestvennom literaturovedenii," 519.

62. E. M. Feoktistov, *Vospominaniia*, 30.

63. "Po povodu 'Ottsov i detei'" was first published in Turgenev's *Literaturnye i zhiteiskie vospominaniia* in 1869. Cited here according to *Ottsy i deti* (2008), 189–99.

64. Feoktistov, *Vospominaniia*, 30.

65. Nikolai Strakhov (using the pseudonym N. Kositsa), "Eshche za Turgeneva," *Zaria*, December 1869; cited here according to N. Strakhov, *Kriticheskie stat'i ob I. S. Turgeneve i L. N. Tolstom (1862–1885)* (Kiev: Tipografiia I. I. Chokolova, 1901), 87. Strakhov's review of *Fathers and Sons* was published in *Vremia*, no. 4 (April 1862), *Kriticheskoe obozrenie*, 50–84 ("Ottsy i deti. I. Turgeneva. Russkii vestnik. 1862 g. no. 2").

66. Strakhov, "Eshche za Turgeneva," 87.

67. Turgenev, "Po povodu 'Ottsov i detei,'" in *Ottsy i deti*, 194–95n.

68. P. V. Annenkov, *Literaturnye vospominaniia*, 477–78.

69. For an overview of both the evolution of the manuscript and of critical attempts to analyze changes made by Turgenev, see the updated notes by A. I. Batiuto in *Ottsy i deti* (2008), 543–77.

70. Turgenev, *PSS Pis'ma* 5:50 (letter of April 10 [22], 1862, to A. I. Gertsen).

71. Turgenev, *PSS Pis'ma* 4:373 (letter of October 1 [13], 1861, to M. N. Katkov). Emphasis added.

72. Turgenev, *PSS Pis'ma* 4:379 (letter of October 30 [November 11], 1861).

73. Turgenev, *Ottsy i deti*, 202–3.

74. Turgenev, *Ottsy i deti*, 18, 21, 24, 33, 186.

75. Turgenev, *Ottsy i deti*, 47. The Herzen reference comes from a letter of February 9, 1862, to Turgenev, cited in Turgenev, *PSS, Pis'ma* 5:409.

76. Turgenev, *Ottsy i deti*, 30.

77. Turgenev, *Ottsy i deti*, 45, 144–45.

78. Turgenev, *PSS, Pis'ma* 5:58 (letter of April 14 [26], 1862, to K. K. Sluchevskii).

79. The other was V. P. Botkin (Turgenev, *PSS, Pis'ma* 5:59 [letter of April 14 (26), 1862, to K. K. Sluchevskii]). See also Turgenev's letter to Dostoevsky of March 18 (30), 1862, *PSS, Pis'ma* 5:36–38. Unfortunately, Dostoevsky's letter to Turgenev with his response to *Fathers and Sons* has not survived.

80. Published in *Vremia*, no. 10 (October 1862), *Sovremennoe obozrenie*, 141–63 (unsigned; Dostoevsky's authorship was attested by Strakhov). Cited here according to Dostoevskii, *PSS* 20:30–49.

81. Dostoevsky's blending of Katkov with Pavel Petrovich is described in the notes to "A Ticklish Question" in *PSS* 20:280, 289–90. See also A. I. Batiuto, "Priznaki velikogo serdtsa . . . (K istorii vospriiatiia Dostoevskim romana 'Ottsy i deti')," *Russkaia literatura* no. 2 (1977): 33–34.

82. Dostoevskii, *PSS* 20:279.

83. Dostoevskii, *PSS* 20:279.

84. Dostoevskii, *PSS* 20:36.

85. Dostoevskii, *PSS* 20:37, 40.

86. Dostoevskii, *PSS* 20:48, 292.

87. Dostoevskii, *PSS* 20:41. Dostoevsky seems to have been very amused by the book-borrowing incident, and mentioned it also in the 1861 article "Literaturnaia isterika (Literary Hysterics)" (*PSS* 19:146).

88. Turgenev, *Ottsy i deti*, 47.

89. Dostoevskii, *PSS* 20:42. See 20:289–90 for more examples of echoes of *Fathers and Sons*.

90. M. A. Antonovich, "Asmodei nashego vremeni (*Ottsy i deti*. Roman Turgeneva. 'Russkii vestnik,' 1862 g., no. 2, fevral')," *Sovremennik* no. 3 (1862), cited according to his *Literaturno-kriticheskie stat'i*, ed. G. E. Tamarchenko (Moscow-Leningrad: Khudozhestvennaia literatura, 1961), 38, 39, 40, 42–43.

91. D. I. Pisarev, "Bazarov," *Russkoe slovo*, 1862, bk. 3, cited according to his *Sochineniia*, 2:7–50, pp. 8, 11.

92. I. V., "Dikovinki russkoi zhurnalistiki (Pis'mo k redaktoru) (Little Marvels of Russian Journalism [Letter to the Editor])," *Russkii vestnik* 39, *Sovremennaia letopis'* 18 (1862): 17.

93. Katkov, "Roman Turgeneva," 403; *SS* 1:467. Katkov's two articles have also been reprinted with commentary in *Kritika 60-kh godov XIX veka*, ed. L. I. Sobolev (Moscow: AST Astrel', 2003), 109–43 and 143–69.

94. Katkov, "Roman Turgeneva," 404; *SS* 1:468.

95. Katkov, "Roman Turgeneva," 410; *SS* 1:473.

96. Katkov, "Roman Turgeneva," 413; *SS* 1:476.

97. Katkov, "Roman Turgeneva," 414–15; *SS* 1:477.

98. Katkov, "Roman Turgeneva," 423; *SS* 1:484.

99. Katkov, "Roman Turgeneva," 423–24; *SS* 1:485.

100. Katkov, "O nashem nigilizme," 405; *SS* 1:510.

101. Katkov, "O nashem nigilizme," 407–8; *SS* 1:511–12.

102. Katkov, "O nashem nigilizme," 413–14; *SS* 1:517.

103. Katkov, "O nashem nigilizme," 410; *SS* 1:513.

104. Katkov, "O nashem nigilizme," 425–26; *SS* 1:526. T. A. Trofimova has traced the "positive principle" as a factor in Katkov's literary policy in her dissertation, "'Polozhitel'noe nachalo' v russkoi

literature XIX veka ('Russkii vestnik' M. N. Katkova)," *Kandidat* diss., Rossiiskii gosudarstvennyi gumanitarnyi universitet, Moscow, 2007.

105. Turgenev, *PSS, Pis'ma* 5:96 (letter of July 19 [31], 1862, to M. N. Katkov).

106. Turgenev, "Po povodu 'Ottsov i detei,'" *Ottsy i deti*, 192.

107. Turgenev, *PSS, Pis'ma* 7:201 (letter of May 10 [22], 1867, to A. I. Gertsen).

108. Katkov, editorial in *Moscow News*, no. 5, January 6, 1880. See *Ottsy i deti*, 599–600.

109. See, for example, *PSS, Pis'ma* 5:37 (letter of March 18 [30], 1862, to F. M. Dostoevskii) and 5:50 (letter of April 10 [22], 1862, to A. I. Gertsen).

110. Turgenev, *Ottsy i deti*, 556–57.

111. Turgenev, *Ottsy i deti*, 554.

112. *Sankt-Peterburgskie vedomosti*, no. 299, 1874.

113. Untitled notice, *Moskovskie vedomosti*, no. 273, November 1, 1874, 3.

114. Turgenev, *PSS, Pis'ma* 13:218 (letter of November 13 [25], 1874, to V. V. Stasov).

115. Turgenev, *PSS, Pis'ma* 13:218. (With restoration of censored word.) Belinsky had used the same unsavory metaphor about Katkov in one of his letters (see chapter 1).

116. Z. "Kastratsiia khudozhestvennykh proizvedenii," *Sankt-Peterburgskie vedomosti*, no. 336, (December 6 [18], 1874), 2. See Turgenev's letters that mention this response, *PSS, Pis'ma* 13:234–35.

117. Turgenev, *PSS, Pis'ma* 5:7, 14, 22, 43–44.

118. Turgenev, *PSS, Pis'ma* 5:57 (letter of April 14 [26], 1862, to M. N. Katkov). Turgenev already knew that a negative review was set to appear in the *Contemporary* (5:431).

119. Northrop Frye, *Anatomy of Criticism: Four Essays* (New York: Atheneum, 1970), 163.

120. Frye, *Anatomy of Criticism*, 171.

121. Frye, *Anatomy of Criticism*, 169.

122. Frye, *Anatomy of Criticism*, 168.

123. Frye, *Anatomy of Criticism*, 170.

124. Frye, *Anatomy of Criticism*, 163, 164.

125. Turgenev, *Ottsy i deti*, 16.

126. Turgenev, *Ottsy i deti*, 157.

127. Turgenev, *Ottsy i deti*, 184–86. Allen sees the celebration scene as anomalous for Turgenev: "Almost nowhere does Turgenev represent a group that can provide psychological strength and moral support for the self. The only significant exceptions prove the rule ... the extended Kirsanov family in *Fathers and Sons* is formed only in the novel's epilogue; it has no place within the body of a Turgenevan narrative" (*Beyond Realism*, 58). In Frye's scheme, of course, this setting apart of the inception of the new ideal society at the end of the work is in line with the poetics of comedy.

128. Turgenev, *Ottsy i deti*, 188.

129. Turgenev, *PSS, Pis'ma* 5:38 (letter of March 18 [30], 1862, to A. N. Maikov). See also the letter to E. E. Lambert of March 2 (14), 1862 (5:28–29). There is no trace in the surviving record of these "insistent demands of Katkov" or of the "shouting and unpleasantness" Turgenev attributes to him in the letter to Lambert.

CHAPTER 4

1. The only lengthy novel that Dostoevsky published elsewhere was *A Raw Youth* (*Podrostok*, 1875), which he published in *Notes of the Fatherland*. Whether coincidentally or not, this novel is considered the least successful of Dostoevsky's major works. William Mills Todd III has discussed Dostoevsky's working relationship with Katkov in several articles: "*The Brothers Karamazov* and the Poetics of Serial Publication," *Dostoevsky Studies* 7 (1986): 87–97; "Dostoevsky's Russian Monk in Extra-Literary Dialogue: Implicit Polemics in *Russkii vestnik*, 1879–1881," in *Christianity and the Eastern Slavs*, vol. 2, *Russian Culture in Modern Times*, ed. Robert P. Hughes and Irina Paperno (Berkeley: University of California Press, 1994), 124–33; "Dostoevskii as a Professional Writer"; and "Tolstoy and Dostoevsky: The Professionalization of Literature and Serialized Fiction," *Dostoevsky Studies* 15 (2011): 29–36. There is some disagreement among translators about how to translate the titles of some of Dostoevsky's

novels, in particular *Besy* and *Podrostok*. For *Besy*, I have chosen to translate the title as *The Devils* (since the demons in the King James Version of the story of the Gadarene swine are called "devils"). For *Podrostok*, I believe that no one has improved on Constance Garnett's choice of *A Raw Youth*. The word "adolescent" in English implies a person of 13 or 14, not the 19-year-old man who is the narrator of Dostoevsky's novel.

2. F. M. Dostoevskii, *PSS* 28/1:288 (letter of November 3, 1857 to M. M. Dostoevskii). Further references to Dostoevskii's *PSS* in this chapter and the next will be given in parentheses in the text.

3. *Poor Folk* (*Bednye liudi*) first appeared in Nekrasov's *Peterburgskii sbornik* (St. Petersburg, 1846).

4. The first chapters of *Notes from the Dead House* (*Zapiski iz mertvogo doma*, often translated as *House of the Dead*) were published in the journal *Russkii mir* in 1860. After Dostoevsky and his brother received permission to start their journal *Vremia*, publication continued there in 1861. A separate edition appeared in 1862. See *PSS* 4:276-77.

5. On the history of *Time* and its successor journal *Epoch* (*Epokha*), see V. S. Nechaeva, *Zhurnal M. M. i F. M. Dostoevskikh "Vremia," 1861-1863* (Moscow: Nauka, 1972); and Nechaeva, *Zhurnal M. M. i F. M. Dostoevskikh "Epokha," 1864-65* (Moscow: Nauka, 1975).

6. On the idea of *pochvennichestvo* elaborated by the editors of and contributors to *Time*, see Ellen Chances, "The Ideology of 'Počvenničestvo' in Dostoevskij's Journals *Vremja* and *Èpokha*," PhD diss., Princeton University, 1972; Chances, "Literary Criticism and the Ideology of Pochvennichestvo in Dostoevsky's Thick Journals *Vremia* and *Epokha*," *Russian Review* 34, no. 2 (April 1975): 151-64; and Wayne Dowler, *Dostoevsky, Grigor'ev, and Native Soil Conservatism* (Toronto: University of Toronto Press, 1982).

7. Nechaeva has described the progressive sympathies of some of the young contributors to *Time* (*Zhurnal "Vremia"*). See also G. F. Kogan, "Zhurnal 'Vremia' i revoliutsionnoe studenchestvo 1860-kh godov," *Literaturnoe nasledstvo* 86: *F. M. Dostoevskii: Novye materialy i issledovaniia* (Moscow: Nauka, 1973), 581-93.

8. Publications in which Dostoevsky addressed or alluded to Katkov include "Gospodin -bov i vopros ob iskusstve," *Vremia*, 1861, no. 2 (will be referred to in text as "Mr.—bov"); "Obraztsy chistoserdechiia," *Vremia*, 1861, no. 3 ("Models of Sincerity"); "'Svistok' i 'Russkii vestnik,'" *Vremia*, 1861, no. 3 ("*The Whistle* and the *Russian Herald*"); "Primechanie k 'Pis'mu s Vasil'evskogo ostrova v redaktsiiu 'Vremeni' L. K.,'" *Vremia*, 1861, no. 4 ("Note to 'Letter'"); "Otvet 'Russkomu vestniku,'" *Vremia*, 1861, no. 5 ("An Answer to the *Russian Herald*"); "Literaturnaia isterika," *Vremia*, 1861, no. 7 ("Literary Hysterics"); "Knizhnost' i gramotnost'," *Vremia*, 1861, no. 7 ("Bookishness and Literacy"); "Po povodu elegicheskoi zametki 'Russkogo vestnika,'" *Vremia*, no. 10 ("Apropos of the Elegiac Note"); "Shchekotlivyi vopros," *Vremia*, 1862, no. 10 ("A Ticklish Question"); "Neobkhodimoe literaturnoe ob"iasnenie po povodu raznykh khlebnykh i nekhlebnykh voprosov," *Vremia*, 1863, no. 1 ("A Necessary Literary Explanation"); and "Zhurnal'naia zametka o novykh literaturnykh organakh i o novykh teoriiakh," *Vremia*, 1863, no. 1 ("A Journal Note"). Publications in which Katkov addressed or alluded to Dostoevsky, or that Dostoevsky referred to, include "Neskol'ko slov vmesto sovremennoi letopisi" ("A Few Words Instead of the Contemporary Chronicle"); "Nash iazyk i chto takoe svistuny" ("Our Language"); "Odnogo polia iagody," *Russkii vestnik* 33 (May 1861): 1-26, reprinted in *SS* 1:369-95 ("Birds of a Feather"); "Po povodu 'Polemicheskikh krasot' v *Sovremennike*," ("Apropos of 'Polemical Beauties'"); "Zametka dlia zhurnala *Vremia*," *Russkii vestnik* 34 (July 1861): 95-98, reprinted in *SS* 1:455-58 ("Note for the Journal *Time*"); and "Elegicheskaia zametka" ("Elegiac Note"). References for the controversy over the Polish question will be given below.

9. See the notes in *PSS* 18:269-92; Robert Louis Jackson, *Dostoevsky's Quest for Form: A Study of His Philosophy of Art* (New Haven: Yale University Press, 1966); Joseph Frank, *Dostoevsky: The Stir of Liberation, 1860-1865* (Princeton: Princeton University Press, 1986), 76-85; Nechaeva, *Zhurnal "Vremia,"* 242-44; and Perevalova, *Zhurnal M. N. Katkova*, 126-29. See also my "Maidens in Childbirth: The Sistine Madonna in Dostoevskii's *The Devils*," *Slavic Review* 54, no. 2 (1995): 261-75.

10. Katkov, "Pushkin," February, 312; *SS* 1:266. See Jackson, *Dostoevsky's Quest for Form*, 38-39; and *PSS* 20:288. Joseph Frank considers Dostoevsky's source to have been the writings of Valerian Maikov, but the passage he cites from Maikov concerns realism rather than usefulness, and is thus

not as close to Dostoevsky's formulation as Katkov's position (Frank, *Dostoevsky: The Seeds of Revolt, 1821–1849* [Princeton: Princeton University Press, 1976], 208; see also *Stir of Liberation*, 84). See also the discussion by Perevalova, *Zhurnal M. N. Katkova*, 75. V. A. Viktorovich traces parallels between "Mr.—bov" and the work of A. V. Druzhinin and V. P. Botkin in "'G-n—bov' i vopros ob iskusstve," in *Dostoevskii: Materialy i issledovaniia*, vol. 13 (St. Petersburg: Nauka, 1996), 227–29. Perevalova quotes a statement by Katkov from an 1859 note to the minister of education that presents a similar idea about "usefulness" [*pol'za*]: "All the interest and usefulness of literature [here meaning "journalism"] consist in its presenting opinions and information with full independence. Only under this condition can thinking minds and talents bring usefulness to the administration." (Perevalova, *Zhurnal M. N. Katkova*, 75.)

11. Katkov, "Pushkin," February, 315; *SS* 1:269. Much closer to the time of Dostoevsky's writing, in January 1861 Katkov referred to "art for art's sake" as a sickly art that turns into a course on aesthetics ("A Few Words Instead of the Contemporary Chronicle," 480; *SS* 1:310). Viktorovich notes the way that Dostoevsky adopts what he finds valuable from both sides of the debate ("G-n—bov," 227).

12. Katkov, "Nash iazyk," 14; *SS* 1:343.

13. Katkov, "Nash iazyk," 15; *SS* 1:343–44.

14. Katkov, "Nash iazyk," 15; *SS* 1:343–44.

15. Quoted in Katkov, "Nash iazyk," 16; *SS* 1:344–45.

16. The quotation about "negation" is from Katkov, "Nash iazyk," 11; *SS* 1:341. The quotation about Pushkin is from "Neskol'ko slov vmesto sovremennoi letopisi," 480; *SS* 1:310.

17. Katkov, "Nash iazyk," 16; *SS* 1:345.

18. Katkov, "Neskol'ko slov vmestvo sovremennoi letopisi," 482; *SS* 1:312. An extreme view of Katkov's position was expressed by a contemporary commentator, the historian M. I. Kastorsky, who viewed Katkov as being moved entirely by personal interests in the polemic, and as having no regard for ideas or principles. M. I. Kastorskii, "Neskol'ko slov o literaturnykh zaslugakh g-na Katkova," *Biblioteka dlia chteniia* 12 (December 1862): 29–30.

19. See also the highly tendentious analysis of V. Ia. Kirpotin, *Dostoevskii v shestidesiatye gody* (Moscow: Khudozhestvennaia literatura, 1966), 96–97.

20. Katkov, "Otzyv inostrantsa o Pushkine," *SS* 1:55.

21. Letter to A. E. Vrangel', April 13, 1856.

22. Katkov, "Nash iazyk," 11; *SS* 1:339; and "Neskol'ko slov vmesto sovremennoi letopisi," 482; *SS* 1:312.

23. Katkov, "Nash iazyk," 17; *SS* 1:346.

24. Katkov, "Nash iazyk," 17, 18; *SS* 1:346, 347.

25. M. T., "Iz putevykh zametok ot S.-Peterburga do Irkutska," *Sanktpeterburgskie vedomosti*, no. 36 (February 14, 1861) (page numbers not visible in my copy). For an outline of the *Egyptian Nights* debate, see Dostoevsky, *PSS* 19:292–95, 300–8. See also my discussion of the *Egyptian Nights* scandal in *Discovering Sexuality in Dostoevsky*, 3–16.

26. See Reginald E. Zelnik, "The Sunday-School Movement in Russia, 1859–1862," *Journal of Modern History* 37, no. 2 (June 1965): 151–70.

27. As the capital of Perm Province, the city of Perm had an Assembly of the Nobility, part of the self-governing system of the noble class since the eighteenth century. The Assemblies usually had their own clubhouses, used for a variety of social gatherings. Since the page numbers are not visible in my copy of the article, I am unable to give precise references.

28. See Leslie O'Bell, *Pushkin's "Egyptian Nights": The Biography of a Work* (Ann Arbor: Ardis, 1984).

29. Kogan, "Zhurnal 'Vremia' i revoliutsionnoe studenchestvo," 584. On Russian feminism, see Richard Stites, *The Women's Liberation Movement in Russia: Feminism, Nihilism, and Bolshevism 1860–1930* (Princeton, NJ: Princeton University Press, 1978).

30. A. N. Maikov, *Sochineniia*, 2 vols., ed. F. Ia. Priima (Moscow: Pravda, 1984), 1:132.

31. Maikov, *Sochineniia*, 1:126. This poem was set to music by Nikolai Rimsky-Korsakov in 1898.

32. Kogan, "Zhurnal 'Vremia' i revoliutsionnoe studenchestvo," 584. Both Kogan and the editors of the Dostoevsky *PSS* identify the author of the article as "Timmerman" (19:292). The author of

the article, who purports to be a traveler passing through Perm', refers in the third person to "M. P. Timmerman" as one of the people participating in the reading. It may well be that "M. T." is also "M. P. Timmerman," but if so he has fabricated a persona in which to narrate the evening as a bystander. The editors of the *PSS* also state that the benefit was for orphanages, while the article itself refers only to a new Sunday school (19:292).

33. Kamen'-Vinogorov, "Russkie dikovinki," *Vek*, no. 8 (February 1861): 289–92.
34. Kamen'-Vinogorov, "Russkie dikovinki," 290.
35. Kamen'-Vinogorov, "Russkie dikovinki," 290.
36. Kamen'-Vinogorov, "Russkie dikovinki," 291. In a memoir published in 1900, Veinberg (Kamen'-Vinogorov) expressed regret for allowing himself this "unchaste" personal remark. He did not, however, express any real regret for it at the height of the polemic in 1861. "Bezobraznyi postupok 'Veka.' [Iz moikh literaturnykh vospominanii]," *Istoricheskii vestnik* (May 1900): 481.
37. Kamen'-Vinogorov, "Russkie dikovinki," 291.
38. [M. L.] Mikhailov, "Bezobraznyi postupok 'Veka,'" *Sanktpeterburgskie vedomosti*, no. 51 (March 3, 1861), page numbers not visible in my copy. Dostoevsky later alluded to the Tolmachova scandal in *Crime and Punishment*, when the sensualist Svidrigailov says to Raskolnikov, "It was the same year, it seems, that the 'Outrageous Action by the *Age*' happened (you know, *Egyptian Nights*, the public reading, remember? Those dark eyes! Oh, where are you, golden time of our youth!)" (*PSS* 6:216). For more on Mikhailov, see M. L. Mikhailov, *Sochineniia*, 3 vols., ed. B. P. Koz'min, M. I. Dikman, Iu. D. Levin, and G. F. Kogan (Moscow: Khudozhestvennaia literatura, 1958); and Stites, *Women's Liberation Movement*, 38–48.
39. "Zametka ot redaktsii," *Vek*, no. 9 (March 1861): 328.
40. "Po povodu stat'i g. Mikhailova: Ob"iasnenie ot redaktsii 'Veka,'" *Vek*, no. 10 (1861), 363.
41. "Po povodu stat'i g. Mikhailova," 363.
42. "Po povodu stat'i g. Mikhailova," 363.
43. Kamen'-Vinogorov, "Otvet Kamnia-Vinogorova," *Vek*, no. 10 (1861), 363.
44. Kamen'-Vinogorov, "Otvet Kamnia-Vinogorova," 364.
45. Kamen'-Vinogorov, "Otvet Kamnia-Vinogorova," 364.
46. Kamen'-Vinogorov, "Otvet Kamnia-Vinogorova," 364.
47. N. N. Strakhov, "Postupok i mneniia g. Kamnia Vinogorova v No. 8 gazety 'Vek,'" in his *Kriticheskie stat'i (1861–1894)*, vol. 2 (Kiev: I. P. Matchenko, 1902), 253. Originally published in *Vremia*, 1861, no. 3.
48. Strakhov, "Postupok i mneniia g. Kamnia Vinogorova," 256.
49. Strakhov, "Postupok i mneniia g. Kamnia Vinogorova," 258.
50. Strakhov, "Postupok i mneniia g. Kamnia Vinogorova," 261–62.
51. Strakhov, "Postupok i mneniia g. Kamnia Vinogorova," 262.
52. Katkov, "Nash iazyk," 22; *SS* 1:351.
53. Katkov, "Nash iazyk," 23; *SS* 1:351.
54. Katkov, "Nash iazyk," 23; *SS* 1:351.
55. Katkov, "Nash iazyk," 23; *SS* 1:352.
56. Katkov, "Nash iazyk," 23; *SS* 1:352.
57. Katkov, "Nash iazyk," 24; *SS* 1:352–53.
58. Katkov, "Nash iazyk," 24; *SS* 1:353.
59. Katkov, "Nash iazyk," 24; *SS* 1:353.
60. Katkov, "Nash iazyk," 25; *SS* 1:353.
61. Katkov, "Nash iazyk," 25; *SS* 1:354.
62. Katkov, "Nash iazyk," 25; *SS* 1:354.
63. Katkov, "Nash iazyk," 28, 29; *SS* 1:356, 357–58.
64. Katkov, "Nash iazyk," 30; *SS* 1:359.
65. Katkov, "Nash iazyk," 30; *SS* 1:359.
66. Katkov, "Nash iazyk," 31; *SS* 1:360.
67. Katkov, "Nash iazyk," 31; *SS* 1:360.

68. Katkov, "Nash iazyk," 32; *SS* 1:361.
69. Katkov, "Nash iazyk," 33; *SS* 1:362.
70. Katkov, "Nash iazyk," 33; *SS* 1:362.
71. Katkov, "Nash iazyk," 34; *SS* 1:363.
72. Katkov, "Nash iazyk," 36; *SS* 1:366.
73. Katkov, "Nash iazyk," 37; *SS* 1:366.
74. Katkov, "Nash iazyk," 35; *SS* 1:364.
75. See V. Kirpotin, "Dostoevskii o 'Egipetskikh nochakh' Pushkina," *Voprosy literatury*, 1962, no. 11:112–21; Joseph Frank, *Stir of Liberation*, 86–87; Lewis Tracy, "Decoding Puškin: Resurrecting Some Readers' Responses to *Egyptian Nights*," *Slavic and East European Journal* 37, no. 4 (1993): 456–71; and S. V. Berezkina (Beriozkina), "F. M. Dostoevskii i M. N. Katkov (iz istorii romana 'Prestuplenie i nakazanie'), *Izvestiia RAN, Seriia literatury i iazyka* 72, no. 5 (2013): 16–25. During the discussion at the conference "Dostoevsky Beyond Dostoevsky" at Brown University in March 2014, Olga Meerson pointed out that the introductory part of *Egyptian Nights* is centrally concerned with the question of usefulness in art that Dostoevsky had discussed in "Mr.—bov." But strangely neither he nor Katkov ever refers to this aspect of *Egyptian Nights* in the course of their polemic.
76. See also the fragment from Strakhov's unpublished article that Dostoevsky appends as a "letter" to the end of "An Answer to the *Russian Herald*": "*Egyptian Nights* is not a fragment at all. Where have you found in it signs of unfinishedness, fragmentariness? On the contrary—what a full picture! What marvelous correlation of the parts, definiteness and finishedness! . . . *Egyptian Nights* is an improvisation, but it is a complete, finished improvisation" (19:137–38).
77. P. A. Kuskov, "Nekotorye razmyshleniia po povodu nekotorykh voprosov," *Vremia*, no. 2 (February 1861): 131–48. (Katkov cites it as being in the April issue, no. 4, but this appears to be incorrect.) According to Nechaeva, Kuskov was a talentless poet whom Apollon Grigoriev, one of the major contributors to *Time*, could not stand: "He demanded his removal from *Time*, accompanying mention of him with epithets and supplements that are not printable" (*Zhurnal "Vremia,"* 214).
78. Kuskov, "Nekotorye razmyshleniia," 136; Katkov, "Odnogo polia iagody," 20; *SS* 1:388.
79. Katkov, "Odnogo polia iagody," 20; *SS* 1:388–89.
80. Katkov, "Odnogo polia iagody," 24–25; *SS* 1:394.
81. Katkov, "Odnogo polia iagody," 25; *SS* 1:394.
82. Katkov, "Odnogo polia iagody," 26; *SS* 1:395. The editors of the Dostoevsky *PSS* agree that Katkov most likely thought Dostoevsky was the author of the feuilleton (19:309–10).
83. Geoffrey Hosking, *Russia: People and Empire, 1552–1917* (Cambridge, MA: Harvard University Press, 1997), 32–33. My summary of the events is indebted to Hosking's account.
84. Katkov, "Pol'skii vopros," *Russkii vestnik* 43 (January 1863): 471–88; reprinted in *SS* 3:14–29.
85. Katkov, "Pol'skii vopros," 473; *SS* 3:16.
86. Katkov, "Pol'skii vopros," 476–77; *SS* 3:19.
87. Katkov, "Pol'skii vopros," 477; *SS* 3:19.
88. Katkov, "Pol'skii vopros," 478–79; *SS* 3:20–21.
89. Katkov, "Pol'skii vopros," 482; *SS* 3:23.
90. For discussion of Strakhov's article, see Nechaeva, *Zhurnal "Vremia"*, 303–5; Frank, *Stir of Liberation*, 210–12; Linda Gerstein, *Nikolai Strakhov* (Cambridge, MA: Harvard University Press, 1971), 103–6; Andrzej Walicki, "The Slavophile Thinkers and the Polish Question in 1863," in *Polish Encounters, Russian Identity*, ed. David L. Ransel and Bozena Shallcross (Bloomington, IN: Indiana University Press, 2005), 89–99; Olga Maiorova, *From the Shadow of Empire*, 100–2; and Edyta Bojanowska, "Empire by Consent: Strakhov, Dostoevskii, and the Polish Uprising of 1863," *Slavic Review* 71, no. 1 (spring 2012): 1–24. See Bojanowska for further detailed bibliography.
91. N. N. Strakhov, "Vospominaniia o Fedore Mikhailoviche Dostoevskom," in *Biografiia, pis'ma, i zametki iz zapisnoi knizhki F. M. Dostoevskogo* (St. Petersburg: A. S. Suvorin, 1883), 247.
92. N. Strakhov, *Bor'ba s zapadom v nashei literature. Istoricheskie i kriticheskie ocherki*, vol. 2 (Kiev: I. P. Matchenko, 1897; Mouton, reprint 1969), 110.

93. Russkii [N. N. Strakhov], "Rokovoi vopros," *Vremia*, no. 4 (186): 152–63. In his labeling of the Russians as barbarians, one cannot help but recall his words during the Tolmachova controversy, when he called the Russian public "northern barbarians" unable to understand *Egyptian Nights* properly (19:138).

94. Bojanowska, "Empire by Consent," 10–11; Strakhov, "Rokovoi vopros," 162.

95. Katkov, "Po povodu stat'i 'Rokovoi vopros,'" *Russkii vestnik* 45 (May 1863): 410; *SS* 3:119.

96. K. Peterson, "Po povodu stat'i 'Rokovoi vopros' v zhurnale *Vremia*," *Moskovskie vedomosti*, no. 109 (May 22, 1863), page number not visible in my copy.

97. Nechaeva, *Zhurnal "Vremia*," 303. See also A. S. Dolinin, "K tsenzurnoi istorii pervykh dvukh zhurnalov Dostoevskogo," in *F. M. Dostoevskii: Stat'i i materialy*, vol. 2 (Petrograd: Mysl', 1922–24), 559–77, for documents and correspondence relating to the opening and closing of *Time* and the opening of its successor journal *Epoch*. Herzen wrote in 1864, "The journal *Time*, moderate but honest and full of magnanimous sympathies, edited by the outstanding writer Dostoevsky, a martyr who had just returned from hard labor, wrote a few humane words about Poland, which most probably would have passed unnoticed, but the *Moscow News* pointed out [*ukazal na*] the article, and the journal was banned" (cited in Nechaeva, *Zhurnal "Vremia*," 308).

98. Strakhov, "Rokovoi vopros," 158. For more of Dostoevskii's *ex post facto* interpretation of the article, see his letter to I. S. Turgenev of June 17, 1863 (28/2:33–34).

99. Katkov, "Po povodu stat'i 'Rokovoi vopros,'" 398; *SS* 3:108.

100. Katkov, "Po povodu stat'i 'Rokovoi vopros,'" 402; *SS* 3:112.

101. Katkov, "Po povodu stat'i 'Rokovoi vopros,'" 402–3; *SS* 3:112–13.

102. Katkov, "Po povodu stat'i 'Rokovoi vopros,'" 411; *SS* 3:119.

103. Katkov, "Po povodu stat'i 'Rokovoi vopros,'" 417; *SS* 3:125.

104. Katkov, "Po povodu stat'i 'Rokovoi vopros,'" 417; *SS* 3:123.

105. Katkov, "Elegicheskaia zametka," 162; *SS* 4:453.

106. Katkov, "Elegicheskaia zametka," 166; *SS* 4:547.

CHAPTER 5

1. See Joseph Frank, *Dostoevsky: The Miraculous Years, 1865–1871* (Princeton: Princeton University Press, 1995), 39. See note 1 to chapter 4 for an explanation of how I have chosen to translate titles of Dostoevsky's novels.

2. Mikhail Katkov, "O nashem nigilizme po povodu romana Turgeneva," 411; *SS* 1:514–15.

3. Katkov, "O nashem nigilizme," 424; *SS* 1:525–26.

4. Katkov, "O nashem nigilizme," 425; *SS* 1:526.

5. L. Grossman, *Dostoevskii* (Moscow: Molodaia gvardiia, 1965), 339. Iu. F. Kariakin disagrees with Grossman's characterization of the letter, and considers the plot as outlined in it to be banal and unrealistic: "Someone other than Dostoevsky could have written the letter to Katkov. No one but him could have written *Crime and Punishment*." I believe that, especially in the context of Dostoevsky's generally not very eloquent letters, Grossman is closer to the truth. "Mif o 'chernoi magii' Dostoevskogo," *Russkaia literatura*, no. 1 (1972): 114.

6. The example Dostoevsky gives of "traces in our newspapers" is the case of "that seminary student who killed a girl by agreement with her in a barn and whom they arrested an hour later over breakfast" (28/2:137). The notes in the *PSS* say that "the source of this fact has not been established" (28/2:424). But G. F. Kogan has found the account of this case in the major Russian newspapers, including Katkov's *Moscow News*, in February 1865. G. F. Kogan, "Iz istorii sozdaniia 'Ispovedi Stavrogina,'" in *Izvestiia Akademii nauk: Seriia literatury i iazyka* 54, no. 1 (Moscow: Nauka, 1995): 70.

7. The notes to the *PSS* state that Dostoevsky received 150 rubles per printer's sheet for *Crime and Punishment*, and give as their source L. K. Ilinsky's article on Dostoevsky's honoraria (28/2:425). But Ilinsky says in that article that the payment was 125 rubles per printer's sheet. L. Il'inskii, "Gonorar Dostoevskogo," *Bibliograficheskie listy Russkogo bibliologicheskogo obshchestva*, no. 3 (1922): 8.

8. Letter of March 16, 1863, from N. F. Shcherbina to M. N. Katkov, in *Literaturnoe nasledstvo* 86, 390.

9. *Troubled Sea*s is ritually referred to by Soviet scholars as a vicious antinihilist screed, although most of the novel is a rather diffuse satire that spends more time among the feckless nobility and civil-servant class than among nihilists; no nihilists appear until the last 100 pages of the 550-page novel. E. N. Dryzhakova calls it "a rather banal family story with intricate romantic adventures.... The depiction of the nihilist-revolutionaries .. looks like a hastily invented appendage to a novel of mores." ("Dostoevskii i nigilisticheskii roman 1860-kh godov," in *Dostoevskii: Materialy i issledovaniia* 17 [St. Petersburg: Nauka, 2005], 15.) Dryzhakova rejects the label "antinihilist," calling it "an unjustified legacy of Soviet literary scholarship," and uses the term "nihilist novel" for "works of Russian literature that depict nihilists, that is, young people who reject old customs, independent of whether the depiction is sympathetic, condemnatory, tragic, or caricatured" ("Dostoevskii i nigilisticheskii roman," 4). For an overview of Pisemsky's career, see Charles A. Moser, *Pisemsky: A Provincial Realist* (Cambridge, MA: Harvard University Press, 1969), 120–30. On Pisemsky's relationship with Katkov, see Moser, *Pisemsky*, 122–23, 144. See also Trofimova, "'Polozhitel'noe nachalo' v russkoi literature XIX veka."

10. Shcherbina letter to Katkov, *Literaturnoe nasledstvo* 86, 390.

11. Quoted in Liubimov, *Katkov i ego istoricheskaia zasluga*, 48–52.

12. Letter to Kraevskii of March 30, 1842, cited in Nevedenskii, *Katkov i ego vremia*, 89. Speaking of Katkov's willingness to help younger writers (she demonstrates that he was active in creating the Literary Fund in 1858–59), Perevalova writes, "It is quite likely that Katkov, at this period more than well-to-do, but having himself in his youth experienced need and repeated blows to his self-esteem [*samoliubie*], understood how painfully such 'trivia' could be felt, and strove to help the people who were materially dependent on him avoid them." (*Zhurnal M. N. Katkova*, 98).

13. A. G. Dostoevskaia, *Vospominaniia*, ed. S. V. Belov and V. A. Tunimanov (Moscow: Khudozhestvennaia literatura, 1971), 101, 105.

14. William Mills Todd III, "Dostoevskii as a Professional Writer," 83. In discussing Dostoevsky's relationship with Katkov, Todd focuses on the damage done to Dostoevsky's reputation by the low rates Katkov paid him, thus "[taking] him out of the first rank of Russian writers" (83).

15. B. L. Modzalevskii, "Dostoevskii—sotrudnik 'Russkogo vestnika': Neizdannye pis'ma F. M. Dostoevskogo 1866–1873 gg.," *Byloe*, no. 14 (1919): 32–33. Vladimir Soloviov also speaks of Katkov's "refined delicacy" in his dealings with him. ("'Dlia blaga Rossii,'" 76).

16. Grossman, "Gorod i liudi 'Prestupleniia i nakazaniia,'" introduction to his edition of F. M. Dostoevskii, *Prestuplenie i nakazanie* (Moscow: Khudozhestvennaia literatura, 1935), 42. See the comment by N. N. Strakhov: "It was the only thing people were reading, the only thing lovers of reading were talking about, usually complaining about the crushing power of the novel, the difficult impression from which people with healthy nerves almost got sick, and people with weak nerves had to stop reading" (Dostoevskii, *PSS* 28/2:438).

17. Konstantine Klioutchkine, "The Rise of *Crime and Punishment* from the Air of the Media," *Slavic Review* 61, no. 1 (spring 2002): 89. Dostoevsky's use of journalistic sources for his work on *Crime and Punishment* has been discussed by many scholars, including V. V. Danilov, "K voprosu o kompozitsionnykh priemakh v 'Prestuplenii i nakazanii' Dostoevskogo," *Izvestiia Akademii nauk SSSR. Otdelenie obshchestvennykh nauk*, no. 3 (Leningrad: Izdatel'stvo Akademii nauk SSSR, 1933), 249–63; Grossman, "Gorod i liudi," 5–52; Grossman, *Dostoevskii*, 333–34; Donald Fanger, *Dostoevsky and Romantic Realism: A Study of Dostoevsky in Relation to Balzac, Dickens, and Gogol* (Chicago: University of Chicago Press, 1965), 185–90; and *PSS* 7:329–41. See also V. D. Rak, "Istochnik ocherkov o znamenitykh ugolovnykh protsessakh v zhurnalakh brat'ev Dostoevskikh," in *Dostoevskii: Materialy i issledovaniia*, 1, ed. G. M. Fridlender (Leningrad: Nauka, 1974), 239–41. For a general discussion of Dostoevsky's use of journalistic material in his art, see Charles A. Moser, "Dostoevsky and the Aesthetics of Journalism," *Dostoevsky Studies* 3 (1982): 27–40.

18. Klioutchkine, "The Rise of *Crime and Punishment*," 100. Anne Lounsbery has done a similar analysis of the ways in which "networks of print" affect "real-world" events in *The Devils*. (Anne

Lounsbery, "Print Culture and Real Life in Dostoevsky's *Demons*," *Dostoevsky Studies* 11 [2007]: 25-37.) See also Ilya Kliger, "Shapes of History and the Enigmatic Hero in Dostoevsky: The Case of *Crime and Punishment*," *Comparative Literature* 62, no. 3 (2010): 228-45.

19. See Fanger, *Dostoevsky and Romantic Realism*, 216, and Klioutchkine, "The Rise of *Crime and Punishment*," 98. Klioutchkine rejects Dostoevsky's claim that he had predicted this murder, seeing the similarity to Raskolnikov's crime as related to Dostoevsky's participation in the "media wave" of crime writing at the time (99).

20. N. N. Strakhov, "Materialy dlia zhizneopisaniia F. M. Dostoevskogo," in *Biografiia, pis'ma i zametki iz zapisnoi knizhki F. M. Dostoevskogo*, 237.

21. G. Z. Eliseev, "Zhurnalistika," *Sovremennik*, no. 3 (1866): 37, 39.

22. N. N. Strakhov, "F. M. Dostoevskii. Prestuplenie i nakazanie," *Otechestvennye zapiski*, 1867; reprinted in Sobolev, ed., *Kritika 60-kh godov XIX veka*, 373.

23. The review by the writer Nikolai Dmitrievich Akhsharumov (an occasional contributor to the *Russian Herald*) contains a similar passage, which sounds like an amalgamation of the positions of the *Russian Herald* and of *Time*. Akhsharumov speaks of the Russian "proletariat," which consists not of factory workers but of scattered groups of students and former students: "The number of students grew quickly, but the need for them, the vital need, has remained almost the same. As a result of this, *supply*, as political economy terms it, *has exceeded demand*, and a very significant number of young people have remained without bread." These students cannot merge with the crowd because they have pretensions to belonging to higher levels of society thanks to their intellectual development. So they have become dissatisfied and embittered. "We cannot finally explain [the possibility of Raskolnikovs] without addressing the very character of our intellectual development. In our country it was not born of life and *did not grow up on its soil*, but was transplanted to us in fragments and in incomplete form from distant lands and from a different climate. Therefore it does not find here, in real life, that firm point of support and that check that would be inevitably necessary in order for it to have a regular growth and to bring practical, mature fruit." (N. D. Akhsharumov, "Kritika: *Prestuplenie i nakazanie*, roman F. M. Dostoevskogo," *Vsemirnyi trud*, no. 3 [1867]: 155-56; emphasis added.) For more on Akhsharumov, see Perevalova, *Zhurnal M. N. Katkova*, 240-41.

24. Strakhov, "Prestuplenie i nakazanie," 377-80.

25. Katkov, "O nashem nigilizme," 407-8; *SS* 1:511-12.

26. [Anon.], "Literaturnye zametki," *Nedelia*, no. 5 (April 10, 1866): 72, 73. On the antinihilist novel, see also Dryzhakova, "Dostoevskii i nigilisticheskii roman"; Charles A. Moser, *Antinihilism in the Russian Novel of the 1860's* (The Hague: Mouton, 1964); T. F. Prokopov, "Vzbalamuchennyi antinigilizm (K istorii 'literaturnogo pokhoda' M. N. Katkova protiv revoliutsionnoi demokratii)," in *Katkovskii vestnik*, 71-82; and Trofimova, "'Polozhitel'noe nachalo' v russkoi literature XIX veka."

27. Katkov's criticism is echoed in Akhsharumov's review, in relation not to Sonia but to Raskolnikov: "We must admit that the author has made an error in not separating himself from his creation with a sufficiently clear line. He was, as they used to say, insufficiently objective." Akhsharumov, "Kritika," 148. For general information on the alterations to *Crime and Punishment*, see *PSS* 7:325-26. At a late stage of my work on this project I became familiar with the studies by S. V. Berezkina (Beriozkina), who has also analyzed the interactions between Dostoevsky and Katkov regarding *Crime and Punishment*. Her work is complementary to mine; she discusses how references to George Henry Lewes, Schleswig-Holstein, and the "woman question" are influenced by the treatment of those topics in the *Russian Herald*. She also offers a somewhat different interpretation of how the figure of Sonia was developed by Dostoevsky. S. V. Berezkina (Beriozkina), "F. M. Dostoevskii i M. N. Katkov"; the discussion of the "woman question" in this article is largely reproduced in her "'Zhivet zhe na kvartire u portnogo Kapernaumova...' (Iz kommentariia k 'Prestupleniiu i nakazaniiu' Dostoevskogo)," *Russkaia literatura*, no. 4 (2013): 169-79.

28. "Soobshcheniia i izvestiia," *Russkii vestnik* 200 (February 1889): 361. The contemporary review by Akhsharumov, who was a contributor to the *Russian Herald* but probably did not know about the editors' view of "the exaggerated idealization of Sonia," nevertheless supports that view. He writes, "This

character is deeply idealized and [the author's] task was inexpressibly difficult; therefore perhaps the execution of her character seems weak to us. She has been well conceived, but she lacks body; despite the fact that she is constantly before our eyes, we somehow do not see her." Akhsharumov perceives her importance in the scheme of the novel, and describes her significance for Raskolnikov as "the only person of all those surrounding him whom he had the courage to confide in, and in whom he could find a point of support for himself." But he finds the artistic depiction of Sonia lacking: "All of this, however, comes out in the novel as inert and pale not so much in comparison with the energetic coloration of the other passages in the story as all by itself. The ideal has not taken on flesh and blood, and so it remains for us in an idealized mist. In short, all this came out as weak and intangible [*zhidko, neosiazatel'no*]" ("Kritika," 151).

29. Grossman, *Dostoevskii*, 366. Grossman's remarks about the red pencil marks are metaphorical, since no such manuscript has survived.

30. Grossman, *Dostoevskii*, 366.

31. V. Ia. Kirpotin, *Razocharovanie i krushenie Rodiona Raskol'nikova: Kniga o romane F. M. Dostoevskogo 'Prestuplenie i nakazanie'* (Moscow: Sovetskii pisatel', 1970), 164.

32. Kirpotin, *Razocharovanie i krushenie*, 167. Beriozkina also introduces an 1895 statement by Liubimov that attributes Katkov's dissatisfaction with the episode to the idea "that the occupation of prostitution could under any circumstances become a lofty feat of self-sacrifice and secrete under itself an innocent purity of soul, preserving its whiteness within the dirty envelope of the body" ("F. M. Dostoevskii i M. N. Katkov," 20–21).

33. Kirpotin, *Razocharovanie i krushenie*, 168.

34. Kirpotin, *Razocharovanie i krushenie*, 169, 174–75. See also Michael R. Katz, "The Nihilism of Sonia Marmeladova," *Dostoevsky Studies* 1, no. 1 (1993): 25–36; and Elizabeth Blake, "Sonya, Silent No More: A Response to the Woman Question in Dostoevsky's *Crime and Punishment*," *Slavic and East European Journal* 50, no. 2 (2006): 252–71.

35. In fact, an inspection of the changes made to the text as published in the *Russian Herald* when Dostoevsky republished the novel as a separate work reveals that in the disputed scene Dostoevsky weakened the romantic coloration of the scene through the removal of several phrases, such as the epithet "darling [*milyi*]" and the following dialogue: "[Raskol'nikov:] 'And you say this while loving me?' [Sonia:] 'Yes, yes, I say it while loving, loving'" (*PSS* 7:288–89).

36. D. I. Pisarev, "Bor'ba za zhizn' ('Prestuplenie i nakazanie' F. M. Dostoevskogo. Dve chasti, 1867 g.)," in his *Polnoe sobranie sochinenii i pisem*, ed. F. F. Kuznetsov et al. (Moscow: Nauka, 2005), 9:134.

37. See *PSS* 28/1:483–44, 487, 494; 9:250–51, 252; and 12:237–46. Unlike most commentators who see the final decision as belonging to Katkov, one scholar has argued that the decision to omit the chapter was actually made mutually between Liubimov and Dostoevsky in October 1872, before Katkov returned from a trip abroad in November. (B. V. Fedorenko, "Iz razyskanii o Dostoevskom. 2. Iz tvorcheskoi istorii romana F. M. Dostoevskogo 'Besy,'" in *Novye aspekty v izuchenii Dostoevskogo; sbornik nauchnykh trudov* [Petrozavodsk: Izdatel'stvo Petrozavodskogo universiteta, 1994], 293.)

38. For a comparison of the two texts and a discussion of "At Tikhon's" as the culmination of Dostoevsky's artistic exploration of the theme of the "insulted female child," see my *Discovering Sexuality in Dostoevsky*, 29–41.

39. *Dokumenty po istorii literatury i obshchestvennosti*, Issue 1 (Moscow: Tsentrarkhiv, 1922), 3–40. The revised, less explicit version was published by V. L. Komarovich, "Neizdannaia glava romana 'Besy,'" *Byloe*, no. 18 (1922): 219–52.

40. As a start, see the sources referenced in *PSS* 12:237–46, as well as Frank, *The Miraculous Years*, 430–34. Komarovich, one of the first scholars to publish a version of "At Tikhon's," himself questioned the advisability of including it in the canonical text.

41. A. S. Dolinin, "'Ispoved' Stavrogina.' (V sviazi s kompozitsiei 'Besov')," *Literaturnaia mysl'. Al'manakh*, no.1 (Petrograd: Mysl', 1922), 145.

42. Dolinin, "'Ispoved' Stavrogina,'" 145. Iurii Kariakin advances a similar argument, and adds that the separate edition appeared just as Dostoevsky was beginning work as the editor of the journal *The Citizen* (*Grazhdanin*), so he would not have had no time to do the necessary revisions to the rest of the

text that the restoration of the chapter would have entailed. (*Dostoevskii i kanun XXI veka* [Moscow: Sovetskii pisatel', 1989], 328.)

43. Kariakin, *Dostoevskii i kanun XIX veka*, 323.

44. See *Discovering Sexuality in Dostoevsky*, 39–41.

45. Kariakin, *Dostoevskii i kanun XIX veka*, 325.

46. Kariakin, *Dostoevskii i kanun XIX veka*, 329–30. The extent to which readings of Katkov's editorial activities have changed in Russia can be seen in the way his interference in the texts of *Crime and Punishment* and *The Devils* is characterized in a recent article that labels Katkov the "savior of the fatherland." After noting his major literary contribution, the authors write, "His contribution as an editor was not at all symbolic: it is well known that he took direct part in preparing for publication the texts of the novels *Crime and Punishment*, *The Devils*, *Fathers and Sons*, and others." (Popov and Veligonova, "Spasitel' otechestva," 152). What had been a "crime" is now called a "contribution."

47. "L'homme qui rit" [D. I. Minaev], "Nevinnye zametki," *Delo*, no. 11 (November 1871): 57, 58.

48. N. N. [P. N. Tkachov], "Bol'nye liudi," *Delo*, no. 3 (March 1873): 151–79; and no. 4 (April 1873): 151–79, this quotation April, 367. Tkachov's reference to Dostoevsky's theory of the Russian person apparently relates to the essay "Vlas" in the *Diary of a Writer* for 1873 (*PSS* 21:31–41).

49. See the discussion in Joseph Frank, *Dostoevsky: The Mantle of the Prophet, 1871–1881* (Princeton: Princeton University Press, 2002), 64, 130–72.

50. "Zametki i raznye izvestiia," *Glasnyi sud*, no. 59, March 16/28, 1867, reprinted in *Kritika 60-kh godov XIX veka*, 355.

51. V. N. Zakharov, "Fakty protiv legendy," in his *Problemy izucheniia Dostoevskogo* (Petrozavodsk: Petrozavodskii gosudarstvennyi universitet, 1978), 105.

52. The most succinct and compelling analysis of this episode (despite the non-succinct title) is found in Robert Louis Jackson, "A View from the Underground: On Nikolai Nikolaevich Strakhov's Letter About His Good Friend Fyodor Mikhailovich Dostoevsky and on Leo Nikolaevich Tolstoy's Cautious Response to It," in his *Dialogues with Dostoevsky: The Overwhelming Questions* (Stanford: Stanford University Press, 1996), 104–20. See also A. G. Dostoevskaia, *Vospominaniia*, 395–406; and L. N. Rozenblium, *Tvorcheskie dnevniki Dostoevskogo* (Moscow: Nauka, 1981), 30–45. Traces of this libel of Dostoevsky can be found as recently as J. M. Coetzee's 1994 novel *The Master of Petersburg*, which assumes that Dostoevsky had to have been involved in a sexually suggestive way with a real little girl in order to be able to imagine the crime of Stavrogin. For an interpretation that absolves Coetzee of what I consider an irresponsible depiction of Dostoevsky, see Gary Adelman, "Stalking Stavrogin: J. M. Coetzee's *The Master of Petersburg* and the Writing of *The Possessed*," *Journal of Modern Literature* 23, no. 2 (winter 1999–2000): 351–57.

53. V. G. Avseenko, "Ocherki tekushchei literatury. Novogodniaia knizhka 'Otechestvennykh zapisok.' Chem otlichaetsia roman g. Dostoevskogo, napisannyi dlia etogo zhurnala, ot drugikh ego romanov, napisannykh dlia 'Russkogo vestnika.' Nechto o plevkakh, poshchechinakh i t. p. predmetakh," *Russkii mir*, no. 27 (January 29, 1875), cited in Dostoevskii, *PSS* 17:347. Zakharov refers, apparently mistakenly, to a different article by Avseenko, in which *A Raw Youth* is also discussed, but without the reference to the *Russian Herald* correcting Dostoevsky's earlier works. This article, published in the *Russian Herald* in January 1876, will be discussed below, but it is clearly not the article to which Dostoevsky is reacting in his notebook entry.

54. Frederick T. Griffiths and Stanley J. Rabinowitz. *Novel Epics: Gogol, Dostoevsky, and National Narrative* (Evanston: Northwestern University Press, 1990), 147. See also their expanded edition, *Epic and the Russian Novel from Gogol to Pasternak* (Boston: Academic Studies Press, 2011).

55. For an informative but tendentious account of Avseenko's career and his association with the *Russian Herald*, see E. G. Gaintseva, "V. G. Avseenko i 'Russkii vestnik' 1870-kh godov," *Russkaia literatura*, no. 2 (1989): 70–84.

56. V. G. Avseenko, "Literaturnoe obozrenie," *Russkii vestnik* 121 (January 1876): 507.

57. Avseenko, "Literaturnoe obozrenie," 502.

58. Avseenko, "Literaturnoe obozrenie," 503.

CHAPTER 6

1. Ė. G. Babaev, *Lev Tolstoi i russkaia zhurnalistika ego epokhi*, 2nd. ed. (Moscow: Izdatel'stvo Moskovskogo universiteta, 1993), 10.

2. William Mills Todd III, "The Ruse of the Russian Novel," in *The Novel*, vol. 1: *History, Geography, and Culture*, ed. Franco Moretti (Princeton: Princeton University Press, 2006), 411. For Todd's discussions of Tolstoy, see "The Responsibilities of (Co-) Authorship: Notes on Revising the Serialized Version of *Anna Karenina*," in *Freedom and Responsibility in Russian Literature: Essays in Honor of Robert Louis Jackson*, ed. Elizabeth Cheresh Allen and Gary Saul Morson (Evanston: Northwestern University Press, 1995), 159–69; "Reading *Anna* in Parts," *Tolstoy Studies Journal* 8 (1995–96): 125–28; "Anna on the Installment Plan: Teaching *Anna Karenina* Through the History of Its Serial Publication," in *Approaches to Teaching Tolstoy's Anna Karenina*, ed. Liza Knapp and Amy Mandelker (New York: Modern Language Association of America, 2003), 53–59; "Tolstoy and Dostoevsky"; and (with Justin Weir) "Fear and Loathing in the Caucasus: Tolstoy's 'The Raid' and Russian Journalism," in *Before They Were Titans: Essays on the Early Works of Dostoevsky and Tolstoy*, ed. Elizabeth Cheresh Allen (Boston: Academic Studies Press, 2015), 193-209.

3. *Semeĭnoe schast'e*, *Russkii vestnik* 20 (April 1859); *Kazaki*, *Russkii vestnik* 43 (January 1863); *Polikushka*, *Russkii vestnik* 43 (February 1863). Like Turgenev, Tolstoy had a contretemps with Katkov as the *Russian Herald* was being launched, in 1856. In the case of Tolstoy, it concerned Katkov's use of his name in an advertisement for the journal and a later notice that Tolstoy had ceased to be a contributor, while in Tolstoy's view he had never formally agreed to be a contributor. See L. N. Tolstoi, *Polnoe sobranie sochinenii*, 90 vols., ed. V. G. Chertkov et al. (Moscow: Jubilee Edition, 1928–58), 60:132–34. Subsequent references to this edition will be given in parentheses in the text. See also Babaev, *Tolstoi i russkaia zhurnalistika*, 50.

4. *Tysiacha vosem'sot piatyi god*, *Russkii vestnik* 55 (January 1865): 48–156; 55 (February 1865): 574–627; 61 (February 1866): 763–814; 62 (March 1866): 312–40; 62 (April 1866): 690–733. Although the *Russian Herald* published a favorable review by P. K. Shchebalsky of the first three volumes of *War and Peace* in January 1868 (73:300–20), the later portions of the novel, with their disquisitions on the philosophy of history, were criticized by Shchebalsky for what he called "nihilism in history": "Both Napoleon and Kutuzov along with Barclay constantly did the opposite of what they should have done, and consequently in essence it's all the same who won the Battle of Borodino, and whose army perished between Moscow and Kovno, it's all the same whether battles were given, armies perished, Napoleons or 'the last soldiers in the artillery train' commanded the armies; whether wise men or idiots were the ministers, whether people killed each other or embraced each other . . . All the same, all the same!" (P. K. Shchebal'skii, "Nigilizm v istorii," *Russkii vestnik* 80 [April 1869]: 862–63). See Babaev, *Tolstoi i russkaia zhurnalistika*, 53–54. See also Maiorova's discussion of *War and Peace* (*From the Shadow of Empire*, 143–54).

5. F. Buslaev, "Perepiska Tolstogo s M. N. Katkovym," *Literaturnoe nasledstvo* 37–38: *L. N. Tolstoi II* (Moscow: AN SSSR, 1939), 195–96. Compare Tolstoy's letter to Katkov of May 17, 1875 (after the publication of *War and Peace*), in which he asserts that every page of his *Azbuka*, a set of readings for children, "cost me even more labor and has more significance than all those writings for which they praise me so undeservedly" (62:185). On Tolstoy's pedagogical activities, see vol. 8 of his *Polnoe sobranie sochinenii*; Boris Eikhenbaum [Eichenbaum], *Lev Tolstoi* (Leningrad, 1928–31; reprint Munich: Wilhelm Fink, 1968), bk. 2; and his *Lev Tolstoi: Semidesiatye gody* (Leningrad: Sovetskii pisatel', 1960).

6. See Todd, "Responsibilities," 162, and "Anna on the Installment Plan," 54.

7. Edward C. Thaden (with the collaboration of Marianna Forster Thaden), *Russia's Western Borderlands, 1710–1870* (Princeton: Princeton University Press, 1984), 159. On Cherkassky, see V. A. Tvardovskaia, *Ideologiia poreformennogo samoderzhaviia*, pp. 33, 42. See also Theodore R. Weeks, "Religion and Russification: Russian Language in the Catholic Churches of the 'Northwest Provinces' after 1863," *Kritika* 2, no. 1 (winter 2001, new series): 87–110; Olga Maiorova, *From the Shadow of Empire*, 99–116; and Alexei Miller, *The Romanov Empire and Nationalism: Essays in the Methodology*

of Historical Research (Budapest: Central European University Press, 2008). Denmark had been forced by the Treaty of Vienna to cede Schleswig-Holstein to Prussia and Austria in late 1864. S. V. Berezkina (Beriozkina), "F. M. Dostoevskii i M. N. Katkov," 18–19.

8. Èikhenbaum (Eichenbaum), *Semidesiatye gody*, 161–62. The letter from Strakhov is in *L. N. Tolstoi—N. N. Strakhov: Polnoe sobranie perepiski*, 2 vols., ed. A. A. Donskov, compiled by L. D. Gromova and T. G. Nikiforova (Ottawa: Slavic Research Group at the University of Ottawa and State L. N. Tolstoy Museum, 2003), 1:185. Strakhov presciently warned Tolstoy about the *Russian Herald*, based on his experience observing Dostoevsky's dealings with the journal, "I have a premonition that you will not get along."

9. See Todd, "Anna on the Installment Plan," 58–59; Èikhenbaum (Eichenbaum), *Semidesiatye gody*, 172–73; V. Zhdanov, *Tvorcheskaia istoriia "Anny Kareninoi"* (Moscow: Sovetskii pisatel', 1957), 57; V. A. Zhdanov and È. E. Zaidenshnur, "Istoriia sozdaniia romana 'Anna Karenina,'" in L. N. Tolstoi, *Anna Karenina: Roman v vos'mi chastiakh*, ed. V. A. Zhdanov and È. E. Zaidenshnur (Literaturnye pamiatniki) (Moscow: Nauka, 1970), 803–33.

10. *Anna Karenina, Russkii vestnik* 115 (January 1875): 243–336; 115 (February 1875): 742–817; 116 (March 1875): 246–316; 116 (April 1875): 572–641. Later installments were in 121 (January 1876): 305–90; 121 (February 1876): 679–745; 122 (March 1876): 291–339; 122 (April 1876): 641–93; 126 (December 1876): 687–737; 127 (January 1877): 267–324; 127 (February 1877): 830–98; 128 (March 1877): 329–82; and 128 (April 1877): 709–763. For analysis of the installments of *Anna Karenina* in the *Russian Herald* in comparison to the final organization of the novel, see Todd, "Responsibilities"; "Anna on the Installment Plan," 57; "Tolstoy and Dostoevsky," 34–36; and Sydney Schultze, *The Structure of Anna Karenina* (Ann Arbor: Ardis, 1982), 44–55.

11. V. G. Avseenko [signed "A."], "Po povodu novogo romana grafa L. N. Tolstogo," *Russkii vestnik* 117 (May 1875): 411.

12. V. G. Avseenko [signed "A."], "Literaturnoe obozrenie," 510.

13. A. L. Bem described Dostoevsky's polemic with Tolstoy in *A Raw Youth* in 1936: "Khudozhestvennaia polemika s Tolstym (K ponimaniiu 'Podrostka')," in *O Dostoevskom: Sbornik statei, Praga 1929/1933/1936*, ed. A. L. Bem (Moscow: Russkii put', 2007), 535–51. See also the discussions by Robert Louis Jackson, *Dostoevsky's Quest for Form*, 113–18; Gary Saul Morson, *Narrative and Freedom: The Shadows of Time* (New Haven: Yale University Press, 1994), 179–80; and Kate Holland, *The Novel in the Age of Disintegration: Dostoevsky and the Problem of Genre in the 1870s* (Evanston: Northwestern University Press, 2013), 116–19 and 211n28.

14. Dostoevskii, *PSS* 13:453.

15. Dostoevskii, *PSS* 13:454. In his notes and sketches for *A Raw Youth*, Dostoevsky refers to Liovin as a "misanthrope" and as "sad," like the "grandson" in Nikolai Semionovich's letter (*PSS* 17:216, 16:420).

16. Todd, "Anna on the Installment Plan," 58; "Ruse of the Russian Novel," 413.

17. *The Law and the Lady* by Collins appeared alongside *Anna Karenina* in the January, March, and April 1875 issues. Trollope's *The Way We Live Now* appeared with *Anna Karenina* in the January, February, March, April, December 1876 and January, February, and March 1877 issues. Todd notes the appearance of Victorian novels in the *Russian Herald* ("Responsibilities," 164; "Anna on the Installment Plan," 55). See also Amy Mandelker, *Framing Anna Karenina: Tolstoy, the Woman Question, and the Victorian Novel* (Columbus: Ohio State University Press, 1993); and Liza Knapp, *Anna Karenina and Others: Tolstoy's Labyrinth of Plots* (Madison: University of Wisconsin Press, 2016), 82–169.

18. Feoktistov, *Vospominaniia*, 93.

19. *Anna Karenina, Russkii vestnik* 127 (February 1877): 842; pt. 6, ch. 19. I will cite *Anna Karenina* (hereafter cited as *AK*) first according to the *Russian Herald* (hereafter *RV*) publication, followed by the part and chapter as in modern editions. With respect to the novel Anna reads in the train, I concur with Gary Saul Morson, who says, "We are told that this novel deals with fox hunts and speeches in Parliament. Anyone who knows the English novel will immediately recognize these incidents as the signature of Anthony Trollope" (*Anna Karenina in Our Time: Seeing More Wisely* [New Haven: Yale University Press, 2007], 96). For more hypotheses on the possible sources, see Edwina Cruise,

"Tracking the English Novel in *Anna Karenina*: Who Wrote the English novel That Anna Reads?" in *Anniversary Essays on Tolstoy*, ed. Donna Tussing Orwin (Cambridge: Cambridge University Press, 2010), 159–82. See also B. Lönnqvist, "The English Theme in *Anna Karenina*," *Essays in Poetics: The Journal of the British Neo-Formalist Circle* 24 (autumn 1999): 58–90; and W. G. Jones, ed., *Tolstoi and Britain* (Oxford: Berg Publishers, 1995). Lönnqvist extensively documents the negative aura of the artificial and mechanical that surrounds the English theme in the novel. On the connections between *Anna Karenina* and French culture, see Priscilla Meyer, *How the Russians Read the French: Lermontov, Dostoevsky, Tolstoy* (Madison: University of Wisconsin Press, 2008), 152–209.

20. D. I. Zhuravskii, "O zheleznykh dorogakh v Rossii," *RV* 3 (May 1856): 440. Martin Katz discusses Katkov's promotion of railroad construction: "As in other financial and economic affairs, his motives were essentially political—to foster the creation of an organic political entity" (Katz, *A Political Biography*, 115).

21. Zhuravskii, "O zheleznykh dorogakh," 442, 444.

22. Zhuravskii quoting Perdonnet, *Traité Élémentaire des chemins de fer* (Paris: Garnier, 1865), in "O zheleznykh dorogakh," 444–45. Emphasis in original.

23. Zhuravskii, "O zheleznykh dorogakh," 455.

24. Zhuravskii, "O zheleznykh dorogakh," 446. Another notable article promoting the growth of railroads is N. A. Liubimov, "Arago o zheleznykh dorogakh i elektricheskikh telegrafakh," *RV* 2 (March 1856): 109–15. The need for railroads for the development of the Russian economy is taken as a given in many of the articles concerning modernization and political economy that appear in the *Russian Herald* in the late 1850s.

25. Katkov's letter is in Buslaev, "Perepiska," 197. Evgenii Markov, "Teoriia i praktika iasnopolianskoi shkoly: Pedagogicheskie zametki tul'skogo uchitelia," *RV* 39 (May 1862): 149–89.

26. Markov, "Teoriia i praktika," 165–66.

27. Markov, "Teoriia i praktika," 189, emphasis added.

28. Tolstoi, "Progress i opredelenie obrazovaniia," *PSS* 8:325–55, this passage on 342. Cited in Elisabeth Stenbock-Fermor, *The Architecture of Anna Karenina: A History of Its Writing, Structure and Message* (Louvain: Peter de Ridder Press, 1975), 66. See also Tolstoi, *PSS* 8:446–52 for variants of this article.

29. Liza Knapp, "The Setting," in *Approaches to Teaching Tolstoy's Anna Karenina*, ed. Liza Knapp and Amy Mandelker (New York: Modern Language Association of America, 2003), 30. See also M. S. Al'tman, "Zheleznaia doroga v tvorchestve L. N. Tolstogo," *Slavia* 34 (1965): 251–59; Elisabeth Stenbock-Fermor, *Architecture*, 65–74; Gary R. Jahn, "The Image of the Railroad in *Anna Karenina*," *Slavic and East European Journal* 25 (1981): 8–12; Schultze, *Structure*, 118–26; and Stephen Baehr, "The Troika and the Train: Dialogues between Tradition and Technology in Nineteenth-Century Russian Literature," in *Issues in Russian Literature before 1917: Proceedings from the III International Congress on Soviet and East European Studies*, ed. Douglas Clayton and R. C. Elwood (Columbus: Slavica, 1989), 85–106.

30. The phrase "bad omen" is in *AK, RV* 115 (January 1875): 315, pt. 1, ch. 18; "goods train" is in *AK, RV* 128 (April 1877): 763, pt. 7, ch. 31; "vengeance and murder," *AK, PSS* 19:392, pt. 8, chapter 16. Jahn argues that the train has both positive and negative associations in the novel. In my view, any positive aspects are overwhelmed by the negative tonality lent to railroad travel, trains, and the commerce enabled by trains.

31. *AK, RV* 122 (April 1876): 669–70, pt. 5, ch. 15.

32. *AK, RV* 122 (April 1876): 675, pt. 5, ch. 17. See Knapp, "Setting," 31.

33. See John Summerson, *Victorian Architecture: Four Studies in Evaluation* (New York: Columbia University Press, 1970), 36–46. See also Henry-Russell Hitchcock, "Age of Cast Iron," in his *Architecture: Nineteenth and Twentieth Centuries, The Pelican History of Art*, 4th ed. (Harmondsworth: Pelican Books, 1977), 169–90. I am grateful to Joseph M. Siry for these references.

34. *AK, RV* 127 (February 1877): 850–51, pt. 6, ch. 20. Knapp has done a brilliant analysis of the ways in which Tolstoy juxtaposes Liovin's estate with that of Vronsky: "The Estates of Pokrovskoe and Vozdvizhenskoe: Tolstoy's Labyrinth of Linkings in *Anna Karenina*," *Tolstoy Studies Journal* 8 (1995–96): 81–98; and her *Anna Karenina and Others*, 19–52.

35. See V. A. Kitaev, *Ot frondy k okhranitel'stvu*, 56–58.
36. "O nekotorykh usloviiakh, sposobstvuiushchikh umnozheniiu narodnogo kapitala," *RV* 4 (August 1856): 142.
37. "O nekotorykh usloviiakh," 148–49.
38. E. L., "Sovremennoe polozhenie kreditnykh uchrezhdenii," *RV* 7 (January 1857): 275–76, 551.
39. Kitaev, *Ot frondy k okhranitel'stvu*, 83. Perevalova writes, "The journal constantly engaged in propaganda for bourgeois reforms, emphasizing the outmodedness of the organization of landownership, the necessity for landowners to create 'rational farms' with the use of machines, fertilizer, etc., the building of factories and plants, the development of foreign and domestic trade, credit institutions, and transport" (*Zhurnal M. N. Katkova*, 68). On de Molinari, see V. K. Ronin, "Bel'giiskii èkonomist v russkoi pechati: Giustav de Molinari v zhurnalakh Katkova," in *Rossiia i Evropa: Diplomatiia i kul'tura* (Moscow: Nauka, 2002), 202–16.
40. Iu. A. Gagemeister, "Vzgliad na promyshlennost' i torgovliu Rossii," *RV* 7 (January 1857): 7, 8. See Kitaev, *Ot frondy k okhranitel'stvu*, 60.
41. *AK, RV* 127 (January 1877): 305–6, pt. 6, ch. 11. The name "Malthus" is a reference to Thomas Robert Malthus and Malthusian economic theory connected to population growth and resource depletion.
42. "Vnutrennee obozrenie," *Vestnik Evropy* 41 (June 1873): 796. My attention was drawn to this reference by Zhdanov and Zaidenschnur, "Istoriia sozdaniia," 824. "Strusberg" refers to Bethel Henry Strousberg (1823–84), a railway entrepreneur who stood trial in Russia in 1875 for fraudulent bank dealings and was deported to his native Germany. He is alluded to in pt. 7, ch. 6 of *Anna Karenina*, in Liovin's conversations in Moscow about the foreigner who is to be deported.
43. *AK, RV* 128 (April 1877): 710, pt. 7, ch. 17.
44. Stenbock-Fermor, *Architecture*, 94. The term "keystone" comes from Tolstoy's letter of January 27, 1878, to S. A. Rachinsky, who had complained of a "radical deficiency" in the structure of *Anna Karenina*, the supposed absence of a link between Anna's and Liovin's stories, which meant that "there is no architecture [in the novel]." Tolstoy responded, "On the contrary, I am proud of the architecture—the vaults have been made to meet in such a way that it is impossible to notice where the keystone is" (62:377; Rachinsky's letter is quoted in the footnote, 62:378). Stenbock-Fermor takes this letter as the point of departure for her analysis (*Architecture*, 7–9).
45. Edward C. Thaden, *Conservative Nationalism in Nineteenth-Century Russia* (Seattle: University of Washington Press, 1964), 47. See also Geoffrey Hosking, *Russia*, 374–76; and Thaden, *Russia's Western Borderlands*, 159–60.
46. Thaden, *Russia's Western Borderlands*, 165.
47. *AK, RV* 121 (February 1876): 712–13, pt. 4, ch. 9.
48. *AK, RV* 121 (February 1876): 715, pt. 4, ch. 10.
49. *MV*, July 13, 1866, no. 147; *1866 god*, 306; quoted in "O dopushchenii russkogo iazyka v inovercheskoe bogosluzhenie," *RV* 71 (September 1867): 387. This article is not signed but is obviously by Katkov.
50. Introduction to Edward C. Thaden, ed., *Russification in the Baltic Provinces and Finland, 1855–1914* (Princeton: Princeton University Press, 1981), 7–9. There is an interesting discrepancy in the way the word for "Russification," "*obrusenie*," is spelled in the *Russian Herald* version and in later editions of *Anna Karenina* before the 1917 reform of the Russian orthography. There is a clear distinction in the way these two verbs are spelled in both pre-1917 and post-1917 orthography: *obruset'* versus *obrusit'*. But the nouns derived from the two verbs become indistinguishable from each other after 1917, because of the elimination of the letter *yat*, which I will represent with a capital letter E. The *yat* was identical in pronunciation to the letter *e*, but its elimination as a separate letter obscured important etymological and historical information in Russian words. Before 1917, the noun derived from *obruset'* was spelled *obrusEnie* (with the *yat*), and the noun derived from *obrusit'* was spelled *obrusenie* (with the *e*). So in texts published before 1917, it would be clear that the word *obrusEnie* referred to a natural, unforced process of becoming Russian, while *obrusenie* referred to the imposition of Russian language and culture on an unwilling subject. In the *Russian Herald* version of the scene at Stiva's dinner party,

the word "Russification" appears once spelled *obrusenie* but three times spelled *obrusEnie*. In the 1878 separate edition prepared by Strakhov and Tolstoy, it is spelled *obrusEnie* all four times. In later, pre-1917 editions of *Anna Karenina*, it is spelled *obrusenie*. Thus for the readers of the *Russian Herald*, the guests at Stiva's dinner party were discussing how the inhabitants of "Poland" could undergo a natural process of becoming Russian, while for the readers of the later separate editions of *Anna Karenina*, the conversation concerned the imposition of Russianness by an external force, presumably the Russian government. In Tolstoy's earlier drafts of this scene, he spelled the word *obrusenie*, not *obrusEnie* (private communication from Liudmila Viktorovna Gladkova, based on unpublished drafts held at the State Tolstoy Museum in Moscow). I would like to thank Liudmila Viktorovna, Tatiana Georgievna Nikiforova, and Donna Orwin for their help with this issue. My initial hypothesis was that Katkov had changed the spelling for ideological reasons. But since it is spelled two different ways in the *Russian Herald*, and Katkov spelled the word *obrusenie* in his own articles and editorials, the discrepancy seems to have been an accident, but one that Strakhov and Tolstoy perpetuated in their own 1878 edition, going so far as to change the one instance of *obrusenie* in the *Russian Herald* to *obrusEnie*.

51. See Katkov, "O dopushchenii russkogo iazyka," for the most comprehensive digest of his views.

52. Weeks, "Religion and Russification," 103.

53. Katkov, "O dopushchenii russkogo iazyka," 360.

54. Gladkova, private communication based on unpublished drafts held at the State Tolstoy Museum.

55. *Ocherki drevneishego perioda grecheskoi filosofii*. On Leontiev, see E. V. Perevalova, "'Ten' Katkova': Pavel Mikhailovich Leont'ev," *Izvestiia vysshikh uchebnykh zavedenii: Problemy poligrafii i izdatel'skogo dela*, no. 1 (2012): 118–24; and *Zhurnal M. N. Katkova*, 38–39. Tolstoy had consulted Leontiev in 1871 about his study of Greek (83:175n8). San'kova hypothesizes that Katkov's experience teaching poorly prepared university students led him to the idea that the classical system would be beneficial for Russian education (*V poiskakh mesta*, 118). See Katkov's account of his teaching difficulties in "Pis'ma M. N. Katkova k A. N. Popovu," 483.

56. Allen Sinel, *The Classroom and the Chancellery: State Educational Reform in Russia under Count Dmitry Tolstoi* (Cambridge, MA: Harvard University Press, 1973), 170. Sinel gives a thorough account of the process of educational reform under D. A. Tolstoy. For Katkov's own summary of Tolstoy's career, see Katkov, "Obzor deiatel'nosti grafa D. A. Tolstogo v kachestve ministra narodnogo prosveshcheniia," *MV*, May 7, 1880, no. 125; *SS* 2:741–50. See also V. N. Bugaeva, *Pedagogicheskoe nasledie M. N. Katkova* (Smolensk: Madzhenta, 2011).

57. Joseph Backor, "M. N. Katkov," 239.

58. G. K. Gradovskii, "Iz minuvshego," *Russkaia starina*, bk. 1 (January 1908): 83.

59. Gradovskii, "Iz minuvshego," 84. For a sampling of Katkov's editorials about education, see Katkov, *SS* vol. 5: *Energiia predpriimchivosti*.

60. Sinel, *Classroom*, 58–59; Feoktistov, *Vospominaniia*, 173–74.

61. *AK, RV* 116 (April 1875): 572–641. The obituary is "Pamiati Pavla Mikhailovicha Leont'eva," 705–44.

62. "Pamiati Leont'eva," 720.

63. *AK, RV* 121 (February 1876): 715–17, pt. 4, ch. 10.

64. A strange sidelight to the story of the Katkov–Leontiev friendship is that Katkov's brother Mefodii twice tried to kill Leontiev, first shooting at him in the halls of the Katkov Lycée in September 1874. He was apprehended and confined to a mental hospital. In January 1875 he escaped and made a second attempt, after which he commited suicide in Butyrka prison, where the Katkovs' mother had been employed and where at least Mikhail, and perhaps Mefodii as well, had lived in their childhood. P. I. Bartenev claimed in his 1910 memoirs that Mefodii was angered by Leontiev's having cut his allowance, which has the ring of truth, since Leontiev handled financial affairs for Mikhail Katkov ("Vospominaniia P. I. Barteneva," http://feb-web.ru/feb/rosarc/ra1/ra1-047-.htm, accessed June 16, 2015). More facetiously, Turgenev claimed that Mefodii was avenging his children, who were studying at the lycée and were "pecked to death by Latin" (letter to A. A. Fet, September 27 [October 9], 1874, *PSS 1960–68, Pis'ma* 10:305). A contemporary death notice reads,

On March 1 in a solitary cell of the hospital of the Moscow Province Prison Castle [the prison known as Butyrka] the brother of the publisher of the *Moscow News*, Mefodii Nikiforovich Katkov, hanged himself. He had for some time lived in a separate apartment at his brother's house; his two sons are studying at the Lycée of Tsesarevich Nicholas. Last year he got the idea of shooting at the Director of the Lycée, P. M. Leontiev. Two shots aimed at him only slightly wounded him, but the third shot seriously wounded a watchman at the Lycée in the stomach. Katkov was seized and taken to the police hospital, where he was placed in the lunatic department, from which he escaped and again with a revolver in his hands, appeared at the Lycée, but was detained, dispatched to the hospital of the Province Castle and placed in a solitary cell. (March 1, 1875, accessed at http://rusgenealogy.clan.su/publ/1-1-0-61, August 30, 2014)

See also Bartenev's footnote to "Pis'ma M. N. Katkova k A. N. Popovu," 484. Tolstoy wrote to A. A. Fet in January 1875 that he was visiting Katkov when the latter got the news of Mefodii's second attempt to kill Leontiev. He sent Katkov his condolences on Mefodii's death (62:133, 135). See Tolstoi, *PSS* 62:133; Kalmanovskii, "Pobezhdennyi pobeditel'," 129-31; and San'kova, *V poiskakh mesta*, 141-42.

65. Editorial of September 2, 1873, cited according to M. N. Katkov, *O zhenskom obrazovanii: Stat'i, sviazannye s vozniknoveniem i postepennym rostom zhenskoi klassicheskoi gimnazii* (Moscow: A. P. Snegireva, 1897), 18, 20. The *Domostroi* was a sixteenth-century code of rules for the household in old Muscovy. By the nineteenth century its title was used as shorthand for outdated patriarchal mores. Tolstoy references it in *The Kreutzer Sonata*. See also G. Golovachov, "O zhenskikh uchebnykh zavedeniiakh," *RV* 28 (July 1860): 267-85, 28 (August 1860): 457-480; and "Obrazovanie zhenshchin v Amerike" (no signature), *RV* 107 (October 1873): 765-85. The latter article describes coeducation in the United States, in particular at Oberlin College. The thrust of the article is that the natural intellectual capacities of women are in no way different from those of men.

66. Katkov, *O zhenskom obrazovanii*, 21-22.

67. Katkov, *O zhenskom obrazovanii*, 37.

68. Katkov, *O zhenskom obrazovanii*, 46-47.

69. Katkov, *O zhenskom obrazovanii*, 47. There is an echo of Katkov's thought in an earlier version of the dinner party scene in *Anna Karenina*. As the men discuss the question of a woman's infidelity, a young student says, "A developed woman will not make a mistake [in context this refers to infidelity]. Do not lock her up, give her a higher education" (*PSS* 20:338).

70. Katkov, *O zhenskom obrazovanii*, 47-48.

71. *AK*, *RV* 121 (February 1876): 718, pt. 4, chapter 10.

72. *AK*, *RV* 121 (February 1876): 718, pt. 4, ch. 10. The prince only gives the first half of the proverb, but all Russian readers would know the ending.

73. *AK*, *RV* 121 (February 1876): 719, pt. 4, ch. 10.

74. *AK*, *RV* 121 (February 1876): 726-27, pt. 4, ch. 13.

75. *AK*, *RV* 115 (January 1875): 301-302, pt. 1, ch. 14.

76. Ilya Vinitsky, *Ghostly Paradoxes: Modern Spiritualism and Russian Culture in the Age of Realism* (Toronto: University of Toronto Press, 2009), xii. See also Michael D. Gordin, *A Well-Ordered Thing: Dmitrii Mendeleev and the Shadow of the Periodic Table* (New York: Basic Books, 2004), 81-110; and Donna Orwin, "Did Dostoevsky or Tolstoy Believe in Miracles?," in *A New Word on The Brothers Karamazov*, ed. Robert Louis Jackson (Evanston: Northwestern University Press, 2004), 125-41.

77. N. P. Vagner, "Po povodu spiritizma: Pis'mo k redaktoru," *Vestnik Evropy* 4 (1875): 855-75.

78. Vinistky, *Ghostly Paradoxes*, 90.

79. Footnote to S. A. Rachinskii, "Po povodu spiriticheskikh soobshchenii g. Vagnera," *RV* 117 (May 1875): 380.

80. Liubimov, *Katkov i ego istoricheskaia zasluga*, 40. Katkov's association with the spiritualists is reflected in the title of a poem by Iakov Polonsky satirizing spiritualism, "Old Spirits and New Spirits [Starye i novye dukhi]," published in *Nedelia* in 1875. The title is an obvious reference to Katkov's

famous article, "Old Gods and New Gods [Starye i novye bogi]." On Polonsky's poem, see Vinitsky, *Ghostly Paradoxes*, 102, 105.

81. Rachinskii, "Po povodu," 386.

82. Footnote to N. P. Vagner, "Mediumizm," *RV* 119 (October 1875): 866. See Vinitsky, *Ghostly Paradoxes*, 94–5, 98–100, 194, 195.

83. A. M. Butlerov, "Mediumskie iavleniia," *RV* 120 (November 1875): 348, cited according to Augustus De Morgan, preface to his wife Sophia's book *From Matter to Spirit: The Result of Ten Years' Experience in Spirit Manifestation* (London: Longman, Green, Longman, Roberts, & Green, 1863), vi, xvlii. According to Vagner, the great chemist Dmitrii Mendeleev considered this quotation from De Morgan to be "an insult cast at him personally." (N. P. Vagner, "Vospominanie ob A. M. Butlerove," in A. M. Butlerov, *Stat'i po mediumizmu*, ed. A. N. Aksakov [St. Petersburg: V. Demakov, 1889], xliii).

84. A. N. Aksakov, "Mediumizm i filosofiia: Vospominaniia o professore Moskovskogo Universiteta Iurkeviche," *RV* 121 (January 1876): 442–69. See Vinitsky, *Ghostly Paradoxes*, 29.

85. Iurkevich, "Iz nauki o chelovecheskom dukhe," *RV*, April 1861 and May 1861, with introductions by Katkov.

86. Aksakov, "Mediumizm i filosofiia," 443.

87. Vagner, "Vospominanie," xlii. See Vinitsky, *Ghostly Paradoxes*, 94. Vladimir Soloviov recalled having discussions with Katkov about "the resurrection of the dead and about spiritual corporality [*dukhovnaia telesnost'*]" (Solov'ev, "'Dlia blaga Rossii,'" 75).

88. See Vinitsky, *Ghostly Paradoxes*, 138–47, on Tolstoy's later response to spiritualism in his 1889 play *The Fruits of Enlightenment*.

89. *AK, RV* 128 (April 1877): 731, pt. 7, ch. 22.

90. See Vinitsky, *Ghostly Paradoxes*, 139.

91. On Brédif, see Vinitsky, *Ghostly Paradoxes*, 19, 24, 90–91.

92. *AK, RV* 128 (April 1877): 723, pt. 7, ch. 20.

93. Aksakov, "Mediumizm i filosofiia," 454.

94. *AK, RV* 128 (April 1877): 724, pt. 7, ch. 21.

95. *AK, RV* 128 (April 1877): 726, pt. 7, ch. 21.

96. *AK, RV* 128 (April 1877): 729, pt. 7, ch. 21.

97. Vagner, "Mediumizm," 922.

98. See Todd, "Responsibilities," 162–63.

99. "Khristiane v Turtsii," *RV* 49 (January 1864): 344–86, and 49 (February 1864): 721–41, translation of Rev. W. Denton, *The Christians in Turkey* (London: Bell and Daldy, 1863). I will quote the text using Denton's original English. Denton also published *Servia and the Servians* (London: Bell and Daldy, 1862), a detailed travelogue based on his visit to Serbia.

100. Footnote to "Khristiane v Turtsii," 344.

101. "Khristiane v Turtsii," 344; *Christians in Turkey*, 1.

102. "Khristiane v Turtsii," 346; *Christians in Turkey*, 2.

103. "Khristiane v Turtsii," 381; *Christians in Turkey*, 31. Denton accuses high Turkish officials of the "deepest immoralities." He explains that high Ottoman officials were trained in iniquities from childhood: "Several at least of the present advisers of the Sultan were educated in the harem (the rest of my sentence must of necessity be in a dead language)." The passage in Latin reads: "There catamites and pathics spent their youth. The first step towards honor and power for their advancement in governing the realm was servicing the lust of the king. However as full-grown men they pursue those very vices that they were imbued with in childhood and youth and they are accustomed to keep in a rather secluded part of the palace no small number of boys, on whom they practice their lust, and also girls" ("Khristiane v Turtsii," 375; *Christians in Turkey*, 27). I would like to thank my colleague Michael J. Roberts for this translation. Katkov appended a footnote approving of Denton's couching of this passage in Latin, lauding "this honorable trait of English morality and the free press" (375).

104. E. M. Feoktistov, "Russkaia politika na Vostoke pred Krymskoiu voinoi," *RV* 73 (January 1868): 24.

105. V. A. Ul'ianitskii, "Turtsiia, Rossiia i Evropa s tochki zreniia mezhdunarodnogo prava," *RV* 127 (February 1877): 450. See Todd, "Anna on the Installment Plan," 59.

106. V. S. Nekliudov, "Politicheskie zametki," *RV* 128 (April 1877): 856. The installment of *Anna Karenina* is on 709–63.
107. M. N. Katkov, editorial of August 14, 1876, in *1876 god*, 446.
108. Katkov, editorial of August 16, 1876, in *1876 god*, 451.
109. Katkov, editorial of August 21, 1876, in *1876 god*, 462–63.
110. Katkov, "Russkoe narodnoe dvizhenie minuvshego goda," *SS* 2:387.
111. Katkov, "Russkoe narodnoe dvizhenie," *SS* 2:388.
112. Katkov, "Russkoe narodnoe dvizhenie," *SS* 2:388.
113. See the analysis by Barbara Lönnqvist, "The Role of the Serbian War in *Anna Karenina*," *Tolstoy Studies Journal* 17 (2005): 35–42. Anna Berman discusses Tolstoy's vision of Slavic brotherhood in the context of sibling relationships in general, in her *Siblings in Tolstoy and Dostoevsky: The Path to Universal Brotherhood* (Evanston, IL: Northwestern University Press, 2015), 98–103.
114. Stenbock-Fermor, *Architecture*, 40. S. A. Kibalnik argues that Tolstoy displays sympathy for the nobility of Vronsky's sacrifice, and compares him to Silvio in Pushkin's story "The Shot." The comparison is apt, but in both cases there is a feeling of self-dramatizing, futile romanticism rather than truly admirable self-sacrifice. S. A. Kibal'nik, "Spory o Balkanskoi voine na stranitsakh 'Anny Kareninoi,'" *Russkaia literatura*, no. 4 (2010): 41–42.
115. A. A. Fet, *Moi vospominaniia*, vol. 2 (1848–1889) (Moscow: A. I. Mamontov, 1890), 346. See also 292–93, 308–9, 312–16, 325, 344–46, 382–83; and Tolstoy 62:217, 253–54, 268, 280–81, 303, 315.
116. Note appended to "Voennoe obozrenie" (signed "M."), *RV* 129 (May 1877): 422–72.
117. *Perepiska L. N. Tolstogo s N. N. Strakhovym, 1870–1894* (St. Petersburg: Obshchestvo Tolstovskogo Muzeia, 1914), 120. On a letter sent to the same newspaper by Tolstoy's wife protesting Katkov's action, see N. N. Gusev, *Lev Nikolaevich Tolstoi: Materialy k biografii s 1870 po 1881 god* (Moscow: AN SSSR, 1963), 257–59.
118. Stenbock-Fermor, *Architecture*, 29.
119. N. P—ov, "Vospominaniia dobrovol'tsa," *RV* 129 (May 1877): 221.
120. "Vospominaniia dobrovol'tsa," 224.
121. "Vospominaniia dobrovol'tsa," 234.
122. M. N. Katkov, "Chto sluchilos' po smerti Anny Kareninoi," *RV* 130 (July 1877): 450. In a study that compares part 8 of *Anna Karenina* to the second part of the epilogue of *War and Peace*, Eric Naiman has done a brilliant analysis of the absence of Anna's name in part 8: "Tolstoy's Hinges," in *New Studies in Modern Russian Literature and Culture: Essays in Honor of Stanley J. Rabinowitz*, ed. Catherine Ciepiela and Lazar Fleishman (Stanford: Stanford Slavic Studies, 2014), vols. 45 and 46; vol. 45, pp. 70–94. Trofimova compares Katkov's note, which violates conventional journalistic practice of the time, to his similarly unconventional essays on *Fathers and Sons*: "In both cases the critical articles were called upon to emphasize the peculiarities of the novels and to underline key points" ("'Polozhitel'noe nachalo' v russkoi literature XIX veka," 131).
123. Katkov, "Chto sluchilos'," 462. Dostoevsky published a fascinating response to *Anna Karenina*, and to part 8 in particular, in his *Diary of a Writer* for July-August 1877. Although Dostoevsky sees *Anna Karenina* as a work that shows Europe that Russia has "our own national 'new word'" to speak, he vehemently rejects Liovin's and Prince Shcherbatsky's, and by extension Tolstoy's, position with regard to the volunteer movement. Dostoevsky sees part 8 as Tolstoy's "separation from a universal and great Russian deed and a paradoxical untruth leveled against the people" (Dostoevsky, *PSS* 25:200, 202).
124. See also Tolstoi, *PSS* 62:159, 186n, 197, 202, 294.
125. *Tolstoi—Strakhov, Polnoe sobranie perepiski*, 1:219; *Perepiska Tolstogo s Strakhovym*, 65–66.
126. Irina Paperno argues that Strakhov "did finish the novel for Tolstoy" by preparing the revised separate edition. "Leo Tolstoy's Correspondence with Nikolai Strakhov: The Dialogue on Faith," in *Anniversary Essays on Tolstoy*, 103.
127. *Tolstoi—Strakhov, Polnoe sobranie perepiski*, 1:345–46; *Perepiska Tolstogo s Strakhovym*, 122–23. See Tolstoi, *PSS* 62:335, 336n8.

CHAPTER 7

1. *Brat'ia Karamazovy, RV* 139 (January 1879): 103–207 (pt. 1, books 1 and 2); 139 (February 1879): 602–84 (pt. 1, bk. 3); 140 (April 1879): 678–738 (pt. 2, bk. 4); 141 (May 1879): 369–409 (pt. 2, bk. 5, ch. 1–4); 141 (June 1879): 736–80 (pt. 2, bk. 5, ch. 5–7); 142 (August 1879): 650–99 (pt. 2, bk. 6); 143 (September 1879): 310–53 (pt. 3, bk. 7); 143 (October 1879): 674–711 (pt. 3, bk. 8, ch. 1–4); 144, November 1879): 276–332 (pt. 3, bk. 8, ch. 5–8); 145 (January 1880): 179–255 (pt. 3, bk. 9); 146 (April 1880): 566–623 (pt. 4, bk. 10); 148 (July 1880): 174–221 (pt. 4, bk. 11, ch. 1–5); 148 (August 1880): 691–753 (pt. 4, bk. 11, ch. 6–10); 149 (September 1880): 248–92 (pt. 4, bk. 12, ch. 1–5); 149 (October 1880): 477–551 (pt. 4, bk. 12, ch. 6–14); 150 (November 1880): 50–73 (epilogue).

2. Marcus C. Levitt, *Russian Literary Politics and the Pushkin Celebration of 1880* (Ithaca: Cornell University Press, 1989). See also Alan P. Pollard, "Dostoevskii's Pushkin Speech and the Politics of the Right under the Dictatorship of the Heart," *Canadian-American Slavic Studies* 17, no. 2 (summer 1983): 222–56; Igor' Volgin, *Poslednii god Dostoevskogo* (Moscow: Sovetskii pisatel', 1986), 214–72; Joseph Frank, *The Mantle of the Prophet*, 497–513; and Iu. V. Klimakov, "Pushkinskaia tema v literaturnom nasledii M. N. Katkova," in *Katkovskii vestnik*, 46–58.

3. On the publication of *The Brothers Karamazov*, see Volgin, *Poslednii god*; Frank, *Mantle of the Prophet*; and several articles by Todd: "*The Brothers Karamazov* and the Poetics of Serial Publication"; "Dostoevsky's Russian Monk"; "Dostoevskii as a Professional Writer"; and "Tolstoy and Dostoevsky."

4. Letter of June 20–21, 1878, to A. G. Dostoevskaia, *PSS* 30/1:32. Mikhail Epstein has written about the disparity in importance and self-confidence between Katkov and Dostoevsky in life: "Posterity doesn't give a damn about Katkov, but reveres the genius of Dostoevsky. But no raptures of posterity can rescind the fact that Mr. Katkov was a more important gentleman than Mr. Dostoevsky—had more power, self-confidence, bearing, and sense of his own worth, made people reckon with him as a personality, inspired respect and even a certain timidity. . . . So it is this physics of influence, which Katkov had and Dostoevsky did not have, that interests me more than anything. What do these people give off, what kind of waves flow out of them? What marks them out, like males in a herd of baboons? And why are talented people, as a rule, devoid of this physics of influence?" Mikhail Ėpshtein (Epstein), "Virtual'nye knigi," *Zvezda*, "Esseistika i kritika," no. 8 (August 31, 2008): 219, 220. Volgin compares Dostoevsky to one of his own characters, calculating his conduct several moves ahead: "The distinguishing feature of this situation is the state of dependence, passivity, and tension" (*Poslednii god*, 238).

5. Frank also discusses this incident (*Mantle of the Prophet*, 404–5).

6. See the remarkable letter of April 25, 1866, from Dostoevsky to Katkov, in the aftermath of an attempt on the life of Tsar Alexander II, in which, while seeming to agree with Katkov's views on the "Polish conspiracy," Dostoevsky affirms the importance of freedom of speech and allowing the "nihilists" to have their say, not censoring them and thus making them into "sphinxes" (*PSS* 28/2:153–55; discussed by Todd, "Dostoevskii as a Professional Writer," 84).

7. L. E. Obolenskii, "Literaturnye vospominaniia i kharakteristiki (1854–1892)," *Istoricheskii vestnik*, no. 2 (1902): 501. See also "Vstupitel'naia stat'ia (K istorii sozdaniia 'Brat'ev Karamazovykh')," in *F. M. Dostoevskii, Materialy i issledovaniia*, ed. A. S. Dolinin (Leningrad: AN SSSR, 1935), 53–54; Volgin, *Poslednii god*, 73–80, 241–44; and Frank, *Mantle of the Prophet*, 417–20. The dinner was the regular yearly dinner of St. Petersburg professors and writers, but it was held early in honor of Turgenev ("Vnutrennee obozrenie, 1 April 1879," *Vestnik Evropy* 76/2, no. 4 [April 1879]: 821). The *Herald of Europe* account of the dinner does not allude to Dostoevsky's renunciation of Katkov, but does describe him (without naming him) as rudely challenging Turgenev to spell out "his ideal"—that is, the liberal-radical hopes of a constitution that he shared with the young generation.

8. "Pis'ma Maikova k Dostoevskomu (za 70 gg.)," ed. E. B. Pokrovskaia, in *F. M. Dostoevskii, Stat'i i materialy*, vol. 2, ed. A. S. Dolinin (Leningrad-Moscow: Mysl', 1924), 364. The "main points" that were "discussed here at the dinner," in Maikov's words, apparently concerned the granting of a constitution to Russia. S. A. Vengerov, who was present at the dinner, told A. S. Dolinin that Turgenev had talked in

his speech of the necessity to "crown the edifice," which was understood as referring to a constitution ("Pis'ma Maikova," 362).

9. "Pis'ma Maikova," 365.

10. The coinage of the phrase is attributed to Markevich, but without a specific citation. It sounds ineffably Katkovian, and was used by him as early as January 26, 1875, in his obituary for M. N. Longinov (1823–75), literary historian and at the end of his life chief censor of Russia: "He was not the obscurantist that people wished to defame him as. He honored the interests of scholarship, highly valued the gifts of civilization, was an admirer of art and a passionate lover of literature. But for that very reason he was an implacable enemy of the swindlers of the pen and bandits of the press" (Katkov, *1875 god*, 59–60).

11. Turgenev, quoted in B. M. Markevich [Inogorodnyi obyvatel'], "S beregov Nevy," *Moskovskie vedomosti*, no. 313 (December 9, 1879): 4. See the original letter in Turgenev, *PSS 1960–68, Pis'ma*, 12:145.

12. Letter to Ia. P. Polonskii, November 10 (22), 1879, *PSS 1960–68, Pis'ma*, 12:173; emphasis in original.

13. Markevich, "S beregov Nevy," 5. After Turgenev's death, Katkov published an article in which he claimed that Turgenev had actually translated Pavlovsky's memoir into French himself ("Turgenev," *MV*, September 20, 1883, no. 261; *SS* 1:718–19).

14. Markevich, "S beregov Nevy," 5. Pierre François Lacenaire (1803–36) was a notorious murderer who captured the imagination of many writers, including Dostoevsky.

15. Markevich, "S beregov Nevy," 5.

16. Markevich, "S beregov Nevy," 5.

17. Turgenev, *PSS 1960–68, Pis'ma*, 12:194, 197.

18. It appeared in *Molva* on December 29, 1879, and in the *Herald of Europe* in early 1880 (Turgenev, *PSS 1960–68*, 15:387).

19. Turgenev, *PSS 1960–68*, 15:184–85.

20. Turgenev *PSS 1960–68*, 15:185. Turgenev was also referring to the accusation that Markevich had taken a bribe in 1875.

21. Markevich, "Spravka dlia g. Turgeneva," *Moskovskie vedomosti*, no. 5, January 6, 1880, cited in Katkov, *SS* 1:792. See Turgenev, *PSS 1960–68, Pis'ma*, 5:97–98. Turgenev's troubles were related to the Polish uprising, as the Russian government was scrutinizing the activities of people connected to Alexander Herzen, who was agitating in the support of the Poles from his base in London.

22. Turgenev *PSS 1960–68*, 15:184.

23. Katkov, "Po povodu polemiki g. Turgeneva s 'Inogorodnym obyvatelem,'" *Moskovskie vedomosti*, no. 5, January 6, 1880; cited according to *SS* 1:697.

24. Katkov, "Po povodu polemiki," *SS* 1:697–98.

25. Katkov, "Neobkhodimost' diktatury dlia bor'by s kramoloi," *MV*, no. 37, February 7, 1880; *SS* 3:410. See Levitt, *Pushkin Celebration*, 60–63.

26. Katkov, "Potrebnost' v tverdoi i energicheskoi vlasti dlia bor'by s kramoloi," *MV*, no. 44, February 14, 1880; *SS* 3:421.

27. Katkov, "Pokushenie protiv gr. Loris-Melikova," *MV*, no. 51, February 21, 1880; *SS* 3:426.

28. Katkov, "Pokushenie protiv gr. Loris-Melikova," *SS* 3:426, 427.

29. Katkov, "Natsional'naia i antinatsional'naia partii v Rossii," *MV*, no. 94, April 4, 1880; *SS* 2:416.

30. Katkov, "Natsional'naia i antinatsional'naia partii," *SS* 2:416.

31. Katkov, "Natsional'naia i antinatsional'naia partii," *SS* 2:417, 418.

32. Katkov, "Natsional'naia i antinatsional'naia partii," *SS* 2:418; emphasis added.

33. See his letters to P. V. Annenkov and V. P. Gaevskii in early May (N.S.) 1880, *PSS 1960–68, Pis'ma*, 12:237–38. See Levitt, *Pushkin Celebration*, 69–70, 76–78.

34. *Russkaia mysl'*, no. 3, 1880, two pages inserted at beginning of issue, undated, unsigned. Iuriev was responding specifically to Katkov's editorials of March 19 and March 21, 1880. In the March 19 editorial Katkov accused the government of halfheartedly struggling with sedition, the intelligentsia of

"giving in" to it, and the "legal press" of "winking at" it (*1880 god*, 159). See Dostoevsky, *PSS* 30/1:341; and Levitt, *Pushkin Celebration*, 69.

35. Levitt, *Pushkin Celebration*, 70.
36. Levitt, *Pushkin Celebration*, 76.
37. Katkov, "Rech' na Pushkinskom prazdnike," *SS* 1:706. See Levitt, *Pushkin Celebration*, 85–88; and Volgin, *Poslednii god*, 232–38. Volgin dryly comments, "Turgenev and his allies could calmly finish eating their dinners" (233). Turgenev's remarks are in a letter of June 6, 1880, to Kovalevsky, *PSS 1960–68, Pis'ma*, 12:270.
38. Letter to V. V. Stasov, January 9 (21), 1882, *PSS 1960–68, Pis'ma*, 13:136.
39. N. Ia. Stech'kin, *Iz vospominanii ob I. S. Turgeneve (S prilozheniem semi ego neizdannykh pisem)* (St. Petersburg: V. V. Komarov, 1903), 25.
40. *Golos*, June 8, no. 158, cited in Dostoevsky, *PSS* 30/1:365.
41. The account of the incident in the introduction to vol. 1 of the Katkov *Sobranie sochinenii* relies heavily on Levitt's book, but turns it into a triumph for Katkov over "ill-intentioned falsehood" (Timofei Prokopov, "'Rossiia ... v nei dva imperatora: Aleksandr II i Katkov'; Vekhi sud'by okhranitelia konservativnoi gosudarstvennosti," 1:47–49). In Ivan Karamazov's conversation with the Devil, published in the August 1880 installment of *The Brothers Karamazov*, the Devil tells Ivan a story that Ivan himself had composed, about a "thinker and philosopher" who rejected the idea of a future life. When the gates of paradise were finally opened to him, "he sang a 'Hosanna,' but he overdid it, so that some of those there, with a somewhat nobler cast of thought, didn't even want to offer him their hand at first: they said he had jumped over into the camp of the conservatives too precipitously" (*PSS* 15:79). Is this a parodic version of the snubbing of the former liberal Katkov at the June 1880 celebration?
42. "Zasluga Pushkina," *MV*, no. 155, June 6, 1880; reprinted in *RV* 147 (June 1880): 957–63; *RV* 261 (June 1899): 403–09; *SS* 1:699–705. I will cite it according to the *Sobranie sochinenii* edition.
43. Marina Kanevskaya, "Pushkin as 'Universal' Poet: Varnhagen von Ense and Dostoevsky," in *Cold Fusion: Aspects of the German Cultural Presence in Russia*, ed. Gennady Barabtarlo (New York: Berghahn Books, 2000), 113–25.
44. The original translation is "Sochineniia A. Pushkina," *Syn otechestva*, 7, no. 4 (1839): 1–37. The translation is unsigned, but Kanevskaya states without citing a source that the translator was Iakov Neverov. Katkov's translation was "Otzyv inostrantsa o Pushkine," *SS* 1:53–84.
45. Kanevskaya, "Pushkin as 'Universal' Poet," 113; her footnote on Katkov is 123n9. Strakhov, "Glavnoe sokrovishche nashei literatury," *Otechestvennye zapiski*, December 1867, republished in his *Zametki o Pushkine i drugikh poetakh*, 2nd ed. (Kiev: I. I. Chokolov, 1897), 17–34. Katkov's translation of Varnhagen is cited on 23–26; his 1856 article is cited on 21–22, attributed to him both by name and as "one of our most famous philologists."
46. Katkov, "Otzyv inostrantsa," *SS* 1:53.
47. Katkov, "Otzyv inostrantsa," *SS* 1:53–54.
48. Katkov, "Otzyv inostrantsa," *SS* 1:55.
49. Katkov, "Otzyv inostrantsa," *SS* 1:56.
50. Katkov, "Otzyv inostrantsa," *SS* 1:58; Varnhagen, col. 483. *The Son of the Fatherland* version uses the word *neobrabotannyi* (unpolished) instead of Katkov's *neobrazovan* (unformed) ("Sochineniia A. Pushkina," 5). I will give Varnhagen's German original when appropriate, after the Russian, from Varnhagen von Ense, review of *Sochineniia A. Pushkina* (*Werke von Alexander Puschkin*), *Jahrbücher für wissenschaftliche Kritik*, 61 (October 1838).
51. Katkov, "Otzyv inostrantsa," *SS* 1:58; Varnhagen, col. 483.
52. Katkov, "Otzyv inostrantsa," *SS* 1:59; Varnhagen, col. 484.
53. Katkov, "Otzyv inostrantsa," *SS* 1:60–61; Varnhagen, col. 486.
54. Katkov, "Otzyv inostrantsa," *SS* 1:61; Varnhagen, col. 486. The distinction between the two words is maintained in the *Son of the Fatherland* version ("Sochineniia A. Pushkina," 7).
55. Katkov, "Otzyv inostrantsa," *SS* 1:62.
56. Katkov, "Otzyv inostrantsa," *SS* 1:63–64.
57. Kanevskaya, "Pushkin as 'Universal' Poet," 119.

58. Katkov, "Otzyv inostrantsa," SS 1:83.
59. Katkov, "Otzyv inostrantsa," SS 1:83.
60. Michael Wachtel, *A Commentary to Pushkin's Lyric Poetry, 1826-1836* (Madison: University of Wisconsin Press, 2011), 227. See also Megan Dixon, "Repositioning Pushkin and Poems of the Polish Uprising," in *Polish Encounters, Russian Identity*, ed. David L. Ransel and Bozena Shallcross (Bloomington: Indiana University Press, 2005), 49–73; Katya Hokanson, "In Defense of Empire: 'The Bronze Horseman' and 'To the Slanderers of Russia,'" in *Beyond the Empire: Images of Russia in the Eurasian Cultural Context*, ed. Tetsuo Mochizuki (Sapporo: Hokkaido University, 2008), 149–66; and T. J. Binyon, *Pushkin: A Biography* (New York: Vintage, 2002), 337–39, 362–67.
61. A. S. Pushkin, *Polnoe sobranie sochinenii*, 10 vols. (Moscow: AN SSSR, 1962–66), 3:222–23. Bojanowska notes the connection between Pushkin's poem and the titles of Katkov's "The Polish Question" and Strakhov's "Fatal Question" ("Empire by Consent," 11).
62. Wachtel, *Commentary*, 230. Wachtel also notes that "The storming of Praga was the scene of Suvorov's brutal suppression of the Warsaw Uprising of October 24/November 4, 1794, celebrated by Russian patriots, but viewed with horror by Poles (and much of Western Europe) because of the indiscriminate killing of civilians" (227).
63. Pushkin, *PSS* 3:224–26.
64. See the discussion in Hokanson, "In Defense of Empire," 150.
65. Wachtel, *Commentary*, 227.
66. *The Letters of Alexander Pushkin*, 3 vols., trans. and ed. J. Thomas Shaw (Madison: University of Wisconsin Press, 1967), 2:446–47; Pushkin, *PSS* 10:325.
67. *Letters of Pushkin*, 2:489; Pushkin, *PSS* 10:351.
68. Quoted in Binyon, *Pushkin*, 367.
69. Katkov, "Otzyv inostrantsa," SS 1:83. The *Son of the Fatherland* version omits the word "dubious" and the phrase "not in shame and slavery."
70. Kanevskaya, "Pushkin as 'Universal Poet,'" 118.
71. Katkov, "Otzyv inostrantsa," SS 1:83.
72. *PSS 1960–68*, 15:73.
73. Levitt refers to the distinction as deriving from Belinsky, but the use of the distinction by Varnhagen and Katkov predates its appearance in Belinsky's writings in 1841 (*Pushkin Celebration*, 107; Belinskii, *PSS* 5:121–27). Belinsky had originally commissioned Katkov's translation of Varnhagen von Ense's article for his own journal the *Moscow Telegraph* (see ch. 1).
74. Turgenev *PSS 1960–68*, 15:68.
75. Turgenev *PSS 1960–68*, 15:68.
76. Turgenev *PSS 1960–68*, 15:68–69.
77. Turgenev *PSS 1960–68*, 15:69.
78. Turgenev *PSS 1960–68*, 15:71.
79. Turgenev *PSS 1960–68*, 15:75. The phrase "as yet unknown chosen one" is from Mikhail Lermontov's 1832 poem "Net, ia ne Bairon, ia drugoi" ("No, I am not Byron, I am another").
80. Levitt, *Pushkin Celebration*, 110.
81. Katkov, "Pushkin," SS 1:290.
82. "Nash iazyk," SS 1:346, 347.
83. Belinskii, *PSS* 7:501–2.
84. Excerpts from Venevitinov's diary are found in *Literaturnoe nasledstvo* 86, 501–9; this quotation on 505.
85. See, for example, Levitt, *Pushkin Celebration*, 122–46, 174–75; Volgin, *Poslednii god*, 254–72; and Frank, *Mantle of the Prophet*, 517–29.
86. Belinskii, *PSS* 7:501.
87. Katkov, "Otzyv inostrantsa," SS 1:56.
88. Kanevskaya, "Pushkin as 'Universal Poet,'" 118.
89. Kanevskaya, "Pushkin as 'Universal Poet,'" 121.
90. Katkov, "Zasluga Pushkina," *MV*, no. 155, June 6, 1880, no. 155; SS 1:699–705.

91. *RV* 147 (June 1880). The Duma speech is on 938–40; Pushkin's Poland poems are on 950–51; "Zasluga Pushkina" is on 957–63; the excerpt from the 1856 Pushkin articles is on 964–74; and the Dostoevsky excerpt is on 992–94.
92. Katkov, "Zasluga Pushkina," *SS* 1:701.
93. Hokanson, "In Defense of Empire," 151–52. See Maiorova, *From the Shadow of Empire*, for discussion of the ramifications of 1812 in Russian culture.
94. Katkov, "Zasluga Pushkina," *SS* 1:699.
95. Katkov, "Zasluga Pushkina," *SS* 1:699.
96. Katkov, "Zasluga Pushkina," *SS* 1:699–700.
97. Katkov, "Zasluga Pushkina," *SS* 1:701.
98. Katkov, "Zasluga Pushkina," *SS* 1:703–4.
99. Katkov, "Zasluga Pushkina," *SS* 1:704. Pushkin, *PSS* 8:427; emphasis in original.
100. Katkov, "Zasluga Pushkina," *SS* 1:703. Katkov had expressed a similar sentiment in February 1843, when he returned from Germany to find his former friends absorbed with issues he had no interest in (including, strangely enough, "*Gogol', da Gegel'* [Gogol and Hegel]"): "It is good to have a little like-minded circle, with a single, identically understood goal; but solitary labor and a more sincere converse with oneself is also good" ("Pis'ma M. N. Katkova k A. N. Popovu," 482).
101. Dostoevsky first offered it to Iuriev, but when they met in Moscow in late May 1880, Dostoevsky felt that Iuriev was unreliable (30/1:158–59). He also worried that because of the intrigues against Katkov, the latter might lose interest in publishing it (30/1:181). See Pollard, "Dostoevskii's Pushkin Speech," 231–32, 239–40.
102. "Iz perepiski K. N. Leont'eva," *RV* 285 (May 1903): 176. Cited in Volgin, *Poslednii god*, 271.
103. Letter of June 13, 1880, *PSS 1960–68, Pis'ma*, 12:272; emphasis in original. Turgenev suggested that Stasiulevich should convey his criticisms of Dostoevsky's speech to the person who was to write about the Pushkin Celebration in the *Herald of Europe*, which he did (*PSS 1960–68, Pis'ma*, 12:565). See Pollard, "Dostoevskii's Pushkin Speech," 252.
104. Volgin, *Poslednii god*, 271.
105. See Dostoevsky, *PSS* 26:129–74. Pollard writes, "Using Pushkin as the text for a sermon, [Dostoevsky] exhorted his intelligentsia audience to Christian humility, repentance, and faith. Why did they applaud the anathema that Dostoevskii pronounced upon them? Briefly put, the answer is that Dostoevskii's rhetorical and histrionic skills misled the audience into believing that they were listening to the panegyric they wanted to hear, and in turn the audience's enthusiasm misled Dostoevskii into believing that they were acclaiming the homily he wanted to deliver" ("Dostoevskii's Pushkin Speech," 255).
106. Unlike the editors of Dostoevsky's *PSS* (30/1:394), Volgin argues that the letter was written the previous day, before the first hemorrhage (*Poslednii god*, 741).
107. Letter of January 29, 1881, from Pobedonostsev to Katkov, *Literaturnoe nasledstvo* 86, 534–35.
108. *MV*, January 30, 1881, no. 30.
109. "Kharakteristika vnutrennego mira Dostoevskogo (Po povodu ego konchiny)," *MV*, no. 33, February 2, 1881; *SS* 1:708–10.
110. Katkov, "Kharakteristika," *SS* 1:708.
111. Katkov, "Kharakteristika," *SS* 1:708.
112. Katkov, "Kharakteristika," *SS* 1:708–9.
113. Katkov, "Kharakteristika," *SS* 1:709.
114. Katkov, "Kharakteristika," *SS* 1:709.
115. Katkov, "Kharakteristika," *SS* 1:709.
116. Katkov, "Turgenev," *SS* 1:717, 718.
117. Katkov, "Turgenev," *SS* 1:718.
118. Katkov, "Turgenev," *SS* 1:718.
119. Katkov, "Turgenev," *SS* 1:718.
120. Katkov, "Turgenev," *SS* 1:719.
121. Katkov, "Turgenev," *SS* 1:719.

122. Katkov, "Turgenev," *SS* 1:720.

123. Note to Katkov, "Istechenie sroka troistvennogo soiuza i strakh Evropy pered svobodnoi Rossiei" (*MV*, no. 66, March 8, 1887), in *SS* 2:834. The story of Katkov's involvement in foreign policy in his last years is told in great detail in George F. Kennan, *The Decline of Bismarck's European Order: Franco-Russian Relations, 1875–1890* (Princeton: Princeton University Press, 1979). Kennan provides a remarkable summation:

> With Katkov's death, Russia lost one of her greatest publicists—a man of outstanding literary and editorial talent as well as intellectual capacity, passionately patriotic and wholly sincere in his defense of Russian national interests as he saw them, but not always well informed about the international affairs he undertook to discuss, easily imposed upon by persons unworthy of his confidence, and often misguided by the intensity of his own political passions. . . . But in the totality of his life's work Katkov remained, for all of that, a great man. It is not without a certain sadness that the writer of these lines has seen himself obliged, by the nature of his subject matter, to occupy himself mainly with the aberrations in matters of foreign policy that marred the final months of the activity of this formidable and talented personality, and to leave aside the great services he rendered to Russia at other times and in other fields. (327)

See also Christy Campbell, *The Maharajah's Box: An Exotic Tale of Espionage, Intrigue, and Illicit Love in the Days of the Raj* (Woodstock: Overlook Press, 2002).

124. K. P. Pobedonostsev, "'Zachem bylo delat' iz Katkova gosudarstvennogo cheloveka?' Pis'mo Aleksandru II ot 11 marta 1887," *SS* 6:255, 256; emphasis in original.

125. K. N. Leont'ev, "G. Katkov i ego vragi na prazdnike Pushkina," *Varshavskii dnevnik*, no. 150, July 15, 21, 1880; *SS* 6:195, 196. Emphasis in original.

126. "Novonaidennye i zabytye pis'ma Dostoevskogo," ed. I. S. Zil'bershtein, *Literaturnoe nasledstvo* 86, 121.

127. "Novonaidennye pis'ma," *Literaturnoe nasledstvo* 86, 148n17.

CONCLUSION

1. Howard S. Becker, *Art Worlds* (Berkeley: University of California Press, 2008), xvi.

2. N. S. Leskov, *Sobranie sochinenii*, 11 vols. (Moscow: Khudozhestvennaia literatura, 1956–58), 10:412 (letter of July 29 [August 10], 1875, to P. K. Shchebal'skii). On Leskov's relationship with Katkov, see William B. Edgerton, "Nikolai Leskov: The Intellectual Development of a Literary Nonconformist," PhD diss., Columbia University, 1954; Nepomnyashchy, "Katkov and the Emergence of the *Russian Messenger*"; and I. P. Viduètskaia, "Dostoevskii i Leskov," *Russkaia literatura*, no. 4 (1975): 127–37.

3. Katkov, "Zasluga Pushkina," *SS* 1:700–1.

4. J. A. Sutherland, *Victorian Novelists and Publishers* (Chicago: University of Chicago Press, 1976), 80.

5. Milan Kundera, *Testaments Betrayed: An Essay in Nine Parts*, trans. Linda Asher (New York: Harper Collins, 1995), 271.

6. On Perkins, see A. Scott Berg, *Max Perkins: Editor of Genius* (New York: Dutton, 1978). On Lish, see "Rough Crossings: The Cutting of Raymond Carver," *The New Yorker* (December 24 and 31, 2007): 93–99.

7. Kundera, *Testaments Betrayed*, 245.

8. Kundera, *Testaments Betrayed*, 246; emphasis in original.

9. Letter to A. V. Druzhinin, November 30, 1860, in Katkov, *SS* 5:595.

10. Vyzinskii, "Kratkoe skazanie," 860.

11. Compare Ian Duncan's discussion of the role of Archibald Constable in early nineteenth-century Edinburgh: "He was able to reclaim the tradition of a professional rather than merely commercial class of men of letters by paying unprecedentedly high fees to his editors and contributors: an investment that saved their status as gentlemen and, conversely, cast the publisher himself as an enlightened patron

rather than a tradesman" (Ian Duncan, *Scott's Shadow: The Novel in Romantic Edinburgh* [Princeton: Princeton University Press, 2007], 25). Duncan cites a nineteenth-century description of Constable's *Edinburgh Review* that sounds strikingly like the role of the *Russian Herald* in its early years, after the Crimean War and the repressive reign of Nicholas I: "Cockburn goes on to credit the *Edinburgh Review*, founded as an organ of polite, moderate, antirevolutionist but proreform liberalism in the brief respite from wartime regimentation opened by the Peace of Amiens, with inaugurating the fitful, contentious rebuilding of a Scottish public sphere in the long dusk of the Dundas despotism" (24).

12. Becker, *Art Worlds*, 103.

13. Michael Baxandall, *Painting and Experience in Fifteenth Century Italy: A Primer in the Social History of Pictorial Style* (Oxford: Oxford University Press, 1972), 1.

14. Baxandall, *Painting and Experience*, 3.

Bibliography

Adelman, Gary. "Stalking Stavrogin: J. M. Coetzee's *The Master of Petersburg* and the Writing of *The Possessed*." *Journal of Modern Literature* 23, no. 2 (winter 1999–2000): 351–57.
Akhsharumov, N. D. "Kritika. *Prestuplenie i nakazanie*, roman F. M. Dostoevskogo." *Vsemirnyi trud*, no. 3 (1867): 125–56.
Aksakov, A. N. "Mediumizm i filosofiia. Vospominaniia o professore Moskovskogo Universiteta Iurkeviche." *Russkii vestnik* 121 (January 1876): 442–69.
Alekseev, M. P. "K istorii slova 'nigilizm.'" In *Sbornik statei v chest' akademika Alekseiia Ivanovicha Sobolevskogo*, edited by V. N. Peretts, 413–17. Leningrad: AN SSSR, 1928.
Allen, Elizabeth Cheresh. *Beyond Realism: Turgenev's Poetics of Secular Salvation*. Stanford: Stanford University Press, 1992.
Al'tman, M. S. "Zheleznaia doroga v tvorchestve L. N. Tolstogo." *Slavia* 34 (1965): 251–59.
Annenkov, P. V. *Literaturnye vospominaniia*. Edited by S. N. Golubov et al. [Moscow]: Khudozhestvennaia literatura, 1960.
Antonovich, M. A. "Asmodei nashego vremeni (*Ottsy i deti*. Roman Turgeneva. 'Russkii vestnik,' 1862 g., no. 2, fevral')." In *Literaturno-kriticheskie stat'i*, edited by G. E. Tamarchenko, 35–93. Moscow-Leningrad: Khudozhestvennaia literatura, 1961.
Arkhipov, V. "K tvorcheskoi istorii romana I. S. Turgeneva 'Ottsy i deti.'" *Russkaia literatura*, no. 1 (1958): 132–62.
Artem'ev, Maksim. "Starinnaia russkaia traditsiia: Kak SMI vliali na vlast' i obshchestvo v Rossii." Forbes.ru, March 21, 2014.
Avineri, Shlomo. "Hegel and Nationalism." In *The Hegel Myths and Legends*, edited by Jon Stewart. Evanston: Northwestern University Press, 1996.
Avseenko, V. G. "Literaturnoe obozrenie." *Russkii vestnik* 121 (January 1876): 496–510.
———. "Ocherki tekushchei literatury. Novogodniaia knizhka 'Otechestvennykh zapisok.' Chem otlichaetsia roman g. Dostoevskogo, napisannyi dlia etogo zhurnala, ot drugikh ego romanov, napisannykh dlia 'Russkogo vestnika.' Nechto o plevkakh, poshchechinakh i t. p. predmetakh." *Russkii mir*, no. 27 (January 29, 1875).
———. "Po povodu novogo romana grafa L. N. Tolstogo." *Russkii vestnik* 117 (May 1875): 400–20.
Babaev, È. G. *Lev Tolstoi i russkaia zhurnalistika ego epokhi*. 2nd ed. Moscow: Izdatel'stvo Moskovskogo universiteta, 1993.
Backor, Joseph. "M. N. Katkov: Introduction to His Life and His Russian National Policy Program, 1818–1870." PhD diss., Indiana University, 1966.
Baehr, Stephen. "The Troika and the Train: Dialogues between Tradition and Technology in Nineteenth-Century Russian Literature." In *Issues in Russian Literature before 1917: Proceedings from the III International Congress on Soviet and East European Studies*, edited by Douglas Clayton and R. C. Elwood, 85–106. Columbus: Slavica, 1989.
Bakunin, M. A. *Sobranie sochinenii i pisem, 1828–1876*. Edited by Iu. M. Steklov. 4 vols. Moscow: Izdatel'stvo Vsesoiuznogo obshchestva politkatorzhan i ssyl'no-poselentsev, 1934–35.
Bartenev, P. I. *Vospominaniia*. http://feb-web.ru/feb/rosarc/ra1/ra1-047-.htm. Accessed June 16, 2015.
Basistov, P. "Nakanune I. S. Turgeneva: Moskva 1860." *Otechestvennye zapiski* 130, no. 5 (May 1860): sec. 3, 1–18.
Batiuto, A. I. "K voprosu o proiskhozhdenii slova 'nigilizm' v romane I. S. Turgeneva 'Ottsy i deti' (Po povodu stat'i B. P. Koz'mina 'Dva slova o slove "nigilizm"')." *Izvestiia AN SSSR. Otdelenie literatury i iazyka* 12, no. 6 (1953): 520–25.

---. "Parizhskaia rukopis' romana I. S. Turgeneva 'Ottsy i deti.'" *Russkaia literatura*, no. 4 (1961): 57-78.

---. "Priznaki velikogo serdtsa ... (K istorii vospriiatiia Dostoevskim romana 'Ottsy i deti')." *Russkaia literatura*, no. 2 (1977): 21-37.

Baxandall, Michael. *Painting and Experience in Fifteenth Century Italy: A Primer in the Social History of Pictorial Style.* Oxford: Oxford University Press, 1972.

Becker, Howard S. *Art Worlds.* Berkeley: University of California Press, 2008.

Belinskii, V. G. *Polnoe sobranie sochinenii.* 13 vols. Moscow: AN SSSR, 1953-59.

Bem, A. L. "Khudozhestvennaia polemika s Tolstym (K ponimaniiu 'Podrostka')." In *O Dostoevskom: Sbornik statei. Praga 1929/1933/1936*, edited by A. L. Bem, 535-51. Moscow: Russkii put', 2007.

Berezin (Beriozin), I. "Stseny v pustyne: Mezhdu Basroi i Bagdadom." *Russkii vestnik* 13 (January 1858): 322-48.

Berezkina (Beriozkina), S. V. "F. M. Dostoevskii i M. N. Katkov (iz istorii romana 'Prestuplenie i nakazanie')." *Izvestiia RAN, Seriia literatury i iazyka* 72, no. 5 (2013): 16-25.

---. "'Zhivet zhe na kvartire u portnogo Kapernaumova ...' (Iz kommentariia k 'Prestupleniiu i nakazaniiu' Dostoevskogo." *Russkaia literatura*, no. 4 (2013): 169-79.

Berg, A. Scott. *Max Perkins: Editor of Genius.* New York: Dutton, 1978.

Berlin, Isaiah. *Russian Thinkers.* Edited by Henry Hardy and Aileen Kelly. New York: Viking, 1978.

Berman, Anna. *Siblings in Tolstoy and Dostoevsky: The Path to Universal Brotherhood.* Evanston, IL: Northwestern University Press, 2015.

Bialyi, G. "V. Arkhipov protiv I. Turgeneva." *Novyi mir*, no. 8 (August 1958): 255-59.

Billington, James H. *The Icon and the Axe: An Interpretive History of Russian Culture.* New York: Knopf, 1966.

Binyon, T. J. *Pushkin: A Biography.* New York: Vintage, 2002.

Blagoveshchenskii, N. "Otvet na 'Ob"iasnenie' pomeshchennoe v No. 10 'Russkogo Vestnika.'" *Moskovskie vedomosti*, no. 138, June 23, 1860, pp. 1093-94.

---. "Redaktsii Russkogo Vestnika." *Moskovskie vedomosti*, no. 151, July 10, 1860.

Blake, Elizabeth. "Sonya, Silent No More: A Response to the Woman Question in Dostoevsky's *Crime and Punishment*." *Slavic and East European Journal* 50, no. 2 (2006): 252-71.

Bojanowska, Edyta. "Empire by Consent: Strakhov, Dostoevskii, and the Polish Uprising of 1863." *Slavic Review* 71, no. 1 (spring 2012): 1-24.

Bowman, Herbert E. *Vissarion Belinski 1811-1848: A Study in the Origins of Social Criticism in Russia.* New York: Russell & Russell, 1954.

Bozherianov, I. "Pamiati M. N. Katkov." *Russkii vestnik* 304 (August 1906): 532-43.

Budanova, N. F. "'Nov": O prototipe Khavron'i Pryshchovoi v romane Turgeneva." In *Turgenevskii sbornik: Materialy k polnomu sobraniiu sochinenii i pisem I. S. Turgeneva*, vol. 3, edited by N. V. Izmailov and L. N. Nazarova, 153-59. Leningrad: Nauka, 1967.

Bugaeva, V. N. *Pedagogicheskoe nasledie M. N. Katkova.* Smolensk: Madzhenta, 2011.

Buslaev, F. "Perepiska Tolstogo s M. N. Katkovym." In *Literaturnoe nasledstvo* 37-38: *L. N. Tolstoi II*, 189-207. Moscow: AN SSSR, 1939.

Butlerov, A. M. "Mediumskie iavleniia." *Russkii vestnik* 120 (November 1875): 300-48.

---. *Stat'i po mediumizmu.* Edited by A. N. Aksakov. St. Petersburg: V. Demakov, 1889.

Campbell, Christy. *The Maharajah's Box: An Exotic Tale of Espionage, Intrigue, and Illicit Love in the Days of the Raj.* Woodstock: Overlook Press, 2002.

Carr, Edward Hallett. *Michael Bakunin.* London: Macmillan, 1937.

---. *The Romantic Exiles: A Nineteenth-Century Portrait Gallery.* Boston: Beacon Press, 1933.

Chances, Ellen. "The Ideology of "Počvenničestvo' in Dostoevskij's Journals *Vremja* i *Èpokha*." PhD diss., Princeton University, 1972.

---. "Literary Criticism and the Ideology of Pochvennichestvo in Dostoevsky's Thick Journals *Vremia* and *Epokha*." *Russian Review* 34, no. 2 (April 1975): 151-64.

Chernyshevskii, N. G. *Polnoe sobranie sochinenii.* 15 vols. Moscow: Khudozhestvennaia literatura, 1939-53.

Chicherin, B. N. *Moskva sorokovykh godov*. Edited by T. F. Pirozhkovaia. Moscow: Izdatel'stvo Moskovskogo universiteta, 1997.
Chizhevskii, D. I. *Gegel' v Rossii*. Paris: Dom knigi, 1939.
Costlow, Jane T. *Worlds Within Worlds: The Novels of Ivan Turgenev*. Princeton: Princeton University Press, 1990.
Cruise, Edwina. "Tracking the English novel in *Anna Karenina*: Who Wrote the English Novel That Anna Reads?" In *Anniversary Essays on Tolstoy*, edited by Donna Tussing Orwin, 159–82. Cambridge: Cambridge University Press, 2010.
Danilov, V. V. "K voprosu o kompozitsionnykh priemakh v 'Prestuplenii i nakazanii' Dostoevskogo." *Izvestiia Akademii nauk SSSR: Otdelenie obshchestvennykh nauk*, no. 3, 249–63. Leningrad: Izdatel'stvo Akademii nauk SSSR, 1933.
"Death of M. Katkoff," *Times*, Tuesday, August 2, 1887, p. 6.
De Morgan, Augustus. Preface to Sophia De Morgan, *From Matter to Spirit: The Result of Ten Years' Experience in Spirit Manifestation*. London: Longman, Green, Longman, Roberts, & Green, 1863.
Denton, W. *The Christians in Turkey*. London: Bell and Daldy, 1863.
———. "Khristiane v Turtsii." *Russkii vestnik* 49 (January 1864): 344–86; and 49 (February 1864): 721–41.
———. *Servia and the Servians*. London: Bell and Daldy, 1862.
"Dikovinki russkoi zhurnalistiki (Pis'mo k redaktoru)." *Russkii vestnik* 39, *Sovremennaia letopis'*, no. 18 (May 1862): 16–18.
Dixon, Megan. "Repositioning Pushkin and Poems of the Polish Uprising." In *Polish Encounters, Russian Identity*, edited by David L. Ransel and Bozena Shallcross, 49–73. Bloomington: Indiana University Press, 2005.
Dobroliubov, N. A. *Polnoe sobranie sochinenii*. Edited by P. I. Lebedev-Polianskii. 6 vols. Moscow: Khudozhestvennaia literatura, 1934–39.
———. *Sochineniia*. 4 vols. St. Petersburg: Ogrizko, 1862.
Dokumenty po istorii literatury i obshchestvennosti, no. 1. Moscow: Tsentrarkhiv, 1922.
Dolinin, A. S. "'Ispoved' Stavrogina.' (V sviazi s kompozitsiei 'Besov')." *Literaturnaia mysl'. Al'manakh*, no. 1, 139–62. Petrograd: Mysl', 1922.
———. "K tsenzurnoi istorii pervykh dvukh zhurnalov Dostoevskogo." In *F. M. Dostoevskii: stat'i i materialy*, vol. 2, 559–77. Petrograd: Mysl', 1922–24.
Dostalov, Khristo [D.]. "Turetskie dela." *Russkii vestnik*, *Sovremennaia letopis'* 13 (February 1858): 245–65; 14 (March 1858): 35–53; and 15 (May 1858): 33–51.
Dostoevskaia, A. G. *Vospominaniia*. Edited by S. V. Belov and V. A. Tunimanov. Moscow: Khudozhestvennaia literatura, 1971.
Dostoevskii, F. M. *Polnoe sobranie sochinenii*. 30 vols. Leningrad: Nauka, 1972–90.
Dowler, Wayne. *Dostoevsky, Grigor'ev, and Native Soil Conservatism*. Toronto: University of Toronto Press, 1982.
Dryzhakova, E. N. "Dostoevskii i nigilisticheskii roman 1860-kh godov." In *Dostoevskii: Materialy i issledovaniia* 17:3–29. St. Petersburg: Nauka, 2005.
Duncan, Ian. *Scott's Shadow: The Novel in Romantic Edinburgh*. Princeton: Princeton University Press, 2007.
Dunn, Dennis J. *The Catholic Church and Russia: Popes, Patriarchs, Tsars and Commissars*. Aldershot: Ashgate, 2004.
Edgerton, William B. "Nikolai Leskov: The Intellectual Development of a Literary Nonconformist." PhD diss., Columbia University, 1954.
Èikhenbaum (Eichenbaum), Boris. *Lev Tolstoi*. Leningrad, 1928–31; repr. Munich: Wilhelm Fink, 1968.
———. *Lev Tolstoi: Semidesiatye gody*. Leningrad: Sovetskii pisatel', 1960.
Eliseev, G. Z. "Zhurnalistika." *Sovremennik*, no. 3 (1866): 32–79.
Èpshtein (Epstein), Mikhail. "Virtual'nye knigi." *Zvezda*, "Esseistika i kritika," no. 8 (August 31, 2008): 218–34.

Fanger, Donald. *Dostoevsky and Romantic Realism: A Study of Dostoevsky in Relation to Balzac, Dickens, and Gogol.* Chicago: University of Chicago Press, 1965.
Fedorenko, B. V. "Iz razyskanii o Dostoevskom. 2. Iz tvorcheskoi istorii romana F. M. Dostoevskogo 'Besy.'" In *Novye aspekty v izuchenii Dostoevskogo; sbornik nauchnykh trudov,* 265-94. Petrozavodsk: Izdatel'stvo Petrozavodskogo universiteta, 1994.
Feoktistov, E. M. "Russkaia politika na Vostoke pred Krymskoiu voinoi." *Russkii vestnik* 73 (January 1868): 21-82.
———. *Vospominaniia: Za kulisami politiki i literatury, 1848-1896.* Edited by Iu. G. Oksman. Introduction by A. E. Presniakov and Iu. G. Oksman. Reprint introduction by Hans J. Torke. Leningrad: Priboi, 1929. Reprint edition Oriental Research Partners, 1975.
Fet, A. A. *Moi vospominaniia.* Vol. 2 (1848-1889). Moscow: A. I. Mamontov, 1890.
Frank, Joseph. *Dostoevsky: The Mantle of the Prophet, 1871-1881.* Princeton: Princeton University Press, 2002.
———. *Dostoevsky: The Miraculous Years, 1865-1871.* Princeton: Princeton University Press, 1995.
———. *Dostoevsky: The Seeds of Revolt, 1821-1849.* Princeton: Princeton University Press, 1976.
———. *Dostoevsky: The Stir of Liberation, 1860-1865.* Princeton: Princeton University Press, 1986.
Frye, Northrop. *Anatomy of Criticism: Four Essays.* New York: Atheneum, 1970.
Fusso, Susanne. *Discovering Sexuality in Dostoevsky.* Evanston: Northwestern University Press, 2006.
———. "Maidens in Childbirth: The Sistine Madonna in Dostoevskii's *The Devils.*" *Slavic Review* 54, no. 2 (1995): 261-75.
Gagemeister, Iu. A. "Vzgliad na promyshlennost' i torgovliu Rossii." *Russkii vestnik* 7 (January 1857): 5-52.
Gaintseva, E. G. "V. G. Avseenko i 'Russkii vestnik' 1870-kh godov." *Russkaia literatura,* no. 2 (1989): 70-84.
Galakhov, A. D. *Zapiski cheloveka.* Edited by V. M. Bokovaia. Moscow: Novoe literaturnoe obozrenie, 1999.
Gershenzon, Mikhail. *Obrazy proshlogo.* Moscow: A. A. Levenson, 1912.
Gerstein, Linda. *Nikolai Strakhov.* Cambridge, MA: Harvard University Press, 1971.
Gheith, Jehanne. *Finding the Middle Ground: Krestovskii, Tur, and the Power of Ambivalence in Nineteenth-Century Russian Women's Prose.* Evanston: Northwestern University Press, 2004.
———. "In Her Own Voice: Evgeniia Tur, Author, Critic, Journalist." PhD diss., Stanford University, 1992.
Golovachov. "O zhenskikh uchebnykh zavedeniiakh." *Russkii vestnik* 28 (July 1860): 267-85, 28 (August 1860): 457-80.
Gordin, Michael D. *A Well-Ordered Thing: Dmitrii Mendeleev and the Shadow of the Periodic Table.* New York: Basic Books, 2004.
Gradovskii, G. K. "Iz minuvshego." *Russkaia starina,* bk. 1 (January 1908): 77-86.
Granjard, Henri. *Ivan Tourguénev et les courants politiques et sociaux de son temps.* Paris: Institut d'études slaves de l'Université de Paris, 1966.
Griffiths, Frederick T., and Stanley J. Rabinowitz. *Epic and the Russian Novel from Gogol to Pasternak.* Boston: Academic Studies Press, 2011.
———. *Novel Epics: Gogol, Dostoevsky, and National Narrative.* Evanston: Northwestern University Press, 1990.
Grossman, L. *Dostoevskii.* Moscow: Molodaia gvardiia, 1965.
———. "Gorod i liudi 'Prestupleniia i nakazaniia.'" Introduction to F. M. Dostoevskii, *Prestuplenie i nakazanie.* Edited by L. Grossman, 5-52. Moscow: Khudozhestvennaia literatura, 1935.
Grot, N. P. [Russkaia zhenshchina]. "Elena Nikolaevna Stakhova." *Nashe vremia,* no. 13 (April 10, 1860): 207-10.
———. "Otvet russkoi zhenshchiny gospozhe Tur." *Nashe vremia,* no. 18 (May 15, 1860): 284-87.
Gusev, N. N. *Lev Nikolaevich Tolstoi: Materialy k biografii s 1870 po 1881 god.* Moscow: AN SSSR, 1963.

Hegel, G. W. F. *Elements of the Philosophy of Right*. Edited by Allen W. Wood. Translated by H. B. Nisbet. Cambridge: Cambridge University Press, 1991.

Hitchcock, Henry-Russell. *Architecture: Nineteenth and Twentieth Centuries, The Pelican History of Art*. 4th ed. Harmondsworth: Pelican Books, 1977.

Hokanson, Katya. "In Defense of Empire: 'The Bronze Horseman' and 'To the Slanderers of Russia.'" In *Beyond the Empire: Images of Russia in the Eurasian Cultural Context*, edited by Tetsuo Mochizuki, 149–66. Sapporo: Hokkaido University, 2008.

Holland, Kate. *The Novel in the Age of Disintegration: Dostoevsky and the Problem of Genre in the 1870s*. Evanston: Northwestern University Press, 2013.

Hosking, Geoffrey. *Russia: People and Empire, 1552–1917*. Cambridge, MA: Harvard University Press, 1997.

Hupchick, Dennis P. *The Balkans: From Constantinople to Communism*. New York: Palgrave Macmillan, 2004.

Iazykov, D. "Literaturnaia deiatel'nost' grafini E. V. Sal'ias (Evgeniia Tur): Bibliograficheskii ocherk." *Istoricheskii vestnik* (May 1892): 485–93.

Il'inskii, L. "Gonorar Dostoevskogo." *Bibliograficheskie listy Russkogo bibliologicheskogo obshchestva*, no. 3 (1922): 4–9.

Iurkevich, P. "Iz nauki o chelovecheskom dukhe. P. Iurkevicha. Trudy Kievskoi dukhovnoi Akademii, 1860 knizhka chetvertaia." *Russkii vestnik, Sovremennaia letopis'* 32 (April 1861): 79–105; and 33 (May 1861): 26–59.

"Iz pis'ma k redaktoru." *Moskovskie vedomosti*, no. 140, June 25, 1860, p. 1110.

Izmest'eva, G. P. "Istoricheskie portrety: Mikhail Nikiforovich Katkov." *Voprosy istorii*, no. 4 (2004): 71–92.

Jackson, Robert Louis. *Dialogues with Dostoevsky: The Overwhelming Questions*. Stanford: Stanford University Press, 1996.

———. *Dostoevsky's Quest for Form: A Study of His Philosophy of Art*. New Haven: Yale University Press, 1966.

Jahn, Gary R. "The Image of the Railroad in *Anna Karenina*." *Slavic and East European Journal* 25 (1981): 8–12.

James, Henry. Review of *Life and Letters of Madame Swetchine*. *North American Review* 107, no. 220 (July 1868): 328–334.

Jones, W. G., ed. *Tolstoi and Britain*. Oxford: Berg Publishers, 1995.

Kalmanovskii, E. "Pobezhdennyi pobeditel': Istoricheskoe esse." *Novaia Rossiia*, no. 3 (1995): 129–43.

Kamen'-Vinogorov [P. I. Veinberg]. "Otvet Kamnia-Vinogorova." *Vek*, no. 10 (1861): 363–64.

———. "Russkie dikovinki." *Vek*, no. 8 (February 1861): 289–92.

Kanevskaya, Marina. "Pushkin as 'Universal' Poet: Varnhagen von Ense and Dostoevsky." In *Cold Fusion: Aspects of the German Cultural Presence in Russia*, edited by Gennady Barabtarlo, 113–25. New York: Berghahn Books, 2000.

Kantor, V. "M. N. Katkov i krushenie estetiki liberalizma." *Voprosy literatury*, no. 5 (1973): 173–212.

———. "O sud'be imperskogo liberalizma v Rossii (M. N. Katkov)." *Filosofskie nauki*, no. 2 (2007): 66–91.

———. *Sankt-Peterburg: Rossiiskaia imperiia protiv rossiiskogo khaosa: K probleme imperskogo soznaniia v Rossii*. Moscow: Rosspen, 2008.

Kapustin, M. "Budushchee Turtsii." *Russkii vestnik, Sovremennaia letopis'* 14 (March 1858): 125–28.

Kariakin, Iu. F. *Dostoevskii i kanun XXI veka*. Moscow: Sovetskii pisatel', 1989.

———. "Mif o 'chernoi magii' Dostoevskogo." *Russkaia literatura*, no. 1 (1972): 113–25.

Kastorskii, M. I. "Neskol'ko slov o literaturnykh zaslugakh g-na Katkova." *Biblioteka dlia chteniia* 12 (December 1862): 20–53.

Katkov, M. N. "Chto sluchilos' po smerti Anny Kareninoi." *Russkii vestnik* 130 (July 1877): 448–62.

———. "Dopolnitel'noe ob"iasnenie po povodu stat'i g. Blagoveshchenskogo." *Russkii vestnik, Sovremennaia letopis'* 27 (June 1860): 462–63.

———. "Ėlegicheskaia zametka." *Russkii vestnik, Sovremennaia letopis'* 34 (August 1861): 162–66. Reprinted in *Sobranie sochinenii*, 4:453–57.

———. "*Istoriia drevnei russkoi slovesnosti: Sochinenie Mikhaila Maksimovicha*. Kniga pervaia. Kiev, 1839." *Otechestvennye zapiski* 9 (1840), bk. 4, sec. 5, 37–68. Reprinted in *Sobranie sochinenii*, 1:171–213.

———. "Kharakteristika vnutrennego mira Dostoevskogo (Po povodu ego konchiny)." *Moskovskie vedomosti*, no. 33, February 2, 1881. Reprinted in *Sobranie sochinenii*, 1:708–10.

———. "Koe-chto o progresse." *Russkii vestnik, Sovremennaia letopis'* 35 (October 1861): 107–27. Reprinted in *Sobranie sochinenii*, 2:7–28.

———. "Nash iazyk i chto takoe svistuny." *Russkii vestnik, Sovremennaia letopis'* 32 (March 1861): 1–38. Reprinted in *Sobranie sochinenii*, 1:329–68.

———. "Natsional'naia i antinatsional'naia partii v Rossii." *Moskovskie vedomosti*, no. 94, April 4, 1880. Reprinted in *Sobranie sochinenii*, 2:415–19.

———. "Neobkhodimost' diktatury dlia bor'by s kramoloi." *Moskovskie vedomosti*, no. 37, February 7, 1880. Reprinted in *Sobranie sochinenii*, 3:409–12.

———. "Neskol'ko slov vmesto sovremennoi letopisi." *Russkii vestnik* 31 (January 1861): 478–84. Reprinted in *Sobranie sochinenii*, 1:308–13.

———. "Nevladeiushchie klassy i mirovaia iustitsiia." *Russkii vestnik, Sovremennaia letopis'* 27 (June 1860): 429–62.

———. "O dopushchenii russkogo iazyka v inovercheskoe bogosluzhenie." *Russkii vestnik* 71 (September 1867): 316–91.

———. "O filosofskoi kritike khudozhestvennogo proizvedeniia (Stat'ia Rëtshera)." *Moskovskii nabliudatel'* 17 (May 1838): bk. 2, 159–95; and (June 1838): bk. 1, 303–34 and bk. 2, 431–57. Introduction reprinted in *Sobranie sochinenii*, 4:7–11.

———. "O nashem nigilizme po povodu romana Turgeneva." *Russkii vestnik* 40 (July 1862): 402–26. Reprinted in *Sobranie sochinenii*, 1:507–27.

———. *O zhenskom obrazovanii: Stat'i, sviazannye s vozniknoveniem i postepennym rostom zhenskoi klassicheskoi gimnazii*. Moscow: A. P. Snegireva, 1897.

———. *Ob elementakh i formakh slaviano-russkogo iazyka*. Moscow: V universitetskoi tipografii, 1845. Reprinted in *Sobranie sochinenii*, 4:12–160.

———. "Ob"iasnenie." *Russkii vestnik, Sovremennaia letopis'* 27 (May 1860): 145–67.

———. "Ob"iasnenie." *Russkii vestnik, Sovremennaia letopis'* 29 (October 1860): 431–34.

———. *Ocherki drevneishego perioda grecheskoi filosofii*. Moscow: Tipografiia Moskovskogo Universiteta, 1854. Reprinted in *Sobranie sochinenii*, 4:161–328.

———. "Odnogo polia iagody." *Russkii vestnik* 33 (May 1861): 1–26. Reprinted in *Sobranie sochinenii*, 1:369–95.

———. "Otzyv inostrantsa o Pushkine." *Otechestvennye zapiski* 3, no. 5 (1839), *Prilozhenie*, 1–36. Reprinted in *Sobranie sochinenii*, 1:53–84.

———. "*Pesni russkogo naroda, izdannye I. Sakharovym. Piat' chastei*. Sanktpeterburg. 1838–1839." *Otechestvennye zapiski* 4 (1839): bk. 6, sec. 6, 1–24, and bk. 7, sec. 6, 25–92. Reprinted in *Sobranie sochinenii*, 1:85–164.

———. "Po povodu pis'ma G-zhi Evgenii Tur." *Russkii vestnik, Sovremennaia letopis'* 26 (April 1860): 468–88.

———. "Po povodu 'Polemicheskikh krasot' v *Sovremennike*." *Russkii vestnik, Sovremennaia letopis'* 33 (June 1861): 138–58.

———. "Po povodu polemiki g Turgeneva s 'Inogorodnym obyvatelem.'" *Moskovskie vedomosti*, no. 5, January 6, 1880. Reprinted in *Sobranie sochinenii*, 1:695–98.

———. "Po povodu stat'i 'Rokovoi vopros.'" *Russkii vestnik* 45 (May 1863): 398–418. Reprinted in *Sobranie sochinenii*, 3:108–26.

———. "Pokushenie protiv gr. Loris-Melikova." *Moskovskie vedomosti*, no. 51, February 21, 1880. Reprinted in *Sobranie sochinenii*, 3:426–27.

———. "Pol'skii vopros." *Russkii vestnik* 43 (January 1863): 471-88. Reprinted in *Sobranie sochinenii*, 3:14-29.

———. "Potrebnost' v tverdoi i ènergicheskoi vlasti dlia bor'by s kramoloi." *Moskovskie vedomosti*, no. 44, February 14, 1880. Reprinted in *Sobranie sochinenii*, 3:421-23.

———. "Pushkin." *Russkii vestnik* 1 (January 1856): 155-72; 1 (February 1856): 306-23; 2 (March 1856): 282-310. Reprinted in *Sobranie sochinenii*, 1:246-303.

———. "Rech' na Pushkinskom prazdnike." *Sobranie sochinenii*, 1:706-7.

———. "Roman Turgeneva i ego kritiki." *Russkii vestnik* 39 (May 1862): 393-424. Reprinted in *Sobranie sochinenii*, 1:459-85.

———. *Sobranie peredovykh statei Moskovskikh vedomostei*. 25 vols. Moscow: V. V. Chicherin, 1863-87. Cited in text according to year.

———. *Sobranie sochinenii*. 6 vols. Edited by A. N. Nikoliukin. St. Petersburg: Rostok, 2010-12.

———. "*Sochineniia v stikhakh i proze grafini S. F. Tolstoi. Perevod s nemetskogo i angliiskogo. Moskva. Dve chasti*." *Otechestvennye zapiski* 12 (1840): bk. 10, sec. 5, 15-50. Partially reprinted in *Sobranie sochinenii*, 1:169-70.

———. "Starye bogi i novye bogi." *Russkii vestnik, Sovremennaia letopis'* 31 (February 1861): 891-904; and 32 (April 1861): 891-904. Reprinted in *Sobranie sochinenii*, 1:314-28.

———. "Turgenev." *Moskovskie vedomosti*, no. 261, September 20, 1883. Reprinted in *Sobranie sochinenii*, 1:718-19.

———. "Zametka." *Russkii vestnik, Sovremennaia letopis'* 30 (November 1860): 100-05.

———. "Zametka." *Russkii vestnik, Sovremennaia letopis'* 30 (November 1860): 210.

———. "Zametka dlia zhurnala *Vremia*." *Russkii vestnik* 34 (July 1861): 95-98. Reprinted in *Sobranie sochinenii*, 1:455-58.

———. "Zasluga Pushkina." *Moskovskie vedomosti*, no. 155, June 6, 1880. Reprinted in *Russkii vestnik* 147 (June 1880): 957-63; and 261 (June 1899): 403-09. Reprinted in *Sobranie sochinenii*, 1:699-705.

Katkovskii vestnik: Religiozno-filosofskie chteniia: K 190-letiiu so dnia rozhdeniia M. N. Katkova. Moscow: Progress-Pleiada, 2008.

Katz, Martin. *Mikhail N. Katkov: A Political Biography, 1818-1887*. The Hague: Mouton, 1966.

Katz, Michael R. "The Nihilism of Sonia Marmeladova." *Dostoevsky Studies* 1, no. 1 (1993): 25-36.

Kelly, Aileen. *Mikhail Bakunin: A Study in the Psychology and Politics of Utopianism*. Oxford: Oxford University Press, 1982.

Kennan, George F. *The Decline of Bismarck's European Order: Franco-Russian Relations, 1875-1890*. Princeton: Princeton University Press, 1979.

Kibal'nik, S. A. "Spory o Balkanskoi voine na stranitsakh 'Anny Kareninoi.'" *Russkaia literatura*, no. 4 (2010): 39-44.

Kirpotin, V. Ia. "Dostoevskii o 'Egipetskikh nochakh' Pushkina." *Voprosy literatury*, no. 11 (1962): 112-21.

———. *Dostoevskii v shestidesiatye gody*. Moscow: Khudozhestvennaia literatura, 1966.

———. *Razocharovanie i krushenie Rodiona Raskol'nikova: Kniga o romane F. M. Dostoevskogo 'Prestuplenie i nakazanie'*. Moscow: Sovetskii pisatel', 1970.

Kitaev, V. A. *Ot frondy k okhranitel'stvu: Iz istorii russkoi liberal'noi mysli 50-60kh godov XIX veka*. Moscow: Mysl', 1972.

Klevenskii, M. "Literaturnye sovetniki Turgeneva." In *Tvorcheskii put' Turgeneva: Sbornik statei*, edited by N. L. Brodskii, 226-43. Petrograd: Seiatel', 1923.

Kliger, Ilya. "Genre and Actuality in Belinskii, Herzen, and Goncharov: Toward a Genealogy of the Tragic Pattern in Russian Realism." *Slavic Review* 70, no. 1 (spring 2011): 45-66.

———. "Shapes of History and the Enigmatic Hero in Dostoevsky: The Case of *Crime and Punishment*." *Comparative Literature* 62, no. 3 (2010): 228-45.

Klimakov, Iu. V. "Pushkinskaia tema v literaturnom nasledii M. N. Katkova." In *Katkovskii vestnik*, 46-58.

Klioutchkine, Konstantine. "The Rise of *Crime and Punishment* from the Air of the Media." *Slavic Review* 61, no. 1 (spring 2002): 88–108.

Knapp, Liza. *Anna Karenina and Others: Tolstoy's Labyrinth of Plots*. Madison: University of Wisconsin Press, 2016.

———. "The Estates of Pokrovskoe and Vozdvizhenskoe: Tolstoy's Labyrinth of Linkings in *Anna Karenina*." *Tolstoy Studies Journal* 8 (1995–96): 81–98.

———. "The Setting." In *Approaches to Teaching Tolstoy's Anna Karenina*, edited by Liza Knapp and Amy Mandelker, 24–34. New York: Modern Language Association of America, 2003.

Kogan, G. F. "Iz istorii sozdaniia 'Ispovedi Stavrogina.'" In *Izvestiia Akademii nauk: Seriia literatury i iazyka* 54, no. 1, 65–73. Moscow: Nauka, 1995.

———. "Zhurnal 'Vremia' i revoliutsionnoe studenchestvo 1860-kh godov." *Literaturnoe nasledstvo* 86: *F. M. Dostoevskii: Novye materialy i issledovaniia*, 581–93. Moscow: Nauka, 1973.

Komarovich, V. L. "Neizdannaia glava romana 'Besy.'" *Byloe*, no. 18 (1922): 219–52.

Kornilov, A. A. *Semeistvo Bakuninykh*, vol. 1: *Molodye gody Mikhaila Bakunina: Iz istorii russkogo romantizma*. Moscow: Izdanie M. i S. Sabashnikovykh, 1915.

Koz'min, B. P. "Dva slova o slove 'nigilizm.'" *Izvestiia AN SSSR, Otdelenie literatury i iazyka* 10, no. 4 (1951): 378–85.

———. "Eshche o slove 'nigilizm' (Po povodu stat'i A. I. Batiuto)." *Izvestiia AN SSSR, Otdelenie literatury i iazyka* 12, no. 6 (1953): 526–28.

Kremenskaia, I. K. "'Moskovskie vedomosti' 1850-kh gg.—Redaktorskii debiut M. N. Katkova." In *Iz veka v vek: Iz istorii russkoe zhurnalistiki 1702–2002*, edited by B. I. Esin. Moscow: No publisher given, 2002.

Kuleshov, V. I. *"Otechestvennye zapiski" i literatura 40-kh godov XIX veka*. Moscow: Izdatel'stvo Moskovskogo universiteta, 1959.

Kundera, Milan. *Testaments Betrayed: An Essay in Nine Parts*. Translated by Linda Asher. New York: Harper Collins, 1995.

Kuskov, P. A. "Nekotorye razmyshleniia po povodu nekotorykh voprosov." *Vremia*, no. 2 (February 1861): 131–48.

L. N. Tolstoi—N. N. Strakhov; Polnoe sobranie perepiski. 2 vols. Edited by A. A. Donskov. Compiled by L. D. Gromova and T. G. Nikiforova. Ottawa and Moscow: Slavic Research Group at the University of Ottawa and State L. N. Tolstoy Museum, 2003.

Leont'ev, K. N. "G. Katkov i ego vragi na prazdnike Pushkina." *Varshavskii dnevnik*, no. 150 (July 15, 21, 1880). Reprinted in Katkov, *Sobranie sochinenii*, 6:185–202.

———. [Anonymous]. "Pis'mo provintsiala k g. Turgenevu." *Otechestvennye zapiski* 130, no. 5, sec. 3 (1860): 18–27.

Leskov, N. S. *Sobranie sochinenii*. 11 vols. Moscow: Khudozhestvennaia literatura, 1956–58.

Levitt, Marcus C. *Russian Literary Politics and the Pushkin Celebration of 1880*. Ithaca: Cornell University Press, 1989.

Literaturnoe nasledstvo 86: F. M. Dostoevskii: Novye materialy i issledovaniia. Edited by I. S. Zil'bershtein and L. M. Rozenblium. Moscow: Nauka, 1973.

Literaturnoe nasledstvo 56: V. G. Belinskii II. Edited by A. M. Egolin et al. Moscow: AN SSSR, 1950.

"Literaturnye zametki." *Nedelia*, no. 5 (April 10, 1866): 72–74.

Liubimov, N. A. "Arago o zheleznykh dorogakh i èlektricheskikh telegrafakh." *Russkii vestnik* 2 (March 1856): 109–15.

———. *Mikhail Nikiforovich Katkov i ego istoricheskaia zasluga*. St. Petersburg: Tovarishchestvo "Obshchestvennaia Pol'za," 1889.

Lönnqvist, B. "The English Theme in *Anna Karenina*." *Essays in Poetics: The Journal of the British Neo-Formalist Circle* 24 (Autumn 1999): 58–90.

———. "The Role of the Serbian War in *Anna Karenina*." *Tolstoy Studies Journal* 17 (2005): 35–42.

Lounsbery, Anne. "Print Culture and Real Life in Dostoevsky's *Demons*." *Dostoevsky Studies* 11 (2007): 25–37.

"M. N. Katkov kak redaktor 'Moskovskikh Vedomostei' i vozobnovitel' 'Russkogo Vestnika.' (Pis'ma ego k A. V. Nikitenko)." *Russkaia starina* 92 (November 1897): 355-73; and 92 (December 1897): 571-89.

Madame Swetchine, sa vie et ses oeuvres, publiés par le Cte de Falloux. 2 vols. Paris: Didier et Ce, 1860.

Maikov, A. N. *Sochineniia.* 2 vols. Edited by F. Ia. Priima. Moscow: Pravda, 1984.

Maiorova, Olga. *From the Shadow of Empire: Defining the Russian Nation through Cultural Mythology, 1855-1870.* Madison: University of Wisconsin Press, 2010.

Mandelker, Amy. *Framing Anna Karenina: Tolstoy, the Woman Question, and the Victorian Novel.* Columbus: Ohio State University Press, 1993.

Markevich, B. M. "S beregov Nevy." *Moskovskie vedomosti*, no. 313, December 9, 1872.

———. "Spravka dlia g. Turgeneva." *Moskovskie vedomosti*, no. 5, January 6, 1880.

Markov, Evgenii. "Teoriia i praktika iasnopolianskoi shkoly: Pedagogicheskie zametki tul'skogo uchitelia." *Russkii vestnik* 39 (May 1862): 149-89.

Markovich, V. M. "Roman I. S. Turgeneva 'Ottsy i deti' v otechestvennom literaturovedenii 1952-2006 godov." In Turgenev, *Ottsy i deti*, 507-40.

Martinsen, Deborah A., ed. *Literary Journals in Imperial Russia.* Cambridge: Cambridge University Press, 1997.

"Materialy dlia zhizneopisaniia M. N. Katkova: Iz pisem M. N. Katkova k materi i bratu." *Russkii vestnik* 250 (August 1897): 132-71.

Mazon, André. *Manuscrits parisiens d'Ivan Tourguénev: Notices et extraits.* Paris: Librairie ancienne Honoré Champion, 1930.

Meshcherskii, V. P. "Vospominaniia o M. N. Katkove (Pis'ma v Tveritino)." *Russkii vestnik* 250 (August 1897): 1-49.

Meyer, Priscilla. *How the Russians Read the French: Lermontov, Dostoevsky, Tolstoy.* Madison: University of Wisconsin Press, 2008.

Mikhailov, M. L. "Bezobraznyi postupok 'Veka.'" *Sanktpeterburgskie vedomosti*, March 3, 1861.

———. *Sochineniia.* 3 vols. Edited by B. P. Koz'min and G. F. Kogan. Introduction by M. I. Dikman and Iu. D. Levin. Moscow: Khudozhestvennaia literatura, 1958.

Miller, Alexei. *The Romanov Empire and Nationalism: Essays in the Methodology of Historical Research.* Budapest: Central European University Press, 2008.

Minaev, D. I. ["L'homme qui rit"]. "Nevinnye zametki." *Delo*, no. 11 (November 1871): 54-75.

Modzalevskii, B. L. "Dostoevskii—sotrudnik 'Russkogo vestnika.' Neizdannye pis'ma F. M. Dostoevskogo 1866-1873 gg." *Byloe*, no. 14 (1919): 30-52.

Morson, Gary Saul. *Anna Karenina in Our Time: Seeing More Wisely.* New Haven: Yale University Press, 2007.

———. *Narrative and Freedom: The Shadows of Time.* New Haven: Yale University Press, 1994.

Moser, Charles A. *Antinihilism in the Russian Novel of the 1860's.* The Hague: Mouton, 1964.

———. "Dostoevsky and the Aesthetics of Journalism." *Dostoevsky Studies* 3 (1982): 27-40.

———. *Pisemsky: A Provincial Realist.* Cambridge, MA: Harvard University Press, 1969.

Mullen, Elizabeth Mary. "M. N. Katkov as Editor of 'Russkii vestnik' from 1856-1862," MA thesis, Brown University, 1965.

Naiman, Eric. "Tolstoy's Hinges." In *New Studies in Modern Russian Literature and Culture: Essays in Honor of Stanley J. Rabinowitz*, edited by Catherine Ciepiela and Lazar Fleishman, 45:70-94. Stanford: Stanford Slavic Studies, 2014.

Nazarova, L. N. "I. S. Turgenev i E. V. Salias-de-Turnemir v nachale 60-kh godov." In *Teoriia i istoriia literatury (k 100-letiiu so dnia rozhdeniia akademika A. I. Beletskogo*, 117-23. Kiev: Naukova dumka, 1985.

Nechaeva, V. S. *Zhurnal M. M. i F. M. Dostoevskikh "Epokha," 1864-65.* Moscow: Nauka, 1975.

———. *Zhurnal M. M. i F. M. Dostoevskikh "Vremia," 1861-1863.* Moscow: Nauka, 1972.

Nekliudov, V. S. "Politicheskie zametki." *Russkii vestnik* 128 (April 1877): 856-65.

Nekrasov, N. P. "Neskol'ko slov o povesti g. Turgeneva: 'Nakanune.'" *Moskovskie vedomosti*, no. 99, May 5, 1860; and no. 100, May 6, 1860.
Nepomnyashchy, Catharine Theimer. "Katkov and the Emergence of the *Russian Messenger*." *Ulbandus Review* 1, no. 1 (1977): 59–89.
Nevedenskii, S. [S. G. Shcheglovitov]. *Katkov i ego vremia*. St. Petersburg: Tipografiia A. S. Suvorina, 1888.
Nikitenko, A. V. *Dnevnik*. 3 vols. Edited by N. L. Brodskii et al. Moscow: Khudozhestvennaia literatura, 1955.
"Novonaidennye i zabytye pis'ma Dostoevskogo," ed. I. S. Zil'bershtein. *Literaturnoe nasledstvo* 86. Edited by V. G. Bazanov et al. Moscow: Nauka, 1973.
"O nekotorykh usloviiakh, sposobstvuiushchikh umnozheniiu narodnogo kapitala." *Russkii vestnik* 4 (August 1856): 141–52.
"O zhenskikh uchebnykh zavedeniiakh." *Russkii vestnik* 107 (October 1873): 765–85.
O'Bell, Leslie. *Pushkin's "Egyptian Nights": The Biography of a Work*. Ann Arbor: Ardis, 1984.
Obolenskii, L. E. "Literaturnye vospominaniia i kharakteristiki (1854–1892)." *Istoricheskii vestnik*, no. 2 (1902): 487–508.
Orwin, Donna. "Did Dostoevsky or Tolstoy Believe in Miracles?" In *A New Word on The Brothers Karamazov*, edited by Robert Louis Jackson, 125–41. Evanston: Northwestern University Press, 2004.
P—ov, N. "Vospominaniia dobrovol'tsa." *Russkii vestnik* 129 (May 1877): 218–54.
"Pamiati Mikhaila Nikiforovicha Katkova. 1887—20 iulia—1897." *Russkii vestnik* 250 (August 1897): 1–182.
"Pamiati Pavla Mikhailovicha Leont'eva." *Russkii vestnik* 116 (April 1875): 705–44.
Paperno, Irina. *Chernyshevsky and the Age of Realism: A Study in the Semiotics of Behavior*. Stanford, CA: Stanford University Press, 1988.
———. "Leo Tolstoy's Correspondence with Nikolai Strakhov: The Dialogue on Faith." In *Anniversary Essays on Tolstoy*, edited by Donna Tussing Orwin, 96–119. Cambridge: Cambridge University Press, 2010.
Passek, T. P. *Iz dal'nykh let: Vospominaniia*. Vol. 3. St. Petersburg: A. F. Marks, 1906.
Pavlov, N. F. "Pis'mo iz Peterburga po povodu vozrazheniia Evgenii Tur, na stat'iu Russkoi zhenshchiny." *Nashe vremia*, no. 17 (April 8–20, 1860): 262–68.
Perepiska L. N. Tolstogo s N. N. Strakhovym, 1870–1894. St. Petersburg: Obshchestvo Tolstovskogo Muzeia, 1914.
Perevalova, E. V. "I. S. Turgenev i M. N. Katkov." *Spasskii vestnik* 14 (2007): 177–86.
———. "'Ten' Katkova': Pavel Mikhailovich Leont'ev." *Izvestiia vysshikh uchebnykh zavedenii: Problemy poligrafii i izdatel'skogo dela*, no. 1 (2012): 118–24.
———. *Zhurnal M. N. Katkova Russkii vestnik v pervye gody izdaniia (1856–1862): Literaturnaia pozitsiia*. Moscow: Moskovskii gosudarstvennnyi universitet pechati, 2010.
Perminov, G. F. "Turgenev o N. A. Dobroliubove: Neizvestnyi fel'eton-parodiia Turgeneva v 'Iskre.'" In *Turgenevskii sbornik: Materialy k Polnomu sobraniiu sochinenii i pisem I. S. Turgeneva*, 3, edited by I. V. Izmailov and L. N. Nazarova, 106–18. Leningrad: Nauka, 1967.
Peterson, K. "Po povodu stat'i 'Rokovoi vopros' v zhurnale *Vremia*." *Moskovskie vedomosti*, no. 109, May 22, 1863.
Pisarev, D. I. "Bor'ba za zhizn' ('Prestuplenie i nakazanie' F. M. Dostoevskogo. Dve chasti, 1867 g.)." In *Polnoe sobranie sochinenii i pisem*. Vol. 9, *Stat'i, 1867*. Moscow: Nauka, 2005.
———. *Sochineniia*. 4 vols. Moscow: Khudozhestvennaia literatura, 1955–56.
Pis'ma M. A. Bakunina k A. I. Gertsenu i N. P. Ogarevu. Edited by M. P. Dragomanov. St. Petersburg: Izdanie V. Vrublevskogo, 1906.
"Pis'ma M. N. Katkova k A. N. Popovu." *Russkii arkhiv*, no. 8 (1888): 480–99.
"Pis'mo iz Bolgrada." *Russkii vestnik, Sovremennaia letopis'* 14 (April 1858): 438–40.
Pobedonostsev, K. P. "'Zachem bylo delat' iz Katkova gosudarstvennogo cheloveka?' Pis'mo Aleksandru II ot 11 Marta 1887." In Katkov, *Sobranie sochinenii*, 6:255–57.

Pokrovskaia, E. B., ed. "Pis'ma Maikova k Dostoevskomu (za 70 gg.)." *Dostoevskii, Stat'i i materialy: Sbornik vtoroi*, edited by A. S. Dolinin. Leningrad-Moscow: Mysl', 1924.

Pollard, Alan P. "Dostoevskii's Pushkin Speech and the Politics of the Right under the Dictatorship of the Heart." *Canadian-American Slavic Studies* 17, no. 2 (summer 1983): 222–56.

Popov, Èduard, and Irina Veligonova. "Spasitel' otechestva." *Moskva*, no. 11 (2013): 148–58.

"Po povodu stat'i g. Mikhailova: Ob"iasnenie ot redaktsii 'Veka.'" *Vek*, no. 10 (1861): 363.

Prokopov, T. F. "Vzbalamuchennyi antinigilizm (K istorii 'literaturnogo pokhoda' M. N. Katkova protiv revoliutsionnoi demokratii." In *Katkovskii vestnik*, 71–82.

Pushkin, A. S. *The Letters of Alexander Pushkin*. Edited and translated by J. Thomas Shaw. Madison: University of Wisconsin Press, 1967.

———. *Polnoe sobranie sochinenii*. 10 vols. Moscow: AN SSSR, 1962–66.

Pustovoit, P. "V pogone za sensatsiei (Po povodu stat'i V. Arkhipova o romane 'Ottsy i deti')." *Voprosy literatury*, no. 9 (1958): 79–88.

Rachinskii, S. A. "Po povodu spiriticheskikh soobshchenii g. Vagnera." *Russkii vestnik* 117 (May 1875): 380–99.

Rak, V. D. "Istochnik ocherkov o znamenitykh ugolovnykh protsessakh v zhurnalakh brat'ev Dostoevskikh." In *Dostoevskii: Materialy i issledovaniia*, edited by G. M. Fridlender, 1:239–41. Leningrad: Nauka, 1974.

Randolph, John. *The House in the Garden: The Bakunin Family and the Romance of Russian Idealism*. Ithaca: Cornell University Press, 2007.

Reitblat, A. *Ot Bovy k Bal'montu: Ocherki po istorii chteniia v Rossii vo vtoroi polovine XIX veka*. Moscow: MPI, 1991.

Renner, Andreas. "Defining a Russian Nation: Mikhail Katkov and the 'Invention' of National Politics." *Slavonic and East European Review* 81, no. 4 (October 2003): 659–82.

———. *Russischer Nationalismus und Öffentlichkeit im Zarenreich: 1855–1875*. Cologne: Böhlau, 2000.

Repnikov, A. V. *Konservativnye modeli rossiiskoi gosudarstvennosti*. Moscow: Rosspen, 2014.

Ronin, V. K. "Bel'giiskii ekonomist v russkoi pechati: Giustav de Molinari v zhurnalakh Katkova." In *Rossiia i Evropa: Diplomatiia i kul'tura*, 202–16. Moscow: Nauka, 2002.

"Rough Crossings: The Cutting of Raymond Carver." *The New Yorker* (December 24 and 31, 2007): 93–99.

Rozenblium, L. N. *Tvorcheskie dnevniki Dostoevskogo*. Moscow: Nauka, 1981.

Ruud, Charles A. *Fighting Words: Imperial Censorship and the Russian Press, 1804–1906*. Toronto: University of Toronto Press, 1982.

San'kova, S. M. *Gosudarstvennyi deiatel' bez gosudarstvennoi dolzhnosti: M. N. Katkov kak ideolog gosudarstvennogo natsionalizma*. St. Petersburg: Nestor, 2007.

———. *Mikhail Nikiforovich Katkov. V poiskakh mesta (1818–1856)*. Moscow: APK and PPRO, 2008.

Sazhin, V. "Ruka pobeditelia: Vybrannye mesta iz perepiski V. Belinskogo i M. Bakunina." *Literaturnoe obozrenie*, special edition: *Èrotika v russkoi literature ot Barkova do nashikh dnei: Teksty i kommentarii*. Moscow, 1992.

Schultze, Sydney. *The Structure of Anna Karenina*. Ann Arbor: Ardis, 1982.

Sementkovskii, R. I. *M. N. Katkov: Ego zhizn' i literaturnaia deiatel'nost'*. St. Petersburg: Iu. N. Èrlikh, 1892.

Shatz, Marshall S. "Michael Bakunin and His Biographers: The Question of Bakunin's Sexual Impotence." In *Imperial Russia 1700–1917: State—Society—Opposition; Essays in Honor of Marc Raeff*, edited by Ezra Mendelsohn and Marshall S. Shatz. DeKalb, IL: Northern Illinois University Press, 1988.

Shchebal'skii, P. K. "Nigilizm v istorii." *Russkii vestnik* 80 (April 1869): 856–63.

Sinel, Allen. *The Classroom and the Chancellery: State Educational Reform in Russia under Count Dmitry Tolstoi*. Cambridge, MA: Harvard University Press, 1973.

Sobolev, L. I., ed. *Kritika 60-kh godov XIX veka*. Moscow: AST Astrel', 2003.

Sokolova, A. I. "Vstrechi i znakomstva." *Istoricheskii vestnik* 124 (1911): 832–43.

Solov'ev (Soloviov), Vladimir. "'. . . Dlia blaga Rossii i vsego mira.'" Edited by Tat'iana Lapteva. *Nashe nasledie*, no. 5 (1992): 69-78.

"Soobshcheniia i izvestiia." *Russkii vestnik* 200 (February 1889): 355-61.

"Sovremennoe polozhenie kreditnykh uchrezhdenii." *Russkii vestnik* 7 (January 1857): 273-310, 491-552.

Sret'kovich, P. "Istoriia odnoi serbskoi derevni." *Russkii vestnik* 14 (April 1858): 562-77.

Stech'kin, N. Ia. *Iz vospominanii ob I. S. Turgeneve (S prilozheniem semi ego neizdannykh pisem)*. St. Petersburg: V. V. Komarov, 1903.

Stenbock-Fermor, Elisabeth. *The Architecture of Anna Karenina: A History of Its Writing, Structure and Message*. Louvain: Peter de Ridder Press, 1975.

Stites, Richard. *The Women's Liberation Movement in Russia: Feminism, Nihilism, and Bolshevism 1860-1930*. Princeton, NJ: Princeton University Press, 1978.

Stoppard, Tom. *The Coast of Utopia: A Trilogy. Voyage. Shipwreck. Salvage*. New York: Grove Press, 2007.

Strakhov, N. N. *Bor'ba s zapadom v nashei literature: Istoricheskie i kriticheskie ocherki*, 2. Kiev: I. P. Matchenko, 1897; Mouton, reprint 1969.

———. "Eshche za Turgeneva." *Kriticheskie stat'i ob I. S. Turgeneve i L. N. Tolstom (1862-1885)*. Kiev: Tipografiia I. I. Chokolova, 1901.

———. "Glavnoe sokrovishche nashei literatury." In his *Zametki o Pushkine i drugikh poetakh*. 2nd ed., 17-34. Kiev: I. I. Chokolov, 1897.

———. "Materialy dlia zhizneopisaniia F. M. Dostoevskogo." In *Biografiia, pis'ma i zametki iz zapisnoi knizhki F. M. Dostoevskogo*. St. Petersburg: A. S. Suvorin, 1883.

———. "Postupok i mneniia g. Kamnia Vinogorova v No. 8 gazety 'Vek.'" In his *Kriticheskie stat'i (1861-1894)*, 2:252-63. Kiev: I. P. Matchenko, 1902.

———. [Russkii]. "Rokovoi vopros." *Vremia*, no. 4 (April 1863): 152-63.

———. "Vospominaniia o Fedore Mikhailoviche Dostoevskom." In *Biografiia, pis'ma, i zametki iz zapisnoi knizhki F. M. Dostoevskogo*, 179-329. St. Petersburg: A. S. Suvorin, 1883.

Summerson, John. *Victorian Architecture: Four Studies in Evaluation*. New York: Columbia University Press, 1970.

Sutherland, J. A. *Victorian Novelists and Publishers*. Chicago: University of Chicago Press, 1976.

M. T. [Timmerman?]. "Iz putevykh zametok ot S.-Peterburga do Irkutska." *Sanktpeterburgskie vedomosti*, February 14, 1861.

Terras, Victor. *Belinskij and Russian Literary Criticism: The Heritage of Organic Aesthetics*. Madison: University of Wisconsin Press, 1974.

Thaden, Edward C. *Conservative Nationalism in Nineteenth-Century Russia*. Seattle: University of Washington Press, 1964.

———. *Russia's Western Borderlands, 1710-1870*. With the collaboration of Marianna Forster Thaden. Princeton: Princeton University Press, 1984.

———, ed. *Russification in the Baltic Provinces and Finland, 1855-1914*. Princeton: Princeton University Press, 1981.

Tkachov P. N. [N. N.] "Bol'nye liudi." *Delo*, no. 3 (March 1873): 151-79; and no. 4 (April 1873): 359-81.

Todd, William Mills III. "Anna on the Installment Plan: Teaching *Anna Karenina* Through the History of Its Serial Publication." In *Approaches to Teaching Tolstoy's Anna Karenina*, edited by Liza Knapp and Amy Mandelker, 53-59. New York: Modern Language Association of America, 2003.

———. "*The Brothers Karamazov* and the Poetics of Serial Publication." *Dostoevsky Studies* 7 (1986): 87-97.

———. "Dostoevskii as a Professional Writer." In *The Cambridge Companion to Dostoevskii*, edited by W. J. Leatherbarrow. Cambridge: Cambridge University Press, 2002.

———. "Dostoevsky's Russian Monk in Extra-Literary Dialogue: Implicit Polemics in *Russkii vestnik*, 1879-1881." In *Christianity and the Eastern Slavs*. Vol. 2: *Russian Culture in Modern*

Times, edited by Robert P. Hughes and Irina Paperno, 124–33. Berkeley: University of California Press, 1994.

———. "Reading *Anna* in Parts." *Tolstoy Studies Journal* 8 (1995–96): 125–28.

———. "The Responsibilities of (Co-)Authorship: Notes on Revising the Serialized Version of *Anna Karenina*." In *Freedom and Responsibility in Russian Literature: Essays in Honor of Robert Louis Jackson*, edited by Elizabeth Cheresh Allen and Gary Saul Morson, 159–69. Evanston: Northwestern University Press, 1995.

———. "The Ruse of the Russian Novel." In *The Novel*. Vol. 1: *History, Geography, and Culture*, edited by Franco Moretti, 401–23. Princeton: Princeton University Press, 2006.

———. "Tolstoy and Dostoevsky: The Professionalization of Literature and Serialized Fiction." *Dostoevsky Studies* 15 (2011): 29–36.

Todd, William Mills III, and Justin Weir. "Fear and Loathing in the Caucasus: Tolstoy's 'The Raid' and Russian Journalism." In *Before They Were Titans: Essays on the Early Works of Dostoevsky and Tolstoy*, edited by Elizabeth Cheresh Allen, 193–209. Boston: Academic Studies Press, 2015.

Tolstoi, L. N. *Polnoe sobranie sochinenii*. 90 vols. Edited by V. G. Chertkov et al. Moscow: Jubilee Edition, 1928–58.

Tracy, Lewis. "Decoding Puškin: Resurrecting Some Readers' Responses to *Egyptian Nights*." *Slavic and East European Journal* 37, no. 4 (1993): 456–71.

Trofimova, T. A. "'Polozhitel'noe nachalo' v russkoi literature XIX veka ('Russkii vestnik' M. N. Katkova)." *Kandidat* diss., Rossiiskii gosudarstvennyi gumanitarnyi universitet. Moscow, 2007.

Tur, Evgeniia [Elizaveta Vasil'evna Salias-de-Tournemir]. "Gospozha Svechina. *Madame Swetchine, sa vie et ses oeuvres publiés*, par le C-te de Falloux, de l'Académie française, 1860." *Russkii vestnik* 26 (April 1860): 362–92.

———. "*La Jeunesse, comédie en cinq actes et en vers*, par Emile Augier, Paris, 1858." *Russkii vestnik* 14 (April 1858): 209–18.

———. "*Le fils naturel, comédie en cinq actes, dont un prologue*, par Alexandre Dumas fils." *Russkii vestnik* 15 (May 1858): 104–22.

———. "Neskol'ko slov po povodu stat'i 'Russkoi Zhenshchiny.'" *Moskovskie vedomosti*, April 17, 1860, pp. 665–67.

———. "Nravoopisatel'nyi roman vo Frantsii: *Madame Bovary, moeurs de province, par Gustave Flaubert*." *Russkii vestnik* 10 (July 1857): 244–84.

———. "Ob izdanii G-zheiu Evgenieiu Tur v 1861 godu gazety Russkaia Rech': Obozrenie literatury, istorii, iskusstva i obshchestvennoi zhizni na zapade i v Rossii." *Moskovskie vedomosti*, no. 258, November 27, 1860, pp. 2051–53.

———. "Ob"iasnenie." *Moskovskie vedomosti*, no. 252, November 19, 1860, pp. 2000–2001.

———. "Pis'mo k redaktoru." *Russkii vestnik, Sovremennaia letopis'* 26 (April 1860): 406–11.

———. *Povesti i rasskazy*. Moscow: V tipografii Katkova i Ko., 1859.

Turgenev, I. S. *Ottsy i deti*. Edited by S. A. Batiuto and N. S. Nikitina. St. Petersburg: Nauka, 2008.

———. *Polnoe sobranie sochinenii i pisem*. 28 vols. Moscow: AN SSSR, 1960–68. Cited in text as *PSS 1960–68*.

———. *Polnoe sobranie sochinenii i pisem*. 30 vols. 2nd ed. Moscow: Nauka, 1978–86.

Tvardovskaia, V. A. *Ideologiia poreformennogo samoderzhaviia (M. N. Katkov i ego izdaniia)*. Moscow: Nauka, 1978.

Ugrinovich, K. "Izvestiia s Kavkaza." *Russkii vestnik, Sovremennaia letopis'* 14 (March 1858): 64–69.

———. "Kratkii obzor voennykh deistvii na Kavkaze v minuvshem 1857 godu." *Russkii vestnik, Sovremennaia letopis'* 13 (February 1858): 165–82, 266–81.

Ul'ianitskii, V. A. "Turtsiia, Rossiia i Evropa s tochki zreniia mezhdunarodnogo prava." *Russkii vestnik* 127 (February 1877): 449–88.

Utin, B. "Svidetel'skoe pokazanie." *Moskovskie vedomosti*, no. 136, June 21, 1860, pp. 1077–78.

"V Ameriku ne vpustiat." Interview with Aleksandr Nikoliukin conducted by Sergei Dmitrenko. *Novaia gazeta, Ex libris*, no. 14, April 18, 2013.

Vagner, N. P. "Mediumizm." *Russkii vestnik* 119 (October 1875): 866–951.

———. "Po povodu spiritizma. Pis'mo k redaktoru." *Vestnik Evropy* 4 (1875): 855–75.
Varnhagen von Ense. Review of *Sochineniia A. Pushkina (Werke von Alexander Puschkin). Jahrbücher für wissenschaftliche Kritik* 61 (October 1838).
[Varnhagen von Ense]. "Sochineniia A. Pushkina." *Syn otechestva* 7, no. 4 (1839): 1–37.
Veinberg, P. I. [Kamen'-Vinogorov]. "Bezobraznyi postupok 'Veka.' (Iz moikh literaturnykh vospominanii)." *Istoricheskii vestnik* (May 1900): 472–89.
Veresaev, V. *Gogol' v zhizni: Sistematicheskii svod podlinnykh svidetel'stv sovremennikov*. Moscow: Moskovskii rabochii, 1990.
Viduètskaia, I. P. "Dostoevskii i Leskov." *Russkaia literatura*, no. 4 (1975): 127–37.
Viktorovich, V. A. "'G-n –bov i vopros ob iskusstve." In *Dostoevskii: Materialy i issledovaniia*, vol. 13, 227–29. St. Petersburg: Nauka, 1996.
Vinitsky, Ilya. *Ghostly Paradoxes: Modern Spiritualism and Russian Culture in the Age of Realism*. Toronto: University of Toronto Press, 2009.
Vinogradov, V. V. *Istoriia slov*. Moscow: Tolk, 1994.
"Vnutrennee obozrenie, 1 April 1879." *Vestnik Evropy* 76/2, no. 4 (April 1879): 821–28.
Volgin, Igor'. *Poslednii god Dostoevskogo*. Moscow: Sovetskii pisatel', 1986.
Vospominaniia o Mikhaile Katkove. Edited by G. N. Lebedeva and O. A. Platonov. Moscow: Institut russkoi tsivilizatsii, 2014.
"Vstupitel'naia stat'ia (K istorii sozdaniia 'Brat'ev Karamazovykh')." In *F. M. Dostoevskii, Materialy i issledovaniia*, edited by A. S. Dolinin. Leningrad: AN SSSR, 1935.
Vyzinskii, G. V. [I. Mai], "Kratkoe skazanie o poslednikh deianiiakh Russkogo vestnika." *Moskovskie vedomosti*, no. 109, May 19, 1860, pp. 858–62.
———. "Ob"iasnenie 'Ob"iasneniia' Russkogo vestnika." *Moskovskie vedomosti*, no. 137, June 22, 1860, pp. 1082–85.
Wachtel, Michael. *A Commentary to Pushkin's Lyric Poetry, 1826–1836*. Madison: University of Wisconsin Press, 2011.
Walicki, Andrzej. "The Slavophile Thinkers and the Polish Question in 1863." In *Polish Encounters, Russian Identity*, edited by David L. Ransel and Bozena Shallcross, 89–99. Bloomington: Indiana University Press, 2005).
Weeks, Theodore R. "Religion and Russification: Russian Language in the Catholic Churches of the 'Northwest Provinces' after 1863." *Kritika* 2, no. 1 (winter 2001, new series): 87–110.
Woodburn, Stephen. M. "The Origins of Russian Intellectual Conservatism, 1825–1881: Danilevsky, Dostoevsky, Katkov, and the Legacy of Nicholas I." PhD diss., Miami University (Oxford, OH), 2001.
Z. "Kastratsiia khudozhestvennykh proizvedenii." *Sankt-Peterburgskie vedomosti*, no. 336, 6 (18), December 1874, p. 2.
Zakharov, V. N. "Fakty protiv legendy." In his *Problemy izucheniia Dostoevskogo*, 75–109. Petrozavodsk: Petrozavodskii gosudarstvennyi universitet, 1978.
"Zametka ot redaktsii." *Vek*, no. 9 (March 1861): 328.
Zelnik, Reginald E. "The Sunday-School Movement in Russia, 1859–1862." *Journal of Modern History* 37, no. 2 (June 1965): 151–70.
Zhdanov, V. A. *Tvorcheskaia istoriia "Anny Kareninoi."* Moscow: Sovetskii pisatel', 1957.
———, and È. E. Zaidenshnur, "Istoriia sozdaniia romana 'Anna Karenina.'" In L. N. Tolstoi, *Anna Karenina: Roman v vos'mi chastiakh*, edited by V. A. Zhdanov and È. E. Zaidenshnur, 803–33. Moscow: Nauka, 1970.
Zhuravskii, D. I. "O zheleznykh dorogakh v Rossii." *Russkii vestnik* 3 (May 1856): 417–57.

Index

Age, 113–17, 118–19, 267n38
Akhsharumov, N. D., 271n23, 271n27, 271–72n28
Aksakov, A. N., 189–91
Aksakov, I. S., 180–81, 195–96, 218, 219, 227, 228
Alekseev, M. P., 82
Alexander I (tsar), 56
Alexander II (tsar), 5, 6, 12, 50, 129, 132, 145–46, 204, 214, 239, 282n6
Alexander III (tsar), 239
Allen, Elizabeth Cheresh, 262n55, 264n127
Annenkov, P. V., 7, 78, 80, 84–86, 87, 93
Ansermet, Ernest, 243
Antonovich, M. A., 81, 89–91
Arkhipov, V., 82–83
Artemiev, Maksim, 248–49n18
Augier, Émile, 55
Austen, Jane, 54
Avineri, Shlomo, 40
Avseenko, V. G., 160–62, 167–68, 273n53

Babaev, Eduard, 163
Babst, I. K., 175–76
Backor, Joseph, 182, 255n10
Bakunin, Mikhail Aleksandrovich, 22–23, 28–33, 39, 250n5, 251n31
Barclay de Tolly, Prince Michael Andreas, 274n4
Bartenev, P. I., 278–79n64
Batiuto, A. I., 81
Baxandall, Michael, 244–45
Becker, Howard S., 242, 244
Beethoven, Ludwig van, 225–26
Belinsky, Vissarion Grigorievich, 17, 2–34, 39, 40–45, 62, 228, 229, 247n8, 250–51n15, 253n73, 254n82, 285n73; *The Fifty-Year-Old Uncle* [*Piatidesiatiletnii diadiushka*], 25–27, 88
Beriozin, I., 75
Beriozkina, S. V., 166, 271n27, 272n32
Blagoveshchensky, N. M., 61, 63, 64, 67–68, 257n70
Bojanowska, Edyta, 130–31, 285n61
Bonaparte, Napoleon, 223–24, 225, 274n4
Botkin, V. P., 27, 29, 30, 42–43, 44

Bowman, Herbert, 23, 254n82
Brasey, Jean-Nicole Moreau de, Comte de Lyon, 233
Brédif, Camille, 191–92
Brontë, Charlotte, 54
Brontë, Emily, 54
Bulgaria, 72–80, 261n32
Burenin, V. P., 94–95
Butlerov, A. M., 189–92
Byron, George Gordon, Lord, 104, 108–9

Carver, Raymond, 243
Catherine II (tsarina), 194
Cervantes, Miguel de, 230
Chateaubriand, François René de, 57
Cherkassky, Vladimir Aleksandrovich, 165
Chernyshevsky, Nikolai Gavrilovich, 14, 31, 65–68, 73, 80, 81, 102, 105, 130, 146–47, 150, 189, 238, 258n87
Chicherin, Boris Nikolaevich, 11
Citizen, 161, 272–73n42
Coetzee, J. M., 273n52
Collins, Wilkie, 169, 275n17
Constable, Archibald, 287–88n11
Contemporary, 7, 44, 65–68, 71–72, 74–75, 80, 81, 86, 87, 89–91, 99, 105, 130, 142, 146, 163, 233, 238
Contemporary Word, 88
Costlow, Jane T., 260n16
Crimean War, 49–50, 54, 72, 76, 78, 170, 171, 175
Cruise, Edwina, 275–76n19

Danilov, A. M., 145
Dante, 140
Davydov, I. I., 48
Decomberousse, François Isaac Hyacinthe, 14
De Morgan, Augustus, 189, 280n83
Denton, W., 193–94, 280n103
Derzhavin, Gavrila, 37
Descartes, René, 91
Dickens, Charles, 169, 243
Dobroliubov, Nikolai Aleksandrovich, 14, 72–75, 79–81, 87, 102–5, 130, 238, 262n49
Dolgorukov, Prince V. A., 206

Dolinin, A. S., 156–57, 282–83n8
Domostroi, 184, 279n65
Dostoevskaia, Anna Grigorievna, 143, 155, 161, 207, 209, 217–18, 226, 227–28, 236
Dostoevskaia, Maria Dmitrievna, 136, 137
Dostoevsky, Fyodor Mikhailovich, 9–10, 14, 16, 18, 19, 46, 47, 53, 69, 83, 93, 97, 98–162, 193, 202, 217–20, 226, 240–41, 242–45, 270n14, 273n52, 275n8, 282n4, 282n6, 282n7, 282–83n8; death, 235–36; evaluation by Katkov, 236–37; and Petrashevsky circle, 102; and *pochvennichestvo* ("return to the soil"), 100–1, 131–36; Works: "An Answer to the *Russian Herald*," 122–25; "At Tikhon's" (chapter excised from *The Devils*), 154–60, 210, 237, 272n38, 272n40, 272–73n42; "Bookishness and Literacy," 109; *The Brothers Karamazov*, 3, 19, 92, 98, 144, 161, 204–10, 216, 227, 234–35, 239, 241, 284n41; *Crime and Punishment*, 3, 18, 98, 127, 136, 137–53, 155, 156, 157, 158, 160–61, 163, 205, 206, 227, 243, 267n38, 269n6, 270n16, 271n23, 271n27, 271–72n28, 272n32, 272n35, 273n46; *The Devils*, 3, 18, 97, 98, 138, 139, 148, 153–60, 163, 164, 206, 209–10, 227, 242, 272n37, 272n40, 272–73n42, 273n46; *Diary of a Writer*, 235, 273n48, 281n123; *Epoch* (journal), 133, 136, 137, 146, 269n97; *The Idiot*, 3, 98, 143, 153–54, 155; "Literary Hysteria," 127–28; "Models of Sincerity," 116–18, 119, 121–22; "Mr.—bov and the Problem of Art," 102–5, 265–66n10, 268n75; *Notes from the Dead House*, 100, 126–27, 141, 159; *Notes from Underground*, 150; Pushkin speech, 98, 205, 220–21, 222, 227–31, 234–35, 286n101, 286n105; *A Raw Youth*, 69, 160–62, 167–68, 204, 206, 264n1, 273n53; "A Ticklish Question," 87–89, 128, 136, 169; *Time* (journal), 84, 87–88, 98–136, 137–38, 142, 148, 179, 228, 269n97; "Uncle's Dream," 99; *The Village of Stepanchikovo and Its Inhabitants*, 98–100, 101, 138, 141; "The Whistle and the *Russian Herald*," 106–7, 108
Dostoevsky, Mikhail Mikhailovich, 99–100, 101, 136, 138, 144
Druzhinin, A. V., 243
Dryzhakova, E. N., 270n9
Dumas, Alexandre *fils*, 55–56, 123
Duncan, Ian, 287–88n11

Eichenbaum, Boris, 166
Eliot, George, 54
Eliseev, G. Z., 146

Elssler, Fanny, 255n17
Eötvös, Jószef, 63–64
Epstein, Mikhail, 282n4
Esakov, Piotr Semionovich, 87

Falloux, Count Alfred de, 57–58, 257n64
Feoktistov, Evgenii Mikhailovich, 28, 54–55, 61, 83–84, 169, 194, 258n87
Fet, Afanasii Afanasievich (Shenshin), 10, 104–5, 118, 124, 166, 197, 228
Fisher, S. N., 185
Flaubert, Gustave, 55
Frank, Joseph, 220, 265–66n10
Freud, Sigmund, 79
Frye, Northrop, 95–97, 264n127
Fusso, Susanne, 157, 272n38

Gaevsky, V. P., 219
Gagemeister, Iu. A., 176–77
Galakhov, A. D., 252n43
Gaskell, Elizabeth, 53
Georgievsky, A. I., 183–84
Gershenzon, Mikhail, 252n34
Gerstein, Linda, 130
Gheith, Jehanne, 53–54, 68, 256n34, 259n102
Gladkova, Liudmila Viktorovna, 278n50
Gladstone, William, 169
Gneist, Heinrich Rudolf Hermann Friedrich von, 63
Goethe, Johann Wolfgang von, 35, 36, 37, 109, 225–26, 235
Gogol, Nikolai Vasilievich, 44, 134, 286n100; *The Government Inspector*, 44, 126
Golokhvastov, P. D., 166
Gradovsky, A. D., 235
Gradovsky, G. K., 182–83
Granjard, Henri, 261n37
Griboedov, Aleksandr Sergeevich, 88–89
Griffiths, Frederick, 161
Grigoriev, Apollon, 268n77
Grossman, Leonid, 140, 145, 151–53, 269n5, 272n29

Hébrard, Adrien, 210
Hegel, Georg Wilhelm Friedrich, 22–23, 29, 35, 38–41, 42, 44, 48, 182, 220–21, 223, 225, 231, 247n8, 253n66, 254n82, 286n100
Heine, Heinrich, 143, 240
Herald of Europe, 177–78, 188, 212, 234
Herzen, Alexander, 15, 22, 86, 87, 93, 113, 132, 169, 213, 251n16, 269n97, 283n21
Hokanson, Katya, 232

INDEX

Home, Daniel Dunglas, 191
Homer, 103, 226
Hosking, Geoffrey, 129

Iazykov, D., 53
Ilinsky, L. K., 269n7
"*Istoricheskii protsess*" (television program), 15–17
Iuriev, S. A., 216–17, 234, 283n34, 286n101
Iurkevich, P. D., 80, 189–91
Ivanov, I. I., 154
Ivanova, Mariia Aleksandrovna, 155
Ivanova, Sofia Aleksandrovna, 144, 155

Jackson, Robert Louis, 103, 273n52
Jahn, Gary R., 276n30
James, Henry, 257n64

Kamen-Vinogorov (pseudonym of P. I. Veinberg), 113–21, 123, 267n36
Kanevskaya, Marina, 220, 223, 225, 230–31
Kant, Immanuel, 91
Kantor, Vladimir, 13, 249n34
Kapustin, M., 75–76
Karakozov, Dmitrii, 145, 148
Karamzin, Nikolai Mikhailovich, 15
Karateev, V., 78, 261n34
Kariakin, Iurii, 157–58, 269n5, 272–73n42
Karr, Alphonse, 198
Kastorsky, M. I., 266n18
Katkov, Mefodii Nikiforovich (brother of Mikhail), 4–5, 247n2, 278–79n64
Katkov, Mikhail Nikiforovich, and aesthetics, 13, 23, 34–38, 51–52, 102–6, 109–25, 266n11; attitude toward England, 54–55, 63, 86–89, 106, 164, 169; attitude toward France, 54–55, 60; and Bakunin, 28–30, 32–33, 250n5, 251n31; brother's insanity and death, 278–79n64; and Catholicism, 58, 59–61; and censorship, 255n32, 261n32; childhood and early life, 4–5; and classical education, 164, 181–84, 185, 278n55; death of, 13, 21, 240; editorial practice of, 36–37, 53, 54–69, 93–95, 101–2, 106, 125, 138, 142–44, 148–53, 154–62, 192–203, 205–8, 237, 242–45, 270n12, 273n46, 281n122, 282n4; and German idealist philosophy, 21–23, 34–42, 46–48, 62, 82, 91, 182, 220–21, 286n100; and "Jewish question," 12; as a model for Pavel Petrovich in *Fathers and Sons*, 86–89, 169; and modernization of the Russian economy, 164, 170, 174–78, 277n39; and nihilism, 80–83, 84–85, 88, 90–92, 97, 105, 120, 123, 130, 135, 138–41, 142, 146, 147–48, 150, 156–60, 185, 189–90, 204, 210–17, 238, 262n50, 282n50; obituary, 21; as patron, 244–45, 287–88n11; and Polish uprising of 1863, 5, 7, 93, 128–31, 178–79, 216–17, 223, 233; professorship at Moscow University, 5, 48–49; and railroads, 164, 170–78, 276n24; reception of, 10–17, 240–41; relationship with Mariia Ogariova, 28–32; romance with Aleksandra Shchepkina, 24–27, 250–51n15; and Russian foreign policy, 287n123; and the Russian language, 4, 6–9, 39, 51–52, 79, 108, 178–79, 221, 232–33, 242–43, 244; and Russian nationalism, 6–9, 12–13, 15–17, 21, 38–40, 50, 51–52, 79, 106, 128–30, 133–35, 165–66, 178–81, 215–16, 221–25, 231–34, 244–45, 248n16; and russification, 164, 165, 178–81, 277–78n50; and Serbia, 164, 168–69, 192–200; and spiritualism, 187–92, 279–80n80, 280n87; studying in Berlin, 46–48, 143; and terrorism, 204, 207, 211–17, 231; as translator, 6, 33, 42, 143, 220; and women's rights, 119–23, 164, 184–87, 279n65, 279n69; *Moscow News* (first editorship), 5, 9, 49–50, 51, 248n17, 255n17, 255n18; *Moscow News* (second editorship), 3, 5–6, 11, 15, 19, 43, 59, 93, 94, 98, 128, 148, 159, 165, 178–84, 204, 205, 206, 211–17, 228, 231, 234–36, 239–40, 269n97; *Russian Herald*, 3, 5, 6, 9–10, 17–19, 43, 46, 50–69, 70, 71–72, 75, 77–80, 82–83, 84, 87, 88–89, 92–95, 98–101, 105, 108, 135–36, 138, 140, 142–43, 144–45, 148–49, 150–53, 154–62, 163–64, 166–203, 204, 205–10, 227, 231, 234–35, 242–45, 248–49n18, 255n20, 273n53, 275n8, 277n39, 277–78n50; Works: "Apropos of the Article 'A Fatal Question' [*Po povodu stat'i 'Rokovoi vopros'*]," 133–35; "Birds of a Feather [*Odnogo polia iagody*]," 125–28; "A Characterization of the Inner World of Dostoevsky (On the Occasion of His Demise) [*Kharakteristika vnutrennego mira Dostoevskogo (Po povodu ego konchiny)*]," 236–37; editorials in the *Moscow News*, 179–85, 194–96, 197–99, 204, 207, 211–17, 233, 239–40, 283–84n34; "Elegiac Note [*Èlegicheskaia zametka*]," 135, 262n57; "A Few Words Instead of the Contemporary Chronicle [*Neskol'ko slov vmesto sovremennoi letopisi*]," 8, 106–8; "The History of Old Russian Literature [*Istoriia drevnei russkoi slovesnosti*]," 33, 38–40; "A Little Something

about Progress [*Koe-chto o progresse*]," 81, 82, 92; Moscow Duma dinner speech, 218–19, 231; obituary for Dostoevsky, 236; obituary for M. N. Longinov, 283n10; "Old Gods and New Gods [*Starye bogi i novye bogi*]," 81–82, 279–80n80; "On Our Nihilism Apropos of Turgenev's Novel [*O nashem nigilizme po povodu romana Turgeneva*]," 70–71, 86, 91–92, 97, 138–41, 147–48, 163; *On the Elements and Forms of the Slavo-Russian Language* [*Ob elementakh i formakh slaviano-russkogo iazyka*], 6, 7, 48, 254n10; "On the Philosophical Criticism of the Artistic Work [*O filosofskoi kritike khudozhestvennogo proizvedeniia*]," 34–38; "Our Language and What Are Whistlers [*Nash iazyk i chto takoe svistuny*]," 104–6, 108–9, 118–22, 227; "The Polish Question [*Pol'skii vopros*]," 129–30, 223, 285n61; "Pushkin," 6–7, 10, 51–52, 60, 70, 88, 103, 107–8, 220, 226, 231, 232; "Pushkin's Achievement [*Zasluga Pushkina*]," 8–9, 205, 223, 229, 231–34, 242–43; "A Review of Pushkin by a Foreigner [*Otzyv inostrantsa o Pushkine*]," 33, 40–42, 107, 205, 220–25, 226, 229–31, 284n44, 285n73; *Romeo and Juliet* translation, 33, 42, 46, 88, 95, 247n7; *Sketches of the Most Ancient Period of Greek Philosophy* [*Ocherki drevneishego perioda grecheskoi filosofii*], 181–82; "Songs of the Russian People [*Pesni russkogo naroda*]," 33, 38–40; "Turgenev," 238–39; "Turgenev's Novel and Its Critics [*Roman Turgeneva i ego kritiki*]," 70–71, 86, 90–91, 97

Katkova, Sofia Petrovna *née* Shalikova (wife of Katkov), 6, 11, 49, 247n2

Katkova, Varvara Akimovna *née* Tulaeva (mother of Katkov), 4–5, 247n2, 278n64

Katranov, Nikolai, 78, 261n36

Katz, Martin, 11–12, 276n20

Kelly, Aileen, 23

Kennan, George F., 287n123

Khitrovo, E. M., 224

Khlopov, Vladimir, 255n17

Khrushchev, Nikita, 83

Kibalnik, S. A., 281n114

Kirpotin, V. Ia., 152–53, 156, 157

Kiseliov, Dmitrii Konstantinovich, 16–17

Kitaev, Vladimir Anatolievich, 13, 176

Klevensky, M., 78

Klioutchkine, Konstantin, 145–46, 271n19

Kliushnikov, V. P., 146, 148, 158

Knapp, Liza, 173, 175, 276n34

Kogan, G. F., 269n6

Komarovich, V. L., 272n40

Kovalevsky, M. M., 218, 219

Kozmin, B. P., 81

Kraevsky, Andrei Aleksandrovich, 46–47, 51, 80, 99, 143, 220

Kramskoi, I. N., 241

Kremenskaia, I. K., 255n18

Krug, Wilhelm, 82

Kundera, Milan, 243

Kuskov, P. A., 125–27, 268n77

Kutuzov, Prince Mikhail Illarionovich, 224, 274n4

Lacenaire, Pierre François, 212, 283n14

Lambert, Countess E. E., 78, 264n129

Lavrov, P. L., 238

Lenin, Vladimir Ilich, 13, 15

Leontiev, K. N., 234, 240

Leontiev, Pavel Mikhailovich, 61, 181–84, 248n18, 278n55, 278–79n64

Lermontov, Mikhail, 285n79

Leskov, Nikolai Semionovich, 16, 158–59, 242

Levitt, Marcus C., 204–5, 217, 220, 226, 285n73

Library for Reading, 135

Lish, Gordon, 243

Liszt, Franz, 31–32

Liubimov, Nikolai Alekseevich, 11, 12, 59, 144, 145, 148–49, 150–53, 154–56, 188, 206–7, 235

Lomonosov, Mikhail, 37

Longinov, N. V., 283n10

Lönnqvist, Barbara, 276n19

Loris-Melikov, Count M. T., 215

Lounsbery, Anne, 270–71n18

Mai, I. *See* Vyzinsky, Genrikh Vikentievich

Maikov, Apollon Nikolaevich, 112–13, 118, 208–9, 240, 282–83n8

Maikov, Valerian, 265–66n10

Maiorova, Olga, 248n16

Maistre, Count Joseph de, 56

Maksimovich, Mikhail, 33, 38–40

Malthus, Thomas Robert, 277n41

Markevich, B. M., 210–13, 283n10, 283n20

Markov, Evgenii, 172

Markovich, V. M., 83

Mazon, André, 78

Meerson, Olga, 268n75

Mendeleev, Dmitrii, 280n83

Meshchersky, Prince Nikolai Petrovich, 11

Meyer, Priscilla, 276n19

INDEX

Michelet, Jules, 112
Mikhailov, Mikhail Larionovich, 114–16, 117–20, 121, 125
Miliukov, A. P., 149, 150, 151
Minaev, D. I., 158–59
Minin, Kuzma, 232
Modzalevsky, B. L., 144
Molière, 225
Molinari, Gustave de, 176
More, Sir Thomas, 212
Morson, Gary Saul, 275n19
Moscow News, 61, 63, 64, 71. *See also* Katkov, Mikhail
Moscow Observer, 41
Mozart, Wolfgang Amadeus, 226
Muratov, Dmitrii Andreevich, 16
Muraviov, Mikhail Nikolaevich, 165, 178

Naiman, Eric, 281n122
Nechaev, Andrei Alekseevich, 16
Nechaev, S. G., 154, 156
Nechaeva, V. S., 132
Nekliudov, V. S., 194
Nekrasov, N. A., 74–75, 80, 99, 166
Nepomnyashchy, Catharine Theimer, 11
Nevedensky, S. *See* Shcheglovitov
Neverov, Iakov, 284n44
New Time, 199, 234
Nicholas I (tsar), 5, 40, 49–50, 100, 129, 253n63
nihilism, 74, 80–84, 88, 90–93, 97, 120, 123, 135, 138–41, 142, 145–49, 150, 153–60, 183–84, 185, 204, 210–17, 238–39, 262n55, 270n9, 282n6
Nikiforova, Tatiana Georgievna, 278n50
Nikitenko, A. V., 49
Nikoliukin, A. N., 14–15
Notes of the Fatherland, 41, 46–47, 51, 99, 135, 137, 160–62, 166, 204, 220, 264n1

Ogariov, Nikolai Platonovich, 28–32, 43, 251n16, 252n34
Ogariova, Mariia Lvovna, 28–32, 252n34
Orlov, A. F., 49–50
Orwin, Donna T., 278n50
Ottoman Empire, 72–80, 164, 168–69, 192–200, 261n32, 280n103

Palmerston, Henry John Temple (3rd Viscount Palmerston), 106, 169
Panaev, I. I., 74
Panaeva, A. Ia., 74
Paperno, Irina, 281n126
Passek, Tatiana Petrovna, 5

Pavlov, I. V., 81
Pavlov, N. F., 79–80
Pavlova, Karolina, 10, 53, 256n37
Pavlovsky, I. Ia., 210–14, 283n13
Peel, Sir Robert, 169
Perdonnet, Auguste, 171
Perevalova, E. V., 5, 7, 255n18, 255n32, 257n69, 266n10, 270n12, 277n39
Perkins, Maxwell, 243
Perminov, G. F., 262n49
Perov, V. G., 240
Peter I (tsar), 38, 230, 233
Peterson, K., 131–32
Phanariotes, 76, 77–78, 261n32
Pisarev, Dmitrii Ivanovich, 14, 72, 89–91, 153
Pisemsky, A. F., 142, 146, 158, 270n9
Pobedonostsev, Konstantin Petrovich, 158, 209–10, 217, 235–36, 239–40
Pogodin, M. P., 166, 254n10
Polevoi, Nikolai, 220
Polish uprising (1830–31), 223–25, 233
Polish uprising (1863), 5, 93, 102, 128–35, 165, 178–79, 214–17, 223, 233, 283n21
Pollard, Alan P., 286n105
Polonsky, Iakov, 279–80n80
Popov, Eduard, 273n46
Pozharsky, Dmitri, 232
Preobrazhensky, S. N., 81
Prudhomme, Louis-Marie, 112
Prutkov, Kozma (invented persona), 128
Pushkin, Aleksandr Sergeevich, 6–7, 10, 19, 37, 40–42, 44, 50, 51–52, 60, 65, 70, 71, 102, 103, 105, 106–25, 140, 164, 204–5, 214–35, 237, 240, 253n73; Works: *The Anniversary of Borodino*, 223–25, 230–31, 233; *Autumn*, 226; *Boris Godunov*, 233, 253n73; *The Captain's Daughter*, 10; *Egyptian Nights*, 102, 109–25, 150, 152, 155, 158, 228, 267n38, 268n75, 268n76; *Eugene Onegin*, 25, 228–30; *The Gypsies*, 229; monument poem, 7, 52; "No, I do not prize the stormy pleasure," 113–14, 117; *Poltava*, 233; "The Shot," 281n114; *To the Slanderers of Russia*, 223–24, 230–31, 232, 233
Pushkin Celebration of 1880, 19, 204–5, 214–35, 240, 284n41
Putin, Vladimir Vladimirovich, 15–17
Putsykovich, V. F., 207

Rabinowitz, Stanley, 161
Rachel (Elisabeth Rachel Félix), 111
Rachinsky, S. A., 188–89, 277n44
Randolph, John, 22–23
Raphael, 51–52, 60, 103

Reitblat, A., 249n19
Renner, Andreas, 9, 248n16
Repin, Ilia, 240–41
Ris, Fiodor Fiodorovich, 202
Romanov dynasty, 232
Rosset, Aleksandr Osipovich, 87
Rötscher, Heinrich Theodor, 34–38, 42, 48
Rozanov, Vasilii Vasilievich, 15
Rumor, 212
Russian Herald. *See* Katkov, Mikhail
Russian Invalid, 68
Russian Literature, 83
Russian Speech, 66–69, 80, 101, 259n102
Russian Thought, 216
Russian Word, 89
Russian World, 141, 161
Russification, 165, 178–81, 277–78n50

Sade, Marquis de, 124, 156
Sailhas-de-Tournemire, Elizaveta Vasilievna. *See* Tur, Evgeniia
Sakharov, I., 33, 38–40
Samarin, Iurii Fiodorovich, 15
Sand, George, 28, 30–31, 53, 54, 252n34
Sankova, S. M., 278n55
Savonarola, 212
Schelling, Friedrich Wilhelm Joseph von, 31, 48, 247n8
Schiller, Johann Christoph Friedrich von, 108–9, 230
Schleswig-Holstein, 165–66
Scott, George Gilbert, 175
Sementkovsky, Rostislav Ivanovich, 11–12, 16
Serbia, 76, 164, 168–69, 173, 192–200
Shakespeare, William, 33, 36, 37, 42, 47, 88, 95, 109, 143, 225, 230, 235
Shalimov, Iurii Iurievich, 16
Shatz, Marshall S., 32
Shchebalsky, P. K., 274n4
Shcheglovitov, Semion Grigorievich, 11, 47, 49, 51
Shchepkin, Mikhail Semionovich, 24, 25
Shchepkina, Aleksandra Mikhailovna, 24–27, 30, 250–51n15
Shcherbina, N. F., 142
Shenshin, Piotr Afanasievich, 197
Sheremetiev, Boris Petrovich, 233
Shevchenko, Maksim Leonardovich, 16
Shevyriov, S. P., 48, 49
Shtakenshneider, Elena Andreevna, 219
Sinel, Allen, 182, 278n56
Sluchevsky, K. K., 87

Sokolova, A. I., 250–51n15
Soloviov, Vladimir Sergeevich, 12–13, 280n87
Solzhenitsyn, Aleksandr Isaevich, 134
Son of the Fatherland, 41, 220
spiritualism, 187–92
Sretkovich, P., 76
Stalinism, 83
Stankevich, Nikolai Vladimirovich, 22, 24, 33, 42, 251n16
Stasiulevich, M. M., 212, 234, 286n103
Stasov, V. V., 94, 210
Stechkin, N. Ia., 219
Stenbock-Fermor, Elisabeth, 178, 197, 199, 277n44
Stolypin, Aleksei Arkadievich, 87
Stoppard, Tom, 251n16
Stowe, Harriet Beecher, 53
St. Petersburg News, 94, 110, 113–15, 117–19, 120–21, 131, 138
Strakhov, Nikolai Nikolaevich, 84, 93, 100, 115–17, 118, 121, 124, 130–35, 145–47, 160, 166, 179, 186, 190, 199, 200–3, 220, 268n76, 269n93, 270n16, 273n52, 275n8, 277–78n50, 281n126, 286n61
Stravinsky, Igor, 243
Stroganov, S. G., 48
Strousberg, Bethel Henry, 178, 277n42
Strusberg. *See* Strousberg, Bethel Henry
Suslova, Apollinaria Prokofievna, 136
Sutherland, J. A., 243
Suvorin, A. S., 234
Suvorov, Aleksandr Vasilievich, 224, 285n62
Svanidze, Nikolai Karlovich, 16–17
Svechina, Sofia Petrovna, 56–61, 257n63, 257n64, 258n87

Tatishchev, S. S., 249n26
Temps, Le, 210–12
Thackeray, William Makepeace, 243
Thaden, Edward, 165, 178–79, 180
Timmerman, M. P., 110–13, 266–67n32
Tiutchev, Fiodor, 240
Tkachov, P. N., 159–60, 273n48
Tocqueville, Alexis de, 57
Todd, William Mills III, 6, 51, 143–44, 163, 169, 194, 248n9, 270n14
Tolmachova, Evgeniia Eduardovna, 109–25, 150, 155, 157, 267n38, 269n93
Tolstaia, Aleksandra Andreevna, 164–65
Tolstaia, Sarra Fiodorovna, 42, 53–54, 262n50
Tolstoy, Aleksei Konstantinovich, 10, 128

Tolstoy, Dmitrii Andreevich, 179, 182–83, 203, 278n56
Tolstoy, Lev Nikolaevich, 9, 13, 15, 16, 18–19, 46, 53, 97, 98–99, 128, 142, 144, 160, 163–203, 242–45, 274n3, 274n5, 278n55, 278–79n64; *Works: Anna Karenina*, 3, 18–19, 69, 97, 161–62, 164, 166–203, 204, 227, 241, 242, 275n17, 275–76n19, 277n42, 277n44, 277–78n50, 279n69, 281n114, 281n122, 281n123, 281n126; *The Cossacks*, 163; *Family Happiness*, 163; *Polikushka*, 163; *War and Peace*, 3, 10, 18, 69, 144, 163–64, 167, 168, 169, 202, 274n4, 281n122; *Yasnaya Polyana* (journal), 165, 172–73
Tolstoy, Mikhail Lvovich, 182
Tretyakov, P. M., 240–41
Trofimova, T. A., 263–64n104, 281n122
Trollope, Anthony, 169, 275n17, 275–76n19
Troppmann, Jean-Baptiste, 212
Tur, Evgeniia (pseudonym of Elizaveta Vasilievna Sailhas-de-Tournemire), 17, 28, 46, 53–69, 80, 88–89, 95, 101, 106, 125, 127, 138, 143, 144, 148, 150, 164, 193, 244, 256n34, 257n63, 258n87, 259n102
Turgenev, Ivan Sergeevich, 9, 13, 14, 16, 17–18, 19, 46, 53, 67–69, 70–97, 98–99, 128, 132, 142, 144, 156, 193, 204–5, 208, 210–14, 216–20, 225–28, 238–39, 242–45, 262n49, 278n64, 282n7, 283n13, 283n20, 283n21, 284n37, 286n103; "Apropos of *Fathers and Sons*," 83–85, 86, 92–94, 210; *Fathers and Sons*, 3, 10, 13, 18, 69, 70–71, 74, 70–97, 128, 138–39, 142, 144, 146–47, 163, 169, 182, 201, 202, 204, 210, 214, 227, 238, 241, 259n102, 262n55, 264n127, 264n129, 273n46, 281n122; *On the Eve*, 17–18, 67, 70–80, 95, 138, 163, 260n16, 261n32; Pushkin speech, 220, 222, 225–27, 230, 231; *Smoke*, 93, 94; "An Unfortunate Girl," 94
Turkey. *See* Ottoman Empire
Tvardovskaia, Valentina Aleksandrovna, 13

Ugrinovich, K., 75
Utin, Boris Isaakovich, 53, 61, 63, 64, 67–68, 256n37, 257n70

Uvarov, Sergei Semionovich, 40

Vagner, N. P., 187–92, 280n83
Varnhagen von Ense, Karl August, 19, 33, 40–42, 50, 205, 220–25, 226, 229–31, 284n50, 285n73
Vasiliev, Andrei Vitalievich, 16–17
Veinberg, Piotr Isaevich. *See* Kamen-Vinogorov
Veligonova, Irina, 273n46
Venevitinov, M. A., 228
Vengerov, S. A., 282–83n8
Viazemsky, Prince P. A., 224–25
Vinitsky, Ilya, 188
Vinogradov, V. V., 14
Vladimirov, Father Artemii, 15
Voice, 219
Volgin, Igor, 220, 234–35, 282n4, 284n37
Vovchok, Marko (pseudonym of Mariia Vilinska), 53, 103
Vrangel, A. E., 137, 138, 141, 142
Vyzinsky, Genrikh Vikentievich, 61–67, 88–89, 127–28, 244, 257n69, 258n87

Wachtel, Michael, 223–24, 285n62
Walicki, Andrzej, 130
War of 1812, 224–25
Weeks, Theodore R., 180–81
Werder, Karl Friedrich, 27, 47
Western provinces, 129, 164, 178–81, 216
Wolfe, Thomas, 243
women's rights ("the woman question"), 110–25, 184–87, 279n65
Woodburn, Stephen M., 247n8, 254–55n10

Zakharov, V. N., 160, 273n53
zapadnyi krai. *See* Western provinces
Zhadovskaia, Iuliia, 53
Zhemchuzhnikov brothers (Aleksandr Mikhailovich, Aleksei Mikhailovich, Vladimir Mikhailovich), 128
Zhuravsky, D. I., 170–72, 176